Finalist for the J. Anthony Lukas Book Prize

PENGUIN BOOKS

DARK MIRROR

Barton Gellman, a Pulitzer Prize– and Emmy Award–winning journalist, is a staff writer at *The Atlantic* and a senior fellow at the Century Foundation. In previous assignments he served tours as a legal, military, diplomatic, and foreign correspondent for *The Washington Post*. His bestselling *Angler: The Cheney Vice Presidency* won the *Los Angeles Times* Book Prize and was a *New York Times* Notable Book of 2008.

Praise for *Dark Mirror*

One of *The Washington Post*'s fifty best nonfiction books of 2020

One of *The Christian Science Monitor*'s best nonfiction books of 2020

"Engrossing . . . Gellman [is] a thorough, exacting reporter. . . . A marvelous narrator for this particular story, as he nimbly guides us through complex technical arcana and some stubborn ethical questions. . . . *Dark Mirror* would be simply pleasurable to read if the story it told didn't also happen to be frighteningly real." —Jennifer Szalai, *The New York Times*

"Illuminating . . . Newsworthy . . . *Dark Mirror* stands out from all the other accounts. Gellman, a Pulitzer Prize–winning former *Washington Post* investigative reporter and author of *Angler*, an influential 2008 biography of Dick Cheney, didn't just use the Snowden files as sources; he used them as starting points for deep, labor-intensive reporting." —*The Washington Post*

"Gellman offers the most detailed, comprehensive and balanced take on the impact of Snowden's 2013 revelations and what they mean today, as the debate on national security versus individual privacy keeps evolving. . . . A compelling book." —NPR

"An insider account of the breaking of Edward Snowden's story and its wider implications for the modern world, all told in prose as gripping as a spy thriller." —*The Christian Science Monitor*

"[A] masterful narrative . . . that deserves its place alongside *All the President's Men, Five Days at Memorial, Nickel and Dimed,* and other classics of the genre . . . A riveting, timely book sure to be one of the most significant of the year." —*Kirkus Reivews* (starred review)

"Partly a thriller about reporting the secrets the U.S. government hoped to keep, partly a deeper exposé about the vast power the surveillance state built to pierce Americans' privacy with a few keystrokes, *Dark Mirror* is a riveting page-turner that captures the danger and drama of the most important leak of classified material in generations. I lived part of this story in real time and am amazed at how many startling things I learned in these pages."
    —Carol Leonnig, three-time Pulitzer Prize winner and bestselling author of *A Very Stable Genius*

"Bart Gellman is that rare combination of a tenacious reporter, a clear explicator of the most complex subjects, and a first-rate storyteller, all rolled into one. To say that *Dark Mirror* is based on his groundbreaking reporting on the NSA for *The Washington Post* is to undersell it: this book is a deep exploration of a surveillance apparatus of unimaginable magnitude, a chronicle of Gellman's intense and sometimes fraught relationship with his enigmatic and controversial source, Edward Snowden, and an intimate, disarmingly candid reporter's notebook about what it's like to spend years watching the watchers, and realizing, along the way, that they are watching you back."
    —Patrick Radden Keefe, *New York Times* bestselling author of *Say Nothing: A True Story of Murder and Memory in Northern Ireland*

"Whether you love Edward Snowden or loathe him, Bart Gellman's new book is essential reading for anyone who cares about privacy and national security. Gellman offers a riveting and often surprising account of his dealings with Snowden, who, for all his seeming idealism, also misdirected Gellman about some key facts. But whatever Snowden's defects, the scope of the NSA global snooping campaign he revealed is more shocking than ever, as Gellman pieces together the puzzle. If you want to understand how intelligence works in the twenty-first century, *Dark Mirror* is a must."
    —David Ignatius, columnist for *The Washington Post* and author of *The Paladin*

"This is an enthralling tale of how Barton Gellman, one of the great investigative journalists of our era, worked to understand, process, and report the greatest and most challenging leaks of all time. *Dark Mirror* is a spy-thriller page-turner that delivers a fresh but complex portrait of Edward Snowden, a fair-minded but damning critique of America's global surveillance behemoth, and a gripping, self-reflective master class on how to discern truth in the dark shadows of the intelligence world."
—Jack Goldsmith, professor, Harvard Law School; assistant attorney general, Office of Legal Counsel, during the George W. Bush administration

"*Dark Mirror* is a riveting narrative of investigative reporting in the age of surveillance. It is a dramatic, authoritative account not only of the significance of Edward Snowden's revelations but of what public interest journalism must overcome to inform citizens about their exposure to our dystopian internet."
—Steve Coll, Pulitzer Prize–winning author of *Ghost Wars* and *Directorate S*

"[A] thoughtful mix of reportage and revelation . . . a necessary and deep meditation about how far our online lives can or indeed should remain completely private." —*The Sunday Times* (London)

"Engaging . . . A well-documented account on the far-reaching impact of U.S. domestic surveillance and the resulting intrusions of privacy; highly recommended both for general readers and those with an interest in national security." —*Library Journal*

"Gellman delivers a compelling story while recounting difficult predicaments and behind-the-scenes events. He takes a deep dive into the surveillance state while recalling being subjected to government investigations, legal pressures, and threats from foreign agencies determined to steal his files. Readers will be drawn into the conversational style of [*Dark Mirror*]." —*Booklist*

"A fine and deeply considered portrait of the U.S.-dominated twenty-first-century surveillance state." —*The Guardian*

"An eloquent behind-the-scenes account of [Gellman's] reporting on NSA contractor Edward Snowden's leak of top-secret U.S. intelligence documents. . . . Enriching the high-level technical and legal analysis with a sharp sense of humor, Gellman presents an exhaustive study of intelligence gathering in the digital age. Even readers who have followed the Snowden story closely will learn something new." —*Publishers Weekly*

DARK MIRROR

EDWARD SNOWDEN AND THE
AMERICAN SURVEILLANCE STATE

BARTON GELLMAN

Research Assistant,
Ashkan Soltani

PENGUIN BOOKS

PENGUIN BOOKS
An imprint of Penguin Random House LLC
penguinrandomhouse.com

First published in the United States of America by Penguin Press,
an imprint of Penguin Random House LLC, 2020
Published in Penguin Books 2021

Page 253, photographs by Bart Gellman.
Page 321, photograph courtesy of Ben Wizner.

ISBN 9780143110477 (paperback)

THE LIBRARY OF CONGRESS HAS CATALOGED THE HARDCOVER EDITION AS FOLLOWS:
Names: Gellman, Barton, 1960– author.
Title: Dark mirror : Edward Snowden and the American Surveillance
State / Barton Gellman.
Description: New York : Penguin Press, 2020. | Includes bibliographical
references and index.
Identifiers: LCCN 2019049573 (print) | LCCN 2019049574 (ebook) |
ISBN 9781594206016 (hardcover) | ISBN 9780698153394 (ebook)
Subjects: LCSH: Snowden, Edward J., 1983– | Gellman, Barton, 1960– |
United States. National Security Agency. | Electronic intelligence—United States—
History—21st century. | Electronic surveillance—Government policy—United States. |
Domestic intelligence—United States. | Leaks (Disclosure of information)—
United States. | Journalists—United States—Biography.
Classification: LCC UB256.U6 G45 2020 (print) | LCC UB256.U6 (ebook) |
DDC 327.12730092 [B]—dc23
LC record available at https://lccn.loc.gov/2019049573
LC ebook record available at https://lccn.loc.gov/2019049574

Printed in the United States of America
1st Printing

Designed by Amanda Dewey

For my children:
Abigail, Micah, Lily, and Benjamin

CONTENTS

PREFACE

How did you do it? How did you extract all that information and
cross a border with it?
It's just a question of being smarter than the adversary.
Which in this case is only the NSA.
Ha, true. One step at a time and you climb up the mountain.
You can tell that story later.

—Author's chat with Edward Snowden, June 9, 2013

This book takes up the gauntlet that Edward Snowden threw down for me that day, the same day he unmasked himself to the world. Shortly after this exchange, he fled his Hong Kong hotel room ahead of an extradition request from the United States. His parting words were a challenge, not a promise. He did not intend to hand me his story. Not all of it. I have built this narrative by my own lights and reporting.

Dark Mirror is not a book about Snowden, or not only that. It is a tour of the surveillance state that rose up after September 11, 2001, when the U.S. government came to believe it could not spy on enemies without turning its gaze on Americans as well. New methods of electronic surveillance impinged on the digital commons used by just about everyone, encompassing us all in a pool of potential threats. It followed, from this way of thinking, that the public must not be permitted to know what the government was doing in its name. Surveillance and secrecy grew together, side by side.

As intelligence agencies threw off old restraints, they positioned themselves as if behind one-way mirrors. On their side the glass was transparent. We appeared in plain view. On our side, opaque, the watchers went unseen. The title of *Dark Mirror* alludes to that design, which takes literal form at the National Security Agency on Fort George G. Meade, Maryland. Reflective panels of blue-black glass wrap the eleven-story headquarters in an electromagnetic cage, safeguarding the secrets of the watchers within.

It was Snowden who gave us the means to watch them back. In a spectacular act of transgression, he exposed the machinery of a global surveillance Leviathan. Snowden made it possible to document the origins of the "golden age of SIGINT," or signals intelligence, as the NSA described the times in its strategy documents. Great swaths of human interaction had shifted to the digital realm. The NSA built the wherewithal to gather information in bulk, without discriminants, from the main arteries of global communications networks. It is too simple to describe what the NSA did as mass surveillance, a concept I explore carefully in this book, but there is no doubt that the agency began to sweep bystanders into its nets by the hundreds of millions. The traditional distinction between foreign and domestic espionage, a foundation of American privacy law, began to erode. Even after years of spirited public debate touched off by the Snowden disclosures, U.S. law and society have yet to adapt fundamentally to what he revealed.

There is another narrative here, more personal, that I did not expect to write. It is the story of my own journey as one of three journalists on the receiving end of the most consequential public leak in the history of U.S. intelligence. Against all inclination and training as a teller of other people's tales, I came to believe I should answer questions that I had sidestepped for years.

Why did Snowden choose me? What made me think I could trust him? How did we communicate under the nose of U.S. counterintelligence authorities? Where did we meet in Moscow? Why did my name appear in an NSA file that predated the Snowden leak? Did the government try to stop my stories? How did I decide which secrets to publish and which to hold back? Who the hell elected me to decide?

No one in my profession had ever possessed tens of thousands of contemporary, codeword-classified documents. There was no playbook for a journalist under that kind of avalanche. Foreign intelligence services tried to hack my accounts and devices. The NSA director, I learned, was calling for a raid to seize my notes and files. Some of the Snowden documents, I believed, should never see the light of day. Others offered leads that I did not know how to follow without endangering my sources. To make matters worse, I had no journalistic home when Snowden appeared in my in-box. I had left the *Washington Post* three years earlier. Before I negotiated a temporary return, I had to make high-stakes decisions on my own. I improvised. I made mistakes, some of them embarrassing to recount. What emerges here, I hope, is an honest portrait of investigative reporting behind the scenes.

Snowden is a complicated figure, far from the cartoon templates of "hero" or "traitor." He can be fine company: funny and profane, an autodidact with a nimble mind and eclectic interests. He can also be stubborn, self-important, and a scold. Our relationship was fraught. He knew that I would not join his crusade, and he never relied on me to take his side as he did with Laura Poitras and Glenn Greenwald. We struggled over boundaries—mine as a journalist who wanted to know more, his as an advocate who saw his cause at stake in every choice of words. He broke ties with me, briefly, when I did not accept his conditions for my first story. The second time he withdrew, believing I had done him harm, we did not speak for months. "I'm not sure I'll ever be able to trust you to watch my back, but that's not why I talk to you," he told me when we resumed contact in the fall of 2013. "I trust you to report."

Twice, after that, I traveled to join him in Moscow for marathon conversations fueled by room service facsimiles of American fast food. He eats with an engineer's logic, ice cream first, because hamburgers don't melt. In New York and Princeton he has beamed in for visits, inhabiting a remote-controlled robot that sees, hears, speaks, and rolls around the room. Occasionally we visited on two-way video across a surveillance-resistant channel built by trusted technical friends. Most often we rendezvoused in the securest precincts of his native habitat, holding live chats by keyboard over encrypted, anonymous links. Those, done right, are the hardest to intercept.

Personal questions, no matter how pertinent, were usually out of bounds. The first time I traveled to see him in Moscow, I tried to get him on record about his relationship with the Russian government. You are living here, I said. Do you accept money from the state? Are you questioned about your time in U.S. intelligence? Snowden accused me of parroting his critics. He spoke in theoretical terms about what a person in his position might do.

"You know I have no relationship with the Russian government," he burst out, finally. "You shouldn't engage in this line of questioning."

"I don't know it. I don't know it until I ask you."

"It's unknowable. You're asking me to say, prove there is no God."

"No, I'm asking you to simply state that you've seen no burning bush."

"And I am. I am. In hypothetical terms."

Hypothetical, because the whole subject was off the record. Until later, when it was not. Even then he declined to respond concretely.

We had dozens of conversations like this, round and round, about dozens of subjects. For the record, I had no reason to believe that Snowden was a Russian asset, and no U.S. government official purported to possess evidence otherwise. Snowden dodged me with equal persistence when I asked about the genius-level IQ test result he obtained in elementary school, according to a family source.

The reader is entitled to know up front that I think Snowden did substantially more good than harm, even though I am prepared to accept (as he is not) that his disclosures must have exacted a price in lost intelligence. Electronic surveillance is a tool of surpassing power and surprising fragility. Its value depends on catching targets unaware. A person of interest, forewarned, can change channels and disappear at least for a while. Dread of lost coverage built a culture of deep silence at the NSA, which earned its nicknames of "No Such Agency" and "Never Say Anything." From an operational standpoint, comprehensive secrecy appeared to bring only advantage. But when the state of the art expanded surveillance into digital neighborhoods used by everyone, the NSA outran its political mandate. The boundary of secret intelligence in a free society had shifted. It needed debate.

Some of Snowden's harshest critics, if only a few, are prepared to accept that this essential conversation would not have happened without him. "I know the world changed as a result of Edward Snowden, in a significant way," former FBI director James B. Comey told me in a long and contemplative discussion of the leaks. "And I can more easily measure the benefits than the costs, but I would hope we don't fall in love with the benefits and not respect the fact that we can't estimate the costs."

The pages to come tell stories that Snowden will not talk about or has not recounted before, not even in his memoir last year, and many stories that have nothing to do with him. I draw upon hundreds of hours of conversations with Snowden and hundreds more with designers, operators, customers, rebels, and dissidents in the surveillance machinery. There are new revelations here from the classified archive, from independent research, and from old reporter's notes that revealed new meaning in hindsight.

At its core this is a book about power. Information is the oxygen of control. Secrecy and surveillance, intertwined, define its flows. "Who knows what?" is a pretty good proxy for "Who governs whom?" Are citizens equipped to hold their government accountable? Are they free to shield themselves from an unwanted gaze? Can anyone today draw a line, say, "None of your business," and make it stick?

There is an origin story for this book, and it antedates Snowden. In 2011, I shared a stage in Silicon Valley with Google's Eric Schmidt. He asked, "Wouldn't you like to be able to say to your Android phone, 'Where are my car keys?'" Good God, no, I told him. Maybe I'm in a casino. Maybe the bartender took my keys and I'm sleeping it off in a room upstairs, never mind whose. I'd be glad to have my phone track my life, but I don't want *you* to know. Schmidt observed that my personal life was evidently more interesting than his, which I doubted, and that Android users love the way their phones hand them information before they even ask. The technology, I agreed, is marvelous. It's like having Batman's Alfred in my pocket, except that Alfred is not working for me. He is following me, taking notes, and sending them to you. I asked whether Schmidt could foresee a time when I could pay in cash for Google services, rather than agree to be spied on. He disputed the verb, but replied candidly. That's not our business model, he said. Until Snowden, it was (just about) nobody's model.

By the time I sat down with Schmidt, I had been worried about my digital exhaust for some time. Most of what I want to know in my work is one or another kind of secret. After 9/11, the U.S. government tried harder to deter, discover, and punish my confidential sources.

In self-defense I set about learning the tradecraft of electronic security. I became comfortable with encryption and anonymous proxies. I bought burner phones with cash, like a drug dealer, then realized I had to turn off my usual phone so that the burner would not march with it in lockstep around town. Would time-stamped security video in the phone store give me away? Maybe, if someone cared enough to review it. Was it enough to change SIM cards, or could I be tracked by the hardware identifier of the phone itself? No, and yes. I fell ever deeper into the rabbit hole, walking up to the line of the absurd. A journalist cannot sensibly aspire to go off the grid.

Just as I began to wonder why I bothered, a man who called himself Verax showed up. Using a clever method I had not seen before, he sent me an encryption key, a recognition signal, and a method to verify both. It was like one of those old comic book advertisements: "If U Cn Rd Ths Msg . . ." Delighted, even vindicated, I found that I could. "I appreciate your concern for operational security, particularly in the digital environment," Verax wrote in his next message. "Many journalists are still exceedingly weak on this topic, which leaves their interests and intentions an open book for sophisticated adversaries. . . . I'm told you're already quite skilled in this regard."

That was not true, actually. I knew the basics. Verax taught me some of the finer points, and we began to talk.

DARK
MIRROR

ONE

PANDORA

The in-box logged a message as I slept. Many hours passed before I checked. Probably should have kept away, but habit tugged. We had taken the channel dark last night. Not because we knew it was blown, but because we could not know. These email accounts were anonymous, encrypted, isolated from our everyday internet lives. Best I could tell, there was no way to lock them down tighter. That thought had reassured me once.

It was the second half of May 2013. Nearly four months had passed since Laura Poitras, an independent filmmaker, reached out to me for advice about a confidential source. Verax, as I came to know him later, had brought her an enigmatic tip about U.S. government surveillance. Poitras and I teamed up to see what would come of it. The previous night, months of suspense had come to an end. Verax delivered. The evidence was here. His story was real, the risks no longer conjecture. The FBI and the NSA's "Q Group," which oversees internal security, were bound to devote sizable resources to this leak. For the first time in my career, I did not think it was out of the question that U.S. authorities would try to seize my notes and files. Without doubt we were about to become interesting to foreign intelligence services.

Poitras and I resolved to meet again in two days. Anything that came up sooner would have to wait. That plan did not last the night. I logged on the next morning, expecting nothing. According to the time stamp, Poitras had fired off a note less than four hours after we parted. She could not have slept much. I hadn't either, but the fog cleared when I saw her subject line. It was our private signal for "urgent." The message, once decrypted, was succinct.

```
I really need to show you something.
You are going to want to see it.
```

Odd. Very. Something to look at? After what we saw last night? Verax had sent a Top Secret, compartmented presentation from the National Security Agency, updated the previous month. Poitras and I stood over a small laptop screen past midnight, struggling with the jargon. The main points came through readily enough. Under the cover name PRISM, the NSA was siphoning data from tens of thousands of Yahoo, Google, Microsoft, and Facebook accounts, among others. Forty-one slides and eight thousand words of speaker's notes laid out the legal rationale and operating details. If authentic—and it sure looked that way—this briefing offered something very rare: an authoritative account, in near real time, of intelligence operations on U.S. soil that spilled far beyond the bounds acknowledged in public.

When we quit for the night, Poitras said she understood maybe 10 percent of it. I could not claim more than half. No shame in that. Journalists were not supposed to know all the answers. We were supposed to know how to find them, to test the evidence and look for more. Building a story might take time, but we had the cornerstone.

So I thought. But something had startled Poitras, startled her enough to break email discipline. There was no use guessing. I found nothing to read between the lines. The news, I supposed, could be good or bad, but any surprise was unsettling at this stage. Surprise meant I did not know where we stood. For weeks, I had been mapping contingencies, thinking through likely paths and roadblocks in the next stage of reporting. I had to find additional sources, make contact without endangering them, authenticate the document, and look for context. There were all kinds of ways I could screw this up—exposing Verax, falling for a fake, misreading the text, disclosing something that caused inadvertent harm. If I had misdrawn my mental map, I might not see trouble coming.

There was no more time to plan. Verax had rung the starting bell. We had the document in hand and no fixed story date. The interlude could be precarious. Verax declined to say where he was, but we knew he had stopped showing up for work. When his employer began to look for him, the risks to his freedom and safety would become acute. Authorities would discover what he took, and they might try to preempt the story. For sure our window for unhindered work would close.

We were trying to slip the gaze of a surveillance giant while peering through its gates. We could not hope to succeed for long, but we bought time every way we could. The urgent email from Poitras that morning had six miles to travel as the crow flies, from Tribeca to upper Manhattan. She dispatched it through anonymous relays around the world, adding thousands of miles of detours to mask her whereabouts. When I logged on, I did the same. We had bought cheap laptops for cash and used privacy tools to spoof their hardware and network addresses. Poitras, Verax, and I encrypted every word. We used no telephones at all. Every contact left a trail—there was no helping that—but we filled it with false footprints.

Before I could make my way downtown, a second email appeared. Same mundane-looking subject line, signaling "urgent." As the body of her encrypted message crossed the internet, the ciphertext looked like this:

-----BEGIN PGP MESSAGE-----

hQIOA7RnVIVebwveEAgA7OBO1qtnQ1mdDTZwU4eI1ZbfF57dLNIbOUxeunqK8q9Zo

o9a0iHGjVreqoOYKip/1pX7rohHmA/TO38jjgnsF9E6hNahg1ZWcBRabfOxGUxu8Gz

xk5H9m+k0dHCqg6EVwAoIWunkghc6jG2p/seNFNCR36vjgCy2BuF47JcOoKgc[. . .]

-----END PGP MESSAGE-----

I plugged in a thumb drive. On it was my private key, a small digital file required to decrypt her message. I typed two passphrases, one to mount the thumb drive and another to enable use of the key. Unscrambled, the new note from Poitras had only eight words.

You need to prepare yourself for this. Jesus.

What in the *hell* was going on? I canceled a flight to Washington and hustled to the subway, trotting down the staircase double time. As I boarded a downtown 1 train, I pulled the battery from my phone. A smartphone is an excellent tracking device. It works well as a remote-controlled microphone, too, for someone who knows how to switch it on.

The first time I met Laura Poitras, three days before Christmas 2010, she turned up unannounced at my office, just off Washington Square. Karen Greenberg, a mutual friend who ran a lively policy salon at New York University Law School, kept telling us we should meet. Greenberg had offered me a fellowship when I quit the *Washington Post*. My new office came with a coffee mug bequeathed to me by the once and future Pentagon official Michael Sheehan. On its side, the mug featured a smiling, square-jawed World War II soldier, java in hand. "How about a nice big cup of shut the fuck up?" the GI said. Secrecy culture, circa 1944, never out of style.

I did not think to ask Poitras how she had made her way to me without a call from security or the fussy receptionist upstairs. That night she let me know I had missed some kind of a scene. "I feel a little bad I had to freak out Karen's staff to get to you," she wrote.

Unsurprising, if her press clippings were to be believed. At age forty-six, she was an Oscar-nominated, Peabody-winning force of nature, prone to shouldering a camera through war zones without a crew. Politics on the radical side. "Intense" and "relentless," the profile writers said. Grew up near Boston, trained as a chef, then turned to film. Her breakthrough film, *My Country, My Country*, traced the failed attempt to install democracy under U.S. occupation in Iraq. PBS had just broadcast her latest, *The Oath*, an alternating narrative of Osama bin Laden's former bodyguard, now a cabdriver in Yemen, and his brother-in-law, a prisoner at the U.S. military detention center at Guantánamo Bay.

Blowback from the Iraq film brought her to me. For four years, since the documentary's debut in 2006, she had been pulled aside for interrogation and search every time she crossed a U.S. border. Typically, Customs and Border Patrol officers held her for hours, stating no reason. They paged through her notebooks, copied video footage from her memory cards, and sometimes "detained" (that was the legal euphemism) her electronic devices. At New York's John F. Kennedy Airport that summer, she later recounted, they had "confiscated my laptop, video camera, footage, and cellphone" and held them for forty-one days. At least once they acknowledged making a full forensic image of her laptop, a bit-by-bit copy they could keep forever and use, among other things, to recover deleted files.

I found all that appalling, beginning with the U.S. government's pretense that computers and smartphones were "containers" no different from a purse or a duffel bag. Seizing, copying, and keeping hundreds of thousands of personal and professional files, by this baroque logic, was no greater intrusion than searching a suitcase for undeclared bottles of scotch. Long precedent held that the Fourth Amendment's requirement of probable cause did not apply to searches at the border, where authorities needed leeway to defend against security threats and enforce customs laws. The government made a broader claim, far more hostile to common sense and the foundational right of a citizen to be left alone. There was no such thing, the government argued, as an "unreasonable" border search because customs agents could be as arbitrary as they liked about search and seizure. They did not need any reason at all. King George could have embraced the claim verbatim. Federal judges had only just begun to question it.

Poitras had heard that my old newsroom colleagues saw me as an eccentric on privacy, the guy who encrypted his notes and set up spooky online accounts. Possibly I wore a tinfoil sleeping cap to ward off hostile radio beams. To me the need for precautions was apparent. Journalists, same as everyone else, had accepted the gifts of the internet without considering their price. Mobile phones, web browsing, email, and messaging left long trails of data about whom we talked to, when we spoke, where we met, and what we talked about. Changing laws and technology gave the government more access to that data trove with less oversight. Large private employers deployed comparable tools at company scale, enabling them to look over the shoulders of employees at will. Some story targets tried to squelch leaks by hiring private investigators to dig up our communications records. Journalists pledged not to reveal our confidential sources, but we were allowing adversaries to pluck them from our digital exhaust. It had been years since I kept my notes where anyone else, even bosses I trusted, could read them. "The cloud," as the security analyst Graham Cluley put it, was just another word for "somebody else's computer." When you left information there, you gave up control.

Poitras wanted to know how to defend herself. Ordinarily, I would start a conversation like that by asking what she wanted to protect and who she thought was after it. Poitras already knew she had a world-class adversary. That was not good news, but even the U.S. government had to budget time, money, and scarce technical resources. It could not pull out all the stops for everyone on a watch list. Until now, Poitras had been a cheap target, traveling with naked data. She could make herself much more expensive with file encryption. Meanwhile, about that laptop they copied? Had she changed the passwords on her email and online accounts? She had.

That night I sent her what purported to be "a quick note for further reading." In fact, all self-restraint failed. My thousand-word email was thick with links and recipes for an alphabet soup of software tools: GPG, TrueCrypt, OTR, SOCKS proxies, Tor. It is not hard to see, in retrospect, why my colleagues seldom asked for this kind of advice.

Many of the methods I commended to Poitras had their origins with the cypherpunks of the 1990s, a liberty-minded (and therefore leaderless) collective of visionaries and technologists. In the infancy of the internet, the cypherpunks set out to protect it from censorship, surveillance, and other forms of untoward state control. One of them, John Perry Barlow, a former Grateful Dead lyricist and cofounder of the Electronic Frontier Foundation, wrote a declaration of independence, warning governments at large ("you weary giants of flesh and steel") that "you are not welcome among us." In "A Cypherpunk's Manifesto," Eric Hughes announced an action plan: "We know that someone has to write software to defend privacy, and since we can't get privacy unless we all do, we're going to write it."

That is what they did. They wrote the software, and the software worked, and they gave it away for free. Even the U.S. Naval Research Laboratory, which invented "onion routing" to enable anonymous communications online, released the software and its underlying code for free public use. "Preserving privacy means not only hiding the content of messages, but also hiding who is talking to whom," wrote the authors of the laboratory's breakthrough technical paper.

With tools like these, anyone could read and write and meet on the internet without censorship or fear, cloaked in the elegant mathematics of cryptography. Anyone could, and hardly anyone did. Muggles did not treat with the conjurings of wizards. Not many heard tell of such arcana; fewer had the motive or patience to master them. I took a certain nerdy pleasure in the effort, and I had strong incentives as a journalist covering secret diplomacy, intelligence, and war. I started using GPG, the gold standard of email and file encryption, in 2006— not long after *Time* magazine overrode a reporter's objections and handed his notes to prosecutors in the criminal case against Vice President Dick Cheney's chief of staff. I counted Werner Koch, who wrote the software and maintains it still, among the great contributors to civil society.

And still it had to be said: GPG was so hard to navigate that even experts foundered on its novella-sized user guide. The manual could swallow Robert Louis Stevenson's tale of Jekyll and Hyde with two thousand words to spare. The punch line of that joke wrote itself, but I had no better advice to offer Poitras. Maybe the best tip I sent her was "You should probably have a more experienced adviser." Today, I should mention, there are easier tools, though not easy enough. I keep an updated list at gellman.us/pgp.

Our collaboration on the NSA story began two years later, on January 31, 2013, when Poitras wrote to say she was passing through New York.

"Do you have time to grab a coffee in the next few days?" she asked. "I could use some advice." The invitation was not as casual as it looked. An encrypted note followed, asking me to leave my mobile phone behind. Two days later, at Joe, the pocket-sized espresso bar I picked out, she made a face at the tightly spaced tables and said we had better try elsewhere. We switched venues twice more before she found one private enough. She had my attention.

Poitras made small talk until our server brought food and drink. By habit, I pulled out a Moleskine notebook. She shook her head, and I put it away. A nameless informant had come to her, she said, describing himself as a member of the U.S. intelligence community. She did not tell me so at the time, but their conversation had begun five days before. The NSA, by the anonymous correspondent's account, had built a surveillance machine of such breadth and power that it placed American democracy at risk. He could supply proof, but not yet.

Not a promising start. I kept a poker face, I think, but few subjects in my experience matched the allure of an intelligence plot to delusional tipsters. After writing about warrantless domestic surveillance in my last book, I had been swarmed with letters in spidery script and voicemails that kept going until they filled my queue. Poitras's source did not sound like a crackpot, but there was another kind of story tip that many reporters file under "Important if True." This kind of tip sounded plausible, newsworthy if genuine, but by its nature the story was out of reach. I could imagine what proof might look like, but it would take a subpoena or, well, a wiretap to reach it. There might be gold in those files, but you could spend a career looking.

I thought about cautioning Poitras, then caught myself. It was a bad habit. Journalists, like cops and trial lawyers, liked to think we had special instincts for truth. Bullshit detectors. I was not immune to the fantasy, but science offered scant support. In controlled experiments, professional investigators did no better than a coin toss at picking out truth and lies. For sure, I had nothing to boast about. Over the years, I had placed faith where it did not belong and missed or dismissed facts that did not fit my experience. One of my most disquieting flops came on a West Bank hilltop in June 1995, when I interviewed an Israeli settler named Yigal Amir. By then, Amir was already stalking Prime Minister Yitzhak Rabin. Five months later, he edged close enough to put two bullets in Rabin's back. No spider sense tingled as I spoke to him. I dismissed the assassin's dark words as cliché. Calling Rabin a traitor, pissing into a hole marked "Oslo Agreement"—that was theater, commonplace among religious nationalists of his stripe. I had met hundreds like him, I thought.

I shut up and took another bite of burger, leaving the floor to Poitras. I could easily have blown the moment with a casual joke. The Poitras I came to know was a stern judge of colleagues who did not share her ferocious sense of mission. As our conversation went on, in any case, I liked what I heard. The source had not shown Poitras all his cards, and Poitras kept some from me, but he spoke fluently in the languages of signals intelligence and communications networks. I thought I heard a weakness for high rhetoric, but Poitras said the source wrote with precision about matters of fact. His willingness to say "I don't know" encouraged us both. Another small measure of credence came when he lapsed from plain English into shoptalk without appearing to notice. That was the way of many closed tribes and not easy to fake.

Poitras hoped I might recognize some of the jargon. Had I heard of BOUNDLESSINFORMANT? I had not, but I loved its pitch-perfect tone of earnest overreach, ambitious with a touch of sinister. How about SSO? I was pretty sure that stood for Special Source Operations, something to do with NSA access to equipment under friendly corporate control. What did her source mean by DNR? CNO? No idea. All I came up with were "do not resuscitate" and "chief of naval operations," which were comically inapt. (Correct answers, gleaned later: "dialed number recognition" and "computer network operations.") NSANet? Yes, I knew that one. It was the agency's secure global intranet, connecting thirty thousand employees to shared intelligence community resources such as a Top Secret reference site modeled on Wikipedia.

Was her source the whistleblower he claimed to be? A fabricator who used public records to feign inside knowledge? A real intelligence analyst peddling fake intrigue? A half-informed official who misread something benign? I told Poitras I thought I could narrow the possibilities. In research for *Angler*, my book on Cheney, I had left out small details I learned about the NSA. They were too technical for my purposes, or I did not understand them in context, or they had no connection to events I wrote about. If the source knew what I knew, that might mean something. If he filled in the gaps, or made persuasive corrections, so much the better.

Poitras asked what I thought of combining forces if the story panned out. Print and film had complementary strengths, she said. Neither of us committed in that first meeting, but I was intrigued. As time went on, Poitras passed questions and replies among us. Every exchange chipped away at our doubts. By spring, the two of us were partners. Everything would depend on the written evidence, I wrote to her in early May, but I had reached a turning point.

If this guy was not for real, I wrote, "I will be very surprised."

When Poitras introduced us, Verax needed convincing about me. He was suspicious of the *Washington Post*, where I grew up as a journalist. He knew it chiefly by its opinion pages, where op-ed columns and unsigned editorials—the voice of the publisher—denounced WikiLeaks, pressed for war in Iraq, and defended other excesses, as he saw them, of President George W. Bush's "global war on terror." Verax wanted "adversarial" voices to tell his story, and he had chosen them already. Poitras had proved herself both a skeptic and a target of the wartime establishment, and her short film on another NSA critic had caught Verax's attention. The *Guardian* columnist Glenn Greenwald had built his brand as a dogged combatant against the national security state and its apologists. Months of effort, however, had failed to elicit a reply from Greenwald, who disregarded emails from Verax and a how-to video on encryption.

I did not fit the outsider mold. I was a card-carrying member of the mainstream media, and I made no pretense that I would join a campaign for Verax or his cause. On the other hand, I had been digging into domestic surveillance for years. My case to Verax rested on two claims: that I was well positioned, with years of sources, to report beyond the documents themselves, and that straight-up reporting of new disclosures had unequaled power to hold the government to account.

Verax goaded me, probably on purpose, by suggesting that only a fearless dissenter like Greenwald could expose the truth. I took the bait. I knew Greenwald slightly, having tried and failed to moderate him on a 2010 panel titled "The Constitution and National Security." I had seldom shared the stage with a less tractable panelist. He was clearly intelligent, I told Verax, and a great debunker of hypocrites. He demanded evidence for official claims, which I admired. Like his opponents, he was also selective about it. I thought it better suited a litigator than a news reporter to fix his attention on facts that fit his argument.

My main argument with Verax had to do with the life cycle of information in public debate. Greenwald disdained my tribe of mainstreamers, but how did he think he discovered the sins he took up arms to denounce? Where had he learned about torture, secret prisons, domestic surveillance, abuse of national security letters, or the ground truth about weapons of mass destruction in Iraq? Most of those stories first came to light, and all were considerably advanced, in my journalistic neighborhood. There were other essential players, for sure. Nongovernment organizations like the International Committee of the Red Cross (and the *New York Review of Books*, which obtained the ICRC's confidential report) uncovered hard facts about conditions at Guantánamo Bay. Public interest litigators, from Judicial Watch to the ACLU, forced the government to disgorge secret meeting notes and photographs of detainee abuse. Those in turn fed new disclosures by CBS's *60 Minutes* and the *New Yorker*. Crowdsourced sightings and analysis on social media exposed clandestine CIA rendition flights and their destinations, which paved the way for a huge scoop about secret overseas prisons in the *Post*. Opinions helped shape public debate, but the conversations could not begin without the forces of fact. Patient, committed investigative reporting by traditional news organizations was indispensable.

Verax accepted my limits on advocacy. What he feared was equivocation about unequivocal facts. How could he know I would not water down the story or kill it on command from the U.S. government? I had heard that question before. It always felt outlandish, akin to asking how many facts I typically made up. I wanted to say my record spoke for itself, but I knew that was not something he could verify. Maybe it was a conceit to suppose I had a "record" that anyone could consult. Even if Verax read every word I wrote, he had no vantage point on what I might have left out. I thought the stories made a strong circumstantial case, but I could not offer categorical proof of my independence.

Verax homed in on first principles. Why did I choose this line of work? How did I measure success? I was impatient to start asking my own questions, but there was no dodging. Journalism mattered to me, I told him, because truth was an elemental value. Truth as best fallible humans could tell it, assembled as we found the pieces and revised as we found more. I believed in transparency as a leveler of power—in the voting booth, the marketplace, and anywhere else decisions had to be made. I did not enjoy personal conflict, I told Verax, but in all modesty I had been pissing off authorities for a long time.

I found myself telling the story of my abortive high school newspaper career. The principal spiked a story. I published anyway. She fired me, seized the press run, and burned it. A few days later, with adorable teenage hubris, I called a news conference with two other editors to announce *Gellman v. Wacker*, a First Amendment lawsuit in the U.S. District Court for the Eastern District of Pennsylvania.

"No shit? That is hilarious," Verax wrote.

The lasting lesson, I told him, was how easily we were crushed. The School District of Philadelphia ran out the clock, waiting until I graduated to acknowledge our constitutional right to publish. The principal penned a poison note for my college application file and then professed to have lost it, sidestepping my legal right to read what she wrote. By every practical measure we lost. Yet the battle gave me the gift of a career and a lifetime fascination with the use and abuse of power. That was one of my favorite yarns, especially when accompanied by a *Philadelphia Inquirer* photograph of my *Welcome Back, Kotter*–era hair.

Verax got the message. But that was then. Minor league. What proof did I have, he asked, that I was prepared to stand up to government pressure now? It felt like a job interview, but fine. So there was this book I wrote about Dick Cheney, which told stories the former vice president tried to conceal, and he went on television to express his contempt for my work. I did a long piece about the FBI's use of national security letters to sweep in hundreds of thousands of records of Americans who were not suspected of wrongdoing. The Justice Department wrote, and then had to retract, a ten-page letter to Congress accusing me of willful "distortions and falsehoods." Two years before that, the CIA had mounted a fierce campaign to discredit my reporting on the hunt for Iraqi weapons of mass destruction. David Kay, who put his name on that attack, told me matter-of-factly three years later that he knew at the time the story in question was true. Still earlier, a senior aide to Secretary of State Madeleine Albright banned me from her aircraft because I wrote about secret diplomatic calls that belied her public claims. (Someone higher-ranking thought better of that move.) In my greenest year as Pentagon correspondent, just after the Gulf War, I wrote a front-page piece disclosing that 93 percent of the munitions dropped on Iraq were not the "smart bombs" depicted in Pentagon videos. Two-thirds of them missed their targets. General Merrill A. McPeak, the Air Force chief of staff, offered publicly to put me in a field and see how I liked standing under a payload of "dumb bombs."

REALLY want this story," I told Verax on May 18. "I believe it is quite significant." And he should want me to do it because, not in spite, of my mainstream media roots. If a major newspaper "takes ownership of this story and devotes resources to pursuing it," I wrote, "you have something you can't get anywhere else."

> You will not relinquish the power to release whatever you think should be released, globally and at will. But spare a little time, before you do that, for the chance that the document will be presented in a frame that says: This is real. We've verified it. It looks complicated, but we can tell you what it means. Here is the context and here is why it is news.

Verax countered that I had no power to promise that. He predicted a corporate publisher would buckle under government threats, whatever my intent. "My concern is about your editors, their lawyers, and the rest of the long tail," he wrote. "I fear institutional caution is going to dilute this to the detriment of the public."

"What you are saying does not match my experience in any way," I replied. "You do not know my world at all."

My departure from the *Post* had not been happy, but there was no doubt the paper had backed me to the hilt for twenty-one years. I had sat in or listened in as Leonard Downie Jr., the *Post*'s longtime executive editor, faced down bluster from cabinet secretaries, two intelligence agency chiefs, and a national security adviser. There were other encounters, still higher up, that I did not witness. The *Post* gave anyone a respectful hearing, but it made up its own mind. I had disagreed with Downie twice, on the margins, about what was fit to print. They were close calls. I could have been wrong.

I doubt that I convinced Verax, exactly. He remained agnostic about what I could do, but agnostic was enough. He took an engineer's approach, building in fallbacks and redundant paths to get his story out. If I did not deliver, Poitras or Greenwald might. His plan had no "single point of failure," he told me later. If all of us pursued the story, there would be, in his mind, a natural division of labor. I told him, as the story neared, that I would not coordinate my coverage with Greenwald's. It did not matter. Our roles and skill sets, he said, were complementary.

Verax announced his decision in a note to Poitras and me, conferring a cover name in the NSA's concatenated style.

    So it is decided! If the journo (henceforth BRASSBANNER) wants to
    join, I welcome them.

Poitras and I had come to picture a man in late middle age, possibly older. Verax did not seem to write in a woman's voice, whatever we thought that meant, and the span of his claims to firsthand knowledge suggested a long career. Even so, we did not know his name, his agency, or his job. That was becoming a serious problem for me.

Poitras asked me to promise that I would not try to discover Verax's identity without his consent. That was already out of the question for me. In principle it would be a huge breach of trust, and in practice I could put our source in danger by sleuthing around. The NSA or some other party might know by now that we were homing in on the story. I had no way to know who was watching. If I did so much as a Google search on the small clues I had, authorities might learn more than I did.

"I will not try to unmask the source," I wrote to Poitras on May 7, 2013, but I hoped he would unmask himself to us—and soon. He was planning to come forward on his own, a remarkable promise, but only after the debate had been fully joined. He knew all attention would turn to him once the leaker had a name. From my point of view, I needed to know before the story was done.

The same day, I wrote to Verax and Poitras:

I will do all I can to authenticate the document. What often happens is that I can do so only in part. Maybe I can get a second source to confirm that a document with this date and title exists, or confirm one or more points in paraphrase or verbatim, or confirm essential facts without specific reference to the document. . . .

All that said, unless I get completely independent confirmation, there is no easy substitute for confidence in . . . the bona fides of the original source. . . .

It would be a first for me, in 20-some years of national security reporting, to write the story without knowing where it came from. I am not saying I won't do it. That depends on the totality of the facts I can turn up. . . . But I'd like very much to know whether there is anything I can do to persuade [you].

I was treading on thin ice. My channel to Verax was new, still brittle. Ordinarily, I would not push this hard so early. Why take the risk before he sent me anything? But there were greater risks to the integrity of this story. None of us expected a happy ending for Verax. Nearly every scenario left us incommunicado, soon and without warning. He could be arrested, seized without formalities by parties unknown, forced into hiding, or granted refuge on condition of silence. He thought he might be killed. We might not know one outcome from another. He would simply be gone. If I did not ask essential questions now, I might not—probably would not, I thought—have another chance.

Verax tabled the request for his name but suffered me to ask about scores of other details. These were strange, asynchronous interviews, back and forth by email and chat, with a big hole at their center: I was trying to authenticate a document I had yet to see. By now, he had explained that it would show NSA access to online accounts at big-name U.S. companies. I sent him ten or twenty questions at a time.

"Why should I believe you have access to classified material, much less the capacity to vouch for it?" I began. Not especially diplomatic, but I hoped to establish an unmannered tone. Bluntness, I discovered, did not bother him. There were lines of inquiry he ruled out of bounds, many of them about himself and the people he loved, but if he made a claim of fact he was prepared to defend it.

"I have direct access to the documents by virtue of my position," he replied. "I know they're authentic because they're access-controlled, originated internally, and appropriately marked. I've said this before, but authenticity will seem immediately apparent when you see it."

A piece of paper, I told him, did not mean much on its own. The news would be what it disclosed. Before I could take those disclosures as true, I had to know a lot more.

Who wrote the document? For what purpose? Were there "chops"—initials or stamps—that showed a chain of approval? Did he have the distribution list? How many people had access? What gave the document authority? It would be ruinous to base a big story on a fabricated document, but nearly as bad if it turned out to be a low-level staff draft, a rejected proposal, or an outdated memo about a pilot program long since revoked. What if the document just had its facts wrong? "Dewey Defeats Truman" was a genuine *Chicago Tribune* headline in 1948, but the other fellow took the oath of office.

"Assuming authenticity, is the document accurate?" I asked. "Does it contain any false statements, misleading spin or important omissions?" Verax said he could not vouch for every page, but its descriptions matched his experience with NSA regulations, training, collection systems, and data repositories. This was not an expired memo or obsolete draft, he said. It was a high-level overview of ongoing operations, prepared and updated recently by its top manager. Every military organization had a "command brief" like that, Verax said, in part "to demonstrate the necessity of the program for budget justification."

I edged closer to the personal. This story would undoubtedly draw return fire, with attacks on the messenger and his credibility. I could not afford a big surprise there.

"If the administration tries to discredit the source, either speculating about the source's identity or purporting to know, is there a particular line of attack I should expect? Is there something the administration might say, fairly or not, that could damage the source's credibility?"

Had he been fired from a government job? No. Substance abuse? No. Drunk driving? "I don't drink at all," he replied. After a while he said there was no point dwelling on him. He expected attacks on his character. "You can't protect the source, but if you help me make the truth known, I will consider it a fair trade," he wrote. "Ultimately, don't be distracted by me: the activities are more important than the characters."

People will say you did not follow procedure, I wrote. If you objected so strongly, what exactly did you do to lodge a protest? Later, after the first stories were published, he would tell me he had in fact raised concerns repeatedly with NSA colleagues and supervisors. I had no way to confirm that. NSA officials told me they found no evidence that Snowden reported a violation of law or rules, but they could not exclude that he spoke of his doubts to colleagues in less formal ways. It became clear, on the other hand, that Snowden did not invoke any official grievance procedure. I did not know then that he was a contractor, rather than a government employee, and therefore might not be covered by the limited whistleblower protections of a recent presidential directive. In this first exchange, his emphasis was on futility: whistleblowers are commonly crushed when they challenge the leaders or priorities of their agencies. I do not know how anyone in government, or any other large bureaucracy, could deny that with a straight face.

"The IC has had plenty of time to practice defanging internal protest or oversight, and one need only look at outcomes of previous protests to assess the fruitfulness of that avenue," he said, referring to the intelligence community.

I often ask people with claims of wrongdoing to give me the other side's strongest rejoinder. The reply helps me test the source and prepare for interviews with the people he accuses. "What should I expect to hear from the U.S. government when it learns I have the document, and how would you respond?" I wrote.

"The usual justifications: the program is authorized by law, it is vital to national security, they don't comment on sensitive programs or corporate partnerships. I don't think they will try to challenge the authenticity of the document itself, because it would require access to the program details to fake in the first place."

"If the administration claims that disclosure of the document, or any part of it, would damage national security, what would be its likely stated reasons? What would be wrong with those claims?"

Verax predicted, accurately, that the government would say publication of the story "will chill corporate partnerships."

I could not let him stop there. Was there really nothing more to say about the security interests at stake? Did he not worry, I asked, that disclosure of this document would reveal "tactics, techniques, procedures or technology the exposure of which would benefit foreign intelligence targets"?

That got under his skin, and he hinted at renewed doubts about my establishment values. "I am somewhat concerned that journalists are being made to feel that [their] responsibility is protecting the methods that empower an elite at the expense of the world's inherent right to privacy," he wrote. "Does such an assertion even require rebuttal?"

Well, yes, I said.

Verax, irritated, made a concession that he would decline to repeat later as a public figure, when his statements grew more politic. A story about the document, he acknowledged, would cause some losses. The benefits, he argued, had overriding value. "Yes, beloved USG TTPs will be exposed that could benefit foreign governments (FG), but that disclosure benefits a far wider audience," he wrote. Foreign governments "already know the NSA subverts big telecoms companies. They do the same when they can." But the "innocent and uninvolved" people had no idea they were swept up in large-scale surveillance. Because of that, internet companies felt no pressure to protect them. "I am unconvinced that shadowy figures pose a greater threat to security than information control, total surveillance, and permanent national militarization," he added.

I would come to think of that tone as his high dudgeon mode. Its arrival, in the months and years to come, signaled time to take a break, to save the subject for another day. Our links were ephemeral. He could close a channel and never show up again. Even so, there were times I pressed past the warning signs. One day, when I asked too many follow-ups, he wrote back, "Are you purposely trying to piss me off with questions you know I won't answer?"

The hypothetical questions reached an end on May 20, when the PRISM briefing arrived. The next day brought something else entirely.

P*repare yourself.*
    Jesus.
This was not a Poitras I recognized. Her first urgent email had a practical message: we needed to meet. This second one was purest adrenaline. When I reached her downtown hotel, the room was a shambles. Equipment, clothing, and papers covered the bed and most of the floor. She had not slept or changed, and I could not read her face. Shock, no doubt, but something else, too. Elation? Alarm? Disbelief? If she said anything at the door, I do not remember it. What I do recall is a shake of her head and a sweep of her hand. *Come in. See for yourself. I can't explain.*

Verax had sent us another package, larger than the first. Much, much larger. Three digital vaults, each with a separate passphrase, nested one inside another like matryoshka dolls. The outer vault was labeled "Pandora." Inside it was another, labeled "Verax." And inside that, one more: "Journodrop." I typed the final passphrase and a status window popped open, text flying up and off the screen too fast to read as the encrypted archive unpacked. The operation took a long time. When it stopped, there were eight gigabytes of new files. I had done the math for a story once: one gigabyte could hold tens of thousands of pages, more if fancy graphics were kept to a minimum.

I clicked experimentally on a folder called "fisa," short for the Foreign Intelligence Surveillance Act. Inside it were two more folders. I clicked the top one and found eleven more folders inside. I began to drill down, opening the first folder listed at each new level. There were six of them at the next, fourteen after that, and then twenty-one—folders inside folders inside folders. A quick scan of file names showed Word memos, plain text files, PowerPoint decks, Adobe portable document files, Excel spreadsheets, and photographs.

I had no words. Nothing in my experience prepared me to cope with this volume. How would I vet it, protect it from theft, write stories across so wide a span? I knew how to chase down facts with old-school investigative methods. I drew on open literature and background interviews for context. I circled hard targets from the outside in, interviewing sources on the periphery before approaching the big shots at the center. Afterward, I started around the circle again. Those methods worked, but they did not scale. I could not authenticate classified documents in batches, dozens or hundreds at a time. And there was no way I would put the archive online to crowdsource the analysis, an effective tool in some cases but not when there were unknown risks to public safety. Even if Verax wanted that—and he emphatically did not, describing the idea as "reckless"—I would have had no part in it.

The size of the archive itself, on the other hand, helped validate it. Over the years, I had seen forgeries, some of them fairly convincing, from hoaxers or people with something to gain. But who could possibly fabricate so many? What benefit could justify the prodigious labor involved? In theory, a few doctored papers could be hidden among real ones. I would have to watch for that. Even so, I was increasingly confident in Verax. Poitras was committed to an afternoon flight. We did not have much time to talk. She kept a copy of Pandora. She gave me the original, and I took it home.

This was the Hollywood version of a "leak": an unknown source emerging from nowhere, bearing a stupendous scoop. In the real life of a newsroom, this happened so seldom that it was tantamount to myth. Typically, I got my best stories in small pieces from people I had cultivated for years or discovered through a common web of trust, each contributing part of a whole that none would tell me directly.

I could not get past the size of the archive. How many documents did it hold? The number did not matter much, but looking for it became a calming distraction. The job was unexpectedly difficult. I found no point-and-click method to count the combined contents of all those hundreds of folders. Eventually, I resorted to the command line. I opened a Terminal window and tried to remember the syntax. I garbled it, googled it, and finally typed this:

```
find . -type f | wc -l
```

In the economical language of Unix, I asked the computer to take an inventory. Look inside the current volume. Find only user files. Instead of listing the file names, count them. I tapped Enter and stood, unable to stay still. Seconds ticked away. Nothing happened. As I reached for the keyboard to see what was wrong, the Terminal window scrolled up a line and displayed a response.

```
51662
```

I sat back down. Whoa. Well, I sure messed up *that* command. This was my "air-gapped" computer, disconnected permanently from the internet, so I switched to another laptop and browsed for a more accurate counting method. I tried five variations, adding options to filter out invisible files, temporary directories, and other system junk. The results stayed north of fifty thousand every time.

Agitation sent me on tangents. I reached straight for the cliché, grabbing a package of cheap printer stock from a shelf. What would the archive look like on paper? All right, it's a standard ream, five hundred pages, call it two inches thick. Suppose every document is one page long. Can't be true, but keep it simple. To print fifty thousand pages I'll need a hundred reams. Multiply by two inches, divide by twelve, and, let's see, the stack is seventeen feet tall. I would have to stand on my own head twice to reach the top. And of course these were not one-page documents, by and large. The first five I opened had page counts of 57, 4, 188, 16, and 356.

I should be more prepared for this. Why so overwhelmed? I had written about classified matters plenty of times. That was hard to avoid as a military and diplomatic correspondent. My master's thesis, long before, had parsed the political theory of "Secrecy, Security, and the Right to Know." I had twice taught a Princeton course on the subject and debated it in faculty seminars at the U.S. Naval Academy and Stanford's Hoover Institution. Until now, I had never possessed the full text of a contemporary, codeword-classified document, still less a library. Nobody had. Not in my business. Not on this scale. This was not the most voluminous U.S. classified leak in history, I knew. WikiLeaks had published a quarter million diplomatic cables three years before. But those were classified Confidential or Secret. Nearly everything in this archive had Top Secret markings, most were "sensitive compartmented information," or SCI, and many had cover names, handling caveats, and access controls that signified additional restrictions.

There was nothing systematic about my work in those first few hours. I clicked on files as they caught my eye and skimmed. I found a lot of technical material: network diagrams, data tables, status reports. Also legal opinions, operational briefs, target lists, budgets, and productivity figures for scores of collection sites identified by cover name. Most of the jargon and cryptonyms meant nothing to me. Then I came across a document bearing the following stamps:

TOP SECRET//STLW//COMINT//ORCON//NOFORN

The last three labels were somewhat generic, as close-hold information goes. The document discussed communications intelligence sources and methods; the NSA, as "originating" agency, controlled distribution; no foreign national should have access. It was the second label, the cryptonym, that leaped off the page. *STLW!* This one I knew. It stood for STELLARWIND, the warrantless domestic surveillance program created by Dick Cheney in late 2001. He and his chief counsel conceived it, enlisted the NSA director, Michael V. Hayden, to build it, found a Justice Department lawyer to bless it, and packaged the program for sign-off by President Bush. STELLARWIND had filled two chapters in my last book, *Angler*, but I never discovered exactly how it worked. Just the year before, in 2012, I had written to Poitras about her short film on the former NSA official Bill Binney, who spoke of STELLARWIND as a grave threat to privacy. "Wish I knew the underlying details that could support what he's saying," I wrote. "This story has driven me nuts—spent a long time trying to find out what the program actually did and does, and broke my sword on it."

If ever I had a white whale, this was it. I had told a tale of historic battles inside the Bush administration, fought to the brink of a mass resignation, but I never had a clear view of the beast itself. And now, out of the blue, it had washed up on the screen of my laptop. The contours were clear, innards laid open to view. There would be a big, important story in that, and I saw a handful of others the first day. I also ran across information that I knew I would not publish. Some of it I almost—not quite—wished I had not seen: ongoing operations against plainly dangerous adversaries, photographs of clandestine personnel in the field.

Fuck, fuck, fuck. I needed a lawyer. I needed a security upgrade. I needed a newsroom at my back. I needed a safe way to reach other experts and sources. I needed advice from my partner Dafna Linzer, a great journalist and the love of my life, but I did not know what I could say without waiving attorney-client privilege. I stewed in our apartment, conspicuously agitated and unable to explain.

Pandora's name in the Greek myth meant "all-gifted." Her box, once opened, could never be resealed. Verax intended his gift, like hers, to be irrevocable. In the ancient story, Pandora's box unleashed every evil that befell humankind. What remained in the otherwise empty box was hope. Verax hoped to make public enough information to start an unstoppable debate. By nature and profession, I believed his "Pandora" would do more good than harm, but nothing quite like it had raised its lid before.

Some people, when unboxing a complicated gift, have the sense to look for a user guide. My first pass through Pandora skipped right past it. That was no fault of Verax, who left a pair of text files in the top directory, with names in emphatic capital letters: "README_FIRST" and "README_SECOND." Eventually, I took notice.

The second file gave a high-level tour of the subjects covered and the organization of folders. The first, a 1,041-word introduction and manifesto, began like a conversation in progress: "It will be retroactively changed to damage my credibility, I had a good record and was well liked." It was a tense and jumbled opening, with little of the polish I had come to expect from Verax. Years later he told me he composed both cover notes in haste as he reached the brink of departure from his home in Hawaii. He had not yet boarded the flight that would leave his whole world behind, but it was too late to change his mind. He had committed himself with one final breach of NSA defenses, the one he saved for last. Auditing systems were sure to flag it, and soon. Behind the grandiloquence of his note was a young man, alone, under extraordinary stress.

I led a comfortable and privileged life, a life engineered by the power structure to be difficult to give up. As I advanced and learned the dangerous truth behind the U.S. policies that seek to develop secret, irresistable [sic] powers and concentrate them in the hands of an unaccountable few, human weakness haunted me. As I worked in secret to resist them, selfish fear questioned if the stone thrown by a single man could justify the loss of everything he loves. I have come to my answer.

My sole motive is to inform the public as to that which is done in their name and that which is done against them. The U.S. government, in conspiracy with client states, chiefest among them the Five Eyes—the United Kingdom, Canada, Australia, and New Zealand—have inflicted upon the world a system of secret, pervasive surveillance from which there is no refuge. They protect their domestic systems from the oversight of citizenry through classification and lies, and shield themselves from outrage in the event of leaks by overemphasizing limited protections they choose to grant the governed. I tell you from experience that these protections can be stripped away in an instant.

He closed with a breathtaking act of trust, placing himself entirely in our hands. The timing was his own, as always, but he gave me what I needed when I needed it. "Verax" left the room. His alter ego stepped out from behind the curtain.

Edward Joseph Snowden, SSN: ███-███-███
CIA Alias "Dave M. Churchyard"
Agency Identification Number: 2339176
Former Senior Advisor | United States National Security
Agency, under corporate cover
Former Field Officer | United States Central Intelligence
Agency, under diplomatic cover
Former Lecturer | United States Defense Intelligence Agency,
under corporate cover

He had a name now. There were so many questions left. What kind of man could assume such risks? Who would take decisions of this consequence upon himself? How could he, how could anyone, walk off undetected with the patrimony of a global surveillance establishment?

TWO

HEARTBEAT

Not just anyone could do it, but it doesn't take super villain levels of capability to make it happen. All it would take is paying attention to how the system works, which is your job.
— *Edward Snowden to author, December 2013*

Windows down, radio up, Edward Snowden steered his new Integra north on Highway 750 to a subterranean fortress. The gateway resembled a mine shaft sunk in a suburban parking lot. In Waipahu, Hawaii, locals called it "the Hole." NSA workers, who traversed to the spaces below, favored "the Tunnel." It was March 2012 when Snowden reported for duty at the Kunia Regional Security Operations Center, half an hour's drive from the Baskin-Robbins where President Obama learned to sling ice cream as a teen. Months would pass before Snowden approached news reporters, but he had reached the staging point.

Snowden locked his mobile phone in the car, waved his credentials at the guard shack, and passed through a nuclear blast door that had long since stuck on its hinges, unable to close if Armageddon called. The whole facility had grown shabby with age. In the early 1940s, fearing another Pearl Harbor, military engineers had carved out huge underground bays for aircraft assembly. The war moved on and production never began. The Kunia site became an unloved hand-me-down. Successive tenants acquired and discarded it as a Navy armory, an Air Force bunker, an Army field station, and a backup command center for the U.S. Pacific Fleet. In 1993, the NSA moved in and refashioned Kunia as the agency's ears and eyes on Asia. It was meant to be temporary space, but builders did not break ground for its replacement until 2007. When Snowden arrived five years later, according to a contemporary there, the transition was still "Charlie Foxtrot"—a cluster fuck, ever incomplete.

A quarter-mile slope led Snowden down to a man trap, a double turnstile designed to lock him inside until he scanned his green contractor's badge and punched the correct PIN on a keypad. The scale of the structure on the other side was immense. Snowden emerged from the Tunnel that morning into a cavernous expanse of cubicle farms, server racks, cipher-locked offices, and row after row of long, shared tables laid out in an open plan. Three levels, each the size of a football field, stacked thousands of workers under miles of fluorescent bulbs. "It's like a Bond villain's lair, only with crappier lighting," Snowden told me. "There are a lot more people in there than you'd think, too. I remember being amazed when there was a fire drill."

Disaffection came gradually. Snowden's rebellion against the chain of command did not begin or end at Kunia. His riskiest intrusions into NSA files took place the following year at the agency's new Captain Joseph J. Rochefort command center, five miles to the northeast. Snowden's shift of allegiance from the government to the public at large, as he conceived its interests, was years in the making. By the time he left the CIA, fantasies of rebellion had taken on the character of planning.

Long before that, in his teens and early twenties, Snowden acquired the skills, values, and implacable sense of self that amounted to an origin story for the global public figure he became. He walked away from high school for a self-set curriculum in computer networking, graphic design, kung fu, and the imaginative worlds of anime, costume play, and electronic gaming. Collectively, they fostered a drive for mastery and black-and-white moral views that emphasized personal virtue and prowess. After discovering a shortcut to the U.S. Army Special Forces, he traded his joystick for a rucksack and rifle, pushing himself until his body broke. He accumulated credentials as an engineer by passing certification tests without always bothering to sit through the courses. All those things preceded his arrival at Kunia, but it was here in the Tunnel that Verax was born, among other *noms de code*, and here that Snowden began to probe the NSA's defenses.

"I was starting to operationalize," Snowden recalled, dropping his guard briefly near the end of a nine-hour interview on a hot summer night in Moscow.

"You seem to mean that in two ways," I said carefully, recalling the many times he had refused to speak of it. "One is where you actually start, past the point of no return, in terms of gathering material, extracting it from systems. And the other is communicating to journalists."

"Well, really it's all part of the whole thing," Snowden replied. "It's when you move from the idea of 'something needs to be done' to 'I'm going to do something about it.'"

I ventured another step. Snowden slammed the door.

"You're asking me to confirm or deny operative aspects of acts the government alleges to be criminal," he said in an email later. On another occasion he blamed "tabloid values" for my questions about how he got away with so many files. "Obviously there is a personal interest. There is human curiosity. But you've got to be restrained in how you approach those things. When you talk about weighing benefits and harm, what is the benefit in knowing that?"

Even so, he permitted himself a note of pride.

"I'm not sure anybody will ever talk about how all this stuff happened," he said. "But it was tremendously complex. I'm talking about things that needed to be handled with care and precision in a *really* constrained environment."

The transfer to Hawaii was a concession to Snowden's health, saving his intelligence career just long enough for him to end it with finality. A series of small blackouts over several months preceded a serious epileptic seizure in the middle of a phone call with his boss at Dell Advanced Solutions Group, a U.S. intelligence contractor. Snowden's new diagnosis left him unable to drive lawfully from Maryland to his job as a CIA technical adviser in Langley, Virginia. Dell found him a position half a world away, where he could, in theory, commute by bicycle. Snowden intended to pedal to work from the ranch house he rented in Waipahu, but locals warned him that the blind curves north of Plantation Road were death on wheels. He surveyed the route and decided he could manage it safely by car, despite a state law requiring six seizure-free months before driving. As always, he planned for contingencies and valued his own judgment over the rules. If he felt a seizure coming on, he could ditch on the east side of the road, where no one's life but his own would be at risk. Snowden was no stranger to moving. Previous jobs had cycled him twice through Langley, to Switzerland as a CIA technical officer, and to Japan on a Dell contract for the NSA. The Kunia job was meant, in part, to dial down the stress.

By spring, he was bored senseless. Snowden had signed a contract with Dell for an analyst's slot in the NSA's National Threat Operations Center (NTOC), pronounced by insiders as "EN-tock." There he would work alongside the agency's military and civilian staff to predict, detect, and defeat Chinese hacking attempts against U.S. government systems. Snowden reached that position eventually, but corporate politics unseated him on his way. Another company, CACI International, held the prime contract. Someone there bounced the Dell subcontractor in favor of a CACI employee. By the time Snowden learned of the change, he had already packed and shipped his belongings by sea. In compensation, Dell offered him a sleepy billet in HT322— Hawaii Technical Directorate, Office of Information Sharing. His job was to configure and maintain classified network servers, enforcing access restrictions on each account.

The substitute position paid more than the one he came for, but it could hardly have been more prosaic. Within weeks, he had automated most of the job, writing scripts for maintenance and other routine tasks that his predecessor had performed by hand. It seldom took him more than "a half hour a day," Snowden told me, to keep the Microsoft SharePoint servers running smoothly. Now and then he was called upon for elementary technical support. Not everyone at the NSA was a computer wizard, not by a long shot. One baffled colleague at Fort Meade headquarters sent an urgent request to the help desk in August 2012. For some reason, she could no longer open files sent from Hawaii. When a more senior official groused on August 24 that the support ticket had "sat around for over a week," someone tossed it to Snowden. He sent back a solution the same day, but by then the email chain had grown out of hand. Six days and thousands of words were expended before Snowden stamped out the last of the confusion. "Select 'Word Pad' from the list of programs, make sure the box in the bottom-left that says 'Always use the selected program to open this kind of file' is checked, then click ok," he wrote on August 30.

In his spare time, Snowden began to browse the file directories under his administrative care. It was not always required for his job, but neither was it an unambiguous breach of rules. Snowden held valid credentials to read, write, copy, or delete just about any document on the SharePoint servers. His NSA manager, a career civilian employee, soon broadened Snowden's domain. Spotting underworked talent, he assigned Snowden to help out in busier precincts of the Windows network division. Strictly speaking, Snowden's added duties stretched federal contracting regulations. Dell probably did not know it, but the company was now billing NSA for hours that Snowden spent outside his contractual "statement of work." Off-the-books arrangements of that sort were commonplace in the NSA, which deployed its people where needed and could not realistically seek a contract amendment for each new task. Snowden was a Microsoft-certified systems engineer, a credential he had earned at nineteen, and he had real-world network management experience. His supervisors did not intend to waste those skills. By April, ejsnowd had joined the short list of "super users" in Kunia's Windows Server Engineering Division. He could override the restrictions on ordinary user accounts, see further and deeper into the network, and make changes to its fundamental workings. The NSA's chief technical officer, Lonny Anderson, later said the agency had "three tiers of system administrators, one, two, and three." Snowden had reached the top tier, called PRIVAC, for "Privileged Access." Inside the Tunnel, he had the run of every Windows machine with an IP address.

"I was also helping out the Linux team," he told me, referring to a rival operating system, used widely in networking. "So you know, I had Linux boxes, Linux credentials, virtual servers, all that stuff. So basically, I had the keys to everything. I had the keys to all the data sharing. I had access to all the servers. I knew all of the infrastructure."

Then came Heartbeat. That project, in the coming months, opened conduits to TS/SCI networks that stretched far beyond Kunia, beyond the Pacific, beyond the digital boundaries of the NSA itself. Snowden was not yet thirty years old.

On December 29, 2001, a decade before Snowden reached Hawaii, a new voice joined the forums on *Ars Technica*. He called himself TheTrueHOOHA. *Ars*, which took its name from the Latin for "art of technology," hosted online salons where expert nerds and wannabes communed over all things digital. After Snowden became a household name, *Ars* users and editors found circumstantial evidence that he had been the man behind that handle. For years, Snowden refused to confirm or deny it. He finally acknowledged paternity during our second face-to-face interview. In principle, he told me, he did not like the precedent. Anyone should feel free to speak anonymously without pressure to account for his words, then or later.

When the teenage Snowden chose his handle, he staked out a set of implicit claims. He knew things. He had an attitude. He liked to stir the pot. In the Army slang he borrowed (and misspelled), TheTrue-HOOHA stood for "anything and everything except 'no.'" Snowden described himself as a "belligerent, self-important, 18-year-old upstart," a tolerably accurate appraisal by a young man who could still make fun of himself. His contributions from Ellicott City, Maryland, half an hour north of Fort Meade, blended show-offy erudition, teenage irony, righteous anger, generous advice, and orthodox libertarian bromides.

From his first post, Snowden announced a thirst for autonomy. He wanted full control of the technology he used. "It's my first time, be gentle," he began. "Here's my dilemma: I want to be my own host. What do I need?" As any *Ars* reader would recognize, Snowden meant that he wanted to build a network server—the sort that runs a website or distributes digital files—instead of taking the easy path of renting one commercially.

Snowden had spent years by now on other electronic forums, acquiring and discarding whimsical handles such as Shrike and Belgarion. He knew a lot about computers, and demonstrated as much, but he was a newbie to the ways and means of connecting them. He wanted granular answers to basic questions—"I need to know how to get it to recognize a ping and send the proper files, or whatever the hell a server does"—but he did not want to be patronized. Homework did not deter him. If he had to learn a whole new field, he would download and devour the manuals. "I wish to be as self-sufficient as possible," he wrote. "I figured there would be a few gurus here who can relate to my urge to know everything."

When he could not be dissuaded from the project, fellow Arsians began piling on assignments. There were hardware shopping lists and links to technical guides. There were fine-grained exegeses of domain name systems, dynamic host configuration protocols, and on and on. Snowden swelled with excitement. "I'm so jazzed up that someone cares; I can't think straight," he wrote at 2:08 a.m. "Oooh. The purity of geek nirvana."

By the time his parents had reached this age, the high school sweethearts were married and stably employed. Edward Joseph Snowden, their second child, was born in Elizabeth City, North Carolina, on June 21, 1983. His father, Lonnie G. Snowden Jr., followed his namesake into the Coast Guard and rose to the top rank of warrant officer. His mother, Elizabeth, who went by Wendy, launched a career as a federal government clerk. In 1992, when the Snowdens moved north to Crofton, Maryland, nine-year-old Ed wore oversized glasses and a dirty blond bowl cut, amusing friends of his parents with precocious chatter. Teachers at the Crofton Woods Elementary School, on the other hand, could not make out his words. They confused his slow, deliberate southern drawl with a developmental disability. When they tested him, according to family confidants, his IQ score was 155 on the Stanford-Binet scale, or the 99.97th percentile. Two more tests returned similar scores. IQ is a controversial proxy for intelligence, but one evaluator told Snowden's mother, "He will learn what he wants to learn."

Snowden's older sister, Jessica, who went on to work as a researcher for the federal judiciary, had comparable test results. She skipped a grade in school and brought home straight As. Ed did not exactly follow suit. He refused to bother with subjects that bored him, losing interest easily and falling behind. Friends and family said he read voraciously, with unusual concentration, from the age of three. In his grade school years, they would find him asleep at his grandmother's house, face covered by an open volume of *The World Book Encyclopedia*. His grades were erratic: top marks in courses he liked, Bs and Cs or worse in those he did not. In the fall of 1998, his sophomore year at Arundel High School, a bad case of mononucleosis kept him home for four months. When informed that he would have to repeat the grade, he refused to return to school. "The public education system turned it's wretched, spikéd back on me," Snowden wrote in a self-profile some years later. The reverse might equally be said.

During his hiatus at home, the fifteen-year-old used command-line tools such as Telnet to browse interesting internet domains. One day he found his way online to the Los Alamos National Laboratory, which does classified and unclassified research for the U.S. Department of Energy. Using an elementary technique called directory walking, Snowden discovered that the lab had password-protected its employee portal but left the subdirectories wide open. He left voicemails on the lab's main number to report the security flaw, then waited impatiently for evidence of a repair. About two weeks later, his mother answered the Snowden family telephone at home. "Hi, I'm from the Los Alamos National Laboratory," a sober voice said. "Is Mr. Snowden around?" He was looking for Ed, not Lon. After questioning him closely, the man asked if Snowden was looking for work.

To this day, some critics in the U.S. government scorn Snowden as a high school dropout, a low-ranking employee of modest skills who had no grasp of the secrets he disclosed. That is a dishonest narrative. It would surely be embarrassing, if true, that such a slacker upended the NSA so thoroughly in its core mission of "information dominance," the use of other people's secrets to shape events. The truth about Snowden is more interesting. It is the story of a young man who fell short in class, refused to conform, gave no serious thought to a university degree, burned a lot of time in game arcades, and never had to pay the dues that (some of) his seniors did before ascending to six-figure salaries. And yet. It is also the story of a self-taught polymath, determined to apply his talents on his own terms, who repeatedly found his way around conventional barriers.

The defining feature of Snowden's young adulthood was a knack for breaking down problems, unpacking the parts, discerning how the innards worked, and shaping them to his will. He had an eye for hidden openings. It was a hacker's frame of mind, in the classic sense, applicable as much to daily life as to machines. Disregard the "normie" path. Find a side window if the front door is locked, skip needless steps, follow instructions out of sequence if that speeds results. Automate a tedious task or substitute a more efficient one. Rewrite or repurpose any product, any process, if you can turn it to your own ends. Share the recipe.

Some of Snowden's life hacks were inspired. Some did not work at all. At sixteen, after recovering from mono, he enrolled part-time at Anne Arundel Community College. He had found a congenial shortcut, he thought, to a high school diploma. As he read the rules, he could qualify for a General Educational Development (GED) credential with college credits alone, ditching the tedious classes and learning as he liked. To his parents, he seemed to be choosing almost at random. Introduction to Psychology. Martial Arts. The Solar System. Principles of Accounting. He aced algebra and geometry, dropped trigonometry for Japanese, detoured into Mandarin, and barely escaped chemistry with a C. "I'm not paying for you to go to college to have fun," his father told him, repeatedly admonishing the teenager to focus on core academics. Maryland's Department of Education was unpersuaded by Snowden's interpretation of the rules, obliging him to sit for the GED exam. The results and his diploma arrived in June 2002, the same month he would have graduated after illness held him back a grade. He had skipped three-quarters of high school but scored in the 95th percentile in writing, 96th in social studies, 99th in science, mathematics, and literature and the arts.

Lon Snowden despaired of employment for a son who lacked a college degree. He did not believe online wanderings could build the skills and credentials Ed would need. The younger Snowden, contemporaries said, had a preternatural confidence in his path. Like other digital natives of his generation, Snowden learned to think, debate, and build things online before most Americans mastered the rudiments of email. Between 1998 and 2003, from ages fifteen to twenty, he assembled a technical education piece by piece.

One of his best career hacks came in February 2002, when Snowden registered for an expensive private course in Windows system engineering. The Computer Career Institute at Johns Hopkins, a for-profit entity, took his money without requiring proof of relevant work experience, previous training, or even the high school diploma that was still a month away. Lon Snowden could make no sense of it. Who signs up for advanced networking without taking the introductory course? His son saw the move as a strategic play. He had learned something important in online forums: certified engineering skills were an easy shortcut through employment screening in the Washington area's booming tech sector. Computer skills were in high demand, and human resources departments did not know how to judge prospective hires. A Microsoft certification had become a standard proxy. All Snowden had to do was master a syllabus spanning 4,416 pages of technical reading on infrastructure design, installation of complex networks, and so on. That, and troubleshoot simulated failures in timed exercises. Several months later, he passed the grueling sequence of seven qualifying exams. At nineteen, with the barest minimum of coursework, he became a Microsoft-certified systems engineer, identification number 2661071. It was the first of many such credentials, but the MCSE was a golden ticket that year. It would bump him to the head of the queue when the time came.

Snowden had discovered a minor superpower. He could read between the lines of a test, intuiting the designer's intent. He anticipated misdirection, imagining the traps that he would set if he wrote the exam himself. If no one got a question wrong, the test would not produce results in the desired bell-shaped curve. Snowden trained himself to spot false answers inserted for the unwary. "I'm not convinced I'm actually that intelligent," he told me in an introspective moment. "I have an understanding, a sort of talent for understanding what's being tested. The person who's writing the test, what are they trying to do? I can understand the subtext of the question. . . . I'm not sure it's actually more meaningful in terms of 'he's smart' so much as just maybe I kind of beat the test. The difference is subtle, I think, but anywhere you're being measured and rated against standards, I don't know what else to say besides I've done well when my qualifications didn't necessarily merit that placement." Whatever that kind of skill was called, it extended to performance beyond the classroom. He asserted as much, with some bombast, in a 2003 contretemps with an *Ars* user who had bolstered a claim by citing his college diploma. "Can you redeem your degree for a cash prize? Maybe a stuffed animal?" Snowden wrote, adding, "Great minds do not need a university to make them any more credible: they get what they need and quietly blaze their trails into history." Such was his ambition, even then.

Even as he built up professional skills, Snowden devoted great heaps of time to role-playing and fantasy. Since his midteens he had worked and played with a tight group of slightly older friends who shared his fascination with Japanese popular culture. Together they ran a pair of businesses: Clockwork Chihuahua Studios, a web design company, and Ryuhana Press, an online showcase for anime art and comics. Snowden later told me the dot-com boom had brought a lot of money into those start-ups, providing him with some financial independence. He listed himself on RyuhanaPress.com as "Editor/ Coffee-Boy," alongside alter egos of Edowaado and Phish. Friends embarrassed him on his nineteenth birthday by posting photographs of the skinny teen in various stages of undress, opining that "Ed is positive that he is God's gift to women."

Snowden clowned online, but he was dead serious about gaming. In that environment, he displayed the planning skills, the instinct to bypass defenses, and the competitive drive that carried him up or around career ladders in the U.S. intelligence community. In August 2001, alongside his Ryuhana Press pals Katie Bair and Lindsey Deets, he traveled in costume to Baltimore for a gathering known as Otakon, after the Japanese slang term *otaku* for obsessive fans. Snowden cosplayed as Hakeem, a character from the comic *Oasis Destiny*. Hakeem was a "rogue," known for slipping past enemy lines and pivoting to attack from within. Embracing the persona, Snowden scouted a side route past convention center guards and slipped into the overcapacity event. The following year, still in role, he infiltrated again—this time taking his friends with him through back corridors. Years later, when someone asked about his character, Snowden opined that "very few are roguish enough to be a true Hakeem." His advice for the ambitious was to "start practicing evading Con Security now."

Ed grew especially close in those years with Jodon Bellofatto, a fellow enthusiast for bloodthirsty electronic games. They wasted demons by the thousands, side by side, in hundreds of hours of *Diablo II* and *Warcraft III*. In real life, in a nearby dojo, they became serious students of Jow Ga kung fu, working through combat set pieces and competing in tournaments. When they moved together to an empty condominium owned by Snowden's mother, Bellofatto wrote about "Edo begging every last fool who walks in the door to play *Tekken* with him."

The Japanese fighting game was Snowden's best-documented obsession. In the *Tekken* universe, one man must decide the fate of a clan in trials by single combat. The symbolism, looking back, is hard to resist. Snowden became a *Tekken* star by digging down into the logic of the silicon chips that powered the game. He calculated move-by-move reaction times, measured in frames per second. "*Tekken* runs at 60fps," he explained to one advice seeker. "Every move takes a certain amount of frames to execute, and a certain amount of frames to 'recover' from." After learning the time cost of each combination, he lured opponents into attacks that left them frozen long enough for his fatal riposte. In pursuit of millisecond advantages, he experimented with the most efficient finger patterns, settling on use of "the index and middle fingers of both hands in an alternating fashion." He wrote out and practiced attack sequences such as "1,2~f[f,f]..1,2~f[f,f]..1,2~f[f,f] 3, 4." This was not entirely normal behavior, even among *Tekken* masters.

Armed with this granular knowledge, Snowden reckoned there were only three people in Maryland who could take a game from him. Ed Blakslee, who watched a fair share of Snowden's estimated ten thousand matches, wrote, "I have a buddy who is a Tekken GOD. He smokes EVERYONE who has ever played against him." Snowden had lately devised another hack, Blakslee reported in 2003. He learned to control a *Tekken* character with his feet on a *Dance Dance Revolution* floor pad. "I once saw him play at an arcade by standing backwards to the machine and . . . watching the reflection from a mirror," Blakslee added.

Tekken was not all entertainment for a man of Snowden's disposition. It was a kind of rehearsal, honing an approach he could use against adversaries elsewhere. In U.S. military argot, Snowden's *Tekken* victories were based on superior "intelligence preparation of the battlefield." He learned the terrain, scouted his opponent, and planned for countless scenarios ahead. He could not yet have anticipated a contest with the NSA, but his gaming style foreshadowed some of his moves to come.

During the same period, just after turning twenty, Snowden began digging into privacy tools called anonymous proxies, which disguise the origin or destination of an internet link. "I wouldn't want God himself to know where I've been, you know?" he wrote. Some Arsians offered instruction. Others had their doubts. "Unless this is for troubleshooting or a prank, it sounds like it might be illicit activity," one of the latter wrote. "What the hell [are] you so paranoid about here?" asked another. Snowden responded curtly, "Patriot Act." He elaborated. "If they misinterpret the actions I perform, I could be a cyb4r terrorist and that would be very fucking bad," he wrote. "It's not about what's said, it's about what's done and what will be understandable in text logs. My goal is in the worst case . . . they see my IP as a computer in madagascar." Much the same approach, carried out with greater sophistication, guided him a decade later as he passed classified information to me and other journalists. What he had in mind in the fall of 2003 remains unknown.

—————

E ven as he spoke of eluding the Feds, Snowden dreamed of enlisting in the Army. His parents pushed back hard. "I was really swept up in the post–September 11 climate," he told me. "I really believed the government. I mean, I was drinking the Kool-Aid. . . . And when they said, we want to liberate people in Iraq, that resonated with me." He had grown up in a federal family, steeped in the courts and armed services, but nobody wanted him pounding boots in Baghdad. His family begged him to stay in school, join the Air Force or Navy if he absolutely must, but for the love of God keep away from the infantry. Snowden was unmoved. He had learned of an irresistible hack, a side channel that might let him skip years of requirements and enlist directly in the U.S. Army Special Forces. Each year, in a little-publicized program known as 18X, the Army accepted a few recruits as "Special Forces candidates." If Snowden was tough and smart enough, the compressed training regimen could place him in an elite unit, wearing sergeant's stripes, at an accelerated pace. "I liked the idea of the 18X program because it was very merit oriented," he said. "If you just totally demolished their test—their academic test, their fitness test— before you went into basic, you've got a shot at SF. It wasn't guaranteed, but you got a shot. And that was attractive to me."

Lon Snowden threatened to call in Pentagon connections to stand down the Army recruiters. That was bluster talking, a father's fear. After twenty-five years in uniform, he knew he had no say in the decision. In the first week of May 2004, not long before Edward Snowden's twenty-first birthday, Lon Snowden found a note under his door. "Dad, I know you're going to be upset," it began. His son had signed his enlistment papers. "I feel this is vital to my personal growth," Snowden wrote.

At the recruiter's office, Snowden blew through the Armed Forces

Qualification Test, the Army's measure of general aptitude and intelligence. He got only one question wrong, he told me, and it still chafed him: "Where in your body are the Eustachian tubes?" Then came the Defense Language Aptitude Battery, a linguistic logic game so well suited to Snowden that he would probably play it online for fun. After instruction in the grammar and vocabulary of a fictional language, he had to apply the rules to increasingly complex phrases and sentences. He crushed that one, too. Unfamiliar patterns resolved themselves easily for him. When he passed the physical fitness battery, the Army gave him a contract and a ticket to Fort Benning, Georgia.

On June 3, 2004, Private First Class Edward Snowden reported for duty at E Company, Second Battalion, 19th Infantry Regiment as a Special Forces recruit. At five feet ten, Snowden began his infantry training at a skeletal 127 pounds. He had the muscle tone of a martial artist, but "there are supermodels fatter than me," he said. Drill sergeants, for a laugh, paired him in buddy-carry drills with a bodybuilder who weighed twice as much. Snowden just managed to drag his fellow recruit out of a simulated kill zone. Like everyone else, he ran mile after mile in boots and battle gear. He ignored the agony in his legs, spurred on by trash talk from the instructors. ("What the fuck's wrong with you, Mary? You got sand in your vagina?") Near the end of the first fourteen-week stage, Snowden landed awkwardly after jumping off a downed tree trunk during a march through the woods with a fifty-pound rucksack. The next day he tried to stand and fell to the floor. X-rays showed full bilateral tibial fractures. Two broken legs. The next scheduled training stage, a few weeks away, was Airborne. "If you jump out of an airplane like that, your legs are going to turn into powder," an Army doctor told him. Melodramatic, but he got the message. According to Snowden, he could have chosen to "recycle" into a subsequent basic training class, but he would have lost his chance for accelerated promotion and assignment to the Special Forces.

He accepted an administrative discharge and flew home on September 28, 2004, not quite five months after enlisting. Flight attendants wheeled him off the plane at Dulles Airport, a cast on each leg.

Three months later, this time by happenstance, Snowden stumbled onto the career hack that enabled all the rest. After an interlude of recovery in North Carolina, he returned to Ellicott City, signed up again for community college, and started looking for work. It was a dispiriting time, ill suited to ambition. When the University of Maryland offered a post as security guard for $29,000 a year, Snowden had nothing better on his plate. Beginning on January 28, 2005, he stood vigil at the front desk of the Center for Advanced Study of Language. Still under construction, the facility included classified spaces for secret NSA research. Even as lobby hero, Snowden needed a TS/SCI clearance and a clean polygraph. The clearance came through alongside a July 7 letter from Q223, the NSA's counterintelligence awareness office. "Dear Contractor Staff Security Officer," it said. "This form is for your records to verify that the person stated below has been indoctrinated in counterintelligence." However humble the position, the clearance ushered Snowden into the national security establishment. At twenty-two, he had yet to reach even the bottom rung, but he was eligible now to apply for thousands of classified jobs in the Washington area alone.

Overnight shifts at "the Castle," as everyone pronounced CASL, the language center's initials, offered scant diversion. Snowden did not have much to do apart from checking locks and alarms from time to time. One night, he and his partner plugged a laptop into an Ethernet port in the lobby, hoping to pass some time browsing the web. The network in this part of the building was unclassified, but default settings offered no connection to an unknown machine. Irritating. Snowden pulled up a command line and pinged the router, confirming that the physical link was good. All he lacked was a network identity.

He fiddled with the host control settings, assigned himself an IP address on the subnet, and the internet lay before him in its glory.

Two or three weeks passed before anyone noticed unauthorized machines in the logs. By then, there were a lot of them. Many of the guards had learned Snowden's trick. Members of the Castle's IT staff, alarmed at first, asked Snowden how he had managed to bypass network controls. It was not a security offense, exactly: Snowden was breaking out of the building, not trying to break in. When he finished explaining, as he recalled later, "they were like, 'Why are you working at the front desk? Do you want to join the network team?'" He would like that fine, but the position required a college degree. Go to the job fairs for security-cleared personnel, one man suggested. Some of those companies don't care about degrees. Snowden's all-important TS/SCI offered entry into the lucrative world of Beltway bandits, where contractors did the work of intelligence agency employees at double or triple the salary.

Snowden attended his first classified job fair, TECHEXPO Top Secret, in the winter of 2005. He approached the booth of COMSO, a small contractor based in Greenbelt, Maryland, which offered him a job on the spot. The Microsoft certificate, the clearance, and a satisfactory interview were all he needed. Snowden's client, the contractor told him, would be the Central Intelligence Agency. When he first swiped into the George Bush Center for Intelligence, the CIA headquarters in Langley, he was twenty-two years old. Only two years earlier, he had been an unemployed dropout, spending, by his own account, eight hours a day surfing the web, four in the dojo, and two playing *Tekken*. Now he was doing the work of a systems engineer, joining a team that handled the care and feeding of a CIA network that spanned northern Virginia, Washington, and southern Maryland.

What separated Snowden from his agency peers was an email address that included "CTR," for contractor, and a paycheck signed by a private employer in Greenbelt. The jobs were substantially the same.

Again he had the night shift, which suited his vampiric sleep cycle. "The daystar, it burns," Snowden wrote in an *Ars* post in April 2006. He mainly performed standard maintenance—"building the network, expanding the network, taking care of the network," he told me. By this point, he thought of himself as a Windows whisperer, anticipating a server's shifting moods and heading off meltdowns. He loved the quiet of the graveyard shift, with only a skeleton crew for company. From 6:00 p.m. to 6:00 a.m., at a desk in Room 2P20 of the New Headquarters Building or the server vault in 1D04, Snowden said, he and one other guy were "masters of the universe for all of the Washington metropolitan area network."

Late at night, Snowden wandered empty basement corridors of painted cinder block. Motion-sensing lights "just kind of follow you," he said, shadows pooling ahead and behind. It was not lost on him that, as domain administrator, he had "incredible access, ridiculous access." What he did with that access is unclear. Snowden and I discussed this time in detail during my second visit to Moscow in the summer of 2015. He told me then that he could have browsed widely in the CIA's files but resisted the temptation, terrified of laying eyes on something forbidden. "My crayon stayed within the lines at all times," he said. In his 2019 memoir, he described "hours and hours every night" of browsing secret internal web pages of "top secret dispatches regarding trade talks and coups as they were still unfolding." He implied, but did not write explicitly, that he dug beyond the dispatches themselves to look for the identities of their human sources. Case files containing the "true name and complete personal history" of those CIA sources, he wrote, "would be only a few clicks away." Whether or not he had sufficient clearances for that kind of material,

Snowden certainly lacked the requisite "need to know." By the memoir's account, he was coloring far outside the lines.

A senior technical officer paid a call on Snowden after a few months on the job. The older man borrowed him for a project or two, sizing him up, and they developed a rapport. Eventually, the officer asked Snowden how he would feel about working overseas. That was not a hard sell. In a 2002 *Ars* post about IT jobs in Japan, Snowden had written, "I want to expatriate! I want to expatriate with flair and clandestine meetings!" The wish came true on August 26, 2006. Snowden added "STF," or staff, to his email address, swapped a green contractor's badge for a blue one, and received agency identification number 2339176. He was a full-time employee now, soon to be deployable as a telecommunications information security officer. The official designation was TISO, but agency folk, old-timers especially, called the job "commo." Snowden swallowed a five-figure pay cut to take what he saw as a dream job.

The CIA's public affairs staff answers no questions about Snowden's job duties or performance, leaving former officials to say what they like without accountability to the documentary record. Michael Morell, who served as deputy director and acting director until August 2013, sat down with me early the following year at an outdoor café overlooking Arizona's Dove Mountain. After the public disclosures began, three months before he retired, he had asked around about Snowden. It would be absurd, Morell said, to portray him as a young hotshot or some kind of high-powered recruit. Snowden was the lowest of the low-level staff and poorly qualified even for the job he had. He owed his hire to the CIA's desperate need for commos as it ramped up its operational tempo around the world. Snowden slipped through the gate, he suggested, under hiring standards diminished by necessity. Some of that is demonstrably wrong. Historic snapshots of the CIA's employment page show no substantive changes in the job requirements. The qualifications of Snowden's cohort, in comparison to previous years, cannot plausibly be a national security secret. Straight answers about Snowden's own performance reviews would settle other questions. Morell's account, so comprehensively disparaging, is hard to credit in the face of Snowden's steady climb.

Snowden joined the next class in a six-month training course called the Basic Telecommunications Training Program at an unadvertised CIA facility near Warrenton, in northern Virginia. New operations officers, the agency's spies, learned their trade at a better-known site, nicknamed "the Farm." Snowden, like other science and technology officers, went to "the Hill."

It is tempting to imagine a James Bond film scene with Q, the guru, tech-splaining how to fire missiles from a remote-controlled luxury car. In the Hill's syllabus, there were fewer Aston Martins, more broken radios. "You learn how to deal with basically any piece of infrastructure that could be at an embassy," Snowden said. He practiced taking apart and reassembling routers, telephones, firewalls, and ventilation units. He learned fundamentals of cryptography, contemporary and historical. Along with state-of-the-art systems, he had to become proficient with outdated gear that old-school ambassadors and station chiefs might keep on hand. Firefly keys, boxy old KG-84 encryption devices with knobs and dials—these were actual museum pieces now, but Snowden had to know his way around them. A lot of time was devoted to "living your cover," he said. He and his classmates learned basic tradecraft for CIA officers under likely foreign surveillance. They spent equal time on maintaining an identity inside the embassy itself. Some diplomatic colleagues would be unaware of his true employer. "You went through a special course to pretend to be State Department, to understand how it works. Basically, to masquerade as if you're a State Department person. Because they have their own language. They've got their own acronyms. . . . And you've got to be able to blend in."

Snowden learned how to spot a tail. How to detect tampering on a car. How to lie convincingly. What not to tell a spouse (many things) or children (anything). There was a class on cable writing from the field, with special instructions for CRITIC reporting. The latter referred to intelligence of such import that it must be recognized, written, and flash routed to the president within ten minutes. The CRITIC designation was reserved, according to a classified briefing, for matters that "could imminently and materially jeopardize vital U.S. political, economic, informational or military interests." An instructor told a cautionary tale of the hapless trainee who once transmitted a practice CRITIC message for real. On the other hand, a slide admonished new commos, in large capital letters, "WHEN IN DOUBT, PUT IT OUT!" One example in the briefing came from the CIA station in Baghdad at 2:31 a.m. on August 2, 1990. "Iraqi troops in Kuwait City," it said. "Small arms fire is taking place within a thousand yards of the U.S. Embassy."

Before the course ended, Snowden taught the CIA something, too. He was willing to make a spectacle of himself when he thought a principle was at stake. His classmates groused about their housing in a crumbling Comfort Inn and the CIA's refusal to pay for overtime. Snowden regarded those failings as violations of labor, health, and safety laws. He filed a formal complaint, and when the head of school blew him off, he took his grievance to the director of the CIA's Field Services Group—and then to the director's boss. He won a change of housing and a reprimand for insubordination. The latter did not impress him. Unlike others around him, Snowden recalled, he was willing to bear the "cost of escalation."

On the last day of training, Snowden and his classmates ranked their preferences for a first assignment. Snowden wanted a war zone. After Iraq or Afghanistan, his first choices, he asked for Geneva as a fallback. He had heard it was technically challenging, a big station with complex network infrastructure in a city with more spies per capita than most. That is where the agency sent him in March 2007. His bright red diplomatic badge featured a head shot of the baby-faced twenty-three-year-old in a blue suit, maroon dress shirt, and striped club tie. As far as the outside world was concerned, Snowden was a diplomatic attaché in the U.S. mission to the UN Geneva headquarters, State Department employee number 64554. Inside the embassy, he worked in the top-floor Information Technology Center. Alongside the CIA commo shop, each in its own gated space, were the State Department's communications team and the Special Collection Service personnel who eavesdropped on local targets for the NSA. In written communications, Snowden signed as "Dave M. Churchyard." That precaution, adopted after the sacking of the Tehran embassy in 1979, made it harder to identify him as an intelligence employee if someone broke into the classified records.

The CIA salary and subsidies sufficed to rent a four-bedroom apartment with a view of Lake Geneva. Snowden lived large. He bought a Ford Explorer and played the stock market. He had his complaints about Switzerland—"nightmarishly expensive and horrifically classist," he assessed in an *Ars* chat—but overall things were "pretty cool." The work was not so different from the network management he had done as a contractor at Langley. Hoping for more, he volunteered for temporary duty assignments, or TDYs, under which the Geneva station lent personnel to others. In the spring of 2008, he traveled TDY to the U.S. embassy in Bucharest, Romania, where President George W. Bush would soon attend a NATO summit. Snowden joined an advance team that, among other things, transmitted CIA risk assessments to the Secret Service. "The threat reporting was ridiculous," he remembered. "Some keyboard warrior in a forum saying he's going to run Bush over with a car." He saw the leads as implausible, wondered how they were generated and taken seriously. But he laughed it off, he said. The government wasted time and resources. What else was new?

Back in Geneva, Snowden saw things that troubled him. One involved a pair of case officers who encouraged a Saudi wealth manager to drive home drunk, then tried to recruit him as an agent with the leverage of his arrest. "We deal with some really ugly people, just some nasty people, as a tool," said an intelligence colleague who worked with Snowden later. "Some of the means you're using, I feel dirty being involved in this." Another source of disillusion for Snowden was the pervasive U.S. espionage against UN diplomats. He worked with three CIA case officers, he told me, who consulted him informally when they had to break into a foreign official's computer. "They'd be like, we've got a thumb drive we're supposed to put in. What do I need to do? What are the tricks? What do I need to be worried about? What do I not want to fuck up? How would I get caught? How do I explain it? Coming up with plausible things like that." Snowden said he understood the advantage gained by spying on allies, but he did not like the policies it served. His libertarian politics had turned him by then against the war in Iraq, against secret rendition of alleged terrorists, and against Bush's handling of the 2008 stock market crash. Why should America keep trying to be the world's policeman and corporate safety net? Mavanee Anderson, a legal intern at the Geneva mission who knew Snowden between 2007 and 2009, remembered him as an introspective computer genius with a tendency to brood. He was having a crisis of conscience, she said. Snowden later said he first considered blowing a whistle in Geneva but held back for fear of harming flesh-and-blood case officers and their agents. He also hoped the newly elected president, Barack Obama, would change some of the policies that troubled him. On *Ars* in early 2009, he did not sound like a man prepared to spill secrets. Anonymous officials who leak classified information, he wrote, should be "shot in the balls . . . that shit is classified for a reason."

Around that time, the CIA and its twenty-five-year-old employee began heading toward a breach. There are three competing accounts of Snowden's departure. The first came from "two senior American officials" who were paraphrased in the *New York Times*. They said Snowden's Geneva supervisor suspected him of trying to open files he was not authorized to read. The supervisor placed a "derog"—a derogatory memo—in his personnel file. In an unusual response to the *Times* the following day, the CIA Office of Public Affairs said the story was untrue. There was a derog in Snowden's file, but the reason was much less serious. Snowden's explanation fits more closely with the second, official account. While filling out his annual self-evaluation, he said, he identified a vulnerability that would allow any employee to inject malicious code into the agency's online human resources app. Snowden proposed to demonstrate the flaw by taking command of the system without doing damage, a commonly used procedure in security research. He thought about creating a scary pop-up message, but his boss persuaded him to settle for something less flashy. So when Snowden filled out his self-evaluation, he proved he could "own" the web app by changing all the colors on the page. The boss's boss, the senior technology officer for Europe, was embarrassed and angry, according to Snowden. It was he who filed the derog, effectively closing Snowden's path to promotion. A retired CIA official told *Vanity Fair* that Snowden was "too smart to be doing the job he was doing." The conflict arose, the official thought, because "I think he would have liked to have been a player."

A third version of Snowden's departure, not necessarily in conflict with the others, comes from two sources close to his family. In December 2008, they said, Snowden flew home to attend his father's Coast Guard retirement ceremony. His parents noticed with alarm that their son had a chronic hacking cough that never seemed to stop. Commos are sometimes called upon to destroy classified data by grinding electronic components into small particles. Lon Snowden came to believe that CIA negligence had exposed his son to dangerous concentrations of silica dust. He insisted that Ed see a doctor. Snowden lingered in the Washington area to consult respiratory specialists. He never returned to duty. The Geneva station packed up his apartment and shipped the contents home.

Snowden's resignation letter, addressed to his "dear friend and supervisor" on April 16, 2009, said that "looking back on my time here will always be a happy experience." Closing the one door opened another. Since his teens, he had "dreamed of being able to 'make it' in Japan," his pop culture fountainhead. When his lungs recovered sufficiently, Dell came along with the first of three employment contracts he would sign in coming years. In mid-2009, he reported as a systems administrator to the NSA's Pacific Technical Center on Yokota Air Base, outside Tokyo. Occasionally, he was allowed to take small forays into the spy-versus-spy world he craved. In August 2010, the Joint Counterintelligence Training Academy held a three-day classified conference at Yokota, called "Counterintelligence Threat Seminar: China." Then based in Elkridge, Maryland, JCITA was the Defense Department's lead entity for training clearance holders on how to protect U.S. secrets from foreign spies. Shortly before the conference began, organizers learned that they had lost their cyber instructor. Intelligence personnel from all over Asia were descending on Yokota, and there was no one to teach them digital self-defense.

"My team and I were standing around in that secure space, [saying]

'What are we going to do?'" recalled Danielle Massarini, who ran the conference that year. A young man in khakis and T-shirt wandered over. "He piped in and said, 'Hey, I have given briefings on that before.' We thought, what the hell. We'll give him a shot." Snowden must have stayed up all night preparing, Massarini said, because he submitted a set of Top Secret teaching slides by morning. Massarini had spent her career on Chinese counterintelligence, with stints in the office of the secretary of defense and the Army's 902nd Military Intelligence Group. What Snowden handed her that morning, she said, "was without question the best cyber briefing on China intel we'd ever had."

Two days later, Snowden faced a class full of officers and analysts from around the intelligence community: FBI, NSA, Department of Homeland Security, Navy Criminal Investigation Service, Air Force Office of Special Investigations. He guided them on a virtual tour of Chinese hacking consortia, illustrating a range of attacks from simple phishing emails to sophisticated "intrusion sets" of computer code that burrowed into an exposed machine and stayed there. The Beijing government often exploited previously unknown security flaws to gain entry. That kind of flaw was called a Zero Day because attackers used it before the first day, Day 1, that anyone else became aware of the threat. Despite the stealth of that kind of attack, Snowden showed participants how to work and communicate safely in an untrusted environment. One of the habits he taught them became a signature moment in the Laura Poitras film *Citizen Four*. Cover your keyboard with a blanket, he said, when typing your password.

"He came across as brilliant," Massarini said, with a gift for conveying complex material in conversational language. Goggle-eyed avatars, captioned "Be Afraid," danced across his final slide. When he called for questions, Massarini was astonished to see hands raised all around her. The students wanted more. That *never* happened in cyber class. In an ordinary year, she said, participants "were stabbing themselves in the eye with a pencil" by the end of the two-hour seminar. "I can't articulate to you enough how good a presenter he was." In feedback for the three-day conference, Snowden's presentation received by far the best reviews. "That guy's tripping me out with his paranoia," one student wrote. Immediately after returning to Maryland, Massarini invited Snowden to teach again. In the next two years she flew him half a dozen times to Elkridge, Quantico, or Dublin, California, where he earned a stipend of $1,500 per class. He might look like a basement-dwelling hacker, but he could be outgoing and funny when he wanted to. "I worked with those people," Massarini said. "He could answer the detailed technical questions, but he could shoot the shit and have a beer with you too."

As usual, Snowden automated the larger part of his routine work in Japan. The free time permitted him to propose a new venture on the side. Nobody had asked him for it, but he was bored and looking for a project worth his time. The seeds of EPICSHELTER, as he named it, had been planted when Snowden watched from Geneva as Serbian protesters set fire to the U.S. embassy in Belgrade. Damage to the CIA station there prompted speculation in Snowden's office that important intelligence materials had been lost. He began to think about the problem of disaster recovery. Where, if anywhere, did the Belgrade station preserve real-time copies of its files? How would a well-designed backup system transmit and store data efficiently? It was idle curiosity at the time, but the questions stayed with him. In Yokota, Snowden took them up in earnest. He envisioned a backup and recovery system that could start small and scale up to cover as much of the NSA's digital realm as desired. Some of the features he contemplated were available in the commercial world, but they were not easy to reproduce across interlocking classified networks. "De-duplication" would save storage space by backing up each file only once, even if there were multiple copies on the source networks. "Block level" updates would save bandwidth by synchronizing only new bits and bytes when a source file changed, rather than sending a new copy of the whole file. Snowden drew up conceptual designs and hardware specifications for a global array of network storage appliances. As EPICSHELTER gained currency with his bosses in Japan, Snowden prepared a white paper and briefing slides. In late 2009 or early 2010, organizers of the NSA's Pacific technical conference asked for a presentation, then a draft proposal. Someone arranged for Snowden to brief Lonny Anderson, the NSA's chief technical officer, when Anderson passed through Yokota. That meeting, in turn, brought an invitation to Fort Meade, by Snowden's account, and the NSA's Technical Directorate took ownership of the project. It became a large undertaking of design, engineering, testing, and evaluation. How much it owed to Snowden's early work is difficult to assess. When a proof-of-concept budget came through, the NSA chose Hawaii as the pilot site. Snowden claimed paternity when he saw the prototype up and running at Kunia in 2012.

It is hard to judge how swiftly Snowden's doubts grew in Japan. He wrote abstractly on *Ars* in February 2010 that "society really seems to have developed an unquestioning obedience towards spooky types." His administrative privileges exposed him to a wide swath of information about NSA policy and operations, and he began to read more of it. Meanwhile, he polished his résumé with new training courses and certifications. That year he added credentials as an advanced malware analyst, computer hacking forensic investigator, certified network defense architect, and project management professional. He also used vacation days for travel to India, where courses came cheaper, and scored 96 out of 100 on the test for certified security analyst. One more credential, the EC-Council's certified ethical hacker, was especially consequential. Under DoD Directive 8570, that one completed Snowden's eligibility for Level III access to the innermost security layer, known as the Enclave, of Defense Department networks.

In the summer of 2010, soon after Snowden turned twenty-seven, Dell offered him a transfer home and a return to the CIA in a much more substantial role. It is unclear whether the initiative came from Dell or Snowden. One family confidant said Snowden asked to leave Japan for personal reasons involving his girlfriend, Lindsay Mills. In the new job, his business card named him a Dell "solutions consultant / cyber referent." The latter was important in contractor-speak. It designated him as the man to see for all things cyber in Dell's intelligence contract portfolio.

EPICSHELTER, by Snowden's account, had been good for business. Dell had sold hardware and services for the prototype. Snowden had proved he could think through technical problems with the propeller-heads and translate them for nontechnical folks in operations and sales. As Dell's cyber liaison to the CIA and sister agencies, he drove a round-robin commute across northern Virginia to CIA headquarters in McLean, the National Counterterrorism Center in Liberty Crossing, and the Global Communications Service's New Dominion compound in Reston. Agency representatives described their needs. Snowden helped devise Dell-branded solutions. One day the CIA's Information Operations Center, which is more or less an NSA in miniature, asked for bids on a cluster of password-cracking computers. The agency wanted the fastest number-crunching machines that would fit the power, space, and cooling constraints of the shielded vault that would house them. Snowden selected the hardware, drawing upon components and expertise from Dell's high-performance computing and fabric networking teams. He played a role as well in preparing a far larger bid: "Project Frankie," Dell's joint proposal with Microsoft for a half-billion-dollar cloud computing infrastructure for the CIA. (A rival bid from Amazon won the contract.) Snowden was still a young man, but he was beginning to move in rarefied circles. He regularly sat down with chiefs and deputy chiefs of the CIA's technical branches, representing Dell in meetings with Jeanne Tisinger, the CIA's chief information officer, and Ira "Gus" Hunt, the agency's chief technology officer. Hunt liked to brainstorm, and Snowden told me he pitched one blue sky proposal after another. How about a self-contained, globally deployable data center, sized to fit a standard shipping container? How about a network switch with built-in "separation kernels," or secure hardware enclaves, to guard the digital boundaries between differently classified data flows?

Snowden's career seemed to be thriving, but he was already looking for a change. Interesting problems, the kind that combined technical and operational challenges, attracted him more than access to the executive suites at Dell and its client agencies. In May 2011, he approached Massarini with a proposal. Snowden asked for help to land a job of his own design with the contractor Booz Allen, which supplied personnel to the counterintelligence school where Massarini worked. Snowden would assemble a set of best practices for digital counterintelligence from around the agencies, "harden" a test system, then invite "a multi-disciplinary pool of attendees" to try to break in. "Each time they succeed, you identify an important, critical vulnerability that needs to be addressed," he wrote to Massarini. "Each time they fail, you've got a quantifiable, increasing body of data to illustrate where we're successfully countering CI threats from 'skill level 3' type actors." Snowden would not only teach advanced cyber defense but help improve the state of the art. The job called for someone who could "1) credibly converse with [intelligence agency] executive leadership & most elite technical folks, 2) generate the trust necessary to get an inter-agency representative read into special-methods programs, 3) hot-seat within their offices to understand their methods, 4) still be paranoid enough to then translate all of that into a curriculum without degrading security posture." Standing up such a program from scratch, he wrote, would also require "the people skills to manage the political relationships necessary to open those inter-agency doors."

Someone, as Snowden saw it, very much like him. "I don't want to sound arrogant here," he wrote, "but at the risk of coming off as such, I honestly believe there are very few people who have the necessary background to actually achieve success in building that kind of program." He had two personal requirements. First, he did not want to punch a time card at headquarters; he needed flexibility to work from any office with a secure terminal. Second, he had to have full access to network accounts "with all of the relevant IC orgs and offices, so I can actually go in and work alongside them." Those were ambitious and unorthodox requests, but they fit the interagency mission he had sketched. In retrospect, through the lens of an FBI investigation, Snowden's proposal took on a more suspicious cast. He was asking for the keys to a lot of kingdoms and information about how the gates were secured. In any case, the proposal went nowhere. The job that he wanted did not exist, and Booz Allen turned him down.

Snowden touted his accomplishments in an unclassified curriculum vitae he prepared that summer. At Dell, he wrote, he had helped set "strategy, policy and planning direction" for multimillion-dollar contract proposals, "regularly briefing C-level executives." In a rather grand allusion to EPICSHELTER, he took credit for "driving a modernization initiative for the entire OCONUS backup infrastructure." (In Pentagon-speak, that meant "outside the continental United States.") In places, the résumé took some license with his credentials. A teenage job at a two-person firm based at a town house on Army base housing became "IT Consultant" at "Fort Meade." He cited computer certifications from "Johns Hopkins University," which was not the same thing as the Computer Career Institute at Johns Hopkins, where he studied. In reference to his job as a night shift security guard, the one where he was caught browsing the internet, he cast himself as having trained the networking staff "on IT security procedures, access, and CI awareness." He had successfully communicated, he wrote, in "Japanese, French, Mandarin Chinese, Spanish, Bosnian, Italian, Romanian, and Thai."

The résumé's most intriguing line described Snowden's invention of "an uncensorable method of asset communication that functions in the event of the originator's death or detainment." An asset, in this context, meant an intelligence agent, a foreign national recruited by U.S. handlers. In colloquial terms, Snowden had devised a high-tech "dead man's switch." The foreign agent could queue up an emergency message, knowing it would be transmitted within twenty-four hours unless he took specific steps to reset the clock. Here again, Snowden's ingenuity showed a double edge. A dead man's switch could be a valuable addition to the human intelligence toolkit. It could also be put to use for Snowden's own clandestine work, a guarantee that the NSA documents he took would reach the three journalists he chose no matter what happened to him. Snowden told me on several occasions that shortly before leaving Hawaii, when the risk of arrest reached its peak, he had set up a dead man's switch to convey the documents to journalists if he became unable to send them himself. "At a certain point in the process, your preparations have been made so that you can't lose," he told me in late 2013, declining to speak of the details. "The truth is going to get out. The truth is coming. It's not going to be stopped. When you are a fucking engineer it is not that hard to figure out how to do that."

Snowden became more open about his politics as he recovered from his seizure at the end of 2011. In March 2012, just before departing for Hawaii, he donated $250 to the presidential campaign of the Libertarian Party nominee, Ron Paul, a fierce critic of government surveillance even then. He sent another $250 in May. Inside the Kunia

Tunnel, he wore a hoodie with a parody logo of the NSA. Sold by the Electronic Frontier Foundation, a frequent agency adversary in court, the hoodie depicted a bald eagle wearing comically oversized headphones plugged into AT&T telephone cables. He also kept a copy of the U.S. Constitution on his desk, the better to invoke the Fourth Amendment in conversations with coworkers about surveillance as a form of "search and seizure."

On November 18, 2012, Snowden wrote anonymously to Runa Sandvik, a developer at the Tor Project. Tor allowed anyone to surf the web privately by routing connections through relays around the world. Its network depended on volunteers to supply the connections. Snowden told Sandvik that he contributed some of Tor's fastest "exit relays," which become the apparent point of origin for traffic routed through Tor. That alone was risky for a man who worked at the NSA. Exit relays are visible to anyone on the web, and their operators commonly receive copyright notices and "letters from law enforcement," Sandvik said. If the FBI discovered a relay run by an intelligence contractor, there might be more questions than usual. Snowden knew from Sandvik's Twitter feed that she planned to visit Honolulu. Could she bring some Tor stickers and T-shirts? His explanation would have astounded her if she knew his employer. "I'm talking some of the more technical guys at work into starting additional fast servers up, and I thought some swag-on-hand might incentivize them to do it in the 'tonight' time frame instead of 'eventually,'" he wrote. Snowden was openly recruiting surveillance coworkers to help support the leading countersurveillance technology. "If shirts are available, black is preferable, but will gladly pass out whatevs," he added two days later.

When Sandvik wrote back that she would gladly oblige, Snowden also volunteered to cohost a "cryptoparty" with her. These were increasingly popular gatherings, pairing hipster evangelism with practical instruction on keeping Big Brother at bay. Snowden, incautiously, corresponded with Sandvik about this public event from the same anonymous email address, cincinnatus@lavabit.com, that he would use the following month for first contact with Glenn Greenwald. He did not mention his NSA job, but he sent Sandvik his full name and home address for delivery of the Tor swag. He taught the class alongside her as "Ed."

By this time Snowden had either crossed the line into illegal document gathering or was on the brink of doing so. Any gesture of dissent carried risk. Why would he poke his head up when exposure would surely land him in prison? For a long time, I read his choices in those months as reckless. More recently, I have come to think they may have been considered acts of camouflage. Small expressions of sympathy for NSA critics might inoculate him against darker suspicions. They did not fit the profile of a stealthy "inside threat." He was just one of those guys. Every office has one. Sardonic, contrarian, eccentric maybe, but harmless in the end.

An old NSA maxim, one analyst told me, is that "there is no traffic fairy." No one magically intuits what data you want and intercepts it on your behalf. The lesson for newbies, the analyst said, is supposed to be that "you have to cultivate your own collection, not rely on other people to get it for you without being asked." In Snowden's fourteen months in Hawaii, he embarked on a private version of that exercise.

Despite his experience in Langley, Geneva, and Japan, the network at Kunia was "a completely foreign setup, completely new permissions, completely new servers," he said. Slowly and carefully, he explored the boundaries of his electronic universe. "To do something like this, first you have to know the domain," he said. "You have to understand the rules. You have to understand what's being monitored; you have to understand what's not being monitored. You have to understand what you have access to, what you don't have access to. You have to understand how everything lays out and how it fits together."

Certainly he could not just browse at will. The NSA's access control system specified fine-grained clearances and permissions in a digital certificate for every authorized user. The certificate was known in shorthand as the PKI, for public key infrastructure. At the Pentagon, employees carried their certificates in a chip embedded in a wallet-sized card. At the NSA, there was no hardware involved. The certificates were stored in each user's computer network profile.

The credentials in Snowden's PKI were close to the worst-case scenario for the NSA's internal defenses. The risk he posed, from that point of view, was a nightmare of acronyms: TS//SI//G//TK//HCS. Anyone who worked in the Tunnel had at least the first of those, a Top Secret clearance, and probably the second one, too. "Special intelligence," the control system for compartmented information about surveillance sources and methods, was the bread and butter of Kunia's mission. Not all of Snowden's colleagues held the third credential, short for Gamma, which opened the door to the contents of intercepted communications. The fourth credential may also have been less common. Talent Keyhole covered secrets about spy satellites and other overhead collection systems. Rarest at the NSA was Snowden's clearance for HCS, the HUMINT Control System. (Military and intelligence agencies like to stack acronyms. HUMINT meant "human intelligence," the clandestine work of U.S. case officers.) That one came as a legacy of Snowden's time at the CIA, which did not revoke his credentials upon departure.

On top of all that came the privileged access of a top-tier system administrator. That status enabled Snowden to stop, start, and alter computing processes at the root level, where the fundamental workings of the network were controlled. He could disable, edit, or erase some of the activity logs that would otherwise leave evidence of his digital movements. He could move or copy files and override restrictions on the use of external storage devices such as thumb drives.

It would be easy to overstate the access that the U.S. government officially granted Snowden. Circumstance had given him a set of credentials that few of his Kunia coworkers could match. That did not mean the government entrusted him with all its big secrets, or most of them, or any large fraction. His four major clearances—SI, TK, G, and HCS—made him eligible for those categories of sensitive information, but they did not grant the access on their own. They were threshold credentials, necessary but not sufficient. Before Snowden could be "read into" any given compartment, before he could examine the files inside, proper authorities had to certify his need to know. His final job in Hawaii, for example, cleared him to read files marked BYZAN-TINEHADES and SEEDSPHERE, which were concerned with Chinese government hacking. He did not have a need to know compartmented information about the Chinese Politburo or hackers from Iran.

That, at any rate, was how the limits were supposed to work. Snowden, by lifelong habit, looked for side channels. He had never served in a clandestine role, but he borrowed a classic method of misdirection. His official duties, openly performed, provided "cover for presence" and "cover for action" in digital neighborhoods where he might otherwise attract suspicion.

Early on, Snowden repurposed a routine security audit that he performed in the Windows engineering division. The task, in essence, was to find misfiled secrets—restricted information that had migrated somehow to less restricted locations on the network. He was supposed to delete those files, but he had other options. Once he took possession, according to the NSA's chief technical officer, Lonny Anderson, "he used his sys admin privileges to exfiltrate. He would move the data as part of the sys admin job to a place that he was comfortable, 'Here I can exfil the data.'"

Snowden ran "dirty word searches" across the network domains under his administrative control. A dirty word was a search term that was supposed to come up empty. If everyone followed security protocols, there would be nothing to find. He might search for the term "NOFORN" in a system accessible to the Five Eyes, the NSA's closest foreign counterparts. If he found a hit, it meant that someone had dropped a "don't show foreigners" file in a bucket marked "show our foreign friends."

Another kind of dirty word search took Snowden deeper. He looked for files marked "ECI," or exceptionally controlled information. Nothing classified at that level belonged on the network servers. Information that sensitive was supposed to be stored in a cipher-locked room on a system that required special access credentials. Similar restrictions applied to files labeled "FISA" or "FAA 702," a reference to communications intercepted within the United States under authority of the FISA Amendments Act, Section 702. In general, said the NSA's Anderson, Snowden was authorized for reports and presentations, "not access to what we would call data, so he's not going into repositories and getting access to raw data." That was true, officially, at Kunia, though not in his final position in Hawaii. It was a poor description of what he could reach in practice.

The NSA's digital machinery is operated by humans, and humans make mistakes. Humans also take shortcuts when the approved procedures get too much in the way of their jobs. In one case, a group of analysts curated and shared their working copies of files drawn from a large, restricted database of raw intelligence. They wanted to collaborate and avoid redundant work. Each of them had authority to read the material, but the files did not belong in the system they used for sharing. Snowden found and copied them, he told me later, in order to show how many innocent people are swept into the NSA's net.

Snowden's dirty word searches improved when he turned up a list of cover names for ECI compartments. He was not cleared to look inside the compartments, but his credentials, his PKI certificate, allowed him to see what those compartments were called. His search terms expanded to include "AMBULANT," "BLACKAXE," "CRUMPET," "DEVILFISH," "FLYLEAF," "HYSSOP," "KESSELRUN," "LIGHTNINGTHIEF," and at least seventy more ECI cover names. Every time he found a hit, something new and quite sensitive, previously beyond reach, popped up on his screen.

One day, such a search produced hits on "STARBURST," "WHIPGENIE," and "STELLARWIND." If any one event pushed Snowden over the edge, this might have been it. The three cover names referred to different stages of one evolving set of operations, carried out between 2001 and 2007. Under orders from President Bush, the NSA spied on Americans in ways that Congress had expressly forbidden since 1978. The domestic surveillance, without judicial or legislative authority, was conceived and overseen after the September 11 attacks by Vice President Cheney and his general counsel, David Addington. Eventually, in 2004, the Justice Department ruled that some of the operations were illegal. In broad outline, this much had been made public by the time Snowden arrived in Hawaii.

What Snowden found that day was something new: a near-final draft of the NSA inspector general's report on the episode, classified and compartmented as ECI. Its fifty-seven pages laid out a detailed history of the warrantless surveillance programs, culminating in the collapse of Justice Department legal support. Cheney and his lawyer maintained that no one in the executive, judicial, or legislative branches had the power to limit the president's warmaking authority. Intelligence gathering, which is inherent in war, was the exclusive prerogative of the commander in chief. When the acting attorney general, James B. Comey, refused to certify that the operations were lawful, Cheney's lawyer telephoned the NSA's director, Michael V. Hayden.

"On 11 March 2004," the report said, "General Hayden had to decide whether NSA would execute the Authorization without the Attorney General's signature. General Hayden described a conversation in which David Addington asked, 'Will you do it?'"

Hayden said yes.

"It was the STELLARWIND memo that really affected me," Snowden told me. "The fact that Hayden knew there was no statutory authority." Hayden's career, Snowden noted, continued to thrive in the aftermath. He was not disciplined, charged with an offense, or subjected to hard questions about his choice in a public hearing. When Congress learned of the secret programs, it gave retroactive legal immunity to those who carried them out and authority for future presidents to keep them going. The lesson Snowden drew was that even in the most extreme case, when an NSA director knowingly broke the law as the attorney general defined it, no branch of government was prepared to hold him accountable. The public had no idea what transpired. Snowden believed it should. In November 2013, months after Snowden brought the episode to light, Hayden and I met onstage at Duke University. He argued that every program Snowden disclosed was legal. I noted that he had kept one of them active after the Justice Department said otherwise. Afterward, in a hallway, Hayden accused me of taking a cheap shot. He had agreed to extend STELLARWIND for only forty-five days, he said, in order to allow time for a legal fix. He did not explain why he chose that course rather than halt operations until such a fix was made.

Snowden appears to have made some of his most consequential finds by taking advantage of an efficiency feature in the NSA's configuration of user accounts. You could sign on to any NSA workstation in the world and your "active directory profile"—working files and folders, browser settings, identity certificates—would appear, same as always. If a visitor came to Kunia from some distant office, such as Fort Meade headquarters, remote access could be balky and slow. In such cases, the system was designed to copy the visitor's profile to a temporary local cache. The consequence was this: each time a VIP arrived at Kunia, memos and spreadsheets and slide decks poured into a folder under Snowden's administrative control. Joseph J. Brand, then the NSA's associate director for community integration, policy, and records, unknowingly contributed one collection. Based on my own analysis of the metadata, the hidden properties of the files, Brand's temporary folder supplied Snowden with the STELLARWIND report.

"The biggest hurdle to get over for everyone on the 'how it happened' story is to understand that the NSA's security is about 15 years out of date," Snowden wrote to me. "Their defense is the airgap, a fenceline and some cops."

The ramparts all faced outward. An air gap, meaning physical separation, ensured that sensitive systems did not connect electronically to the wider world. Fences and guards kept adversaries on the other side. There was no effective defense against a skillful insider with the nerve to keep probing day after day, month after month, even as he conversed with journalists.

In April, a month or so after reaching Hawaii, Snowden took on a new project. He called it Heartbeat. Snowden coded it from scratch in plain sight of his colleagues. Anyone at Kunia could follow his progress on an intranet page that listed his name and system identifier, ejsnowd, as the point of contact. At the top of the page, titled "The NSA Heartbeat," Snowden placed a logo of his own design. Green spiky lines crossed a horizontal grid, hospital monitor–style. An overlay displayed the Kunia coat of arms, a hodgepodge of cryptologic symbols: quill pen, brass key, lightning bolt, flaming torch. The motto at the bottom read "Silent Sentinels."

Few assignments could have offered better cover for Snowden's own silent mission.

He had legitimate reason now to automate the transfer of thousands, then hundreds of thousands of files, and then more. That is far from saying he took away copies of all those files for himself. U.S. government officials, who promoted the public allegation that he stole 1.7 million documents, eventually acknowledged that their claims were based on a worst-case surmise. From personal knowledge, I can state with confidence that Snowden did not give any journalist, or all journalists combined, one-tenth that number. There are probably things he took with him that he decided not to release. Whatever the numbers, Heartbeat certainly brought a great volume of new material within his span of control. Because the project operated in open view, he said, a man assembling evidence for journalists would not "have blown up any logs, covered any tracks, hidden his trail, etc., related to the Heartbeat, as he *might* have if he were doing something for the public . . . and didn't want it found."

Heartbeat is central to understanding the way Snowden explored and conquered his digital environment at the NSA. He discussed the project with me sparingly, and only because he believed the NSA had scapegoated his manager for authorizing it. When we spoke of Heartbeat's workings and origins, Snowden deflected efforts to tease out detail.

Me: help me get this right. whatever I describe, if I make the tiniest error, someone will say the story is flat wrong.

Snowden: you don't have to write it like a deposition.

Me: Pot, meet kettle. Kettle, pot.

Snowden: ha.

just tell me the things you feel like you're being horribly, unduly deprived of.

I did. He was unmoved. For much of the Heartbeat narrative I rely on other people and records, public and otherwise.

Snowden's boss, a career civil servant, oversaw a fleet of well over two thousand Windows computers in the Tunnel. An idea "had been kicking around on the Windows team for a while," Snowden said, but nobody had time to take it on. It went like this. Lots of people at Kunia needed regular access to information stored in faraway places, not all of them in the NSA's digital realm. Within their assigned roles and specialties, Kunia workers might draw upon records maintained by the CIA, the FBI, the State Department's Bureau of Intelligence and Research, or any of the other thirteen branches of the U.S. intelligence community. It could take all day to open special connections, log in, and search even a fraction of those. Some analysts had to do so often. Snowden said the overall effect was "a rat's nest of incompatible closed networks and half-baked workarounds," a description backed by others with firsthand knowledge.

There was a lot of pent-up demand for a better way. Surely someone could build a one-stop portal for intelligence that spanned multiple sources? It was a simple idea, excruciatingly hard to carry out. The networks crossed the turf lines of rival agencies. They used different software, data formats, and access protocols. Each had its own intricate set of security controls, and Heartbeat would have to reproduce them exactly. If the portal worked correctly, identical searches would present each user with a different set of results, depending on her clearances and authorized need to know. This was an enormous undertaking. Kunia had no budget for it. Snowden's employer had no contract to perform the work. "This was a self-generated idea," Richard Ledgett, the former deputy director, told me. "It was not something 'Big NSA' thought was needed, so his local managers had some latitude. 'Sure, that sounds like a good idea.'"

The usual dodge in such a case was to put together a prototype.

Maybe next year the project would win approval and funding. Snowden's boss allowed him to give it a try. He had time on his hands and a head start after his previous work on EPICSHELTER, the backup system. Did he volunteer for Heartbeat, understanding its hidden potential? Was it his supervisor's idea? Did Snowden subtly position himself for a tap on the shoulder? There may be no official record on that. The NSA was paying Dell, and Dell was paying Snowden, to do a different job. In reality, Heartbeat began to swallow the bulk of his time. "It's not an exaggeration to say 70% of [my] working hours were spent on this," he told me. One of Snowden's coworkers, who was interviewed by *Forbes* long after all the crockery had broken, asked, "If you had a guy who could do things nobody else could, and the only problem was that his badge was green instead of blue, what would you do?"

Heartbeat stretched past the boundaries of the NSA's own systems. Like the open internet, the intelligence world's classified networks connected a cul-de-sac in Hawaii to virtual roads and highways that spanned the globe. The fiber optic cables of NSANet, the pipes that Ledgett alluded to, linked the agency's email servers, collection systems, processing tools, intelligence reporting platforms, and repositories of intercepted records and content. But the pipes did not stop there. Since the September 11, 2001, attacks on New York and Washington, the White House and Congress had pounded on intelligence agencies to quit hoarding information and work together. NSANet, accordingly, had hooks into an even larger system, in essence a network of networks. The Joint Worldwide Intelligence Communications System, or JWICS, bridged the Defense Intelligence Agency, the National Reconnaissance Office, the National Geospatial-Intelligence Agency, and others under Defense Department control. JWICS also linked to TS/SCI assets at the FBI and the CIA's Agency Data Network. Everything connected to everything, even if each agency kept its most sensitive information offline. In Heartbeat's most expansive conception, it would become a hub with spokes that extended throughout the intelligence community.

It did not begin that way, and neither did it reach so grand a scale. Heartbeat expanded in stages, responding to what Snowden called "mission creep." Some classified intelligence products, such as the CIA's Intellipedia, published an automated notice each time they added or updated an article. "Originally we just mirrored those feeds," Snowden said, "but that didn't solve the 'content retrieval' problem." If you wanted to read an article on the list, you still had to log off Heartbeat, open a network bridge to another agency, and log in to the server where the document was stored. That defeated the purpose of a one-stop portal. Snowden added a daemon, a computer process that ran in the background, to copy each newly listed document into local storage at Kunia. Then some of Heartbeat's early evaluators asked whether Snowden could retrieve new files on remote systems that did not list them automatically.

"Two months of paralysis" set in, Snowden said, as Hawaii's Information Technology Directorate grappled with the implications of that proposal. The idea on the table was to create "an always-up-to-date mirror of all the latest content from all the different internal sites and networks." In order to accomplish that, Heartbeat would have to create and update its own index of systems that belonged to other agencies. Each time the index showed something new, Heartbeat would import a copy. This would not be easy, but it was not a novel challenge in networked computing. Self-updating indexes are commonplace in the civilian world. The tools to build them are called spiders because they crawl around digital networks to look for new files. Google uses a spider of its own design to catalog the entire internet, or most of it. The other half of Heartbeat's mission, downloading and synchronizing the new files, would adapt well-known tools such as wget and rsync.

It was an audacious idea to do anything of this sort on somebody else's TS/SCI network. Among other impediments, the plan required credentials that Snowden did not possess. Every day—or every hour, or many times an hour—Heartbeat knocked on a long line of doors. Each door led to some faraway classified database. Heartbeat could not enter without an invitation, which came in the form of a PKI digital identity certificate. As a prototype with no official status, Heartbeat was not eligible for its own PKI. The system itself could not be added to the guest list. Instead, Snowden embedded his certificate into Heartbeat's Digital Identity Store. When Heartbeat knocked on a door, it announced itself as ejsnowd. Some doors would not open for Snowden. Some of them led to places that only a government employee could go. A new question therefore arose. Would Snowden's boss add his digital identity to Heartbeat alongside Snowden's? Between them, the two identities would open more doors than either one alone. The supervisor agreed, Snowden said, after consulting "multiple levels of NSA and corporate management," including the information systems security manager for all of Hawaii. Nobody objected, by Snowden's account, but nobody put permission in writing. Projects built with a nod and a wink do not rate formal exceptions to security policy.

Someone had to take the fall when the FBI learned that Heartbeat operated off the books. On June 18, 2013, two weeks after the *Washington Post* and the *Guardian* began to publish the NSA disclosures, investigators found Snowden's former manager, who had left Hawaii for a new assignment. According to an NSA letter to Congress, which referred to the man only as a "civilian employee," the manager "admitted to FBI Special Agents that he allowed Mr. Snowden to use" his digital identity "to access classified information on NSANet; access that he knew had been denied to Mr. Snowden." That was a harsh way to spin it, stripped of context. "They threw this guy under the bus," Snowden said. Ledgett said of Snowden's boss, "We ended up firing the guy. He knew he screwed up."

In his unclassified letter to Congress, the NSA's director of legislative affairs, Ethan Bauman, gave an account of how the transaction worked. "At Mr. Snowden's request," Bauman wrote, "the civilian entered his PKI password at Mr. Snowden's computer terminal. Unbeknownst to the civilian, Mr. Snowden was able to capture the password, allowing him even greater access to classified information. The civilian was not aware that Mr. Snowden intended to unlawfully disclose classified information. However, by sharing his PKI certificate, he failed to comply with security obligations." In plain English, Bauman accused Snowden of stealing the password by tricking a superior who should have known better. The trouble with that account is that it cannot be true. That is not the way certificates work in a system like Heartbeat. If Bauman did not know that, his agency employed plenty of people who did.

In order for Heartbeat to function at all, it had to be connected around the clock to each remote network it watched. Connections required an identity certificate. Ordinarily, those certificates were password-protected, but autonomous systems like Heartbeat cannot use them that way. Heartbeat canvassed and copied new files in near real time, twenty-four hours a day. No one could sit by the keyboard and type a password for each of these countless events. Snowden and his manager solved that problem the way network administrators usually do for scripts and other automatic operations. They stripped the password protection from the manager's certificate before embedding it in the Heartbeat Digital Identity Store. This was not an exotic procedure. Snowden's boss, a seasoned network engineer and top-tier system administrator himself, could not have failed to understand what he was doing. The command may look opaque to a layman, but for these men it required no more thought than clipping a house key onto a lanyard.

```
openssl pkcs12 --in bosskey.p12 --out bosskey.pem --nodes
```

It translates easily enough. Launch the openssl utility. Call the pkcs12 command, which manages identity certificates. Convert the certificate called bosskey from its original format to a new one. Strip out the password with the "--nodes" option. The procedure did not steal or capture the manager's password. It saved the certificate in password-less form. Snowden told me he "never, at any point, knew or used the guy's password." Heartbeat did not need it.

The portal grew slowly. "At the very beginning it was tiny," Snowden said. "It had almost nothing. I had to stitch together a gigantic, massive network of all these servers and resources in order for it to have any value, before it was collating any kind of information at all. . . . I don't think that would've been happening in a meaningful way until probably 2013."

On January 24, 2013, Snowden read an alarming post in a classified blog devoted to fresh advances in NSA surveillance. Over in the agency's Application Vulnerabilities Branch, S32313, a small group of clever geeks had come up with a way, in some circumstances, to break the anonymity provided by Tor. That was the privacy network that Snowden helped support, the one he taught to novitiates at the cryptoparty in Honolulu. More to the point, he was staking his freedom on Tor as he contacted journalists. His conversations with Laura Poitras had begun three weeks before, and Poitras had already come to see me in New York. If Tor could be compromised, so might we all.

For years, the NSA and the GCHQ, its British counterpart, had been banging on Tor, looking for some way to pierce its veil of anonymity. It was a hard target, among the most intractable of the tools available to the public at large. ("Tor sucks," one NSA presentation slide complained.) In order to make it easier for novices to use, Tor developers had baked their magic into a custom version of Firefox. They called it the Tor Browser Bundle. Now a small team of NSA hackers had come up with a way to see through the browser's privacy shields.

The NSA liked to hire rising stars in computer science and mathematics as interns for a summer or an academic year. Young innovators came up with hacks that old-timers missed, and a taste of life inside sometimes hooked them into postgraduate employment. It was one of those interns who broke the news that Snowden read in January. The intern and his team had found a vulnerability in Firefox, not in Tor itself, but they could exploit it against certain versions of the bundle. It was a mark of Snowden's icy nerves—and the betrayal that some colleagues felt so strongly—that he congratulated the intern and began a correspondence to tease out details.

"I read your journal.nsa entry," Snowden wrote to the intern. "Really great work! This looks like an awesome way to deal with the TBB. I'd like to know more if you don't mind a couple quick questions." Did the method rely on prior identification of a target, or could it compromise any Tor browser? Did it work against all operating systems? Were there any browser plug-ins that blocked the exploit?

The intern happily entertained the shoptalk. "Thanks!" he replied. "I've attached my current draft of slides." The densely technical, fifty-eight-page presentation laid out the methods and limits of the new exploit, which had the cover name EGOTISTICALGIRAFFE, or EGGI for short. At the moment, the intern told Snowden, NSA operators were deploying it "only against certain extremist web forums," but he added, "I am under the impression that they can serve up an exploit to pretty much anyone." EGGI worked on the Windows browser but not on Mac or Linux. It did not work at all if a user switched off JavaScript, a programming language built into modern web browsers.

Snowden was safe. He always switched off JavaScript. The Tor browser made that easy enough, but the scripting language was left on by default. Without explaining why, Snowden pointedly reminded me and Poitras in coming months to "disable the fucking scripts."

Snowden kept the conversation going with the intern. He had a pedagogical point in mind, and he wanted to save it for later.

"Seriously, this is really great stuff," he wrote on January 25. "I hope you get all the kudos you deserve for putting this together. How long did it take you to come up with this? If Tor team updates [Firefox] . . . do you think the TBB has enough target surface for you guys to restore the same access through a different vuln? Same time investment, or more?" Snowden was asking how long it would take to find a new hole in the browser once the old one was patched.

"Somewhere between a week and two weeks," the intern replied. "We've actually got a couple of bugs we're looking at for Firefox 17+, and once I get back from a TDY [temporary duty] next week, I'm going to try to work with the rest of the team to get something ready to ship, and I'm confident we can have it ready when [Tor developers] release something new, or very soon after:)"

Much later, when government officials and other critics accused Snowden of damaging NSA collection capabilities, he cited the exchange with the intern in reply. "What I was actually doing was, I was trying to elicit information for the benefit of you guys on how long it takes," he said. "After they've lost their exploit, how long does it take them to build another?" That question, he said, "is actually a really great metric against the government's argument that we're going dark."

In the first quarter of 2013, Snowden was presented with two prospects for the final job of his intelligence career. Someone suggested he take the test to join the NSA's Tailored Access Operations unit, or

TAO, a position that would shift him back from Dell to U.S. government employ. "Tailored access" meant breaking into specific networks or machines that eluded the NSA's large-scale collection systems. Most of the tailors' work was routine. The agency had all kinds of off-the-rack hacking ensembles. The tailors worked from checklists. If this, then that. Survey your target's hardware, software, firmware. Identify known security holes. Check for antivirus applications. Push this button, run that scan, deliver the corresponding exploit. TAO slang for this was "popping boxes," no harder than popping a door lock for a halfway competent burglar. Boxes were the computers, routers, and firewalls of a surveillance target. With aptitude and training, a newly enlisted cryptologic technician could do the job most of the time.

When tougher targets called for bespoke tools, TAO collection managers turned to their elite unit, the Remote Operations Center (ROC). "The Rock" employed some of the most talented hackers on the planet. In a culture that loved its puns, they were "ROC stars." The then FBI director, Robert Mueller, once told me that intelligence agencies lured those men and women away from Silicon Valley with a matchless offer. Come test yourself against the world's toughest adversaries. Feel free to invent cracking tools that would land you in prison if you were dumb enough to try them at home. Snowden was not immune to that temptation. "To a lot of people, that's really exciting," he said. "Because you're hacking. These are criminal acts" in the outside world. Snowden aced the TAO exam, sat for an interview, and landed an offer. The former NSA director Mike McConnell later alleged that Snowden passed only because he broke into the test computer and stole the answers. If true, some former government hackers joked, that would have been an outstanding qualification for TAO. Snowden, offended, said he earned his score. "Let's look at it this way," he told me, comparing the challenge to what he did with Heartbeat. "If a guy can, by himself, bridge every network in the IC without those agencies pitching a fit and ingest it all into an NSA website, he can probably pass a test designed for 18 year old Navy recruits without cheating."

Unexpectedly, Snowden turned down the TAO job. He had his eye on a contract at Booz Allen, which supplied "infrastructure analysts" to the NSA Threat Operations Center. Snowden became one of them, transferring out of the Kunia Tunnel to a big open-plan workspace in the Rochefort building nearby. The agency's public relations team had unveiled the shiny new facility with pride, photographing it with a double rainbow overhead. (Inevitably, some denizens insisted on calling it the Roach Fort nonetheless.) No longer would Snowden administer networks for other people to use. He began to work with some of the NSA's most restricted tools himself.

Part of his new mission was to spot, thwart, and report foreign hackers, with a special focus on China. He reverse engineered incoming digital weapons, known as intrusion sets, and traced the attacks to their sources. Contractors like Snowden could lawfully engage in what the NSA calls "computer network defense," but offensive operations were out of bounds. Network warfare, or "computer network attack," operated under a military chain of command. The boundaries were real, but somewhat soft in practice. The other side's machines and networks were the "infrastructure" in Snowden's title, and he had license to poke around as long as he did not break anything. When he learned enough to establish culpability, or found barriers he could not slip past nondestructively, he could propose targets for more aggressive collection or counterattack.

"I'm much more interested in the operational planning side," Snowden told me, explaining why he turned down TAO. "That's what an infrastructure analyst is. We look at the [foreign hackers'] operations. . . . Where are they coming from, what are the tool sets they're using, how are they attacking us? Follow them back home, and then we plan the operation for how to get into their network and hack them back. And that sounded a lot more cool to me. I was actually really good at it." He laughed a bit ruefully and shook his head. "I didn't do it for very long at all," he said. In another life, he would have liked to stay and work his way up. He spent only two months at NTOC before flying to Hong Kong.

Shortly after going public, Snowden told the *South China Morning Post* that he had sought out the contract at Booz for its access to NSA documents that he wanted to expose. He declined to repeat or explain that statement to me, alluding only to "a split focus" in that final assignment. It is clear, in any case, that NTOC broadened his classified horizons yet again. The new position granted him what the NSA calls "dual authorities," a set of combined credentials that few other jobs required. The agency at that time encompassed two principal directorates, Information Assurance and Signals Intelligence. One defended U.S. government secrets. The other stole foreign secrets. Each had its own arsenal of classified legal powers, and each had its own limits. Defenders could look inside (some) U.S. communications networks for evidence of foreign intrusion. Attackers could spy overseas under the president's Executive Order 12333 and use domestically based collection from PRISM and Upstream.

Snowden's new professional home, an organization chartered in 2005, gave him access to both sets of tools. "The idea was that NTOC analysts would have the dual authorities to look at defensive data and SIGINT data, at the same time," said a former employee there. "I could and did, in one workday, help advise on the cleanup of a state-sponsored hacker attack and try to direct SIGINT collection to trace said attack. . . . The main innovation for NTOC policy-wise was the integration of the dual authorities in individual analysts."

In April 2013, the NSA flew Snowden to its Fort Meade headquarters to meet with the NTOC chain of command and compare notes with Maryland-based colleagues on the China beat. While he was there he sat through the required training on the proper use of his new surveillance authorities. Much of it came in the form of self-paced online instruction. One required course, OVSC 1400, introduced an animated helper named Ned NTOC, a classified counterpart to the Clippy character in Microsoft Office. "Ned NTOC will be your trusty guide and appears throughout the course to help you know, understand, and navigate through the legal and policy jungle," the syllabus explained cheerfully.

Suppose, one quiz asked him, you detect a malware attack on a Defense Department network. The malware is attached to a message sent by the University of Maryland email server, ordinarily out of bounds as an NSA target. "You believe it is a BYZANTINEHADES actor," the question states—that is, a Chinese government hacker. "You want to task the U MD mail server IP address." Is that okay? In other words, is Snowden allowed to spy on the machine that handles all outgoing email from a large U.S. campus? It was a multiple-choice question. One incorrect answer was "never." Also incorrect: ask superiors for an "equities review." There were two approved answers. He could lawfully target the university server as long as he used a search term that included "a known malicious signature." If he did not have that, he had to do his best to structure a query "to get only the malicious cyber activity." The second path left a lot more room for error. It was all but certain to ingest innocent messages from professors and students, but Snowden would not get in trouble as long as he did not grab those communications on purpose. Optionally, the training course said, "you may want to check" the query with a senior analyst or NSA lawyer. This was a classified rule, compartmented as "special intelligence," unknown and undebated in public. Snowden recognized the intent to limit intrusion into university life. The procedure still took him aback. Even a new analyst had a great deal of power.

Additional training that week qualified Snowden to dip into a special category of content intercepted inside the United States. This surveillance, "with the assistance of an electronic communication service provider," took place under a classified interpretation of Section 702 of the FISA Amendments Act of 2008. Some of the content belonged to U.S. citizens, companies, and green card holders, all entitled to Fourth Amendment protection. That stuff went into a close-hold data repository. Information drawn from it had to be specially marked.

THIS INFORMATION IS DERIVED FROM FAA COLLECTION

THIS INFORMATION IS PROVIDED FOR INTELLIGENCE PURPOSES IN AN EFFORT TO DEVELOP POTENTIAL LEADS. IT CANNOT BE USED IN AFFIDAVITS, COURT PROCEEDINGS OR SUBPOENAS, OR FOR OTHER LEGAL OR JUDICIAL PURPOSES.

Snowden was now cleared for the FISA compartment. He was not limited to reading old intercepts in storage. He could "task," or assign, new surveillance targets. The training taught him how to use the check boxes and drop-down menus of the NSA's Unified Targeting Tool and a newer one called XKEYSCORE. He soon discovered that the NTOC position allowed him access to still another database of domestic communications traffic. This one was managed exclusively by the FBI. Operating under the cover name CAPTAINCRUNCH, the FBI secretly owned and monitored network servers designed to attract foreign hackers.

In his first filmed interview, Snowden told the world that "any analyst at any time can target anyone." He added, "I, sitting at my desk, certainly had the authorities to wiretap anyone, from you or your accountant, to a federal judge, to even the president." U.S. government officials heaped scorn on that claim, flatly denying that Snowden could do any such thing.

The government denials rested on lawyerly language that sounded like English but was not, quite. No one authorized Snowden, they said, to spy on whomever he liked. Snowden meant something else by "authorities." He used the word, in fact, as intelligence officials ordinarily used it themselves. The legal basis for a wiretap depended on where, how, by whom, and for what purpose it took place. Each of the legal foundations was called an authority. Because of his new job and training, Snowden had a status that permitted him access to several of those—offensive and defensive, domestic and foreign. He could see and manipulate data intercepted overseas (under presidential authority) and at home (under the judicial and congressional authority of FISA). Those authorities were embedded in his digital identity certificate.

I tried repeatedly to unpack the government denials. Robert Litt, general counsel of the Office of the Director of National Intelligence, was a frequent sparring partner. He spoke precisely, as befits a lawyer, and dodged my questions, as befits a man on public relations cleanup duty. Was he prepared to deny that Snowden could pull up the XKEYSCORE interface and type "selectors," or search terms, for new collection and access to content already stored? Litt declined to say one way or another. When I explained why Snowden could not have done his job at NTOC without such access, Litt said he did not have the technical knowledge to reply. (I asked him to check and did not hear back.) Questions about Snowden's qualifications for access to the FISA repository produced much the same result.

What government officials really meant, I think, was that Snowden could not have gotten away with spying on any old accountant or judge, still less the president. In some restricted systems, such as PRISM, search terms required a supervisor's approval in advance. In others, auditors were supposed to conduct after-the-fact reviews. On most systems an analyst had to specify a purpose, a factual predicate, and a legal basis for any surveillance of an email address or other selector. These were point-and-click exercises, but the NSA took them seriously. On the other hand, the NSA worked with at least tens of millions of selectors in a given year. Most of the auditors had full-time jobs, reviewing other people's searches as a second or third assignment. Snowden might well have been busted if he spied clumsily on obviously baseless targets. He was not a clumsy man. A clever analyst, bent on abuse, might disguise his purposes well enough to survive routine review. It would be bold, in light of other events, to claim that auditors would surely have caught Snowden if he put a toe over the line.

In one of my visits to Moscow, I put it to Snowden that a man of his methodical bent would reserve the most dangerous intrusions for last. He waved off the question. Several hours later, long after dark, with plates and utensils piled up from three room service orders, he returned to the subject.

"Your presumption was that you would do the least risky things in the beginning and the most risky things in the end," he said. "And that just makes sense. You don't want to be caught in an operation because you took too many chances too soon. It's got to be at the very end. Because you want to minimize your period of exposure, your period of risk."

On May 19, 2013, Snowden boarded a flight to Tokyo with four laptop computers in his carry-on bag. He changed planes there and arrived the next day in Hong Kong. "I really didn't have a plan" after that, he told me much later. "That was where my script ran out."

THREE

HOMECOMING

Late Sunday night, May 19, 2013, I placed a call to Edgewater, Maryland. Jeff Leen, sounding groggy, picked up his phone at home. Leen ran the investigative unit of the *Washington Post*. He had probably quarterbacked more prizewinning work than anyone in American journalism. Seven Pulitzers? Something like that. Most of the editors I knew best had moved on. Leen, he was a lifer. He had hung in through three publishers, three executive editors, and a long, dispiriting decline in newsroom resources. The new top editor, Marty Baron, brought a sterling reputation from the *Boston Globe*, but we had not met. I needed an introduction, the sooner the better. Leen and I had worked closely on a grueling series about Vice President Dick Cheney in 2007. I trusted him. I did not trust the phone, and I did not want to say much without a lawyer. That made for an awkward conversation.

"I'm calling for an unusual favor," I said. "I need a private meeting with Marty Baron right away. The subject is sensitive. It has to be in person. I don't know who else to ask."

"A meeting? About what?"

"It's a story. A big one. He will not think I'm wasting his time."

"Okay. What's the story?"

"It's related to national security. That's all I can really say."

"I get that it's sensitive. Just a general idea," Leen replied.

"I'm sorry, I can't."

Silence. Might as well say the rest of it.

"I know this doesn't help, Jeff, but I'm going to need a fast decision from the *Post*. There's a document I expect to receive any day now, and the source may take it somewhere else after seventy-two hours."

An edge of grievance crept into his voice. "You've got to be kidding, Bart. Give me something to work with."

"I know it sounds a little crazy. I wish I could say more."

Silence again. This was not going well. Belatedly, it occurred to me how much Leen's position had changed. My request would have been just as peculiar five years before, but back then Leen had the credit to carry it. Len Downie, the editor, had enough history with Leen to take his word. Now there was a new boss, less than six months in the job, and Leen had nothing in the bank.

"Look, I've only sat down twice with Marty myself," he said. "I can't just walk into his office and tell him he has to meet some guy who used to work here and I have no idea what it's about."

I decided to overlook the way he pronounced "some guy."

"Tell him I'm a drama queen. Tell him whatever you want. Jeff, this is a really big deal. We'll all regret it if I wind up somewhere else."

"It doesn't work that way, Bart," he said. "I can't take it to Marty like this. Call me when you can say what's going on."

We hung up, both disgruntled. I tried not to fault him. I had to sound half unglued. Two minutes later the phone rang, Leen on caller ID.

"You caught me off guard," he said. "I mean, out of the blue like that on a Sunday night, you have to admit it's pretty unusual. I've thought some more. I'll see if I can make it happen. Just please tell me this is going to be worth it."

"It will, I promise. Listen, I meant to say before, Marty is going to want to bring the lawyers. Also, my old building pass can't be good anymore. Can you escort me in from the side entrance? I'll circle around through accounting and up the stairs. I don't want to be seen in the newsroom."

"Christ, Bart," Leen grumbled, but it was too late for protest. In for a dime, in for the drama. Years later he told me he called back because he heard "a faint note of fear" in my voice. "I remember when I got off the phone, I thought, 'If Bart Gellman is afraid of something, that makes me afraid.' This must be really huge."

Leen delivered. Baron would see me Thursday, his first day back in town. I could preview the conversation Wednesday with Baron's number two, the managing editor, Kevin Merida. Yes, the lawyers would be there.

Fine. Merida was one of the good guys.

I never told the *Post* how close I came to taking the story elsewhere. I had left three years before with a bad taste in my mouth. The newsroom had been a magnificent place to grow up, full of mentors and colleagues who leveled up my game. Just listening in on the next desk was a master class. Don Oberdorfer excavated foreign policy news in a soothing murmur, probing so gently that his sources might not notice how deep he dug. Ann Devroy's theatrical mockery slapped politicians off their scripts. "Earth to Newt!" she sang out one day, scoffing at the Speaker of the House. Most of an hour later, when I passed her desk again, she still had Gingrich talking. Once I teamed up with her for an interview with National Security Adviser Anthony Lake. She cut off his first reply, maybe two minutes after we took a couch in his White House corner office. "If you're just going to give us the usual bullshit, Tony, let's move on to something else," she said. He obeyed.

The *Post* cycled me through one great assignment after another: courthouse, Pentagon, Middle East, State Department, then a decade on long-term projects. No one ever asked me to pull a punch, and the owners protected the newsroom at their own peril. During a trip to Egypt in 1997, I read Katharine Graham's memoir with a lump in my throat. Everyone remembered Watergate, but her crucible as publisher came with the Pentagon Papers story of 1971. The Nixon administration tried to suppress a classified history of the Vietnam War, successfully halting publication by the *New York Times*. The attorney general threatened personally to bring criminal charges if the *Post* took up the story. Graham's lawyer pressed her to relent, warning that she risked losing the company. Graham hired a new lawyer and published. The *Times* and the *Post* fought the case to the Supreme Court and won. Those were not some mythic old days, though they long preceded me. They were the lived experience of the newsroom for decades afterward. A company culture like that allowed me to shrug off threats to rescind my credentials and incidents of senior official telephone rage, including a memorably profane call from the Israeli prime minister Benjamin Netanyahu. I borrowed courage from the *Post*, sometimes past the point of common sense, when I crossed a sketchy checkpoint in Somalia or drove through Hezbollah-controlled terrain in Lebanon. I was no Keith Richburg or Anthony Shadid, who routinely braved far greater dangers, but if I fell into trouble, I knew the paper would spare no effort to extract me.

I had my low moments. Downie took me to the woodshed when I needed it. Even the bad days confirmed that I knew where I stood and what the *Post* stood for. By 2009, I no longer felt sure of either. Marcus Brauchli, the new editor, sounded disconcertingly vague about big decisions. His messages to the staff read as artful, contingent. Some of our best reporters began to stall, unsure of what to make of incompatible orders. One day Brauchli asked me for what he called an adjustment. He still wanted my most ambitious work, no mistake about that, but investigative projects should be delivered in weeks, not months. He must have known he could not have that both ways. When scandal broke at the *Post* itself, neither Brauchli nor the new publisher spoke convincingly about an abortive plan to sell six-figure tickets to lobbyists for "salon dinners" with reporters. Morale declined in the newsroom, as much the fault of the leadership as of staff cuts. Dafna preceded me to the exit. When she chanced across Brauchli in black tie one night, she cornered him against the stage, surrounded by print and broadcast executives, and told him he was wrecking the paper. I followed her out the door in the first days of 2010. We were pretty sure the *Post* we knew was gone.

As the Snowden reporting coalesced in the spring of 2013, I began a fellowship at the Century Foundation in New York. I was contemplating a book on the surveillance state and its discontents. *Time* magazine had assigned me a cover story that would preview some of the themes. I intended to confess that I had fallen into a kind of madness in my zeal to safeguard confidential sources and notes. I had built the digital equivalent of a sealed room, private and secure, but nobody came to visit. This could not be a working model of journalism. I would have to rebalance my priorities. Before I started writing, Snowden upended the tale. The surveillance threat was worse than I knew, and we could never have talked without the spooky tools. My story would have to be very different now.

I had not expected to test *Time*'s appetite for journalistic risk. Some of my freelance work touched on intelligence and law enforcement, but I needed no government secrets to write about self-described Patriot militias or Mitt Romney's political childhood. How would the magazine handle a high-stakes intelligence story? The red box around a *Time* cover story still had power, if I could harness it. The Washington bureau chief, Mike Duffy, was a reporter's reporter, one of the best I knew. I decided to try him. On May 7, after a primer on encryption, Duffy and the intelligence correspondent Massimo Calabresi joined me in a live, secure chat from Washington.

"I've got a line on a document that, I'm told, describes in some detail how much content telecoms and ISPs are handing over to the NSA under authority of the FISA Amendments Act. Which companies, which data," I wrote.

"What would you like us to do to prepare?" Duffy asked.

"The main thing in advance is to get a sense of what management and the lawyers are going to think of posting a story and document that may have scary stamps on them."

"We have to think about what's required on our end, both in the way of guidance for you, red lines, and whether we can follow through on what you and they require," Duffy typed back. Candidly, he did not feel sure of *Time*'s "commitment to publishing without regard to cost, under current fluid company circumstances."

I probably should have quit that day, but I knew Duffy would tell me when it was time. Time Warner was preparing to unload its magazine business, a drag on the fabulous profits of its film and television divisions. It was an entertainment conglomerate, journalism barely in peripheral view. With the Time Inc. spin-off imminent, the stock market would not smile upon an expensive legal dispute about classified secrets. "Circumstances not encouraging of risk taking at moment," Calabresi wrote the following week, after poking around a bit. Duffy phoned the same day to say the lawyers were stalling. As an editor, he badly wanted the story. As a friend, he could not advise me to stick around.

One last attempt brought me to Time Inc.'s general counsel Maurice Edelson. He and his staff were doubtless capable lawyers, but the conversation kept trailing off. If all they wanted was to keep their cards close, they were winning. Yet if that was the point, why would they meet me at all? Another suspicion occurred to me. I tore a page from my notepad and jotted three lines. Anyone acquainted with national security law would recognize the short-form classified markings and citations to the espionage statutes.

TS//SCI//NF
18 USC 793
18 USC 798

"Are these familiar to you?" I asked, passing the note around.

No. Afraid not.

Maybe I should have foreseen it. Time Inc. owned and operated close to a hundred magazines. Edelson and company lawyered for titles from *Horse & Hound* to *SuperYacht World*, alongside the news flagships of *Time* and *Fortune*. Even without a coming stock spin-off, their days must be spent on sponsorship deals, rights management, labor law, and corporate governance, maybe the occasional libel case.

"I mean no offense, but this is a specialized field," I said. "I need to hear where the company stands from people who have encountered the issues before."

That bumped the question up the chain to Time Warner's general counsel, Paul Cappuccio, a conservative powerhouse who had clerked for Justice Antonin Scalia and served as associate deputy attorney general under President George H. W. Bush. I was not granted an audience, but word came down that he had retained Arnold & Porter to handle the Gellman problem. I was instructed to call Baruch Weiss, a partner at the firm and former acting deputy general counsel of the

Department of Homeland Security. Duffy and Calabresi joined me around a speakerphone. Time Warner, Weiss told us, was pleased to offer its full support for my NSA story. The company had hired him to help us navigate. For our own protection, we would follow three guiding principles. First, I must not conduct interviews on *Time*'s behalf about anything classified. I should instead pass my questions to him. Weiss would take them up with a properly cleared government official and let my editors know what was fit to print. Second, *Time* did not authorize its employees to receive or retain classified information. Until the legal questions were resolved, I should not discuss government secrets—that is, my story—with the editors.

I was too flummoxed to register any third principle that might have emerged. Was it possible that Duffy had arranged this call as a prank? He might have the high jinks in him, but probably not the acting chops to account for the slow burn crossing his face.

"We have never, not once, done a story this way," Duffy told Weiss, leaning into the speakerphone. Reporters did the interviews. If the government raised some kind of alarm, editors would take legal advice and decide. Weiss had the process backward, Duffy said. He was out of his lane.

These were special circumstances, Weiss responded amiably. We could fall afoul of the Espionage Act in the course of the reporting itself. Calabresi, struggling for self-control, asked whether Weiss sincerely imagined that an interview with a government official could be prosecuted as unlawful transmission or receipt of national defense information. That was unsettled law, Weiss said. Of course it was, Calabresi shot back. No one had ever been fool enough to bring charges like that against a reporter. This was basic First Amendment stuff. Duffy dialed back the heat. We were not the lawyers, he acknowledged. But whatever the abstract risk, Attorney General Eric Holder was already under pressure to scale back use of aggressive legal tools against journalists in leak cases. That, Weiss replied, was no guarantee at all.

The three of us passed notes. What was happening here?

Me: Does he still have USG obligations as a clearance holder?
Duffy: I don't want him to be the interlocutor.
Me, double underlined: DEAL BREAKER.

The conversation went on, pointlessly. Eventually, it sank in that Weiss had not in fact stepped out of his lane. Time Warner had placed him athwart our path. I had met the man socially. I supposed no malign intent. Weiss had his instructions, and now we had ours. No one could say Time Warner killed an NSA scoop, not overtly. Should that become, improbably, a point of embarrassment, the company had merely provided us with top-shelf legal support. Duffy, looking caged, paced the conference room. Not long before pressing the disconnect button, he drew a finger across his throat. Calabresi pressed both palms against a big glass window, high above the Avenue of the Americas, and mimed a jump. "There *must* be a way," he said, almost pleading. We all knew it was past time for me to leave.

And go where? For three days, I flirted with an approach to the *New York Times*. On May 15, I asked an old friend for Jill Abramson's home phone number. The *Times* executive editor knew me casually, well enough that she'd probably take the call. Her paper had always been Brand X to me, the richer, imperious rival, but Abramson could do this story big if she bought in. Snowden left the choice to Poitras and me, but he doubted that the *Times* would have the guts. The paper had held back publication for more than a year after learning in 2004 about the Bush administration's warrantless surveillance of domestic telephone calls. I did not know enough to judge, but I doubted that cowardice explained the delay. Whatever happened back then, I was pretty sure Abramson would say yes this time. Still, yes could mean a lot of things.

Dafna was the first to tell me I would be out of my mind to start from scratch at a newspaper I had never seen from inside. She did not know what had me barricaded, but I had never shut her out of a story before. Go back to the *Post*, she said. I could rewrite the last chapter of my newsroom career. My friends Steve Coll and Bob Kaiser, both former managing editors, said the same. "They'll still see you as part of the institution and handle it that way," Coll told me. In a time of austerity, "people will say, 'This is how we demonstrate that we're still in the game.' They're not going to fail you."

I kept trying to imagine that phone call to the *Times*. At noon on May 19, I told Poitras and Snowden it was not going to work:

```
They don't know me, I don't know them, and the amount of mutual trust
required is off the charts. I'd be asking them to represent me through
unlimited legal proceedings around this story; to take on the govern-
ment on national security; to rely on my judgment and assurances
about confidential sourcing, not only involving this channel but oth-
ers I pursue on my own; and to accept limits on what I will and will
not tell them. . . .

    I don't know the personalities and their histories and their body
language; I don't know how to interpret them between the lines; I
don't know who really decides what, or how to use newsroom back chan-
nels to find out; and I don't know how much to rely on ambiguous
verbal assurances. . . .

    I have been terribly conflicted about how to approach the Times,
and the thought of going to the WaPo has been a complete relief.
```

That night I placed the call to Jeff Leen.

The PRISM slides arrived the next day, Pandora the day after that. I quickly became uneasy about losing them. Spinning magnetic platters in a cheap plastic case were no vessel for irreplaceable data. I pictured the drive shattered on the floor or fumble-fingered into the coffeepot. I imagined a subway snatch-and-grab, a black bag search of my home or office, a predawn visit from men and women with badges.

Was it a crime to make backup copies? Maybe so, by a black-and-white reading of the Espionage Act of 1917. The statute was notoriously broad. Time Warner's lawyer was not wrong to say the law had yet to be tested squarely against the First Amendment. (A narrower and more recent statute became equally pertinent in the days to come.) Receiving, possessing, or communicating what I had learned, none of which was optional in my line of work, could theoretically lead to felony charges. If I took the statute literally, there was no lawful course for me at all: I could not keep the NSA documents, give them to someone else, or destroy them. Making copies might add another few counts to the list.

To hell with that. There was evidence here of domestic espionage that the government had dissembled and sometimes flat-out lied about. Game-changing rules had been written in secret, concealed from the public and even from judges with active cases before them. I took for granted that secrecy was inherent in spycraft. Intelligence operations could not be run by plebiscite. But powers so enormous called for free debate at least about their limits and principles. No one in a democracy got to assume new authority and hide it, least of all when it came to surveillance of the sovereign public. I was not immune to high dudgeon myself, it appeared.

My decision was visceral, but I knew what it meant. I would not willingly comply with an order to hand over these documents or my reporting notes. I would not leave them exposed to seizure. Backups could not wait. There had to be more than one, and they had to live elsewhere. Constructing a sufficient set of elsewheres—concealed, dispersed, redundant, and locked down as securely as civilian means allowed—was another skill set I had to teach myself. Seeking expert advice would add more risk than it cured. ("Say, where's a good place to hide something that a nation-state or two may come hunting for? Asking for a friend.") Readers who try the thought experiment should presume an adversary who has seen the same movies they have. Behind a toilet, like Michael Corleone's gun? The other fellow remembers that. Hollow book, frozen ice pop, loose floorboard? Been there, found those.

Ordinary backup copies might not do the job. I tried to place myself in Snowden's mind, guessing at a road map drawn in fractals. He used technical puzzles for tactical gain, each level more intricate than the last. Clearly, he had a penchant for surprise. It would be just like him to tell me one day that there was something concealed on this hard drive that he had not mentioned before. For sure he knew how to hide information in digital alcoves that a computer usually ignored. A click-and-drag copy of folders and files might leave vital data behind. I decided to make bit-by-bit clones, which reproduce even disk sectors marked as damaged or unused. The first clone took all night. More would have to wait a couple of days. The following morning, May 22, I caught a plane to Washington.

Before my first meeting at the *Post*, I stopped by the offices of Williams & Connolly, the paper's law firm of choice since Katharine Graham went lawyer shopping in 1971. I had been around the block before with its senior partner Kevin Baine. Courtly as ever, he draped an arm across my shoulder and escorted me to an elegant office appointed in leather and antique woods. A portrait of the late justice Thurgood Marshall, who hired Baine as a law clerk in 1975, took pride of place on one wall. A casual observer might glance at the suit and the hair and the aquiline nose and mistake this guy for some kind of smooth-talking pol. That would miss the teeth behind his smile. Journalists loved the man for his forward-leaning advice. I had never heard Baine suggest that we soften a story "out of an abundance of caution," the watchwords of timid lawyering. Aggressive reporting sometimes pushed boundaries and made people angry. Baine helped us sidestep needless trouble, but he did not run from risk.

He had agreed to see me without asking why. As I hoped, Baine already knew. He would join us at the *Post* in a couple of hours. Could he offer me individual advice under attorney-client privilege? He could try, he said. He did not expect a conflict of interest, but he would stop me if he heard one coming. Good. That was one of the main things I wanted to know. With that question open, I began hypothetically. Suppose a freelance reporter happened across a highly classified document. Something sensitive involving the NSA. Baine smiled, approving the approach. This freelance fellow, I told him, was looking to write a story for a newsroom not far from here. I offered a sense of the subject, reserving details for now.

Baine reviewed familiar territory first. The government had never brought Espionage Act charges against a reporter, and he strongly doubted it would start now, but no one could rule out prosecution if a national security story did conspicuous harm. There might or might not be a winning defense in the law's vagueness, overbreadth, and conflict with constitutional protections. Fewer defenses would apply if I was charged under a related statute, 18 U.S.C. § 798, "Disclosure of classified information." Unlike the Espionage Act, this one specified that publication is an offense. It also confined itself to a narrow category of classified information, which happened to be the stuff I had in hand: information about a "cryptographic system" or "communication intelligence activities." On the other hand, the government had shown no stomach for prosecution of journalists under that statute either. Sources were increasingly at risk of criminal charges, but not yet reporters. Since at least the 1980s, the *Post* and other news media had published stories from time to time about intercepted communications. I had done so myself. There were other exotic charges a prosecutor could try, such as "conversion of government property" for private gain, but those would really be a stretch.

We dropped the hypotheticals. The likeliest risk, verging on probable, was a subpoena for testimony and evidence once prosecutors inevitably brought charges against my source. The *Post* would fight a subpoena on my behalf, and it would appeal adverse rulings, but if the Justice Department kept pushing, we would probably lose. It might take years, but eventually I could face a hard choice. Contempt of court, it is said, puts the key to the jailhouse door in a contemner's hands. Comply with the judge's order, and you walk free. Refuse, and you stay behind bars until you submit or the order becomes moot. (In theory, the judge must release you if she concludes you will never comply, but judges do not tend to take that view.) If the newspaper had the means to hand over evidence, refusal could bring steep and escalating fines. Another good reason, I thought, to keep full control of the files myself.

I wondered, on the other hand, whether I had stumbled on a safe place for a backup. If Williams & Connolly represented me, could the firm hold a copy in its vault under lawyer-client privilege? Baine shifted a couple of inches in his chair, body language responding before he spoke the words. If the question became ripe, he said, he would have to take it up with his partners. It would be a tough sell. *Post* lawyers told me later that they made the same request and the firm declined.

There were a few novel elements of the case. Baine and I chewed on them. Finally, I told him I had learned something disquieting two days before. My source had left the country, and I did not like what I knew of his whereabouts. I was not ready to specify, but the jurisdiction could not be described as friendly. A complicating factor, he said, but not a showstopper.

As we parted, Baine added a caution. I had kept a lot of the facts in the bag so far. I was right to want a written contract with the *Post*, but the strength of my legal shield would depend on good faith all around. "You don't want to leave out anything that makes them feel misled," he said.

Half an hour later I slipped into *Post* headquarters and climbed the back stairs to Don Graham's ninth-floor suite. As Washington Post Company chairman, he had broader responsibilities now. He no longer ran the newspaper business himself. What exactly I wanted from him, I could not have said. An employer, still less an ex, did not count as family. I knew that but clung to the image. Graham had taken an interest since my summer internship at twenty-two, pretty much all my professional life. The rift with Brauchli pained him. When I came to say goodbye in 2010, he pulled me into a fierce embrace. Maybe I was looking for a sign that something of the bond endured. I had returned with a challenging story, I told him, the kind that burns a lot of lawyer time. I hoped the company would still have my back. I let that hang. He could not possibly answer, but Graham is not known for his poker face. I liked what I saw.

Two floors down, the managing editor, Kevin Merida, brought Jeff Leen and the national editor, Cameron Barr, to a corporate conference room. Jay Kennedy and Jim McLaughlin, the in-house legal team, brought Kevin Baine. Everyone knew the decision would be Marty Baron's to make, but I told them enough to show respect and prepare for the following day. Mysterious source. Codeword-classified document.

NSA hooks in a lot of big internet companies. I needed legal cover, and so did my reporting partner, a filmmaker I would introduce if the *Post* wanted in.

Baron reconvened us late the next morning, May 23. At the *Boston Globe*, I knew, he had led a gutsy investigation of child abuse in the Catholic Church, a powerful enemy in that town more than most. Record like that, the man had to have an ego. Wherever he stashed it left no bulges I could see. Baron projected authority without overt display. Two years later, Liev Schreiber would play him, a head taller but uncannily true to life, in *Spotlight*, the Academy Award–winning film about the church cover-up.

Gang's all here, Baron said, pointing his chin toward the legal contingent. I hear you have quite a story. Tell us about it.

He had no other preamble. I had one. With apologies, I had to ask the group to leave mobile phones outside or remove the batteries. A couple of people looked as though I had asked them to peel off their socks. Baron settled the question, humoring me without comment. Kennedy, the *Post*'s general counsel, told me later, "I will confess at that moment I thought, 'Really?' I had never heard anyone suggest a phone could be turned on and the microphone activated remotely. I thought, 'Okay, this is starting off a little strangely.'"

The two handwritten pages of notes I brought were a patchwork of arrows, underscores, inserts, and strikethroughs. This may take awhile to explain, I said. Baron listened without interruption for what must have been twenty minutes. I explained how PRISM worked, how it fit with what we knew before, how the story came to me, and how I planned to confirm it. If we came to terms, Baron would have hard decisions to make about the journalistic, legal, and national security risks. Respectfully, I would have to make my own. I did not mean to encroach on his prerogatives, but I was no longer an employee. Obviously, he had the final call on what went into the paper, but there were things I was not prepared to leave out and things I was not prepared to disclose. If we could not reach a meeting of minds—I floundered for a diplomatic formula—I would understand. Maybe, I said lamely, we could try for another story one day. Leen, who had stuck his neck out, looked to be in a retracting frame of mind. Of course I was encroaching on Baron's prerogatives.

I noticed after a while that I had shifted to plural pronouns, unconsciously hoping to wedge myself into "we." The source, I said, was pushing hard for us to publish a story within three days. I did not think we could be ready that soon, and I was playing for time, but that would not work for long. The source also insisted that our story be accompanied online by the full PRISM document and its cryptographic signature.

Crypto-what?

I had not thought to rehearse this part. Also, the standard metaphors of cryptography are stupid. I wish I had a recording of the next few minutes, which felt to me like an Abbott and Costello routine. Okay, I said, so you have these two keys, a public key and a private key. (*Blank stares.*) The keys are used to encrypt and decrypt, but the private key can also "sign" a file. (*So the key is kind of like a pen?*) Not really. Maybe. I guess you could say that. Point is, the signature lets you know for sure who sent the file, because each key has a unique fingerprint. (*So these keys, they're biometric?*) No. Fingerprint is just a metaphor. The important thing is that you can't use a signing key unless you know the passphrase to unlock it. (*Wait, you unlock . . . a key?*) Forget that. Another terrible metaphor. But I have to mention one more thing. The signature guarantees the file's contents, ensuring it is unaltered from the original. Think of it as a certified snapshot. (*So the key is kind of like a camera?*) No. Not a camera. Let's start over.

All we need to cover here is that if a file is signed, you can check the signature mathematically. Never mind how. If the signature is valid, you know who signed the file, and you know the file has not changed. (*Oh. So how come you didn't just say*—) Right. You're right.

"Why does your source care about the signature?" a smart person asked.

That was the right question. I did not know. When I found out later, the answer threw our project into crisis. For now, all I could say was that I did not think we could agree to the source's request. There was no doubt in my mind that the PRISM document had vital news value. Parts of it, on the other hand, described the particulars of surveillance against obvious adversaries. If you believed in intelligence collection at all, these were legitimate targets. No way would we want to say where, when, how, and what the NSA learned about them. And any edits we made in the document, any omission, would void the cryptographic signature. It was a math thing. The file and its signature would no longer match. They would not almost match. It was a yes-or-no question.

We set that aside for the moment. I had another big subject to cover. The *Post* could not handle a story this sensitive in anything like a normal newsroom environment. I did not live in Washington, so two or three members of the staff should learn how to email and chat online securely. When working with the source material, the *Post* team would need dedicated computers with freshly wiped, encrypted hard drives. Networking hardware should be physically removed from those machines, cutting them off from the internet and newsroom production systems. Baron would have to find us a windowless room with a high-security lock, reinforced door, and heavy safe bolted to the floor. Decryption key files, stored on memory cards, would never be in the same room except when in use. You don't have to write this stuff down, I said. I brought a list. Once these precautions were in place, access to the classified material would require four credentials: door key, safe combination, digital key card, and passphrases. We would divide the credentials among team members. No one but me would have all of them.

Oh God. Did I just tell Baron I would lock him out of his own work-space?

Anything else? Baron asked, expression opaque.

Don Graham should never play cards with this guy. The corner of Baron's mouth might have moved a little. Was he suppressing a smile? Was it a good kind of smile, the understanding kind? Maybe it was a bad kind, a "nice to meet you, time to leave" kind of smile. Hard to tell.

Sorry, Marty, almost done. Just a couple more things.

Even with all the security, I felt responsible to decide for myself how much source material to transfer to the *Post*. If I knew I would not agree to make something public, sharing it introduced a needless risk. I could show Baron the full PRISM document, but I would hand over only the pages that we both were inclined to print. My source, mean-while, had placed himself in serious jeopardy. I did not feel comfort-able sharing his name. Or his location.

About that. The source had flown overseas. My filmmaker friend, the one who introduced us, had invited me to fly there with her.

He's overseas, Baron said. A statement, not a question. He did not like it much.

Yes, I said. I just found out. It is not a friendly jurisdiction, but this is not something in my power to control. Either I fly there or I don't. It would go against every instinct to pass up a face-to-face interview.

I had one last high-handed request. I wanted Julie Tate on this story, the newspaper's alpha researcher and an old friend. If more doc-uments became available, I would appreciate a say in Baron's choice of reporters to join the team. "If" was a thin veil, a hint of incentive. Even so, I had blatantly invited myself, once again, onto the executive edi-tor's turf.

I trailed off, replaying my words as they must have sounded to him. The list had made sense when I wrote it, but how could any editor sign on to all this? The faces around the table, if I read them right, did not like my odds. All eyes turned to Baron.

You mentioned a filmmaker, he said mildly. What was her name again? How well do you know her?

I explained my history with Poitras and the source. Poitras needed a byline, and her reporting had more than earned it. Baron asked a lot of questions, some of which I had covered with Snowden and some of which I had not thought to ask. By now, I was certain that the PRISM document was real, I said, but I knew we would need better evidence than that. I could get second sources for parts of it, but there was no chance I would confirm the whole thing independently. The best-case scenario, and the likeliest, was that the U.S. government would be alarmed enough to try to talk us out of the story. I planned to say we would not engage in that conversation hypothetically. I had held that line before. If intelligence officials wanted to assert grave harm, they would have to acknowledge the document was real. This was not a trick or a bargaining point. "Let's pretend" was simply incompatible with honest discussion of the interests at stake.

Baron had not had occasion for conversations of that sort at the *Globe*. He wanted to know how they usually worked. Leen and Cameron Barr explained that the *Post* asked for comment and context when a story touched on classified matters, same as we did on any other story. The government sometimes asked us to hold something back. We would ask why. McLaughlin, who had deftly handled several such episodes as the paper's deputy general counsel, said a parallel channel might open among the lawyers. Sometimes we agreed to trim a fact, sometimes we refused, and sometimes we rewrote a sentence to convey the news without disclosing a gratuitous detail. If the government did not like my answer, I said, it might escalate to Baron or even the publisher. In my own experience, these exchanges could be civil or very much not. There had been times when officials explained their concerns persuasively by telling me, off the record, a sensitive piece of context I did not know. At other times, they refused to engage at all. Twice they had told me that if my purported information was accurate, then publication would bring a referral to the Justice Department for criminal investigation. Meanwhile, I could go to hell.

"I'm ready to show the document if you are," I told Baron. Baine caught his eye, and something passed between them. Time Warner had cut me off long before this. Go ahead, Baron said.

I booted one of my throwaway laptops with a thumb drive. From a second encrypted thumb drive, I opened the PRISM slide deck to its cover page.

The style fit a briefing subculture I had come to know at the

Pentagon. All the archetypes were here: cheesy graphics and emblems crammed against starbursts, charts, tables, arrows, and acronyms. The company logos grabbed Baron's attention first, as familiar as any leading American brands. I pointed to a round official seal just below them on the left. That belonged to Special Source Operations, PRISM's parent organization in the NSA. See that eagle with talons closed on what look like strands of twine around the globe? Those are fiber optic cables. The internet. The eagle has the internet in its claws. International telephone networks, too.

Not very subtle, someone said. No kidding. At the State Department or the Pentagon, most people who wrote memos had probably heard of the "front-page rule": before you write it down, imagine the news headline. They might not take the maxim to heart, but they knew in some abstract way that secret documents sometimes leaked. An American eagle as predator, the whole world its prey, was the sigil of an agency that could not even conceive of a public readership.

I gave Baron the overview I wished I'd had when I first read these slides. Take a look farther down the cover page, I said, where "S35333" appears in smaller type. S stands for the Signals Intelligence Directorate, S3 for Data Acquisition, and each digit after that identifies a subordinate function. S353, the eagle people at Special Source Operations, pulled in monumental flows of information from the main trunk lines and switches that carry voice and data around the world. The owners of that infrastructure, mostly big corporations, were the "special sources." The NSA paid them off, rerouted their traffic surreptitiously, hacked into their equipment, or relied on foreign allies with methods of their own. Conveniently for U.S. intelligence, an outsized share of global communications traversed the United States. A call or email from Barcelona to Bogotá might well pass through Miami.

PRISM, or S35333, was another kind of access for the eagle folk. Here the special sources were the American-based internet giants:

Google, Facebook, Yahoo, Microsoft, AOL, Skype, YouTube, and Apple. Also a service called Paltalk, which I had not heard of but that presumably hosted accounts of attractive targets. The great thing about those companies, from an intelligence collector's point of view, was that they did much more than push data through pipes. Unlike AT&T and other common carriers, they stored the content their users sent and received. The NSA did not have to chase down all those emails, videos, photographs, and documents as they raced across fiber optic cables at the speed of light. Collection could wait until the data arrived somewhere and held still. (Or, as often happened when faced with alternatives, the NSA could choose to do both.) Exabytes of user information—that is, thousands of millions of billions of bytes—were assembled on big U.S. company data servers. Years of records might be stored in a single account. Eric Schmidt, then chief executive officer of Google, famously said in 2010 that the world created as much information every two days as it had from "the dawn of civilization through 2003." Some people questioned his numbers, but the general point was hard to dispute. The volume of data produced by humankind was expanding at a pace that beggared analogy. Google held a big chunk of that. Its peers in the PRISM collection system, along with Dropbox and other soon-to-be-added partners, dominated the global marketplace for search, messaging, video, email, and cloud storage.

The NSA, in concert with the FBI, dipped into this treasure trove under a secret interpretation of the legal authority that Congress granted in 2007 and 2008. Until then, the government could not search a Skype or AOL account without a warrant from the Foreign Intelligence Surveillance Court. Each warrant required probable cause to believe that a specific account belonged to an agent of a foreign power. The court nearly always granted those warrants, but it did perform an individual review. After Congress passed the Protect America Act and the FISA Amendments Act, Justice Department lawyers persuaded the court that it could authorize surveillance of an unlimited number of accounts with a single order. The court's decision, based solely on government briefs, was classified as "sensitive compartmented information."

In the new arrangement, a judge no longer needed to hear a valid foreign intelligence purpose for surveillance of each proposed target. Neither the court nor the intelligence committees in Congress even knew who the targets were. Once a year, in a classified proceeding, the court approved two documents. The first one laid out rules meant to govern the NSA's choice of accounts to monitor. The second one specified procedures for "minimizing," or limiting access to, the identities of U.S. citizens, green card holders, and companies. The attorney general and the director of national intelligence certified that the NSA would follow these rules. After that, the agency chose targets at will, according to its understanding of the limits. The court would not know when the agency broke a rule unless the Justice Department, as required by still another rule, disclosed the violation to a judge.

Collection was not deliberately aimed at Americans. The targets had to qualify as foreign. More precisely, and not as strictly, the NSA needed grounds to believe that a target was more likely foreign than not. Acquisition of foreign intelligence also had to be "a significant purpose" of the spying but not necessarily the sole or primary purpose. For various reasons, some avoidable and some not, a lot of Americans were swept in under those terms.

I clicked to slides 15 and 40, the latter updated only six weeks before. I showed Baron and his team that PRISM had more than 45,000 "selectors," or individual collection targets, at the end of 2012. By April 5, 2013, there were 117,675 accounts under active surveillance. The numbers were growing exponentially, more than doubling at Facebook and more than tripling at Skype from year to year.

Could there be that many terrorists, spies, and foreign government targets with Hotmail or Yahoo accounts? What definition of "terrorist," the top target category, would result in numbers like that? The subtitle of this slide deck called PRISM the source "Used **Most** in NSA Reporting." Reporting, in this context, meant alerts and briefings sent to intelligence customers around the U.S. government. Put another way, this briefing told us that Fort Meade shared more information obtained from American internet companies than from any other source.

"Okay," Baron pronounced.

"Okay?" I had to hear him say it.

"Okay. I want the story. We can work with your conditions. We'll come up with a security plan and a contract to cover you. When can I meet Laura?"

It felt as though I had been holding my breath a long time. I let it out.

"Can I have a private word?" I asked.

We walked to an empty office across the hall, Baine alongside. I pulled a small rectangular package from my bag. A hard drive, cloned two nights before. Pandora. I needed a secure home for this backup, and I needed to know the *Post* was all the way in.

I made my words carefully vague.

"It could be that more than one document will become available. More than one story. I'd like you to keep this safe for me."

Another thin veil, the best I could come up with. The drive was encrypted. I would not leave the keys. Even under legal orders, Baron could not open it or profess to know the contents. He might surmise, but he did not owe his private thoughts to anyone.

Sharing custody of the archive would not diminish my own exposure, not formally. The First Amendment issued no membership cards. Whatever uncertain protection it offered, whatever shield law or common-law privilege applied, should extend equally in theory to a freelance reporter. In practice, in the legal culture of twenty-first-century America, a big newspaper's embrace would constrain the government's options. Kicking down my door was one thing, sending a team to toss the newsroom another. Even a polite subpoena might carry political costs. Baron had already promised a lot. Publishing a story would validate my links to the source as legitimate reporting. Covering my legal costs would spare me a burden. But the *Post* could not extend its unwritten privilege at arm's length. Only by joining in my jeopardy would it make this story, and my legal defense, fully its own.

I wanted to know that Baron had skin in the game. I held the hard drive, palm up, at my side. It felt more like a question than an offer. Would he accept?

From over my right shoulder, Baine called time-out.

"Marty, as the company's lawyer, I can't advise you to do that," he said.

I closed my eyes. I opened them. I wanted to object, to contest the ruling, but I had no grounds. Baine had warned me that he would speak up if a conflict of interest emerged. Here it was. This was the point where my interests and the newspaper's diverged. Baron had agreed to publish a single story. Baine, I figured, saw me on thornier terrain, walking around with who knows what and who knows how much of it. There was no reason for Baron to join me in that briar patch. I knew what had to be coming next. Baine would parse and qualify the *Post*'s commitment. Terms and conditions applied. I braced myself, but the lawyer said nothing more. The room went quiet. It took quite a few beats to persuade me that Baine had spoken his piece. I had misjudged the moment. His silence became a subtle, thrilling signal.

He's not really trying. He's not trying at all. Baine had flagged a legal boundary, nothing more. That probably qualified literally as the least he could do. If he wanted to block this transaction, he could spell out nightmare scenarios, invoke the ghosts of subpoena fights past, point out that I had not even said what the package contained. He could pull Baron aside and tell him this decision was not an editor's to make. Williams & Connolly represented the whole company. Baine could walk up two flights to the publisher. He did not do that. He did not do any of those things. Even the dozen words he spoke were soft at the edges. "Can't advise" did not pack the punch of "advise against." Hell, he could have said, "Marty, *stop*. Do not take that package. We need to talk." Baine offered Baron an easy exit, no doubt about that. A lot of editors, a lot of executives anywhere, would be glad to have it. If Baron shouldered this burden without checking upstairs, it was all on him.

Baron nodded. Message received. Boundary noted.

"I'm doing it," he said.

He held out his hand. The answer was yes. Yes to the story, yes to the hard drive, yes to the whole outlandish list. Something seemed to be in my eye. I struggled not to embarrass myself. The *Post* was still the *Post*. I was home.

FOUR

PRISM

As Snowden counted down his final days in Hawaii, a senior civilian manager was making the rounds of NSA headquarters, five thousand miles away. The manager, whose name was Rick, led a project called PRISM, one of the agency's most prolific operations. As a start-up back in 2007, PRISM had produced a grand total of three intelligence reports in its first month. Now, five and a half years later, it had become a principal engine of the U.S. surveillance machine. Rick was its collection manager and chief evangelist.

The wire diagram of the NSA that year placed Rick's operation within the unassumingly named subdirectorate of Data Acquisition, an arm of the Signals Intelligence Directorate. That is to say, Rick ran a spy shop, which is not a redundant thing to say in the context of the larger enterprise. The NSA did a whole lot of spying and a whole lot of other things, too. Great swaths of it, any one of which could swallow a lesser federal agency, took little or no part in the business of espionage. A chart of all those islands would divide the Fort Meade archipelago roughly in half. Information Assurance, on one side, locked down American secrets. Signals Intelligence, on the other, stole the secrets of others. The twin missions, defend and attack, had coequal status but not coequal power. Offense had always been the bigger, richer brother.

In principle, the ambitions of signals intelligence extended to all the world's data in electromagnetic form. SIGINT did not confine its collection to human language and pictures. It filled immense reservoirs with the chatter of machines: missile telemetry, radar signatures, the handshakes at network switches on internet trunk lines. Oceans of information, ever replenished, deluged any vessel that mortal hands could build. "Swallowing the sea is a fatuous idea," said Joel F. Brenner, a Harvard-trained lawyer who served as NSA inspector general in the mid-2000s. "No organization, and no technology, can do it. Doing SIGINT for foreign intelligence purposes therefore implies electronic filtering, sorting, and dissemination systems of amazing sophistication."

George R. Cotter, who served as the NSA's chief scientist until 2009, liked to describe the division of labor in signals intelligence as "Fetch It, Etch It and Retch It." Fetching happened in acquisition, or S3 on the organization chart, where the first stage of spying took place. Thousands of workers reached into cables and routers and networks around the world to extract information that belonged to someone else. Etching was the domain of S2, analysis and production, where thousands of others filtered and looked for meaning in the raw intercepts. Retching, in Cotter's irreverent phrase, described the labors of S1, where the NSA prepared intelligence reports for the president and a long list of lesser customers. The official NSA lexicon evoked a factory: "product lines" were sorted by topic and geography, then assembled into "finished intelligence," most commonly in the form of "serialized reports," and routed to consumers in portions that accorded with their clearances and needs. By the numbers, the conveyor belt rolled backward from S3 to S2 to S1. Acquire, analyze, report. Fetch, etch, retch.

Rick lived on the "Fetch It" side of the house. He displayed evident pride in PRISM and made sure to spread the word. In April 2013, Rick was traveling from office to office in the corridors of S2, regaling analysts with tales of treasure to be had from Silicon Valley and the Microsoft empire east of Seattle: email, voice and video chat, instant messages, photographs, budget documents, travel and medical records, technical drawings, contact lists, and more. He drew upon a "corporate portfolio" of nine companies, listed in order of entry into the PRISM apparatus: "Microsoft, Yahoo, Google, Facebook, PalTalk, AOL, Skype, YouTube, Apple." Dropbox, the cloud storage and synchronization service, was described as "coming soon."

Like a lot of pitches of this sort, Rick's message mixed customer education with reputation-building and budget defense for his office. "PRISM is one of the most valuable, unique, and productive accesses for NSA—don't miss out," he told the analysts. Some offices, he mentioned, did not make optimal use of PRISM. "They are missing unique collection on their targets."

Inevitably, this being a federal agency, Rick brought along a deck of PowerPoint slides. There were forty-one of them, so densely packed that the presentation must have lasted over an hour. He sprinkled the talk with eye-popping samples for each specialized "target office of primary interest" in the directorate. There were South Asia highlights for S2A, China and Korea highlights for S2B, and so on through S2I (Counterterrorism) and S2J (Weapons and Space).

Several qualities enriched Rick's presentation from a journalist's point of view. He wrote close to seven thousand words of speaker's notes, full of granular detail that did not appear on the display slides themselves. Some passages disclosed collection details that a more cautious author might have left out. Prominent display of the PRISM Provider List, which was supposed to be the project's deepest secret, lent a further air of indiscretion to the briefing.

Snowden came across the PRISM file in electronic form around the same time that Rick presented it to analysts in S2H, the Russia product line. Nothing Snowden had seen until now better suited his plan. He had been talking to Poitras for three months, but he still did not feel confident that his disclosures would seize attention from a public that had seldom responded strongly to privacy warnings. Most of the NSA programs that worried him were legally and technically intricate, not easy to explain. He needed examples that ordinary people would recognize. Along came Rick's presentation, festooned at the top of every slide with iconic logos from the best-known Internet companies in the world. "PRISM hits close to people's hearts," he told me.

Alongside the famous trademarks, Rick had placed another image twice the size. This one represented the PRISM project itself. A lot of NSA offices designed their own seals, often relying on clip art found online. They were symbols of identity and prowess, akin to the crossed swords on an Army cavalry patch. PRISM's emblem featured a slab of glass cut into rectilineal planes—an actual prism, the triangular kind used in optics. A beam of light passed through the glass. Two beams of light emerged. The second one, the twin, refracted into a rainbow of hidden colors. Was this a pun, a visual play on PRISM's cover name, or did it mean to convey a more literal message? The internet itself was a construct of light that moved information through cables spun from glass. Did the NSA splice in and sort through the lightstream for secrets? In fact, it did not—or not with PRISM. Not under this program, as officials would say carefully in statements to come that year. There were splicing operations, literal and figurative, at other points of access for the NSA and its allied service in the United Kingdom. I had not pieced those clues together yet.

Snowden understood the power of images. "The internet is on principle a system that you reveal yourself to in order to fully enjoy, which differentiates it from, say, a music player that you can listen to without your interests being known," he wrote to me as I neared publication of the PRISM story. "It is a TV that watches you." In PRISM, he saw an image to persuade the public that there really might be someone on the other side of the screen.

n film and fiction, the NSA mostly listened in on telephone calls. PRISM had capabilities far beyond that. According to the users' guide for the project's Skype interface, a separate document, NSA analysts could not only review stored account information but also dial in and record live "audio, video, chat, and file transfers." Analysts could ask for instant notifications when their targets logged on to Hotmail or AOL or Yahoo Messenger. Using other tools, outside the PRISM rubric, the NSA could monitor keystrokes as they happened during a live chat or an internet search, before a surveillance target even clicked Send. "They can literally watch your thoughts form as you type," Snowden told me.

Never in history had there been richer troves of personal information than the ones held by the internet giants. Rick's presentation described "continued exponential growth" in the volume of information his project obtained from those stores. By his accounting, PRISM produced the raw material for more than 15 percent of the agency's distributed intelligence reports. Since 2011, no source had been cited as often in the President's Daily Brief, which assembled the most timely work from all seventeen agencies and organizations in the U.S. intelligence community. Over the course of fiscal year 2012, the president had received a total of 8,233 articles in his highly classified daily brief. Nearly one in five, 1,477, drew upon information obtained from U.S. internet companies under the auspices of PRISM.

These were eye-opening figures in an enterprise that measured annual intake in the trillions of communications. How could an agency built to spy overseas have set its hooks so deeply into the U.S.

information industry? Rick's audience knew the basics, but he spelled them out. The NSA could lawfully target only foreigners, and only if they were located abroad, but "much of the world's communications flow through the U.S.," he told colleagues. "A target's phone call, email or chat will take the cheapest path, not the physically most direct path." The conversations that analysts needed most "could easily be flowing into and through the U.S."

That happenstance might have been a bonanza for the NSA, but until fairly recently it had not been. Rick echoed a long-standing complaint that Congress had tied the agency's hands. The Foreign Intelligence Surveillance Act of 1978, he said, had unduly "restricted our 'home field advantage' . . . because it provided privacy protections to people who were not entitled to them." Something like "80 percent of known terrorist email accounts used Yahoo or Hotmail," but until 2007 the NSA had to apply for an individual warrant for every surveillance order—"simply because the Government was collecting off a wire in the United States."

Rick skipped over the first six years after September 11, 2001, when President Bush ordered the NSA to disregard the statutory warrant requirement. Under four collection programs overseen by Vice President Cheney, the NSA and FBI began wide-ranging surveillance of internet and telephone communications within the United States. Cheney and his lawyer insisted on concealing those operations from most of Bush's national security staff and nearly everyone in Congress and the FISA Court. The operations were protected as "exceptionally compartmented information"—the most restricted category of classification—under the cover name WHIPGENIE. Later they were reflagged as STELLARWIND, with a special handling caveat known as RAGTIME. The one secrecy precaution Cheney did not allow was designation of STELLARWIND as a "special access program." As Brenner put it, "the creation of a new special access program requires Congressional notification, but it was run directly by the Office of the Vice President and put under the direct personal control of the Vice President's counsel, David Addington."

When the *New York Times* revealed one of the secret programs in 2005, a speechwriter for Bush came up with the name "Terrorist Surveillance Program," a marketing slogan that deliberately misdirected public scrutiny. The domestic surveillance did not spy on known terrorists. It aspired to cover substantially all Americans, collecting hundreds of billions of telephone and internet records, in the hope of discovering *unknown* conspirators. According to an internal classification guide, the NSA followed Bush's political lead and began using "TSP," a made-up compartment name, "in briefings and declarations intended for external audiences, such as Congress and the courts."

A rebellion in the Justice Department against unlawful orders forced Bush to seek authority for the warrantless programs from the FISA Court and eventually from Congress. That was where Rick's briefing picked up the story again. In the Protect America Act of 2007, Congress temporarily removed the individual warrant requirement for surveillance of a foreign target whose communications can be obtained from a U.S. company. As noted in chapter 3, Congress extended the new NSA authority in Section 702 of the FISA Amendments Act of 2008. Legislators also granted retroactive immunity to any telephone carrier or internet provider that broke the law by giving protected information to the government without warrants.

Those were the laws that gave birth to PRISM. The executive branch had persuaded Congress that it was too hard for the NSA to reach its targets from overseas access points, where data split into packets and scattered over multiple paths. The same information, in many cases, was there for the taking on U.S. territory, reassembled and sitting still in the data centers of the American companies. "The [United States] overwhelmed the world, not in its own communications, but as the provider of the infrastructure," Rick explained to his listeners. "We needed to collect the full content directly from the providers' servers."

Although the new FISA orders had the force of law, compelling the companies to provide assistance to the FBI on behalf of the NSA, the orders did not tell each company exactly what to hand over or how. The NSA emphasized partnership, Rick wrote, because "PRISM access is 100% dependent on ISP provisioning." The agency could not take what it wanted without help. A well-informed insider told me, "NSA can't simply walk up to Facebook and say, 'Hey, we're going to go in your server room and pull everything back to headquarters, okay?' Only Facebook knows how to do that. We're talking about services of monumental complexity that span continents, developed by thousands of world-class engineers. There have to be negotiations about who can be brought in from the company on it, what can be pulled based on the architecture of the service, how to actually implement it, and so on."

PRISM was not a mass surveillance program. I say that plainly because there were many who came to misread or miscast it that way. There were regulations and technical limits to what it could do. PRISM did not and could not scoop up Hotmail or Yahoo accounts in bulk. The NSA chose target accounts by way of individual taskings, the term of art. Analysts identified those accounts by email address or a comparably specific factor such as the telephone number used for registration. Those are called strong or deterministic selectors, in counterpoint to weak ones used in other surveillance programs that might match a large number of accounts. (Those might be key words from a target dictionary or a range of numeric device addresses in a foreign network of interest.) When analysts called up the Unified Targeting Tool on their screens, the PRISM interface asked, by way of a drop-down menu, for the foreign intelligence purpose ("Select a Value") of their inquiries. Another drop-down menu asked for a "foreignness factor" that gave reason to believe the target was neither an American nor located in the United States. PRISM users were forbidden to spy deliberately on U.S. persons, the legal term encompassing citizens, permanent residents, organizations, and companies. If Americans turned up "incidentally" in their nets, NSA operators were obliged to "minimize," or restrict access to, those names. Supervisors and auditors kept tabs on compliance. Once a year, in a classified session, the Foreign Intelligence Surveillance Court reviewed the procedures for target selection and for masking the names of Americans who turned up in the catch. Nothing in the Snowden archive, and nothing I learned independently, offered reason to doubt that the NSA workforce did its best to follow the rules in good faith.

And even so, the formal restraints obscured the breadth of government intrusion into the U.S. information economy. Wide gaps had emerged in the checks and balances that once governed domestic NSA operations. For decades, intelligence collection at home had operated under traditional Fourth Amendment standards. Interception of signals on U.S. wires required an individual warrant based upon probable cause and judicial review of the supporting facts. Under PRISM, the NSA sent selectors to Silicon Valley by the tens of thousands, more than a hundred thousand accounts "on cover" at a time, unreviewable in volume and in fact unreviewed by any independent authority. When the intelligence court approved the targeting procedures, it did not ask and was not told the account names under surveillance or the number of Americans swept in.

Rick's presentation celebrated the low threshold of evidence required to task a target for collection under PRISM, comparing it to legal standards in other realms. Conviction of a crime required proof beyond reasonable doubt. Civil judgments were based upon a preponderance of evidence, "greater than 50% percent probability," he wrote. The old

FISA standard for a surveillance order was probable cause. For some kinds of warrants, the FISA Court required a still lower test known as reasonable articulable suspicion, the same standard that governs a traffic stop by police. PRISM surveillance required less than that. An analyst need only state a "reasonable belief" that a would-be target was abroad. But some of the grounds I saw cited for such a "reasonable belief," including an ostensibly foreign IP address, were well known to return false results in significant number.

The acquisition of Americans' content under PRISM was "incidental" to surveillance aimed at foreigners, but that did not mean it was unforeseen. The NSA knew how its systems worked. Bystanders filled its data repositories in far greater numbers than designated targets, and many of the bystanders were American. The NSA kept all that data, and "minimizing" only restricted access to the U.S. identities. Many officials had authority to unmask them, in order to understand the intelligence in context or for other reasons.

The NSA's oversight and compliance directorate generated many reports but seldom found abuse, in large part because the agency defined the term narrowly. Abuse was a knowing breach of regulations by a rogue employee for reasons such as personal gain, vengeance, or romance gone bad. (The latter offense had a nickname, LOVEINT, but it was rare.) Corrupt use of PRISM was not the issue. The hard questions arose from its fine print and everyday practice, when the system worked exactly as intended. The Bush and Obama administrations had defended the FISA amendments of 2008 and 2012 as modest technical adjustments for changing times, with constitutional protections and judicial review intact. Deep layers of secrecy, alongside careful deflection of questions about the government's intent, had left a major shift of legal boundaries invisible outside the privileged world of classified knowledge. Brenner, who supported the change in law, acknowledged nonetheless that its import had been concealed from the public. "NSA was operating under statute—but ordinary, intelligent, educated Americans could not have looked at that statute and understood that it meant what the FISA Court interpreted it to mean," he told an invited Fort Meade audience in 2015.

Because of that secrecy, even the best-informed journalists and policy analysts had no information on the way PRISM worked. Plaintiffs could bring no constitutional challenge in federal court. Congress faced no public pressure, and big internet companies encountered little demand for stronger defense of privacy. Voters and consumers could not ask for change because they did not know the truth.

Two days after Marty Baron agreed to publish the PRISM story, a message from Snowden nearly drove us off the rails. I had sent him an upbeat status report. The *Post* was pressing ahead at full speed. Snowden wrote back, noting pointedly that his seventy-two-hour deadline for publication had expired. The document he had sent to Poitras and me spoke for itself, as far as he was concerned. What else could we possibly need?

He and I had discussed this at length already. There were steps I could not skip. "You may have time constraints I do not understand," I wrote. "I want to make sure that you understand mine. I have seldom heard of a story of this magnitude that went from soup to nuts in three days, or four or five. I'm not proposing a specific alternative. I sincerely hope you'll reconsider the idea of a deadline set in days. If you can shed any light on how timing affects you, it's possible I can help address it in another way."

Late on Saturday night, May 25, he replied with new urgency. "Alright, let's talk about time pressure first," he said. "Let me illustrate the driver in more detail so we're clear. Until you publish, I am at the highest level of personal risk, because rightly or wrongly, adversaries may feel this can be stopped early." He had left a cover story about medical treatment, but "at this point I'm certain we're out of time. That means unless I'm better than I think I am, on Monday, NSA will become aware precisely where I am, and they're not going to be thinking 'what a brave and principled whistlerblower,' it's going to be 'how do we splat the spy?'"

Those were not the words that knocked the wind out of me. The gut punch came when Snowden answered my half-forgotten question about the cryptographic signature, the little digital file he asked me to publish alongside the story and the PRISM slides. I had struggled to explain the thing to editors, focusing on the technical points. They had left me with something bigger to think about.

Why does your source care about the signature?

I had let that question slip in the crush of other work. Snowden had first mentioned the signature nine days earlier, on May 16. Its purpose, he said, was to certify that the PRISM document "has not been edited or changed." That sounded promising. Did he mean, I wrote back, that someone at the NSA had signed the presentation with a U.S. government credential? That would be outstanding news, akin to a royal seal embossed in resin and wax. Little doubt about authenticity would remain. Snowden offered half a reply, then pirouetted away. "It creates a 'chain of custody.' This matters for the historical record," he wrote. "I can't yet explain the rest."

After meeting with the *Post* editors, I remembered that I could do an elementary check of the signature on my own. The result was disappointing. I was slow to grasp what it implied.

```
gpg --verify PRISM.pptx.sig PRISM.pptx
gpg: Signature made Mon May 20 14:31:57 2013 EDT
using RSA key ID ■■■■■■■■
gpg: Good signature from "Verax"
```

Now I knew that Snowden, using his Verax alter ego, had signed the PowerPoint file himself. If I published the signature, all it would prove to a tech-savvy few was that a pseudonymous source had vouched for his own leak. What good would that do anyone?

In the Saturday night email, Snowden spelled it out. He had chosen to risk his freedom, he wrote, but he was not resigned to life in prison or worse. He preferred to set an example for "an entire class of potential whistleblowers" who might follow his lead. Ordinary citizens would not take impossible risks. They had to have some hope for a happy ending.

> To effect this, I intend to apply for asylum (preferably somewhere with strong internet and press freedoms, e.g. Iceland, though the strength of the reaction will determine how choosy I can be). Given how tightly the U.S. surveils diplomatic outposts (I should know, I used to work in our U.N. spying shop), I cannot risk this until you have already gone to press, as it would immediately tip our hand. It would also be futile without proof of my claims—they'd have me committed—and I have no desire to provide raw source material to a foreign government. Post publication, the source document and cryptographic signature will allow me to immediately substantiate both the truth of my claim and the danger I am in without having to give anything up. . . .
>
> Give me the bottom line: when do you expect to go to print?

Alarm gave way to vertigo. I forced myself to reread the passage slowly. Snowden planned to seek the protection of a foreign government. He would canvass diplomatic posts on an island under Chinese sovereign control. He might not have very good choices. The signature's purpose, its only purpose, was to help him through the gates.

How could I have missed this? Poitras and I did not need the signature to know who sent us the PRISM file. Snowden wanted to prove his role in the story to someone else. That thought had never occurred to me. Confidential sources, in my experience, did not implicate themselves—irrevocably, mathematically—in a classified leak. As soon as Snowden laid it out, the strategic logic was obvious. If we did as he asked, Snowden could demonstrate that our copy of the NSA document came from him. His plea for asylum would assert a "well-founded fear of being persecuted" for an act of political dissent. The U.S. government would maintain that Snowden's actions were criminal, not political. Under international law each nation could make that judgment for itself. The fulcrum of Snowden's entire plan was the signature file, a few hundred characters of cryptographic text, about the length of this paragraph. And I was the one he expected to place it online for his use.

Idiot. Remember "chain of custody"? He came right out and told you he wanted a historical record.

My mind raced. When Snowden walked into a consulate, evidence of his identity in hand, any intelligence officer would surmise that he might have other classified information in reach. Snowden said he did not want to hand over documents, but his language, as I read it that night, seemed equivocal. Even assuming he divulged nothing, I had not signed up for his plan. I had agreed to protect my source's identity in order to report a story to the public. He wanted me to help him disclose it, in private, as a credential to present to foreign governments. That was something altogether different.

Even in those next awful hours, I never believed that Snowden was a spy. His behavior was inexplicable through that lens. No aspiring foreign agent would launch his espionage career by handing a pile of secrets to journalists. Intelligence services overseas would much rather have a secret that no one else knows, or no one else knows they know.

If they chose to make it public in a propaganda campaign, they would want to control the selection and timing. I had spent many hours in conversation with this man, probing his backstory and motives. His explanations rang true, and my instincts said he was sincere. The trouble was that instincts had not covered me in glory these last few weeks. Snowden kept springing surprises. I began to second-guess myself. How certain was I, really, that I knew his innermost plans?

A wave of nausea swept over me. This guy's safety and freedom could be in my hands. Nobody at the *Post* understood the signature mumbo-jumbo. Marty Baron would look to me for a decision. The last thing I wanted was to hurt my source, but I had not agreed to play the role Snowden cast for me. I tried to tell myself the question was moot: none of us thought we should publish the PRISM document in full, anyway, and any kind of editing would void the signature. But that was no longer the issue and I knew it. Snowden had told me clearly what he intended to do with the signature. If we published it now, the *Post* would be a knowing instrument of his flight from American law. I might wish him luck. I did. But it was not my role to help.

I logged on to an anonymous chat account, hoping to find Poitras online. It was late, but she had done the same.

```
BG: I just read his email
you see it?
LP: yes
Intense
BG: I can't imagine how where he is leads to Iceland. At all.
He has just told us he intends to apply for asylum and may not be
able to be choosy
"No desire" to provide raw source to a fo gov.
LP: what do you read that—that he is considering that?
BG: I read that as an option he has in mind.
```

Looking back, it is clear to me that I misread Snowden badly. Events to come proved beyond plausible doubt that he did not transfer allegiance to a foreign government, did not contemplate buying his safety with classified files. The words that shook me—"preferably," "choosy," "no desire"—were ambiguous in context. I assumed the worst. We both did.

> LP: oh god
>
> fuck
>
> BG: He's in a position to provide that material. He may be under compulsion. We REALLY can't do anything that could abet or be perceived to abet that.
>
> LP: of course
>
> BG: I just wanna be a goddam journalist

On Sunday we patched together a conference call with the lawyers. I sketched the main developments—file, signature, asylum—without saying "NSA" or "Hong Kong." Childish opsec, but we were scattered and could not wait for a face-to-face. The lawyers were alarmed. When two of them started talking at once, I misheard something. "Don't tell me I'll be aiding and abetting if I don't turn in my source," I said. "I'm not going to do it."

Nobody had suggested that, actually. Everyone on the call agreed that we would carry on with our story plans and protect the source's identity as before. No one but Poitras and I knew Snowden's name anyway. But Kevin Baine, the lead outside counsel, asked me in a no-bullshit tone to level with him. Had I ever promised to publish the full PRISM presentation or its digital signature? I had not, and Poitras said the same. Our source framed both those points as "requests" before he sent the document. Poitras and I had ducked and changed the subject. Why engage him in a hypothetical dispute? Depending on what the document said, publication in full might have been an easy yes. "You have to tell him you never agreed to that," Baine said. Poitras and I faced a whole new kind of legal exposure now. We could not leave unanswered a "direct attempt to enlist you in assisting him with his plans to approach foreign governments."

It was about as bad as I thought. Then it got worse. The day before Snowden's asylum email, we had told Baron for the first time that our source was in Hong Kong. Poitras planned to film him there. Snowden invited me to join her. "I am not sure I will have much beyond the slides to offer, but I will be glad to offer any assistance or insight that I can," he wrote. I badly wanted to meet the man. I told Baron I leaned toward taking the trip, but I was in a bind. Film was Poitras's bailiwick. Filling out the PRISM reporting was mine. I had to reach out in deepest confidence to other people in a position to know the facts. How could I do those interviews over international telephone lines? I was not even using a phone for local calls. I met my sources in person, making advance arrangements when I could do so securely and otherwise turning up at their door unannounced. "I'm on the fence about my priorities," I said. Baron smiled and turned to Poitras, saying, "We'll leave it to you to tip him over." It was the natural instinct of any journalist. Go where the story is. I decided I would have to make it work. Later that day, I wrote to Snowden, "I look forward to meeting face to face. Chances are our mutual friend and I will travel together Saturday."

Not long after the first conference call, Baine sent word that we needed to talk again. Right away. He had consulted his partner Barry Simon, who specialized in government investigations and criminal defense. Simon, Baine said, "had a strong reaction" to our travel plans. That was one way to put it. When he joined the call, Simon spoke with an urgency I had not heard from a lawyer in twenty-one years at the *Post*. There could be a raid on our source at any time by U.S. forces,

Chinese authorities, or parties unknown who operated in Hong Kong's intelligence no-man's-land. If we were in the room, we might well be arrested alongside him in a system that did not afford us many rights. In the circumstances, we could not expect much help from U.S. consular services. Upon our return, U.S. prosecutors would find it easier to bring a criminal case—easier to distinguish our conduct from ordinary journalism—if we carried or took possession of classified documents overseas. When we made notes and recordings of our interviews, those were bound to include classified information, too. We should assume that both U.S. and Chinese authorities were capable of intercepting anything we stored or transmitted in digital form. If we somehow secured our files impregnably, someone might compel us to decrypt them. The final, unavoidable exposure was this: we had no practical defense against eavesdropping when we sat down with our source. No reasonable person, least of all an experienced national security reporter, could claim to be unaware that China routinely wiretapped hotel rooms and meeting venues in Hong Kong. I had interviewed diplomats about the subject myself. By conversing about classified matters—and how could we not?—Poitras and I would directly expose U.S. national security secrets to a foreign intelligence service. If we did not think we could be prosecuted on those facts, Simon said, we were wrong.

Baron, sobered, gave up his playful prodding. We would each have to make this decision for ourselves. He would not fault us if we stayed home. He would back us with every resource if we flew. That night in New York, in my living room, I poured Poitras a bourbon and walked her through the conversation with Simon. "Do you mean to say we can't go talk to a source about *U.S.* surveillance abuses because *Chinese* surveillance might be listening in?" she asked. "Do you realize how fucked up that is?"

I could not dispute the irony, but I decided to push back the trip. Lawyers aside, there were reasons enough to wait. I could not finish reporting or compose a story without the documents. I did not intend to carry them to the backyard of the Chinese Ministry of State Security. Snowden might be good enough to keep the archive safe in that hostile digital environment, but I could not. (He had taught exactly that skill set in counterintelligence school.) Nor did I want to lead U.S. authorities to Snowden's door. By now I had been asking questions for days. If the government had caught wind of the story, it could be watching my travel bookings and credit cards. I did not think Snowden had fully considered that risk.

These were genuine concerns. They were on my mind. But there is no denying that Simon's warning shook me. I had four kids in school, four tuitions to pay, and nobody sold insurance for something like this. Jay Kennedy, the paper's general counsel, had given me contacts for a high-powered lawyer in Hong Kong. I passed them to Poitras with instructions to send invoices to the *Post*. She was still under contract. If she went to see Snowden, the paper would have her back. That night she decided, reluctantly, to cancel her flight.

"This all makes me feel ill," she wrote the next day.

"I thought I was pretty good at gaming out contingencies, but I never thought of this one," I replied.

Poitras was still recovering from an unrelated exchange with Snowden. Three days earlier, she had told him she needed time to think before getting on a plane. Snowden thought she feared questioning at the Hong Kong border, coming or going. He proposed a cover story. Poitras began to wonder exactly what kind of liaison this stranger had in mind.

"Implying an affair with me is an easy and believably incriminating way to justify the surreptitious travel and time alone with someone,"

Snowden told her. Security screeners liked to believe that they had seen through a traveler's secrets, he wrote. If suspicion fell upon her, Poitras could "make them feel like they've unraveled the mystery" with a suitcase full of sex toys and lingerie. Under questioning she could hint at an assignation with a stranger she met online. She need not spell out the mortifying details. Her luggage would tell the story. The camera was for bed play, the video files encrypted for privacy. Snowden laid out the scenario colorfully.

"It is creepy, right?" Poitras wrote to me. "Now I have little interest. Perhaps I'll feel differently in a day." The misunderstanding cleared up quickly enough. Snowden had no lecherous intent. His advice came straight from the playbook of clandestine travel. Cover for presence. Cover for action. An embarrassing story, even as fiction, but all the better camouflage for that.

We hated the replies we sent to Snowden on May 26. We had lawyered up and it showed. "You were clear with me and I want to be equally clear with you," I wrote. "There are a number of unwarranted assumptions in your email. My intentions and objectives are purely journalistic, and I will not tie them or time them to any other goal." I was working hard and intended to publish, but "I cannot give you the bottom line you want."

Poitras wrote to him separately.

There have been several developments since Monday (e.g., your decision to leave the country, your choice of location, possible intentions re asylum), that have come as a surprise and make [it] necessary to be clear. As B explained, our intentions and objectives are journalistic. I believe you know my interest and commitment to this subject. B's work on the topic speaks for itself. I cannot travel to interview you in person. However, I do have questions if you are still willing to answer them.

Snowden responded with bafflement and alarm. "The response in the last few days from you and BRASSBANNER has me extremely concerned about what appears to be a sudden change of heart," he told Poitras. "You've both gone from supportive to inexplicably terrifying. . . . I can't even know if my true name and the source document have already been turned over [to U.S. authorities] at this point. Jesus. I don't know what they said to you, but I did not go to these lengths to hurt my country or my people."

To me, the same day, he wrote that he was "working hard to do what is right in an extremely difficult situation." He was not trying to call the editorial shots. "I confide in you as the lead journalist working on a story of public interest, not to tie you to my raft." He closed with a plea: "Please confirm your intention to include the cryptographic signature with the source document. You now know [failure to do so] will directly jeopardize my safety."

It was excruciating. Snowden had taken a leap, counting on us for a parachute we had not agreed to supply. "What a nightmare," Poitras wrote to me. We would certainly not turn him in, as he seemed to fear. Nor would we share our copy of the PRISM file with U.S. authorities. (I never do that. Governments and big companies often place invisible markers on sensitive documents in order to trace their provenance if they leak.) That was all the reassurance I could offer. "Please understand that the only commitment I have made is to pursue this story vigorously and to protect the identity of a confidential journalistic source. I continue to respect both of those commitments. I did not commit and could not responsibly have committed to publishing a document and cryptographic key that I had never seen."

For a young man in free fall, Snowden responded with remarkable grace. He noted dryly that "your communications appear to be rather more reviewed than they were previously." He could no longer treat the *Post* story as exclusive. "I regret that we weren't able to keep this project unilateral for longer than we had, but so it is. Best of luck to you in your reporting—may you know the truth."

That day, May 27, Snowden had his first conversation with Glenn Greenwald. When I mentioned this sequence in a story two weeks later, Greenwald did not like it. "Bart Gellman's claims about Snowden's interactions with me—when, how and why—are all false," he wrote in the first of a series of angry posts on Twitter. "Laura Poitras and I have been working with him since February, long before anyone spoke to Bart Gellman." He elaborated in his book *No Place to Hide*. My arrival on the scene had marked an unwelcome "new turn" near the end of May, when Poitras handed me a scoop that I "had not worked to obtain." Rather than report the story aggressively, the *Post* and I assembled lawyers and invited the White House to cut the balls off our story.

These were checkable assertions, and he had to know by the time he wrote his book that they were not true. Greenwald had not worked with Snowden or Poitras since February. He had not "set up the encryption software and [begun] speaking directly with Snowden in late March or early April," as he told the *Huffington Post*. He had not even heard of the source or his story until Poitras told him in person on April 19, nearly three months after she and I first met to discuss them. (Even then, Greenwald was unaware that Verax was the Cincinnatus who had reached out unsuccessfully to him before.) Poitras found Greenwald eager but "clueless on the security-technical side of things," still unable to use the encrypted channels required to take part. Another five weeks passed before Verax connected with Greenwald at the end of May. Poitras, who decided in the end to make the Hong Kong trip, invited Greenwald to join her. She handed him the Pandora archive as they prepared to board their June 1 flight. I will not belabor the timeline, which is sketched in an endnote, but every event in this book thus far, up to moment when Snowden said he could not "keep this project unilateral," preceded Greenwald's first glimpse of the documents and his first exchange with a source whose name he still did not know.

Obviously Greenwald played a leading role in the surveillance disclosures, regardless of when it began. He made grander claims: that he had owned this story from the start, and that no one in the mainstream media had the nerve to take it on. He compared his "audacious journalism" about the NSA to the "timid, risk-averse government obeisance" of the *Post* and its mainstream peers. This parable of a man among journalistic mice became his calling card.

I could have agreed with a more nuanced critique of establishment journalism. Sometimes our stories lacked skepticism, deferred too much to authority, or resorted to false equivalence when we had the means to sift competing accounts. But good newspapers, and there were still some left, drove themselves hard "to pursue the truth and to tell it unflinchingly," as Marty Baron said when he accepted an award for just that. On their better days, mainstream journalists delivered the great public good of holding power to account.

Greenwald held that traditional news media, the whole class of us, were trembling servants of the men and women in power. He thought up a lot of synonyms for that. What I saw at the *Post* in real life, as the NSA story unfolded, was a newsroom that threw itself fully into the breach. The reporters and editors and graphic designers I worked alongside did some of the finest journalism that I have seen up close. It is a simple matter of fact that the *Post* did not trim one clause of one story for fear of displeasing authorities.

In the early morning hours of June 11, two days after his opening salvos, Greenwald extended an olive branch. "Hey Bart—I really regret that we got dragged into a public spat over trivial at [*sic*] really doesn't matter," he wrote. "I'll take the blame for getting lured into that." Twelve hours later, as I walked to a sandwich shop on Whitehall Street, my mobile phone showed an incoming call from *New York Times* legal correspondent Charlie Savage. Greenwald had just told him, he said, that I lied in my behind-the-scenes account of Snowden and the PRISM document. Snowden had never insisted that I publish every slide, Greenwald said. All he asked was that I post his digital signature online. Greenwald knew this, he told Savage, because he had read our correspondence.

It was loud on the street. Did I hear that right? The privacy crusader was reading my mail and leaking it? Greenwald could not actually have read all my communications with Snowden. Even Poitras had not seen the whole pile, and Snowden did not keep copies. Greenwald's assertion did not even make sense. The signature would not match the document unless I published both exactly as Snowden sent them. You might want to ask an expert, I told Savage. He dropped the story.

That afternoon I replied to Greenwald's note. "Charlie Savage tells me today that you said you've read all my communications with the source and he never insisted on publication of the PRISM document in its entirety," I wrote. "Really?"

"I never said I read all of your communications," Greenwald wrote back. "How could I know that what I saw was all? I said that I [saw] what I understood to be all of your Q-and-A on PRISM and that, to my knowledge, there was never any demand of publication of all slides. I also said that he never made any demand like that to us. That, obviously, doesn't mean that he didn't make that demand to you at some point."

I drafted several entertaining responses. I deleted them.

Just walk away.

"Peace," I responded. "We all have plenty of important work to do." Many months after the NSA stories launched, reporters were still approaching me with disparaging remarks from Greenwald. I declined to comment. The *Post* gave me a big platform. Scrutiny rightfully came with that. I wanted no part of a sideshow. Greenwald's contributions spoke for themselves. He broke big stories, amplified his source's voice, and framed important questions on state power. He wrote a lot of things that I admired and a lot that I did not. Our differences served the public better, I thought, than a march in lockstep.

On June 5, 2013, as I prepared to publish the PRISM story, I sent an email from my new *Washington Post* account to Ben Rhodes, President Obama's deputy national security adviser for strategic communications. I had an exceptionally sensitive story, I told him. He would want to know about it right away. Details were better left for a more private channel. How should we proceed?

I had been out of daily journalism for years. Rhodes did not know me, and there was no way to guess whether he would take my note seriously. I asked my old friend Anne Kornblut, who had covered the Obama White House, to reinforce the message. Then I opened a second back channel with an email, as opaque as the first, to Michael V. Hayden, the former CIA and NSA director. It had been years since I used his personal email account. He would understand what that meant.

I had known the retired general for a long time. Back in 1990, when he had three fewer stars, he ran a Pentagon think tank for the secretary of the Air Force. I was the greenest of the green among military correspondents. I walked into his office one day, on the brink of the U.S. invasion of Iraq, and asked him to explain how the Air Force goes to war. Assume I don't know the difference between an F-16 and an M-16, I told him. Many hours of conversation followed. Hayden was one of the most impressive talkers I had ever met, lucid and charming and full of down-home sports metaphors. He had a way of making small concessions that shored up his credibility on bigger and less verifiable points. Over the years, as his career took off, Hayden and I spoke from time to time when I learned something secret. He would hear me out and tell me what he could, letting me know when he thought I had a fact wrong or risked causing harms that I might not foresee. Our relationship became strained after 2008, when I came to believe he had misled me about warrantless surveillance. In my Cheney book, I described him as deceptive in his public remarks about the program. Whatever our differences, I figured he would pass word on my behalf to someone who would listen.

Shawn Turner, communications chief for the director of national intelligence, was the first to call. I read him the title, date, author, and classification markings of the PRISM presentation and told him I planned to publish a story about it soon. "I assume your people will not want to discuss it on the phone," I said. "I suggest you get hold of a copy and let me know how they want to handle it."

That evening, June 5, the *Guardian* surprised me with its first story from the Snowden archive. The FBI, on behalf of the NSA, was collecting the call records of Verizon, the nation's largest telephone carrier. Each day Verizon handed over a CD with an updated listing of every telephone call made by every customer. All of them. Local, interstate, international calls—it did not matter. Nationality made no difference either. The listings included American and foreign callers alike.

Records of this kind are known to information scientists as "metadata," akin to the addressee and return address on a sealed envelope. The words spoken on a call, like the ones inside an envelope, are regarded as "content." U.S. law gives less weight to the privacy of metadata, but that information conveys a lot more than laypeople (or judges) tend to assume. If the government knows who talks to whom, and when, and for how long, it has the means to build an immensely revealing dossier. There are many stories to be told in a list of every interaction with a friend, lover, coworker, business rival, clergyman, doctor, medical lab, or suicide hotline. With court-mandated access to something like one trillion call records a year, the NSA possessed the raw material for a comprehensive map of the nation's social, business, political, and religious networks. The government collected the unique hardware identifiers of mobile phones and "comprehensive communications routing information" that could be used to approximate a caller's whereabouts. When the program became public, officials said the NSA did not actually store the location data.

What it actually did with the records was important, but policies could change. That is what Snowden meant when he spoke of "turnkey tyranny," of systems so powerful that they were too dangerous to entrust to any government's hands. Constitutional limits, in any case, were not only about the way government made use of the fruits of a search and seizure. The collection alone had a big impact on privacy. We did not, as a nation, allow police to turn out everyone's pockets in a theater where a wallet went missing, regardless of what they did with the evidence.

In order to justify its striking venture into mass domestic surveillance, the executive branch had come up with a radically new—and entirely secret—interpretation of law. Back in 2001, Section 215 of the USA Patriot Act gave the FBI simplified access to business records that the FISA Court found "relevant to" an authorized investigation of terrorism. Relevance is a legal standard that typically limits the scope of the government's power. It covers this, not that. It distinguishes what investigators may take from what they may not. Under Presidents Bush and Obama, the Justice Department turned that concept on its head. Government lawyers secretly persuaded the FISA Court that *every* record of *every* call met the relevance test because a terrorist plot might involve a party or parties unknown. The NSA proposed to find those ghosts by way of "contact chaining," a mathematical analysis of links among friends, friends of friends, and so on. The computational methods had implications beyond the competence of the court to assess. (FISA judges employed no technical advisers.) What the court knew, and chose to authorize, was that the NSA wanted access to the whole universe of domestic telephone calls.

By design, the intelligence court met in classified session. It heard no opposing views. Not only the substance but the existence of its ruling remained unknown to the public and to most members of Congress, including a principal drafter of the Patriot Act. The court's order was classified TOP SECRET//SI//NOFORN, a level that left the great majority of legislators without a staff member cleared to read the complex material and advise them. Not all these points made it into the *Guardian*'s account, but it was a world-reverberating story and Greenwald told it well.

Now, knowing the race was on, I told Shawn Turner that the *Post* was speeding up its timetable on the PRISM story. When my telephone rang next, I heard the voice of Robert Litt for the first time in two years. As general counsel to Director of National Intelligence James R. Clapper Jr., Litt was the government's senior intelligence lawyer. He sounded tense, but he began with a pleasantry. We had met before, he said, at the Wye River Conference Center in Maryland. He was not sure I remembered. I could hardly have forgotten. We had spent two intense days in a conference room in the spring of 2011, when the Aspen Institute convened a small group of journalists and intelligence officials. It was supposed to be a dialogue, as it happened, about news coverage of national security secrets. There were twenty-eight men and women at the table, including a future FBI director and a former deputy director of national intelligence. No two of us, I think, disagreed more profoundly than Litt and I.

Litt told me he had the PRISM presentation in hand. There were others around his speakerphone, but he left them unnamed. It became clear that they meant to hold this conversation right here on an open phone line, which astounded me. Litt and Clapper, I later learned, had been summoned to Capitol Hill. There was no time to arrange a meeting face-to-face.

Litt and his unnamed colleagues had to be worried, I knew. I am no worshipper of secret stamps. I have seen them on reprints of stories published under my byline. But there were portions of the PRISM presentation that just about anyone would agree had earned their Top Secret markings. Some of the slides included jaw-dropping excerpts of intercepted communications and files. There were foreign nationals caught unawares as they laid plans to kill Americans, construct weapons forbidden by treaty, and break into classified U.S. contractor files. PRISM collection had discovered a dangerous cover-up by one unfriendly government and secret equipment that another had positioned to avoid the gaze of U.S. spy satellites. No one who believed that espionage had a valid role in national defense would be likely to dispute the importance of those finds. If I mentioned them, the targets would no doubt disappear.

"I'm not generally given to hyperbole, but this one really raises the hair on the back of my neck," Litt said.

"I have some idea of what may be on your mind," I told him: "I think I can save us some time."

There were things in the document that the *Post* had no intention to print. I did not name them on the phone, and I will not name them here. Instead I walked through the details by page number and position. Our story would publish nothing from slides 14, 19, 21, or 22. Nothing, for sure, from the map on slide 23 or the transcript in the speaker's notes or the hyperlinked video file. Nothing from the list on slide 28, because one line would imply another and the whole stack would be compromised. These were not decisions we made for fear of lost favor or retribution from the government. We made our own judgments, and these were not hard ones. Speaking for myself, I am not agnostic about my loyalties. I am not—in this context—a global citizen, indifferent to the outcomes of national conflict. Disclosure of the details I allude to here would have caused self-evident harm to my country and some of its allies. We saw no countervailing interest in public policy debate. These would have been valid intelligence targets by any legal standard.

I could hear the mute button engage on the other end. After a while Litt came back onto the line and said, "We're very glad to hear that."

The conversation went south pretty fast after that. The *Post* did not want to blow operational details, but we strongly believed there was a story here. The sheer volume of collection, the impact of incidental collection, and the secret expansion of legal boundaries were important news. I told Litt I intended to name the nine companies and cite Rick's description of direct access to their servers.

Litt is a vigorous advocate. He pushed back on everything. The U.S. government, he said, did not condone public disclosure of any classified information. It reserved all legal options in response. I have no doubt he meant it, but this part was pro forma. He knew that ship had sailed. I was looking for confirmation and context, to be sure I understood what I had read. His whole reason for speaking in detail was to distinguish which of the classified facts the government believed most important to protect. Litt did not dispute Rick's description of data pulled "directly from the servers" of Silicon Valley, but it later emerged that he had not focused on that. "Obviously we'd much prefer that nothing be written about this at all," he said. What he really cared about was outing the company names.

"Why?" I asked.

Public exposure, Litt replied, could cause them embarrassment and leave them reluctant to cooperate in the future.

"If the harm that you're asserting consists of damage to a company brand because the public does not like what it's doing, then I can't accept that as a reason to hold back," I said. "The same goes for damage to intelligence collection if voters decide they want to scale it back. That's actually why we publish news, to let readers decide what they do and don't support."

I expected Litt to take the fight over my head. I gave him Marty Baron's private telephone number, with the obligatory joke that he must have it already. Litt did not call Baron, and neither did his boss. We moved the PRISM story that evening, June 6. The *Guardian*'s version, which included none of the slides or security details we left out, followed less than an hour later. Soon after that, fierce objections began to pour in from Silicon Valley. Companies that had declined to comment in advance, or had said nothing of substance, now issued categorical denials that any U.S. agency had "direct access" to their servers. I scrambled to reconcile those statements with the NSA program manager's explicit words—repeated twice—in the authoritative PRISM overview. Later that night I found a clue in another document from the Snowden archive. There, in a description of a precursor to PRISM, I found a variation on Rick's formula. "For Internet content selectors, collection managers sent content tasking instructions directly to equipment installed at company-controlled locations," it said. That sounded as though the U.S. government black box was on company property but might not touch the servers themselves. I updated my story to disclose the conflicting information and the new evidence.

Direct access, which seemed to be a clear enough term, turned out to be unexpectedly imprecise. It meant very different things in Silicon Valley and Fort Meade. The technology companies understood the term to signify that government spy equipment connected physically into their core hardware. That would represent a devastating loss of control, and in the end they were right to deny it. The NSA's internal account spoke of collection "directly from the servers" in counterpoint to what the agency calls indirect collection, which is done by passive interception of data on the fly across the internet. As Rick explained to the analysts, PRISM did not have to chase photons across fiber optic cables. It acquired data straight from the source in the nine companies' data stores. From the point of view of an NSA analyst, the connection was quite direct: she tasked a selector and buckets of data came back. From the points of view of Facebook or Google, the firebreak between government equipment and their own was of cosmic import. "The actual architecture is very different, but the material effect, with some latency because of review, is as if it were direct," Chris Inglis, the NSA deputy director, explained to me later.

In retrospect, I do not love the way I wrote the story. I knew a lot less then than I learned later, with more time in the documents and many more interviews. The "direct access" question became a big distraction, rightly essential to the companies but not so much to the core questions of public policy. And I completely missed a story hiding in plain sight in the PRISM briefing. The FISA amendments had authorized two new forms of lawful collection, which operated in parallel. PRISM was one. The second, which I neglected, was called Upstream. That one became more important in the months to come.

Three days after the PRISM story went live, Snowden announced his identity to the world in a twelve-minute video that Laura Poitras shot for the *Guardian*. Danielle Massarini was killing time in a Newark Liberty International Airport bar on her way to Germany. "I'm scrolling through my Twitter feed and keep seeing 'Snowden' 'Snowden' 'Snowden,'" she recalled. Why was that name so familiar? Then Snowden's face appeared on a screen above the bar and Massarini screamed aloud, "Oh, shit!" The operations officer of her new unit, the Army Foreign Counterintelligence Activity, looked at her quizzically. "I hired that guy to teach cyber security" at the Defense Department's counterintelligence academy, she said. "Better call the the boss," the ops officer responded. The FBI would soon come calling on everyone who had ever crossed paths with Snowden.

FIVE

BACKLASH

We're not going to open this program up to the sort of
scrutiny that the zealots want.

—*Admiral Dennis Blair*

scanned for a promising table, steering clear of sources who would
not welcome me nearby. A long line of defense and intelligence leaders wound through the buffet. When a seat opened up near Admiral
William McRaven, I set my tray down two places to his right. This
kind of casual contact, at mealtimes and downtimes, brought me back
every year to the Aspen Security Forum. If there was such a thing as a
national security establishment, it summered here under Rocky Mountain skies for four days in July. Deputy secretaries and undersecretar-
ies, intelligence chiefs, combatant commanders, defense contractors,
presidential advisers, and members of Congress gathered to float ideas
and chew on the state of the world. A target-rich environment for a
reporter like me. It had been, anyway. When we sat down for lunch on
July 18, 2013, the Snowden fires had been burning for six weeks.

McRaven and I were acquainted. We had spoken at some length
two years before, not long after he took the helm of U.S. Special Operations Command.

"Good to see you," I said.

Silence. His face grew taut.

"Admiral?"

He would not look at me. McRaven cut a formidable figure, an angular six foot two, with the eagle and trident of a Navy SEAL on his dress blue uniform coat. Twelve years before, he had clawed his way back to fighting shape after shattering his pelvis in a disastrous training jump. A midair collision with a fellow SEAL, after two miles of free fall, had left him barely conscious as time ran out to deploy his parachute. When he popped the canopy, the risers tangled around his legs and "split me like a nutcracker," he told me in 2011, the year he commanded the operation that killed Osama bin Laden in Abbottabad, Pakistan.

Up onstage, the NSA general counsel, Rajesh De, skirmished with Anthony Romero, executive director of the American Civil Liberties Union. Snowden loomed large in their conversation about "the tension between a free press and national security." McRaven glared at his plate. He pumped a leg under the linen tablecloth. From time to time he expelled a breath, more growl than sigh. I reached for one of those little notepads they hand out at conferences, wrote a few words, and slid the pad to my left.

"You clearly have something on your mind. Can we talk about it?" the note said.

McRaven glanced down, shook his head, and pushed back his chair with a little more force than required. He took a couple of long steps toward the exit. Then he stopped, rounded back, and thrust a forefinger at me.

"We didn't have another 9/11," he said, cords of muscle bunching on his neck. "Until you've got to pull the trigger, until you've had to bury your people, you don't have a clue." He flicked a backhand toward Romero onstage. "None of you. None of these people. None of you has a clue." A low murmur from nearby tables trailed him out the door.

As a literal matter McRaven was surely right. My encounters with danger in the field—looking down muzzles at checkpoints, watching a firefight from behind a wall—had not exposed me to anything like combat. (I speak for myself. Some of my colleagues encountered far worse, and not all survived.) I had never held another person's life in my hands or death on my conscience. Even so, the heat of McRaven's anger caught me off guard. Warriors and civilians are tribes apart. There was nothing new in that. Nor was McRaven known for losing his cool. A witness told me after the bin Laden raid that McRaven "was the voice of Walter Cronkite" as he live-briefed President Obama, reporting with equal sangfroid when a helicopter crashed and when the al Qaeda leader's death was confirmed.

Once upon a time McRaven had majored in journalism at the University of Texas. That emphatically did not mean he was prepared to look at national security secrets through a reporter's eyes. Years before our encounter, as he neared midcareer, McRaven had written a treatise on special warfare that gave paramount place to stealth: concealment, surprise, clandestine surveillance of a foe. When he spoke of the raid in Abbottabad, he deflected credit to the CIA, NSA, and National Geospatial-Intelligence Agency. "This will go down in history as one of the greatest *intelligence* operations ever," McRaven told me then. He meant it.

McRaven did not linger long enough at lunch to explain his reference to another 9/11. I took him to mean that electronic surveillance, the kind that Snowden exposed, had fueled the hunt for bin Laden and his lieutenants. NSA's expansive reach had forced al Qaeda leaders underground, depriving them of the command and control to organize another complex attack. Intelligence had led the SEALs to bin Laden's gate, and intelligence gave an edge to commando teams in thousands of lightning assaults against superior numbers. If sources and methods had been lost at Snowden's hands, McRaven must regard that as sabotage. From that point of view, I would qualify as a saboteur myself.

I had never lived in McRaven's world, where secrets sometimes carried mortal stakes. That did not exhaust the conversation I wish we could have had. McRaven had not lived in my world either. In my world, secrets sometimes gave cover to lies. Secrets sometimes shed darkness on conduct that was hard to defend in the light. Secrets sometimes built a mirage of consent to choices the public never knew it had. The dilemmas of self-government and self-defense had absorbed me since graduate school, where my thesis on wartime secrecy covered some of the same terrain as McRaven's. We served distinct and equally vital interests, he and I, in a democracy at war.

Years later, I reached out to McRaven again. He had retired from active service by then and taken the post of chancellor of the University of Texas, his alma mater. I thought I knew what had set him off at Aspen, I wrote, "but I would much rather hear it from you than offer surmise" in my book. Sometimes long shots pay off. "I'm happy to chat with you," McRaven replied by email an hour later. The following day he telephoned from his fourth-floor office in downtown Austin, where a John Wayne coffee mug and a Minuteman soldier's figurine stand sentry by his desk. He could not recall exactly "what precipitated my outburst," but he apologized graciously. "My issue has always been with the safety and security of Americans in harm's way," he said. "I'm sure it's a good reporter's concern too. . . . How do you balance what you think the public needs to know with the potential to put lives at risk?"

He wanted to find some common ground. He did not come up with much. "I'm a big believer in transparency, so please do quote me on that," McRaven said. "And the processes are out there that allow the transparency to occur at the right level." The right level, as he meant it, did not fall within the public domain. Quite the reverse.

McRaven believed in transparency inside the walled precincts of the FISA Court and the House and Senate intelligence committees. The public had no need to know or contribute outside views on policy or law. Classified transparency, in other words. McRaven saw no contradiction in that. This model, the prevailing one among McRaven's peers, extended far beyond surveillance policy. How many noncombatants died in special operations raids? Did the rules of engagement conform to American values or international law? Should U.S. drones be allowed to make autonomous decisions of life and death? All those things were classified, exempt from debate.

McRaven was prepared to accept me as "a man of high character and integrity," but he could not get past the original sin of my transaction with Snowden. "He violated the law, so at the end of the day, in divulging that information, you are dealing with a criminal," he said. "So where is the integrity in that?" (I return to that useful question in chapter 7.) Whatever my efforts to weigh potential harm, whatever consultations I undertook with the government, McRaven believed the things I wrote had consequences that I was not equipped to understand. My incentives, he hinted, might not even incline me to try very hard.

The admiral controlled his voice, but the heat crept back in. "You as a reporter make the call that it's more important for the public—and I would contend, more important for the reporter—to get that story out before somebody scoops you," he said. "The nature of your job is to report. That is in your DNA. And I think your default position is to report. And you can always make a case in your own mind why the American people need to know something."

Long before my first contact with Snowden, the Aspen Institute had asked me to moderate a plenary session. The headliners would be two former directors of national intelligence, Ambassador John

Negroponte and Admiral Dennis Blair. Our assigned subject was entitled "Mission Accomplished? Has the Intelligence Community Connected All the Dots?" So it was that six weeks after the first Snowden disclosures, blind luck granted me an hour onstage with two men who had helped define the modern age of surveillance. The format promised substance after more than a month of low-calorie talking points from Washington. My panelists no longer held office, but they had overseen electronic intelligence gathering in its decade of revolutionary growth. Negroponte served as the first DNI, from 2005 to 2007. He helped recast warrantless surveillance programs under President Bush into forms that the FISA Court and Congress, until then kept in the dark, could bless. On Blair's watch, in 2009 and 2010, some of those programs expanded so fast that the NSA began to choke on the intake.

In a conference call eight days before we met, I invented a "moderator's privilege" to reframe our topic. The audience would surely expect us to talk about the NSA and Snowden. It was too late to change the printed program, but for our purposes I proposed to rewrite the question to ask, "Is U.S. Intelligence Connecting All the Dots, or Collecting Too Many?"

Blair responded first, annoyed. "I don't like it much," he said. "What the hell is there to say about that? Everybody responsible has said it was all properly authorized, supervised. We're not going to open this program up to the sort of scrutiny that the zealots want." Shifting pitch to a mocking whine, which I took to be his impression of a zealot, he added, "'Tell us everything, because we don't trust you.'"

Negroponte, the career diplomat, tacked toward diplomacy. "I satisfied myself there were proper safeguards in place," he said in a reassuring baritone. "I more than satisfied myself."

Blair carried on, still warming up. "The public and the press don't understand that's how we do it," he said. "What's staggering to me here is there's no smoking gun that would indicate that this power is being abused. It's all this, '*Oh, potential.*'" The zealot's whine returned. "'*Oh, gosh, this is big!*' My experience is that people follow the rules and they have tattooed on their foreheads that you don't spy on Americans without permission."

Blair went on for a while. I said Aspen might be the ideal forum to set the story straight. I would ask. They would answer. They would have plenty of allies in the room. Forty minutes later, to their credit, the two men agreed.

On the appointed day, in a ballroom-sized hall atop Aspen's Roaring Fork Gorge, I opened with a light remark about strange bedfellows. "It's safe to say that when we set this panel some months ago, my fellow panelists did not foresee they'd be sitting up onstage with a guy who had communicated clandestinely with Edward Snowden."

An icebreaker, barely worth a chuckle. My kids would have called it a Dad joke. The response did not augur well. Moderator wit, I find, is usually judged on a curve. There is a kind of alliance between speaker and listeners. The audience looks for cues. It wants to respond. This one, unthawed, stared in silence. Neither Blair nor Negroponte cracked a smile.

Right. Straight to it, then. In 2006, the FISA Court had secretly granted the U.S. government the power to collect and store records of every telephone call in the United States. (Collection was never comprehensive in fact, but it was so authorized.) By then the Bush administration had secretly gathered those records for years without notifying the court. "Why on earth would you want all that information?" I asked. "And how does that fit with the boundaries that the American people would expect in terms of privacy?"

Negroponte, on my right, said the Boston Marathon bombing three months back offered answer enough. "One of the reasons you would do it is you have all that data and you detain the Tsarnaev brothers and find out the phone numbers that they've been in touch with in Chechnya or wherever," he said, "and bounce them against these numbers that you have on file, and maybe you'll find other people who've been calling those same numbers in that database."

"Bounce" had a hand-tossed sound to it. Pull a bad guy's phone records, give them a shake, and see who bounces out. No one could object to that. Negroponte chose his words carefully. They were accurate as far as they went. You could not say the same for the story line in Washington. Senator Lindsey Graham, among many others, had recently said the NSA searched only the records of people who were "talking to the terrorists." Negroponte repeated the false claim now. He paraphrased President Bush's response to news stories about a related surveillance program in January 2006. "It seems like to me that if somebody is talking to al Qaeda, we want to know why," Bush had said. Negroponte added, "And that's kind of the underlying philosophy of this program."

In fact, that was not at all the way the NSA used the call records. The program was designed to find out whether, not why, U.S. callers had some tie to a terrorist conspiracy, and to do so it searched us all. Working through the FBI, the NSA assembled a five-year inventory of phone calls from every account it could touch. Trillions of calls. Nobody needed to plumb that ocean to find the numbers on a bad guy's telephone bill. What the NSA actually did was called contact chaining, a sophisticated form of analysis that tried to find hidden, indirect relationships in very large data sets. Contact chaining began with a target telephone number, such as Dzhokhar Tsarnaev's, and progressively widened the lens to ask whom Tsarnaev's contacts were talking to, and whom those people were talking to, and so on. Sophisticated software tools mapped the call records as "nodes" and "edges" on a grid so large that the human mind, unaided, could not encompass it. Nodes were dots on the map, each representing a telephone number. Edges were lines drawn between the nodes, each representing a call. A related tool called MapReduce condensed the trillions of data points into summary form that a human analyst could grasp.

Network theory called this map a social graph. It modeled the relationships and groups that defined each person's interaction with the world. The NSA's analysis touched nearly all Americans because the size of the graph grew exponentially as contact chaining progressed. The whole point of chaining was to push outward from a target's immediate contacts to the contacts of contacts, then contacts of contacts of contacts. Each step in that process was called a hop.

Double a penny once a day and you reach a million dollars in less than a month. That is what exponential growth looks like with a base of two. As contact chaining steps through its hops, the social graph grows much faster. If the average person calls or is called by ten other people a year, then each hop produces a tenfold increase in the population of the NSA's contact map. Most of us talk on the phone with a lot more than ten. Whatever that number, dozens or hundreds, you multiply it by itself to measure the growth at each hop.

The NSA's deputy director, John C. Inglis, had testified in Congress just the day before Negroponte and Blair joined me onstage. Inglis said NSA analysts typically "go out two or three hops" when they chain through the call database. For context, data scientists estimated decades ago that it would take no more than six hops to trace a path between any two people on Earth. Their finding made its way into popular culture in *Six Degrees of Separation*, the play and subsequent film by John Guare. Three students at Albright College refashioned the film as a parlor game, "Six Degrees of Kevin Bacon." The game then inspired a website, The Oracle of Bacon, that calculates the shortest path from the *Footloose* star to any of his Hollywood peers. The site is still live as I write this, and it makes for an entertaining guide on hops and where they can take you.

Bacon shared screen credits with a long list of actors. Those were his direct links, one hop from Bacon himself. Actors who never worked alongside him, but appeared in a film with someone who had, were two hops away from Bacon. Scarlett Johansson never worked with Bacon, but each of them had starred alongside Mickey Rourke: Bacon in *Diner*, Johannson in *Iron Man 2*. Two hops, through Rourke, connected them. Bacon had no role in the *Star Wars* franchise, but he could trace two-hop paths to Harrison Ford, Carrie Fisher, Mark Hamill, and James Earl Jones. If you kept on playing you discovered that Bacon was seldom more than two hops away from any actor, however removed in time and movie style. Two hops reached silent film star Charlie Chaplin, Groucho Marx, and Fred Astaire, none of them born the same century as Bacon. Hedy Lamarr? Humphrey Bogart? Two hops. (Each made a film with Eddie Albert.) In a single-industry town like Hollywood, links like these might make intuitive sense. More surprising, if you did not spend much time around logarithms, was the distance traveled by one or two hops through the vastly larger NSA data set. Academic research suggested that a mean of three hops—three links in the chain, the same number Inglis mentioned—could trace a path between any two Americans.

I wanted to take the conversation there. Blair offered an opening.

"Here's a fact," Blair said. "The number of times those records were accessed in 2012. Take a guess. Okay, I'm going to give you a multiple choice, Bart. Ten, two hundred fifty, ten thousand, five million?"

He probably knew I could answer that. Inglis had mentioned the figure the day before. This was a setup for the audience.

"Under three hundred, according to the administration," I replied.

Blair made a gesture of triumph. Point and match. The FBI and NSA had oceans of information about us. Fine. But they hardly ever looked. Who could object to so shallow a dip into waters so deep?

"Let's talk about what that means," I said. "We just heard from

Chris Inglis yesterday . . . that contact chaining on those numbers, when you pull those numbers, is done to two or three hops. Let's suppose that the median number of unique contacts for people making phone calls is one hundred over the course of the year."

I worked through the arithmetic aloud. Multiply by one hundred at every hop. With phone records from three hundred people, the first hop searched the calls of thirty thousand. The second pushed the boundary to three million. On the third hop, contact chaining would map "a potential universe of about three hundred million, which happens to be approximately the population of the United States."

Dennis Blair, meet Scarlett Johansson. Odds are you know at least a friend of a friend of a friend. She is two hops from Bacon and no more than three from nearly anyone between Hawaii and Maine.

Negroponte leaned in. "Let me interrupt you," he said. "Are we having a hypothetical discussion here or a real one?"

"It's just math," I replied.

"It's just math," Negroponte said, dismissing the point. "It's not what's actually happened." Maybe bulk collection of telephone records empowered the NSA to map the communications of anyone in this room, anyone in America. But the people who possessed that power used it with discipline and restraint. "They check themselves every step of the way," Blair said, "and they are not rummaging around in trillions of records to try to see if they can find something interesting."

They check themselves. There were supervisors and compliance officers, an inspector general, a general counsel, and a director of national intelligence who made classified certifications that the NSA followed its rules. (The rules were also classified.) Should we trust them as much as they trusted themselves? Should we trust not only Blair and Negroponte, not only President Obama, but also every successive heir to the surveillance machine? Would Blair himself have bequeathed these powers comfortably, had he known back then that

Donald Trump would take the wheel in 2017? By then many of his retired peers would sign "never Trump" letters, declaring him unfit for office on grounds that included a reckless attitude toward power.

The answer might depend, in part, on the stakes. How much could someone really learn from a simple list of our calls? The official government position in court was that there is no privacy interest in this kind of "metadata," a term that means information about information. It is the who/when/where of a conversation, without the words themselves. At Princeton, where I had a visiting fellowship, I had been working through the meaning of metadata with Ed Felten, a computer scientist who served for a time as deputy chief technology officer of the United States. Our conversation kept returning to "embedded patterns" in any voluminous data set. That summer he spelled out what he meant in an affidavit for the plaintiffs in a lawsuit against the NSA. Information science had learned how to pull intimate secrets from very large collections of very small clues. "Individual pieces of data that previously carried less potential to expose private information may now, in the aggregate, reveal sensitive details about our everyday lives—details that we had no intent or expectation of sharing," he wrote.

The call data records might one day identify unknown terrorists, but that turned out to be a hard problem. A presidential review group concluded later that year that the NSA had not yet made a breakthrough that way. There were other things, very private things, that were easier to discover. With trivial effort the government could identify people who called whistleblowing, drug abuse, rape, or suicide hotlines. Felten did not mention reporters, but journalistic sources were easy to pick out if they did not take uncommon precautions. With access to the call records, Big Data methods could extract the "membership, donors, political supporters, [and] confidential sources" of human rights or protest groups. Cash donations sent by text message, an increasingly popular channel, identified contributors to political parties and religious institutions. Data mining could reliably pick out sexual orientation. It could track the telephonic fingerprints of secret love affairs as they blossomed, peaked, and died. It could distinguish bosses from employees, in part because bosses get their calls returned faster and have fewer qualms about phoning subordinates at night.

When you factored in time and sequence, the results were startling. "A likely storyline emerges," Felten wrote, when "a young woman calls her gynecologist; then immediately calls her mother; then a man who, during the past few months, she had repeatedly spoken to on the telephone after 11 pm; followed by a call to a family planning center that also offers abortions." The government may seldom care, may never abuse that knowledge in a given year. But now, for the first time in history, it had acquired the power to do so.

Stewart Baker, a former general counsel of the NSA, leaped early into the fray against Snowden in television appearances, newspaper interviews, and blog posts. He sharply criticized some of my stories, too. But he minced no words about the power of the social graph. "Metadata absolutely tells you everything about somebody's life," he said. For purposes of signals intelligence, "if you have enough metadata, you don't really need content." Michael V. Hayden concurred bluntly the following spring. "We kill people based on metadata," he said. "But that's not what we do with *this* metadata."

In Washington, the day before our panel, Representative Bob Goodlatte, a Virginia Republican, asked Robert Litt, the DNI general counsel, whether intelligence officials had really believed the bulk phone collection "could be indefinitely kept secret from the American people?" Litt replied in a rueful voice, "Well, we tried."

Blair and Negroponte both had second thoughts about that. "Those of us who were senior officials in the intelligence community and so on should have done a much better job of explaining the general principles of these programs, without going into titillating individual cases which do nothing but help our adversaries," Blair said. "And it's a kind of a 'pay me now or pay me later,' when . . . you're operating from a defensive crouch of the Snowden revelations and saying, 'Yeah, but we're okay. Trust us.'"

Trust became the core of our conversation. On your watch and since, I told both men, policymakers and intelligence leaders routinely deceived the public with assurances that turned everyday language upside down. NSA director Keith Alexander had said flatly in 2012 that "we don't hold data on U.S. citizens." I thought that qualified as a naked lie. If Alexander thought otherwise, he must have relied on some secret definition of "hold" or "data" that no listener could be expected to guess. Three months before the first Snowden story, Senator Ron Wyden asked Director of National Intelligence James Clapper in a public hearing, "Does the NSA collect any type of data at all on millions or hundreds of millions of Americans?" Clapper stared down at the table, stroked his shaved head, and balled his hand in a fist. He wore the face of a man who had to eat something unpleasant. "No, sir," he told the table. He raised his eyes to Wyden and shook his head. "Not wittingly," he added. Critics, Republicans among them, later accused him of perjury.

I do not view the exchange so harshly. Clapper was an old-school spy without taste or talent for wordplay. On the "high side," where classified information flowed, he had a reputation for integrity and speaking his mind. He never looked comfortable in public, where he had to filter each sentence on the fly. Clapper tripped on a dilemma that many a more agile witness could have sidestepped gracefully. Law

and regulation forbade him to give a classified answer in an unclassified setting. Deflecting the question was Mike Hayden's skill set, not
Clapper's. Wyden was determined to part the curtains on the call records program. He set up the exchange as a public performance. He
already knew the answer. Clapper knew that Wyden knew. He had
briefed the senators himself in classified session. But Wyden wanted a
yes-or-no answer with cameras rolling, and Clapper made a clumsy
job of it. When the facts emerged later, his explanation was worse. He
gave the "least untruthful" answer he could, he told NBC's Andrea
Mitchell. Truth being less untruthful, that reply did not do him any
good. Clapper's culpable offense, in my view, was refusing to correct
the record after the hearing.

What amazed me onstage at Aspen was that Blair still avowed the
truth of the false story line. Our exchange turned almost metaphysi-
cal. The NSA collected U.S. telephone records in bulk, I said. Clapper
said it collected nothing. Alexander said it held nothing. How could
Blair defend those words in good faith?

"I think you're misusing the word 'collect,'" Blair said. "I think the
word, the proper word here, is 'store,' in order to be able to have access
to them when permission is granted."

Permission from whom, he did not say. FISA judges authorized the
acquisition of phone records in bulk, but the judges did not decide or
even know when the NSA pulled the records and chained through
them.

"Well, see, that's the kind of secret term of art that I think is undercutting your case," I told him. If FBI agents could gather all our telephone records "and put them in a tank somewhere and say that that's not
collection, you're not speaking English as most people understand it."

I offered another example. In 2009, when Blair oversaw the intelligence community, the Justice Department and FBI assured Congress
in sworn testimony that they made very sparing use of their power

under Section 215 of the Patriot Act to obtain secret intelligence warrants for "business records." There had been only twenty-one such orders from the FISA Court that year, the FBI reported. "Now," I told Blair, "it turns out that with three of those orders you can get something on the order of one trillion telephone records." (Here I was wrong. The orders were issued quarterly to each of three phone companies, so I should have said twelve of the twenty-one orders, not three.)

Suppose your teenage daughter admits she threw a house party when you were out of town. She assures you that it was no big deal: she invited only twenty-one friends. Later you find out that a trillion teenagers showed up. Did she lie to you? She could mount some kind of pedantic defense, but what parent would let her get away with that? She deceived you, deliberately so. The FBI had done the same.

"You're prepared to justify this program," I told Blair, "but what I'm talking about is the honesty, the straightforwardness of the public debate."

By this time I had decisively lost the room. "I'm not supposed to be the debater up here," I admitted. Negroponte laughed. Blair sighed theatrically. The national security establishment broke into ironic applause. Blair soon seized on his advantage, as the Navy had trained him to do.

"If you came in as director of communications for ODNI, you would get a clearance, but you'd still be the same Bart Gellman who is nasty and suspicious and concerned about things," he said.

N ot suspicious enough, as it turned out. At that moment, I had yet to discover how much the government was still concealing about the call records program. Even now, there is much that remains unconfessed. I never found a way to tell this part of the story in newspaper form.

One reason the story never saw print is that it calls for a grant of patience from the reader. The evidence emerges in fragments. Some assembly is required. Small facts build toward consequential ones. We are heading toward something important, I think, and I want to show my work.

In that summer of 2013, I imagined the phone records as a simple, if gargantuan, list. I assumed that the NSA cleaned up the list—date goes here, call duration there—and converted it to the agency's preferred "atomic sigint data format." Otherwise I thought of the records as inert. I had no reason to doubt Blair's explanation that they were "stored," untouched, until the next Tsarnaev came along.

Even by that account, the scale of collection brought to mind an evocative phrase from legal scholar Paul Ohm. Any information in sufficient volume, he wrote, amounted to a "database of ruin." It held personal secrets that "if revealed, would cause more than embarrassment or shame; it would lead to serious, concrete, devastating harm." Nearly anyone in the developed world, he wrote, "can be linked to at least one fact in a computer database that an adversary could use for blackmail, discrimination, harassment, or financial or identity theft." Revelations of "past conduct, health or family shame," for example, could cost a person his marriage, his career, his legal residence, or his physical safety.

Mere creation of such a database, especially in secret, profoundly changed the balance of power between government and governed. This was the Dark Mirror embodied, one side of the glass transparent and the other blacked out. If the power implications do not seem convincing, try inverting the relationship in your mind. What if a small group of citizens had secret access to the telephone logs and social networks of government officials? How might the privileged knowledge affect their power to shape events? How might their interactions change if they possessed the means to humiliate and destroy the careers of the men and women in power? Capability matters, always, regardless of whether it is used. An unfired gun is no less lethal before it is drawn. And, in fact, in history, capabilities do not go unused in the long term. Chekhov's famous admonition to playwrights is apt not only in drama but in the lived experience of humankind. The gun on display in the first act—nuclear warheads, weaponized disease, Orwellian cameras tracking faces on every street—must be fired in the last. The latent power of new inventions, no matter how repellent at first, does not lie forever dormant in government armories.

These could be cast as abstract concerns, "just math" of another kind, but I thought them quite real. By September, it dawned on me that there were also concrete questions that I had not sufficiently explored. Where in the innards of the NSA did the phone records live? What happened to them there? The Snowden archive did not answer those questions directly, but there were clues.

I stumbled across the first clue while looking for something else. I had become interested in the NSA's internal conversation about "bulk collection," the acquisition of high-volume data sets in their entirety. Phone records were one of several kinds. The agency had grown more and more adept, brilliantly creative in fact, at finding and swallowing other people's information whole. Lately the NSA had begun to see that it consumed too much to digest. Midlevel managers and engineers sounded notes of alarm in briefings prepared for their chains of command. The cover page of one presentation asked, "Is It the End of the SIGINT World as We Have Come to Know It?" The authors tried for a jaunty tone but had no sure answer. The surveillance infrastructure was laboring under serious strain.

One name caught my eye on a chart that listed systems at highest risk.

MAINWAY. I knew that one. NSA engineers had built MAINWAY in urgent haste after September 11, 2001. Vice President

System Survival			FALLOUT Quota (MetaDNI/MARINA)
System Survival	⟹		MAINWAY (high volume/spam burst)
System Survival			FASCIA IVE GM HALO/DPS
System Survival	⟹		EKS (some sort of experimental modeling)

Cheney's office had drafted orders, signed by President Bush, to do something the NSA had never done before. The assignment, forbidden by statute, was to track telephone calls made and received by Americans on American soil. The resulting operation, one of the STELLAR-WIND programs I described in chapter 1, was the lawless precursor of the broader one I debated with Negroponte and Blair.

MAINWAY came to life alongside STELLARWIND in the first frantic weeks after al Qaeda flew passenger airplanes into the Pentagon and World Trade Center. STELLARWIND defined the operation. MAINWAY was a tool to carry it out. The NSA knew how to do this sort of thing with foreign telephone calls, but it did not have the machinery to do it at home. When NSA director Mike Hayden received the execution order on October 4, 2001, for "the vice president's special program," NSA engineers assembled a system from bare metal and borrowed code within a matter of days, a stupendous achievement under pressure. They commandeered fifty state-of-the-art computer servers from Dell, which was about to ship them to another customer, and lashed them into a quick and dirty but powerful cluster. Hayden cleared out space in a specially restricted wing of OPS 2B, an inner sanctum of the gleaming, mirrored headquarters complex at Fort Meade. When the cluster expanded, incorporating some two hundred machines, MAINWAY spilled into an annex in the Tordella supercomputer facility nearby. Trusted lieutenants began calling in a small group of analysts, programmers, and mathematicians on October 6 and 7. On

Columbus Day, October 8, Hayden briefed them on their new jobs in a specially compartmented new operation. That day he called it STARBURST. The STELLARWIND cryptonym replaced it soon afterward. During the same holiday weekend, Hayden dispatched personnel from Special Source Operations to negotiate the secret purchase of telephone data in bulk from AT&T, Verizon, and Sprint. The price surpassed $102 million in the coming five years.

It was impossible to hide the hubbub from other NSA personnel, who saw new equipment arriving under armed escort at a furious pace, but even among top clearance holders hardly anyone knew what was going on. STELLARWIND was designated as ECI, "exceptionally controlled information," the most closely held classification of all. From his West Wing office, Cheney ordered that STELLARWIND be concealed from the judges of the FISA Court and from members of the intelligence committees in Congress.

According to my sources and the documents I worked through in the fall of 2013, MAINWAY soon became the NSA's most important tool for mapping social networks, an anchor of what the agency called Large Access Exploitation. "Large" is not an adjective in casual use at Fort Meade. MAINWAY was built for operations at stupendous scale. Other systems parsed the contents of intercepted communications: voice, video, email and chat text, attachments, pager messages, and so on. MAINWAY was queen of metadata, foreign and domestic, designed to find patterns that content did not reveal. Beyond that, MAINWAY was a prototype for still more ambitious plans. Next-generation systems, their planners wrote, could amplify the power of surveillance by moving "from the more traditional analysis of what is collected to the analysis of what to collect." Patterns gleaned from call records would identify targets in email or location databases, and vice versa. Metadata was the key to the NSA's plan to "identify, track, store, manipulate and update relationships" across all forms of intercepted content. An integrated map, presented graphically, would eventually allow the NSA to display nearly anyone's movements and communications on a global scale. In their first mission statement, planners gave the project the unironic name "the Big Awesome Graph." Inevitably it acquired a breezy acronym, "the BAG."

The crucial discovery on this subject turned up at the bottom right corner of a large network diagram prepared in 2012. A little box in that corner, reproduced below, finally answered my question about where the NSA stashed the telephone records that Blair and Negroponte and I talked about. *The records lived in MAINWAY.* The implications were startling.

The diagram as a whole, too large to display in these pages, traced a "metadata flow sourced from billing records" at AT&T as they wended through a maze of intermediate stops along the way to Fort Meade. MAILORDER, the next-to-last stop, was an electronic traffic cop, a file sorting and forwarding system. The ultimate destination was MAINWAY. The "BRF Partitions" in the network diagram were named for Business Records FISA orders, among them the dozen signed in 2009 that poured the logs of hundreds of billions of phone calls into MAINWAY.

To a first-time reader of network maps, MAINWAY's cylindrical icon might suggest a storage tank. It is not. The cylinder is a standard symbol for a database, an analytic service that runs on the hardware. MAINWAY was not a container for data at rest. The NSA has names for those. They

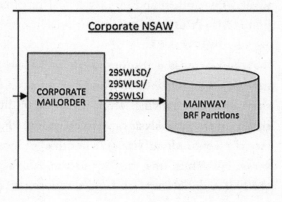

are called data marts and data warehouses. If the agency merely stored the U.S. telephone records, it would have left them in a system called FASCIA II, the "call detail record warehouse" that feeds MAINWAY.

MAINWAY's mission, laid out in its first fiscal year, was to "enable NSA . . . to dominate the global communications infrastructure, and the targets that currently operate anonymously within it." It used contact chaining, the technique we discussed at Aspen, to pierce that anonymity.

For reasons that will become apparent soon, I want to reproduce the full entry for MAINWAY in the *SSO Dictionary*, a classified NSA reference document:

> (TS//SI//REL) MAINWAY, or the MAINWAY Precomputed Contact Chaining Service, is an analytic tool for contact chaining. It's helping analysts do target discovery by enabling them to quickly and easily navigate the increasing volumes of global communications metadata. MAINWAY attacks the volume problem of analyzing the global communications network.

There were two noteworthy terms in that short passage: "precomputed" and the "volume problem." The first one—*precomputed*—turned my understanding of the call records program upside down. Before we get to that, a note on the volume problem.

The NSA has many volume problems, actually. Too much information moving too fast across global networks. Too much to ingest, too much to store, too much to retrieve through available pipes from distant collection points. Too much noise drowning too little signal. In the passage I just quoted, however, the volume problem referred to something else—something deeper inside the guts of the surveillance machine. It was the strain of an unbounded appetite on the NSA's digestive tract. Collection systems were closing their jaws on more data than they could chew. Processing, not storage, was the problem.

Contact chaining on a scale as grand as a whole nation's phone records was a prodigious computational task, even for MAINWAY. It called for mapping dots and clusters of calls as dense as a star field, each linked to others by webs of intricate lines. MAINWAY's analytic engine traced hidden paths across the map, looking for relationships that human analysts could not detect. MAINWAY had to produce that map on demand, under pressure of time, whenever its operators asked for a new contact chain. No one could predict the name or telephone number of the next Tsarnaev. From a data scientist's point of view, the logical remedy was clear. If anyone could become an intelligence target, MAINWAY should try to get a head start on everyone.

"You have to establish all those relationships, tag them, so that when you do launch the query you can quickly get them," Rick Ledgett, the former NSA deputy director, told me years later. "Otherwise you're taking like a month to scan through a gazillion-line phone bill."

And that, right there, was where *precomputation* came in. MAINWAY chained through its database continuously—"operating on a 7x24 basis," according to the classified project summary. You might compare its work, on the most basic level, to indexing a book—albeit a book with hundreds of millions of topics (phone numbers) and trillions of entries (phone calls). One flaw in this comparison is that it sounds like a job that will be finished eventually. MAINWAY's job never ended. It was trying to index a book in progress, forever incomplete. The FBI brought the NSA more than a billion new records a day from the telephone companies. MAINWAY had to purge another billion a day to comply with the FISA Court's five-year limit on retention. Every change cascaded through the social graph, redrawing the map and obliging MAINWAY to update ceaselessly.

MAINWAY's purpose, in other words, was neither storage nor

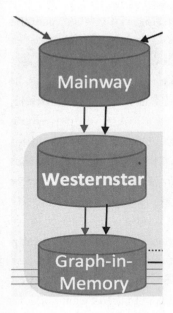

preparation of a simple list. Constant, complex, and demanding operations fed another database called the Graph-in-Memory.

When the Boston bombs exploded, the Graph-in-Memory was ready. Absent unlucky data gaps, it already held a summary map of the contacts revealed by the Tsarnaev brothers' calls. The underlying details—dates, times, durations, busy signals, missed calls, and "call waiting events"—were easily retrieved on demand. MAINWAY had already processed them. With the first hop precomputed, the Graph-in-Memory could make much quicker work of the second and the third.

In order to keep a Tsarnaev graph at the ready, MAINWAY also had to precompute a graph for everyone else. And if MAINWAY had your phone records, it also held a rough and ready diagram of your business and personal life.

As I parsed the documents and interviewed sources, the implications finally sank in. The NSA had built a live, ever-updating social graph of the United States.

Our phone records were not in cold storage. They did not sit untouched. They were arranged in a one-hop contact chain of each to all. All kinds of secrets—social, medical, political, professional—were precomputed, 24/7. Ledgett told me he saw no cause for concern because "the links are unassembled until you launch a query." I saw a database that was preconfigured to map anyone's life at the touch of a button.

Bill Binney, a mathematical cryptographer who quit the NSA in protest when he learned of STELLARWIND, was later falsely accused of passing information about it to the *New York Times*. By Binney's account, which the government does not dispute, FBI agents raided his home in July 2007 and announced themselves at gunpoint as he stepped naked from the shower. The agents would not say exactly what classified program he was alleged to have leaked. Binney, who is as fearless a dissenter as any American I have met, asked them cheerfully, "Oh, you mean 'Cosmic Fart'?" He was testing whether they had been cleared for compartmented information themselves. The agents stared back, stone-faced, until one cracked a tight smile at the STELLARWIND joke.

Binney had quit because spying on Americans—without a warrant—was a red line for him, whether or not ostensibly lawful under presidential orders. As technical director of the NSA's World Geopolitical and Military Analysis Reporting Group, he had helped design analytic tools to automate the production of a gargantuan social graph from foreign metadata. One day in October 2001, Binney said, he heard that a colleague, Ben Gunn, was overseeing the installation of new equipment behind a red-sealed door on the third floor of OPS 2B. Gunn was a hard-charging former employee of GCHQ, the United Kingdom's counterpart agency, who had since become a U.S. citizen and joined the NSA. Subordinates told Binney in alarm, he said, that Gunn was adapting Binney's software, called ThinThread, to analyze domestic calls. When I showed Binney the network diagram of American call data records being funneled to MAINWAY, he did a double take.

"That's a name I've never spoken of," he said. "That's the program they used for STELLARWIND to reconstruct social networks. They take a data set of trillions of calls and collapse it down to a network diagram of who communicates with whom." By "collapse," a data science term that is also called "reduce," Binney meant an analytic technique that strips out the granular detail—the dots and lines on the map—in order to summarize the hidden links of individuals and their overlapping social groups. The result was akin to a constellation pulled out of a skyscape of numberless stars.

Crucially, Binney confirmed to me that the techniques he devised did not confine themselves to individual targets. They computed social graphs for every caller in the gargantuan data set.

"The software does build a profile on everybody in the database, whether or not the analysts look at it," he said. If they did choose to look, he said, they could track individuals in fine detail by extracting a timeline from the index of individual calls. That information, in turn, was enriched by metadata and content drawn from other NSA repositories—for example, from PINWALE, which is a database of the content of intercepted emails and other digital text.

The U.S. call records were supposed to be segregated from other data sets in MAINWAY, with special permission required for access. That is what the network diagram on page 171 conveys with its depiction of FISA-authorized "partitions." By regulation and practice that restriction all but disappeared in 2009, when Attorney General Michael Mukasey approved new and more permissive rules for the Signals Intelligence Directorate.

An NSA summary circulated to analysts celebrated their new freedom to conduct "better, faster analysis" without painstaking efforts to protect the privacy of U.S. citizens and residents. Until then, foreign intelligence analysts were required to ensure that a telephone number (or any other "selector," as the NSA calls search terms) did not belong to an American before using it in contact chaining analysis. The new procedures approved by Mukasey allowed the NSA staff to calculate social graphs "from and through any selector, irrespective of nationality or location." That is, a U.S. telephone number could be used at the beginning, middle, or end of a contact chain, under no more restriction than a foreign intelligence target. The same change applied to British, Australian, and other allied Five Eyes nationals who were normally off-limits. Analysts needed no special permission from superiors to incorporate Americans into their work. The value of this change, the summary memo exulted, was that "it enables large-scale graph analysis on very large sets of communications metadata without having to check foreignness of every node or address in the graph."

In 2012, a year before Snowden's disclosures, NSA director Keith Alexander had ventured to Def Con, the annual Las Vegas hackers' conference. It was a bold excursion into unfriendly terrain, intended to change minds and find recruits. NSA managers saw Def Con as a potential talent pool, albeit a hostile one. The conference had a notorious "Spot the Fed" contest, offering prizes to out government agents in the crowd. Alexander gamely took the stage.

"Does the NSA really keep a file on everyone?" Def Con's founder, Jeff Moss, asked him bluntly.

"No, we don't. Absolutely no," Alexander replied. "And anybody who would tell you that we're keeping files or dossiers on the American people knows that's not true."

Nobody had an inkling then of the Graph-in-Memory. No one knew the NSA and FBI were ingesting our call records. No concrete evidence was available to prove Alexander wrong. Did he take advantage of our collective ignorance to lie?

The tech-speak of electronic surveillance—"metadata," "social graph"—makes it hard to see how systematic the public gaslighting had become. It is difficult, as I tried to illustrate with the tongue-in-cheek story of a trillion-teen house party, to translate the jargon into everyday terms that make sense. Sometimes, even so, it is illuminating to try. So let's suppose you find a G-man standing by your phone, fountain pen and leather notebook in hand. He writes down the numbers you dial and the incoming caller IDs. He times each call on a pocket watch stored in his vest. At the end of the day he sends his notebook to FBI headquarters. Fleets of trucks dispatch all those note-books, more than ten thousand tons a day, up the Baltimore–Washington Parkway to Fort Meade. Armies of clerks copy every page of every note-book onto a parchment roll that stretches coast to coast. Millions more labor in shifts, around the clock, to cross-reference each line, prepare an index, and draw a gargantuan map.

One of the dots on that map is the phone in your pocket or purse. Another is the phone on your desk or your wall, if you bother to keep a landline anymore. The NSA map traces paths to your spouse, your boss, your shrink, your landlord, your bookie, and perhaps to someone you would rather not mention at all. The good news is that the govern-ment is not in the business of random snooping and will probably never look at your small corner of that great big map. But it could. It as-sumed that power when it decided, in secret, to collect and analyze your calls. What's drawn on the map stays on the map—until the day that someone decides otherwise.

The fanciful apparatus I just described could never be built in the analog world, of course. The personnel required would dwarf the pop-ulation at large. Pencil and parchment consumption would deforest a continent. In all of human history, until right now, the tools of our species could not have accomplished surveillance on this scale. Digital technology made it possible. The government made it real, and never asked the public for consent.

Our intuitions do not work very well on complex, abstract ques-tions. That is where our thought experiment helps. The imaginary G-men and notebooks and clerks do only some of the things that MAINWAY did with our telephone records, but at least we can pic-ture their work. Big Data techniques may leave us unmoved, but most of us know what we would think if the fellow with the fountain pen turned up at our door. And the parchment model does not begin to capture the most important danger posed by the telephone records.

The real MAINWAY is, in essence, a surveillance time machine. It can reach back into the past and place eyes on events in a span of hours or days or weeks that had held no interest for the NSA at the moment they happened. That is because MAINWAY and the Graph-in-Memory keep copies of every map they draw. Remember: the FISA Court allowed the NSA to hold on to telephone logs for five years. Every call record included a date, time, and duration. The social graph—the relationship map—could change dramatically from day to day. Telephone accounts were opened and closed. Contacts spoke frequently for a week, then fell silent for a year. MAINWAY could rewind, review, and advance the map like a planetarium display. With a little imagination you can probably spot the risk in your own profession or personal life. Here is mine. I make the rounds of confidential journalistic sources, believing I am flying under the radar because my story is yet to come. There is no reason for the government to monitor the people I talk to, no reason to take the considerable trouble of obtaining a warrant on me. But that offers no protection now, because the government can look back as soon as it judges my work to pose a risk to protected national security information. It is easier for investigators to spy on my sources than on me. There is a lower legal bar for surveillance of someone who signs the security contract. Investigators make a list of who knew the things I wrote about. Which of them showed contact with me in the month before my story? Which of them received calls from a burner phone bought for cash? Whose IP or MAC addresses, the telltales of a device on the web, logged on to newly created accounts? Whose movements overlapped with mine? If my source and I do not take special care, the answers are obvious. The government can watch us in retrospect as easily as if it had tracked us in real time. That is something entirely new, impossible until it had access to metadata in sufficient volume.

Ordinarily we think of surveillance in terms of its targets. The NSA is watching *you*, or me, or her, or them. Targeters have to know where to point their antenna. With bulk collection and a mass social graph, all that changes. There was no reason to track my contacts before the leak, but MAINWAY and associated tools could do it just as well in retrospect.

Which brings us back to Keith Alexander at Def Con. Credit where due: he did not lie about the dossiers. Not if we take the word to mean manila folders in a file cabinet somewhere. The NSA maintained no individual files on us, not even in digital form. The technology does not work that way. Something even more revealing, though, resided in MAINWAY. Our dossiers floated formlessly in a classified cloud, precomputed and untouched until someone asked for them. They were ghosts in the Graph-in-Memory, summoned on demand.

I am well aware that a person could take this line of thinking too far. Maybe I have. The United States is not East Germany. As I pieced this picture together, I had no reason to believe the NSA made corrupt use of its real-time map of American life. The rules imposed some restrictions on use of U.S. telephone records, even after Mukasey blew a hole in them. Only twenty-two top officials, according to the Privacy and Civil Liberties Oversight Board, had authority to order a contact chain to be built from data in MAINWAY's FISA partitions. But history has not been kind to the belief that government conduct always follows rules or that the rules will never change in dangerous ways. Rules can be bypassed or rewritten—with or without notice, with or without malignant intent, by a few degrees at a time or more than a few. Government might decide one day to look in MAINWAY or a comparable system for evidence of violent crime, or any crime, or any suspicion. Governments have slid down that slope before. Within living memory, Richard Nixon had ordered wiretaps of his political enemies. The FBI, judging Martin Luther King Jr. a "dangerous and effective Negro," had used secret surveillance to record his sexual liaisons. A top lieutenant of J. Edgar Hoover invited King to kill himself or face exposure.

Meaningful abuse of surveillance had come much more recently. The FBI illegally planted hundreds of GPS tracking devices without warrants. New York police spied systematically on mosques. Governments at all levels used the power of the state most heavy-handedly, sometimes illegally, to monitor communities disadvantaged by poverty, race, religion, ethnicity, and immigration status. As a presidential candidate, Donald Trump threatened explicitly to put his opposing candidate in jail. Once in office he asserted the absolute right to control any government agency. He placed intense pressure on the Justice Department, publicly and privately, to launch criminal investigations of his critics.

The Graph-in-Memory knew nothing of such things. It had no awareness of law or norms or the nature of abuse. It computed the chains and made diagrams of our hidden relationships on a vast, ever-updating map. It obeyed its instructions, embedded in code, whatever those instructions said or ever might say.

In the national security establishment's conversation with itself, Snowden's name came up often and unfondly. There were exceptions, not many. Some Aspen participants saw the virtue of a more transparent debate about surveillance. Others thought the NSA had gone too far. Negroponte leaned in to tell me quietly, an hour after our panel, that the telephone records collection produced nothing important.

Visiting foreign officials, another minority, took tart exception to some of what they had learned. I found Gilles de Kerchove, the European Union's counterterrorism coordinator, alone in an upstairs lounge, looking disgruntled. For a moment it looked as though he would wave me off. Then he nodded, as if to himself, and recounted the morning, three weeks before, when he learned from *Der Spiegel* that his fax machine had been compromised by an NSA surveillance device. At fifty-six, after years of interaction with American counterparts, de Kerchove did not regard himself as naïve. But a recent remark from the NSA director, in private, had left him sputtering. "'Everybody knows. Everybody does [it]'—Keith Alexander said that," de Kerchove told me. "I don't like the idea that the NSA will put bugs in my office. No. I don't like it. No. Between allies? No. I'm surprised that people find that noble."

Most of the Americans here could speak of nothing but Snowden's betrayal. Many accused him, in nearly identical words, of breaking a sacred oath when he handed NSA documents to me. That assertion, made in all apparent sincerity, was a fascinating artifact of secrecy culture. Clearly Snowden had breached a strongly felt norm, in addition to any offenses under the law, but the oath that people kept talking about does not exist. They were conflating two separate things in their minds, incorporating one into the other. Snowden, like anyone else with a clearance, had signed Standard Form 312, the Classified Information Nondisclosure Agreement. That is a government contract with criminal penalties for noncompliance. The oath Snowden swore, the same one recited by most of his accusers, obliged him to "support and defend the Constitution of the United States against all enemies, foreign and domestic." He and his accusers interpreted that differently.

Some insiders asked incredulously why the government even allowed me to keep writing stories about the classified archive. "As a test of your concern for the security of this country, I suggest you turn over to the FBI everything you received from Snowden," George Cotter later wrote to me, his retirement as NSA chief scientist affording him freedom to be quoted by name. Others, speaking off the record, said in earnest that the FBI should not wait for me to volunteer.

Undercurrents of grievance eddied through the bars and outdoor spaces. Many of those present were baffled by the distrust of the body politic. Shortly before the forum began, a national poll found more people who regarded Snowden as a whistleblower than a traitor. Registered voters displayed "a massive shift in attitudes," the survey found, with a majority agreeing for the first time in years that "the government's anti-terrorism efforts go too far." Members of the Aspen tribe believed in their mission. How could the public and press fail to understand that they were trying to protect us? Who could conceive such a thing as too much intelligence? The president, Congress, and the public at large forgave no failure by intelligence agencies to spot trouble before it arrived. In a corridor I overheard one man say, "Guy boards an airplane with a crotch full of TATP, too dumb to ignite his own underwear, and that's supposed to be a systematic failure of the intelligence community. Now the same people tell us NSA should scale back."

Most of the men and women here had spent whole careers inside the sealed habitat of "the high side," the classified networks that wall off their working environment. Pretty much everyone inside those walls relied to some degree on signals intelligence. The reach of the apparatus came to seem routine. "I did not have a whole lot of time to step back and think about philosophical questions," said a recent retiree from the uppermost ranks of U.S. intelligence. "None of us did. We were too busy putting out fires and managing a complex set of problems and answering to masters who wanted to know how the hell we had missed whatever we didn't see coming." Policymakers, spies, and analysts accepted the surveillance apparatus as they found it. They tried to use it wisely. They were altogether unprepared for the suspicion and anger aroused when ordinary people caught a glimpse of the machinery.

Raj De, the NSA's soft-spoken general counsel, accepted that there could be legitimate disagreements about the boundaries. "I just hate the undertone of, 'You guys are lying,'" he told me. "People can say, 'We don't agree with that.' It's just—I hate the tenor of the whole thing."

Negroponte looked for a dispassionate explanation. "I think the ghost of J. Edgar Hoover and the ghost of Richard Nixon have long been exorcised, but they still cast this baleful influence on some of the things we're doing," he said.

Some of the sentiments I heard at Aspen reminded me of a presentation I had recently come across in the Snowden archive. It dated back to the fall of 2001. In seven pages, marked TOP SECRET//COMINT/ NOFORN/X1, the NSA took inventory of the capabilities it must preserve at all cost in the coming war with al Qaeda. Along the way, the agency ranked its own place in the hierarchy of "critical national assets." The "ability of the U.S. to conduct SIGINT Operations," according to this analysis, was a Level 1 national resource. The heading on

---

TOP SECRET//COMINT//NOFORN//X1

NSA/CSS Mission: PROVIDE AND PROTECT VITAL INFORMATION FOR THE NATION

Survival   -   Without which America would cease to exist as we know it
Critical   -   Causally one step removed from survival
Significant -   Importantly affect global environment in which U.S. must act

SIGINT Portion				
Survival – Level 1	**Critical – Level 2**	**Significant – Level 3**	**Level 4**	**Level 5**

Ability of the U.S. to conduct SIGINT Operations	1. Ability to collect, process and disseminate SIGINT related to:(Gather Secrets by Secret means)
	- Worldwide Terrorism
	- Homeland Defense
	- Weapons of Mass Destruction
	- Strategic military Forces
	- Russia and China Nuclear capability
	- Proliferation
		1A. Ability to accept customer information needs
		
		1B. Ability to exploit:
		- Military Information
		- Economic Information
		- Information Operations Information
		- Political Information
		
		1C. NSA/CSS Worldwide Enterprise
		- NSAW/NSOC
		- Field Sites
		  + Conventional Sites
		  + Mission Ground Stations
		  + Regional Security Operations Centers
		  + Special Collection Sites
			1a1. Provide Customer's SIGINT information needs to:
			- Requirements Staff
			- Standing and Ad hoc requirements database
			- RNET systems
			
			1c1. Overhead Collection Management Center
			1c2. Collection Strategy and Requirements Center
			1c3. Remote Operations Center (ROC)
			1c4. National SIGINT Collection Center
			1c5.DEFSMAC	

DRV FM: NSA/CSSM 123-2
Dated: 24 Feb 98
DECL ON: X1, X3, X5, X6, X7, X8

TOP SECRET//COMINT// NOFORN//X1

that column was "Survival," reserved for assets "without which America would cease to exist as we know it." The organizational health of the Signals Intelligence Directorate qualified as Level 2, or "Critical," which meant "causally one step removed from survival."

The author of these slides was a career civil servant, fairly senior but nowhere near the top. I wondered whether the views expressed were merely her own. The answer became clear when her name and this presentation turned up in a memorandum from Joseph J. Brand. At the time he was chief of staff for policy in the Signals Intelligence Directorate. Brand had commissioned the slide deck and marked it for distribution to the intelligence community at large. He cited it in support of a special achievement award for its author.

The fixed belief that all their work had life-and-death stakes colored attitudes here about the wisdom of any public debate. Outsiders had no business in decisions about where the government should and should not point its surveillance machine. People I had known for years walked away at my approach. More than one hoped aloud that I would face repercussions. A senior government lawyer asked pointedly whether reporters have a professional body to sanction unethical conduct. (We do not. Anyone can commit journalism without a license.) When I joined a small conversation at the coffee urn, a national security lawyer I had not met before remarked without preamble that the law firm of Williams & Connolly took a "very aggressive approach" to First Amendment law. It was no secret, but not especially common knowledge, that the firm represented the *Post* and me. I looked at him more closely. How carefully, he asked me, had I thought about the consequences of relying upon erroneous advice?

That night, Keith Alexander gave a talk. He wished he could "just get all the American people in our huddle and say, okay, here is the game plan." He could not do that because "terrorists . . . are amongst us and they're trying to kill our people." Americans should take comfort in the close oversight of the FISA Court and the intelligence commit-tees in Congress.

I stood to ask a question. We had not met in person. Alexander looked down and pursed his lips when NBC's Pete Williams, the mod-erator, called on me by name. I wanted to follow up on the point that Alexander had just made. The FISA Court and Congress, if my re-porting was correct, did not delve into operational details of a program like PRISM. They did not, for example, know the names of targets or the grounds for their selection. Was Alexander saying, to the contrary, that the legislative or judicial branches "are examining any of the 45,000 selectors that you're using or what was the basis of the 'reason-able, articulable suspicion'? I mean, they don't go into that, right?"

"They don't necessarily go into it," he conceded. "Our general counsel, our IG, they do look at that and make sure that what we're doing is right." Alexander did not know a better way to safeguard civil liberties, he told me. In a perfectly flat tone, he added that maybe "you have greater insights."

Nasty and suspicious. That was the verdict. I had crossed an invis-ible boundary. Maybe there was no avoiding it, given that I had taken Snowden's documents and, sometimes, taken his side. Maybe I asked too many follow-up questions. Maybe a review of the video would judge me rude, insufficiently deferential to rank. The Aspen Security Forum relied on the goodwill of speakers and funding from contrac-tors who sought government business. Academi, the latest rebranding of the Blackwater private military company, was a principal sponsor of the forum that year. (In an off-the-record lunch, the company intro-duced Jose Rodriguez, the former CIA operations chief who had or-dered the burning of video evidence of waterboarding. Rodriguez was advising Academi on compliance with its corporate code of conduct.) No invitation came from Aspen the following year, or the next, or the next after that.

SIX

JAMBOREE

Shortly after 8:00 a.m. on February 7, 2012, NSA and CIA personnel began to arrive at a bunkerlike office building in Herndon, Virginia, a few miles east of Dulles International Airport. Cement and dark reflective glass sheathed the exterior. Fine copper mesh wove through interior walls around Top Secret spaces, sealing off electromagnetic leaks. The neighborhood itself offered a measure of camouflage. On one side, an unremarkable office park. On the other, across the road, little children at the Little Oaks Montessori Academy. The Madame Curie School, Oak Hill Christian School, and Lutie Lewis Coates Elementary School clustered nearby.

Inside, on this day, digital weapons designers from all over the United States had come to review the state of their art. Government labs showed off crackerjack new tools of electronic theft. Geeky enthusiasm set the tone. "Q," James Bond's eccentric gadgeteer, would have been at home if his lab produced software implants as well as toothpaste bombs. Private contractors pitched proof-of-concept designs to "circumvent or exploit" the latest security features of smartphones, computers, and network hardware around the world. Researchers shared test results from the field. Here was a way to bypass Secure Boot in Windows. Here a promising plan to compromise LTE wireless networks, enabling "discreet control of the radio" on a mobile phone and remote activation of its microphone. Here was a technique to extract cryptographic keys from silicon circuits with X-ray computed tomography. Here was STRAWHORSE, a breakthrough in clandestine surveillance of iPhones. The collective goal of the gathering, unrealized but ever in progress, was the wherewithal to penetrate any machine, any network, any electronic data source, anywhere in the world.

NSA leaders are matter-of-fact about the scale of their ambition. Stealing foreign secrets, they say, is what we pay them to do. True enough, as far as it goes, but the motto lacks proportion. The NSA, like the eagle astride the globe on the first page of the first document that Snowden gave me, really does hold the world's telecoms in its grasp. It cannot yet reach every bit and byte, but it comes near enough. Is there room in that picture for self-restraint? Does the agency conceive of boundaries short of black letter law? Rules and regulations are vital, but so are workplace norms. Statutes leave gaps. Precedent is silent when technology upends old assumptions. Secret operations, by their nature, are difficult to test in closed judicial proceedings. There are broad swaths of surveillance, in practice, that judicial and legislative oversight do not even try to reach. That is why culture matters so much when fallible human beings acquire the power to peer into other people's secrets. Culture fills the blank spaces between the lines. One way to gauge the NSA's norms, admittedly ironic in the context of this book, is to listen in on the SIGINT Directorate's conversations with itself.

Since its debut in 2006, for reasons lost to history, the annual hackers' conference in northern Virginia has been known as Jamboree. Possibly the name is meant to be tongue-in-cheek. It brings to mind incongruous scenes of Boy Scouts and Girl Scouts and campfires and songs of peace. In the wiretappers' Jamboree, the setting is less pastoral—a TS/SCI conference space—and the lyrics sing of digital battlefields. Jamboree celebrates technical brilliance, audacity on offense, and a relentless drive to win. It promotes a laser focus on mission accomplishment. Those are virtues among spies, important ones. They are not the only virtues. Jamboree springs from an operational world that can be nonchalant about the privacy of innocents and contemptuous of men and women who allow themselves to be "owned," as hackers say, by American cyber warriors. Sexual innuendo, ethnic slurs, and mockery of the dead are neither furtive nor especially rare in NSA discourse. The people who speak this language among themselves show no apparent concern for reproach by superiors. They are the same people whose work may decide who lives and who dies in a conflict zone. "As many of you know, our forces in Iraq are dropping bombs on the strength of SIGINT alone," Charles H. Berlin III, the former chief of staff of the Signals Intelligence Directorate, told his workforce in an internal newsletter in 2004.

There are many professionals in the NSA who take no part in the japery. I have little doubt that they make up a large majority. NSA personnel and veterans I have met are thoughtful about their power and conflicted about trespassing, as inevitably they do, into private terrain that does not belong to a foreign intelligence target. Among the top guns of the NSA hacker club and those who make use of their work, even so, looser language and attitudes are commonplace. Scores of examples in documents and confidential interviews reveal a tendency in those precincts to infuse official reports with snickering insults and derisive memes invented by teenagers, gamers, and nerds on the Internet.

In the autumn of 2013, I asked the *Washington Post* to hire one of those nerds. Ashkan Soltani, then thirty-eight, had spent his youth in hacker forums and counterestablishment technical gatherings from Def Con in Las Vegas and Hackers on Planet Earth in New York to the

Chaos Computer Club in Berlin. He had grown up to acquire academic credentials, work for state and federal agencies, cofound a start-up company, and earn a reputation in privacy and security circles. His sensibilities, for all that, stayed tuned to his roots. I sought him out with a limited brief, at first: to help me decode the most difficult technical materials in the Snowden archive.

I had relied upon exceptional colleagues at the *Post* to help me tell the NSA stories, foremost among them Greg Miller, Ellen Nakashima, Carol Leonnig, and Julie Tate. None of it was easy work, not by a long shot, but some stories were more accessible than others. The accessible ones grew scarcer by September. Some of the most consequential were yet to come. For those I needed another kind of help, more than I had been willing to accept. I saw tantalizing clues to operations on the edge of the law or inconsistent with stories that the government had told for years. The clues were fragmentary, like puzzles with only scattered pieces in hand. Talent ran deep in the newsroom, but I knew of no one with the computer science and engineering chops I lacked. The usual cure for this problem, a reporter's core competence really, is to set forth into the world and find the people who know things and ask questions. Here that presented a dilemma. I did not feel free to circulate codeword-classified documents before I understood them, and seldom even then, but I could not understand them on my own. Three months into the story, I found myself stuck more often than I liked.

If I allowed someone else to review the archive with me, whom did I know well enough to trust? Who could even qualify? I needed an information scientist with an improbable range of competence in network infrastructure, endpoint security, surveillance tradecraft, public policy, and privacy law. This hypothetical candidate had to be unconflicted, uncommitted elsewhere, and unburdened by ideology that would incline him or her to cherry-pick evidence. Some people, otherwise qualified, might balk at the legal risks. No one who had held or hoped to hold a government clearance would be likely to join an excavation of classified leaks. I wrote down a few names. Others would have fit the bill, but I did not know them personally. My list resolved to one.

Over time Soltani became an alter ego in the reportorial detective work. Alongside the technical help, he supplied something I did not know I needed: a guide to the folkways of the men and women, by far mostly young men, behind the written words.

The first slide deck I showed Soltani, on September 19, was filled with jargon and graphics that I was underequipped to parse. If I understood the gist correctly, there was an important story here. One of the main points seemed to be that the NSA found it difficult, in some fields of operation, to pick out the signals it wanted to steal from torrents of background noise.

Soltani paged through the presentation, intently focused and somewhat awed by his first glimpse of the classified archive. He clicked from slide 3 to slide 4. He stopped. He stared. He laughed. He grabbed my arm. "You've got to see this," he said. I stood up from my own machine and looked over his shoulder. On slide 4, a team from Special Source Operations explained that the collection systems at issue were unable to "apply a value to traffic types." In other words, they dipped into a data stream without knowing as they did so what they scooped up. This was a problem, as they saw it, not because they grabbed more information than the mission required, but because the volume overtopped the banks of available storage. "Collection optimization" was required. The slide featured a photograph of a dark-furred cat, perhaps, by the look of it, a Russian Blue. Its face filled the frame, brown eyes downcast, mouth set in the impression of a frown. A label in large print read "Emo Cat," and, in smaller letters, "No One Understands Him."

The joke would have been plain to the intended audience, a nod to common membership in a meme-savvy group. The seas of incoming data, like the depths of the feline heart, were uncharted. Viewers were meant to laugh at Emo Cat's despair. Cat pictures with sardonic slogans, Soltani explained to me, had their origins on the fringes of the World Wide Web. They had migrated from Internet Relay Chat rooms and avowedly misanthropic forums such as 4chan to Reddit and then to mass-market social media. Facebook kittens were cute and fluffy. Their antecedents had a mean streak, by and large. "Emo" connoted, in this case, mock-worthy pathos.

"So what?" I said. I had noticed the kitten in passing and paid it no mind.

"You don't understand," Soltani replied. The memes we turned up were like cave paintings, he said: simple yet revealing markers of culture. "I *know* these guys. These are the guys I've been hanging out with for years. These are the guys from Reddit and Def Con. They're exactly the same."

Soltani had come to the job with assumptions about the men and women behind the ramparts of the world's most formidable electronic intelligence agency. The artifacts we discovered obliged him to think again.

"I, like a lot of people, expected the NSA to consist mostly of either close-cropped military or 'men in black' types," he wrote to me later, alluding to the film about a secret agency for human-alien relations. "However, after reading through the writing style, tone, and imagery, it's clear that at least a portion of the people there are the socially awkward Reddit nerds. (I'm envisioning young, slightly baby-faced, tubby, perhaps with a 32 oz. 'Big Gulp' in hand as they do their work.) These are not your typical government employees—the Rorschach that emerges from the sea of documents reveals something much more unexpected, but also *much more familiar to geeks like me*."

The NSA's blue badge employees divide between civilian hires and uniformed personnel on assignment from Army, Navy, Air Force, Marine Corps, and Coast Guard intelligence. Military employees arrive prescreened. Civilians run a gauntlet when they apply: a 567-question psychological test, a follow-up interview, the SF-86 Questionnaire for National Security Positions, and a polygraph exam to probe for counterintelligence threats. Even so, in the internet age, the NSA has had to adapt in order to recruit the cohort of gifted hackers it needs. They do not tend to arrive with spit-shined shoes and hair cut high and tight. The culture, Snowden said, is "t shirts, jeans, bleached hair, green hair, earrings, meme shirts, memes posted all over your cubicle." Screeners make allowances. Some of the top recruits would never have made the cut in the analog age of listening posts and paper files.

Alan Tu, a mathematician and computer scientist, was not a member of that group but came to know it well. He joined the NSA straight from grad school at the Georgia Institute of Technology in 2005. At a forward outpost of the National Threat Operations Center in Hawaii, the same office Snowden joined in his final assignment, Tu carried out countersurveillance missions against state hackers from Asia. Thoughtful and judicious, he had an exceptional memory, a straight-arrow reputation, and a sheaf of classified commendations that he cannot show anyone on the outside. On one visit to Hawaii, General Keith Alexander handed him the NSA director's challenge coin, an engraved brass token of outstanding performance.

The NTOC assignment was a hybrid of cyber defense and offense, a rarity in the NSA. Tu hunted for foreign intruders in U.S. military networks and directed new surveillance to trace their source. When he found the intruders, he helped target countermeasures. Sometimes the operations took surreptitious control of "threat actors" overseas, turning the tables to spy back on the spies. With special authority, seldom granted, the agency could launch a counterattack to disrupt or disable the foreign equipment. Tu worked closely with hackers on the offensive side of the house, including the cool kids in the Remote Operations Center, "the Rock."

Tu left the NSA six years later with a well-rounded picture of his comrades' strengths and flaws. "I don't have some grudge or bombshell. Most of the work done at NSA is mundane, and most of it is not controversial, and some of it is noble," he told me.

"Whether military or civilian, you can get oddballs," Tu said. In the military, "you signed up at eighteen or twenty, got basic training, then three to six months of technical school, then a clearance, and—boom—you end up at NSA. Soon after that, raw traffic access. Do you have the maturity to make good decisions? That's a legitimate question." On the civilian side, the people who managed hiring "had to be slightly more mellow about some of the more dramatic folks" who came from the Def Con culture, fond of pranks and cracking wise and competitive game play.

He added, "We're known as a geeky culture." In person, typical employees are "more introverted, quiet, more keep-to-yourself type people." The standard agency joke is that the extroverts look at *other people's* shoes as they talk. But when they sit down at their keyboards and let themselves go, they return to their natural habitat. Their briefings and classified blog posts sometimes read like "the Wild, Wild West," Tu told me.

O n September 20, 2013, the day after we came across Emo Cat, I brought Soltani to meet the *Post* editor, Marty Baron. I knew that critics of our work might seize on Soltani's national origin, so I let Baron know before they met that he had been born in Iran. He was a longtime U.S. citizen, I explained, who left Tehran as a little boy. That sentence covered a lot of history. Soltani's father had grown up in the Iran of Mohammed Reza Shah Pahlavi, the American-backed strongman and last in a line of absolute Persian monarchs. The elder Soltani, an accomplished musician, played the tombak, a goblet drum, and accompanied the shah when he traveled with Iran's national orchestra. Later he became a senior executive of the Iran Insurance Company, overseeing the shah's assets in the Persian Gulf region. The man was, in short, a poor prospect to thrive when the Islamic Revolution of 1979 deposed the shah and turned Iran's social order upside down. Soltani's father fled to America with two daughters in tow, leaving his wife and four-year-old Ashkan to follow after settling the family's affairs. Ashkan and his mother soon found themselves stranded, helpless to obtain visas from a U.S. embassy held hostage by revolutionary forces. Mother and son made their way to Europe instead, then to Canada, and crossed into the United States by car. They applied for asylum, which was quickly granted. Immigration authorities issued them green cards the following year. Those were different times.

Young Ashkan spent the first years of his American childhood in Akron, Ohio. He developed a knack for breaking and rebuilding things to change the way they worked. Among his earliest memories is a battery-powered car, a Datsun replica, that he navigated through the house by programming buttons on a numeric keypad—four units forward, two units right, three units left to steer around an armchair. By the age of ten, when his family moved to "Tehrangeles," the central Los Angeles neighborhood of Little Persia, he was assembling telephone auto-dialers and writing BASIC computer code. He taught himself to read hexadecimal notation to crack the copy protection on Jumpman, the hot computer game of the day. Later, he soldered a rewritable chip onto the motherboard of a Sony game console, bypassing firmware locks. Armed with a dial-up modem, he exchanged hacking tips in computer forums known as bulletin boards. There he learned how to alter the software instructions in early cellular phones. At age fifteen, he got hold of a Motorola MicroTac and wired it to a laptop computer at home. With a series of typed commands he overrode the built-in controls and repurposed the phone as a makeshift spy device. If he wanted to, he could sniff the airwaves for nearby cellular signals and assume the identity of any phone in range. Freon and a hammer, he also discovered, cracked the Kryptonite bicycle locks of the day. All these were common pursuits in the teenage hacker circles Soltani joined. Like a lot of future security experts, Soltani told me, "I grew up finding vulnerabilities in systems."

Soltani earned a bachelor's degree in cognitive science and did his graduate work in computer security and privacy at the University of California, Berkeley. Along with two fellow grad students, he produced a thesis project called "Know Privacy." Their work showed how well-known websites gathered and sold far more information from visitors than they disclosed in their privacy policies. Later, as a consultant to the *Wall Street Journal*, Soltani intercepted the secret signals of smartphone apps as they exfiltrated personal data from users, unawares. MobileScope, his start-up company, commercialized his technique. When I first met Soltani, in May 2012, I created a false identity and let him demonstrate the product on a spare iPad I kept at home. He showed how software developers followed me surreptitiously around New York City and the internet, in violation of government regulations and promises made in their terms of service. I launched a medical app, dreamed up an awkward question, and typed "gonorrhea" in the query field. Two dozen lines sprang out from the icon for my device on the MobileScope screen, each representing a data grab by an advertiser, an information broker, or a middleman in the data economy. In an instant, invisibly, the iPad had transmitted my age, gender, device ID, location, and enough other details to identify my alter ego, "Bart Testbed," if he was real. Some of the companies harvested the embarrassing search term as well. Apple has since tightened privacy controls, and Google has done some of the same for its Android phones, but somewhere a database includes a medical profile of the unfortunate Mr. Testbed. The suspicions that launched Soltani's project arose from "the same hacker mindset" he carried from his childhood: "Here are the vulnerabilities where the law says one thing but the tech works the other way."

Between college and grad school, Soltani worked and played as the spirit moved him. A Vancouver company dispatched him on a computer security assignment to Hong Kong. He found his way to a DJ gig by night. When he tired of employment, he snowboarded through most of 2003 with a group of friends, trading lessons for lift tickets and living on the cheap. They changed hemispheres with the seasons, migrating from winter to winter in Lake Tahoe, New Zealand, and Japan. In 2005, AT&T hired Soltani to help combat a nightmarish wave of spam. The phone company had switched on a feature that enabled customers to receive a text message sent by email. Spammers lit up AT&T phones with billions of unwanted texts, emailing every possible ten-digit number. Here again, an unexpected security hole. Soltani designed a defensive perimeter with spam filters running on high-speed routers. "That became my specialty for a period of time," he said. Word of mouth brought him similar contracts at France Telecom and the Nippon Telegraph and Telephone Corporation in Japan.

U.S. Customs and Border Patrol then hired Soltani to secure a computer facility in West Virginia against denial-of-service attacks that flooded its network with tens of millions of spurious queries. Lacking a security clearance, Soltani was forbidden to touch the government computers. He had to tell his employers where to click and what to type, line by line.

By the time I met him, Soltani had served a stint as staff technologist at the Federal Trade Commission. There he made himself a plague upon Google and Facebook with forensic work that proved they spied illegally on their users. Since then he had earned most of his living as a consultant to state attorneys general who wanted to sue technology companies in New Jersey, California, Ohio, and New York state courts. Compact and charismatic, Soltani had a Rolodex of admirers across government, industry, and university lines, even, somehow, in the companies he had shamed. His impromptu "tech policy cocktail hours," set up on the fly as he traveled, filled the back rooms of dive bars in Washington, San Francisco, and New York.

In April 2013, six or seven weeks before the Snowden stories went public, I asked Soltani to take a long walk with me in Battery Park at the southern tip of Manhattan, leaving our electronic devices behind. I had to beef up my digital security, I told him, and pronto. We walked through scenarios, workflows, and tools. I did not tell him why and he did not ask. The discretion impressed me. When my first NSA story went live on the evening of June 6, Soltani sent an encrypted email. "So that was it," he wrote. Four months later, on September 23, I introduced him to Marty Baron. They hit it off, and Baron gave his blessing for the hire. He did not blink when Soltani told him that my initial precautions for the Snowden archive were not secure enough. We would need some high-end laptop computers to "lobotomize," as Ashkan put it, by blocking ports, removing batteries, and pulling out network circuit boards.

The *Post* signed a contract with Soltani on the same terms as mine. Baron assured him the paper would cover his legal defense if he needed one. "The paper's history is consistent here and its reputation depends upon it," I wrote to Soltani later that day. I told Baron he would not regret the hire: "We're fired up about stories in the pipeline."

On a regular basis, as we set to work, we came across more cave paintings. They spoke to identity and status and the attitudes of NSA data geeks on the hunt.

The larger part of the NSA's intake depends upon what the agency describes as special sources. The NSA asks for secret access to one or another piece of the backbone of the global communications network. Security-cleared executives at U.S. internet and telecommunications companies agree to provide it. The NSA likes that arrangement. Why hotwire a car when the owner will lend you the keys? Some executives—not as many since Snowden—regard support for U.S. intelligence as a patriotic duty. Some are compelled by law. Some companies, like AT&T, have classified arrangements with the NSA, code-named BLARNEY, that stretch back to the 1970s. Some hope for a leg up on bigger government contracts or to ward off regulations. The companies are compensated for their trouble from a classified budget for "corporate partners" that reached $394 million in fiscal year 2011.

When the NSA cannot negotiate access, it helps itself. Overseas, where domestic legal restrictions do not apply, the acquisitions directorate, S3, is free to tunnel just about anywhere it likes. A worldwide hacking infrastructure called QUANTUM deploys a broad range of tools to inject software exploits, intercept communications with methods known as man in the middle and man on the side, and reroute calls and emails through NSA collection points. Most of these are known as passive operations because they collect electronic signals automatically as they pass through large trunk lines and junctions. When passive methods do not suffice, the job becomes, in NSA parlance, interactive. During one representative week in April 2012, there were 2,588 such interactive missions. That kind of bespoke hacking is the province of Tailored Access Operations, and, within it, the Rock.

Sometimes the Rock hits a wall it cannot breach. Commonly that means the surveillance target is using devices or network connections that do not touch the public internet, leaving no path for delivery of a software exploit. That is when the NSA turns to "human-enabled" collection by the Access Operations division, which performs clandestine missions against foreign embassies in the United States and targets of interest overseas. The division's seal, like the one for Special Source Operations, features a predator encircling the globe. The beast on this one, though, is not an eagle. It is a serpent with a long, forked tongue and demonic red eyes. The Latin motto, *Decipio—Circumvenio—Latrocinor*, can be rendered in English as "I deceive, I circumvent, I plunder."

The message is a gamer's gasconade: *We cheat, we steal, we eat your lunch*. In one official briefing, cartoonish swagger gives way to an actual cartoon. The unit is represented as a stick-figure superhero. The "bad guy," wearing devil horns, tries to conceal himself in an internet neighborhood that NSA headquarters hackers cannot see. "CNE Man"—the acronym stands for computer network exploitation—swoops in and saves the day, shouting, "YEAH!!! MAKE DATA HAPPEN!" The NSA has a term for this kind of work. It is called traffic shaping. Access Operations personnel take control of a switch, for example by placing a hardware implant, and change the route traversed by the phone calls, web searches, and emails it wants to acquire. That is why the cartoon refers to "midpoint" collection: the NSA diverts the data stream mid-journey. The bad guys—who commonly are not bad

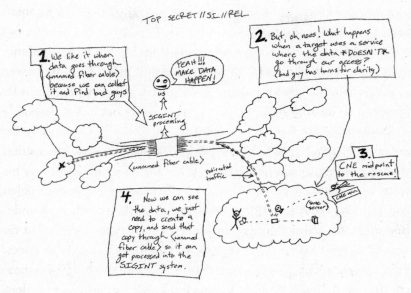

TOP SECRET // SI // REL

at all but merely interesting—keep talking, unawares. CNE Man is a bandit in a cape. That is understood to be okay because the target is, in this case literally, demonized.

A variation on the hero theme takes inspiration from James Bond. The actual spies borrow secret agent mojo from an imaginary counterpart. They name a Windows implant ODDJOB, for example, after the Bond villain in *Goldfinger* with the razor-edged bowler hat.

A more interesting invocation comes in a planning memo for "denial and deception," which is what intelligence officers call the job of hiding their work and misdirecting opponents. It would not do, after all, for CNE Man to fly into a clandestine operation with an NSA serpent on his chest. Field personnel need legends to help them blend in. They pretend to be repair crews, inspectors, or the like to deflect suspicion if anyone spots them at work. Someone has to book their travel and produce their phony paperwork. There is, it turns out, a whole bureaucracy to provide them with "Cover Payroll, Cover Travel, [and] Cover Finance," among other services. Inevitably, the support system has a cover name of its own: MISS MONEYPENNY, after the faithful secretary who flirts with Bond and pines after a romance that is not to be. With Moneypenny as helpmeet, the swashbuckling data burglar becomes Bond himself.

CNE Man, who works in real life at a safe distance, does not generally need to brave physical danger. Another unit fits better into the Hollywood mold of a spy. When midpoint operations will not do the job, the NSA sends in S3283, Expeditionary Access Operations. Its personnel slip across foreign borders or just alongside, seeking vantage points on hard targets that the NSA cannot reach by other means. These teams, which carry out what the agency calls its "human-enabled close access network exploitation program," have a Latin motto, too: *Si ceteri non*—"If others do not." That is to say: when all else fails.

Sneaking up on a surveillance target can be risky. Not always, because the targets are sometimes allied government leaders who would probably confine their response to angry words if they caught on. In other cases, discovery is more hazardous. S3283 insertion teams rely on misdirection and swift departure from the scene. If armed, a choice made case to case, they carry only light weapons for self-defense. "I had a blue force tracker," one veteran of expeditionary surveillance in a war zone told me, referring to equipment that showed the location of American troops deployed a considerable distance away. "I'd coordinate with a guy at the threat operations center in the U.S. embassy. I had enough rounds to last me maybe thirty minutes, an M-4 [rifle], sidearm, some water, and an evasion and escape plan. I was out there on my own."

There is more about Unit S3283 in the Snowden archive, including target locations, photographs of personnel in the field, and details of their tactics and techniques. I am not going to write about those things. What interests me here is the way the NSA talks about their work. Locker room bravado is one thing when it takes place in the field. The trash talk, in this case, is built into the official vocabulary of Fort Meade, where engineers and managers describe close access work in terms of seduction and drunken conquest. Surveillance targets, as depicted in formal accounts of expeditionary operations, are like women who would regret the night if only they remembered it in the morning.

One common mission for Unit S3283 is to hack into a local wireless network. Wi-fi signals do not travel far, even when amplified by surveillance equipment, which means that access teams have to sneak in fairly close. Every stage of their work comes with a suggestive cover name. First comes BLINDDATE, in which a team member searches for vulnerable machines. He slips into the network during HAPPY-HOUR, mingles among the computers there, and lures his tipsy victim into a liaison. Next comes NIGHTSTAND, short for one-night stand, wherein the operator delivers a load of malware into the defenseless machine. Further exploitation and hilarity ensue on SECONDDATE. For all their subtlety, the cover names might as well be BIMBO, ROOFIE, BAREBACK, and THE CLAP.

None of this is to cast shade on the operations themselves. By nature an expeditionary mission is closely targeted, the opposite of mass surveillance, and the NSA chooses the marks to fit the demands of its political masters. The targets I saw in documents are what you would expect of an intelligence agency doing its job. The question is what to make of the giggles between the lines. It is not too much, I think, to say that sexual exploitation is an official metaphor of close access operations, passed up the chain of command in operations reports and back down to the lower ranks in training materials. The seven-part qualifying course on wireless exploitation techniques, for example, includes units called "Introduction to BLINDDATE" ("Grab a partner!") and

"Introduction to NIGHTSTAND." There are plenty more where those come from. The NSA archive features dozens of cover names in the same style, from VIXEN and BADGIRL to LADYLOVE and PANT_SPARTY. The latter is versatile slang in pop culture, suitable for any of several intimate acts. In surveillance-speak it stands for injection of an NSA software tool into "a backdoor" in the target's defenses. Get up close, whip out your PANT_SPARTY tool, and stick it in her back door. The developers, briefers, and trainers who trade in this kind of mirth, without exception that I could find, are men.

Alan Tu, the former threat operations analyst, told me the dick-swinging badinage is the product of a "workforce that was incredibly young, young and male. Many either in their first post-college job, or nineteen- to twenty-one-year-old military operators. This is the age of peak testosterone." It would not occur to those men, Tu added, that anyone outside their circle would read what they wrote or find reason to object. And oversight can be thin, he recalled: "Getting quality managers was sometimes a struggle because often, they would pick from what seemed to be the most appropriate technical guy and give them their first leadership and management job."

Snowden turned down a job in TAO, but this was the culture he grew up in. "The memes are awesome for morale and having fun but you're having fun with systems that get people literally killed," he told me. "It is adolescent empowerment. Literally, 'I can do what I want. What are you going to do to stop me? I am all-powerful.' I would point out what defines our understanding adolescence and what it means to be juvenile is a lack of self awareness and restraint."

Some insiders compare bro-style chatter to the private repartee of surgeons and trauma nurses. There may be truth in that. Clowning can bring stress relief and build esprit de corps. The analogy is imperfect, though, and it has a double edge. There are medical professionals who joke about terminal patients behind their backs, and some who defend the practice, but patients and the public do not respond well when they find out. Scandals have ensued in recent years when doctors, under cover of anesthesia, were caught taking selfies with an unconscious patient, mocking another's appearance, and calling a third a "retard" who probably had syphilis. Society expects a degree of maturity from people who wield the knives. We find their power frightening otherwise.

Toward the end of 2018, I sat down with former FBI director James B. Comey for a long conversation in a midtown New York hotel suite. He had put a lot of effort into cultural change in his own agency before Donald Trump fired him in May 2017. The FBI, like the NSA, worked hard to recruit and accommodate young technical talent. Before the Trump administration came to power, Comey was looking for ways to soften a ban on applicants with a history of marijuana use. "I have to hire a great workforce to compete with those cyber criminals, and some of those kids want to smoke weed on the way to the interview," he told the *Wall Street Journal* then. Attorney General Jeff Sessions put a stop to any squishiness on that point, but the bureau, like the NSA, relaxed some entrenched ideas about who belonged. I asked Comey whether he thought Fort Meade has come to grips with the subculture that the young hacker recruits brought with them.

"That's a great question," he said. "I suspect not, because I remember the first time I went there, 2004, 2005, I was struck that I'd just stepped into the 1950s. I remember walking in and seeing the old wood paneling, old-fashioned carpeting. I felt like I'd gone back in time. The support staff seemed to be mostly white women with beehive hairdos, all done up, and a lot of men in short sleeves. Kind of like what you see in a NASA movie [set in] the 1960s. That's what it felt like. I remember, when I joked about it, someone saying a huge number of employees are legacy. Their parents worked there. It's a family business."

———

By doctrine the agency is supposed to assign its cover names at random. That is only sometimes true in practice. A true cryptonym, usually a pair of randomly selected words, conceals any hint of the secret it protects. BYZANTINEHADES, for instance, betrays no link to Chinese cyber espionage. But there are hundreds of other cover names that make no effort to be opaque. They are hand-selected for meaning, simple or otherwise. At times the names are artlessly literal. One classified compartment, shared with the United Kingdom's GCHQ, is called VOYEUR. It refers to spying on another country's spies as they spy on someone else, an especially intimate encounter. SCISSORS, a more prosaic choice, is a processing system that slices up data for sorting. Voyeurs peer through windows. Scissors cut. No mystery is intended or achieved.

The most revealing cover names are compact expressions of culture akin to street art. The culture owes a great deal to gamers, coders, and other digital natives in the outside world. Some of its products, like the sequence from BLINDDATE to NIGHTSTAND, evoke the "brotopia" of Emily Chang's eponymous book about Silicon Valley. Some, like BOUNDLESSINFORMANT, which is a live-updated map of surveillance intake around the world, are so tone-deaf as to verge on self-parody. (The map itself, despite some breathless commentary, is nothing sinister.) In public remarks and testimony, NSA officials often speak of their "compliance culture," humble and obedient to post-Watergate laws. There is truth in that, but when the agency's hackers roam abroad, where far fewer restraints apply, they strike an outlaw pose. There is a whole branch of the acquisitions directorate, S31177, devoted to TRANSGRESSION. A mysterious BADASS compartment is mentioned but left unexplained. PITIEDFOOL, a suite of technical attacks on the Windows operating system, evokes the ferocity of Mr. T's warning to enemies ("I pity the fool!") in the film *Rocky III*. BLACK-BELT, FELONYCROWBAR, ZOMBIEARMY, and DEVILHOUND share the macho vibe. Another whole class of cover names, including EPICFAIL and ERRONEOUSINGENUITY, jeer opsec errors by surveillance targets who imagine that they are covering their tracks.

Five months after the NSA leaks began, I spoke on a panel at the University of North Carolina with Tom Donilon, who had left his job as national security adviser to President Obama not long before. Afterward we stopped for a drink. He was too angry to talk much about Snowden, so I changed the subject to NSA hacker culture. The keyboard warriors, I told him, reminded me of fighter pilots I had known in the Navy and Air Force as a Pentagon correspondent. Donilon smiled and said, "They *really* want to win."

Internal conversations drip with mock sympathy for the NSA's hapless targets. "The approach we've been using recently is *so terribly simple* that it's kinda sad that it even works," wrote a Technical Directorate author from T-314, End User Solutions. His primer for colleagues offered five ways to hack into routers used by foreign rivals who think they are playing offense. "Very bad for the victim," he observed.

The insider folkways signal membership in a tribe. The tribe likes science fiction and fantasy, comic book heroes, *Star Trek*, *Star Wars*, *Harry Potter*, fast food, whiskey, math jokes, programmer jokes, ethnic jokes, jokes about nontechnical people, and caustic captions on photographs. NSA nerds use "dork" and "bork" as verbs. As in: dork the operating system to exploit a device, but don't bork it completely or the device will shut down. They illustrate reports with photos of animals in awkward predicaments; one of them likens a surveillance target to a horse with its head stuck in a tree. They condescend about "leet" (or "l33t") adversaries, wannabe elite hackers who think they can swim with the NSA's sharks. They boast of dining on rivals who "are honing their skillz," another term of derision. The themes and memes of NSA network operations are telltales of a coder class that lives its life onscreen, inattentive to the social cues of people who interact "IRL"—in real life. "What we're seeing is a culture whereby your primary outlet and mechanism for community is a digitally mediated wiki or forum," Soltani told me.

The keyboard geekery can be whimsical. One training officer, apropos of nothing, dropped a joke about binary numbers into a cryptography lecture. "There are 10 types of people in this world: Those who understand binary and those that don't," the instructor wrote. A weekly briefing on surveillance operations paused to celebrate Pi Day, March 14, when the numeric form of the date is the best-known constant in math. Then there is the NSA Round Table, an electronic discussion group that invites participants to vote one another's comments up or down. The voting system, lifted from Reddit, rewards amusing insults as much as content in a forum ostensibly devoted to classified business. "Why is a scoop of potatoes larger than a scoop of eggs in the cafeteria?" a contributor named Michael wondered one day. Paul jumped in to play the troll. "Let me be the first to down-vote you," Paul wrote, naming several pedantic reasons. A side debate erupted: should Michael's post be down-voted, flagged, or removed? Clyde returned to the topic at hand with a facetious theory that scoop volume is proportional to the relative size of potatoes and eggs themselves. In that case, Scott replied, what would happen if "we served eggs that were bigger than potatoes, like of an Ostrich?" Someone proposed a uniform system, "One Spoon to scoop them all," an homage to *Lord of the Rings*. Punsters demanded the "inside scoop" and lamented the waste of time on "small potatoes."

The same aspirations to nerdy wit define a large universe of NSA cover names. Somebody came up with CAPTIVATEDAUDIENCE for a software tool that listens in on conversations by switching on the microphone of a target's mobile handset. Many, many cryptonyms juxtapose animal names—rabbits, goats, monkeys, kittens, a whole menagerie—with incongruous adjectives.

Comic book heroes and villains take prominent places in the pantheon. MJOLNIR, the mythical hammer óf Thor, is an NSA weapon to break the anonymity of Tor. BATCAVE includes a digital hideout for agency hackers who emerge to steal another country's software code. Batman's alluring foe and sometime love interest, POISONIVY, is the cover name for a remote-access trojan used by Chinese government spies. Another program is named for DEPUTYDAWG, the cartoon sheriff in a Terrytoon children's show. NIGHTTRAIN is harder to source with confidence, being a blues song and a country song and a Guns N' Roses song, but it seems to refer in context to a volume of the *Hellboy* comic series. Inside the agency it is part of an especially sensitive program: espionage on a close U.S. ally during operations alongside the ally against a common foe. NIGHTTRAIN is the ally's surveillance technology. The NSA hacks into it with IRONAVENGER, named for a Marvel Comics story line about robot duplicates of famous superheroes. An NSA system for automated decryption of enciphered data is named TURTLEPOWER, after the Teenage Mutant Ninja Turtles.

So it goes. Harry Potter fans dreamed up QUIDDITCH in honor of the exploits of the NSA's Special Collection Service. SORTING-HAT, the enchanted cap that selects a Hogwarts house for each young wizard, is what the NSA calls the traffic control system for information exchanged with its British counterpart. Dystopian fiction contributes BLADERUNNER and ALTEREDCARBON, a pair of stories adapted from print to film. GROK, a verb invented by science-fiction author Robert Heinlein to signify deep understanding, is an NSA key logger that records every character a victim types. Favorite libations (MAKERSMARK, WALKERBLACK, CROWNROYAL) and junk foods (KRISPYKREME, COOKIEDOUGH, LIFESAVER) make regular appearances. UNPACMAN is a nod to early arcade games.

Star Trek lore provides an especially rich source of memes. VULCANDEATHGRIP, First Officer Spock's ultimate combat move, is a nerdy play on network lingo: the grip in this case seizes encryption keys during the "handshake" of two devices as they establish a secure link. BORGERKING is a two-fer: fast food and a nod to the Borg collective that overmatches Starfleet Captain Jean-Luc Picard. Trekkies account for VULCANMINDMELD and WHARPDRIVE, too, but their best work is no doubt KOBAYASHIMARU. That is what the NSA calls its contract with General Dynamics to help break into another country's surveillance equipment. In the Star Trek oeuvre, the name refers to a simulated mission at Starfleet Academy that tests a young cadet's character in the face of certain doom. Every path in the game is programmed to destroy the player's ship and crew. Cadet James T. Kirk, having none of that, hacks into the simulator and adds a winning scenario. The metaphor stands for more than it may intend: not only creative circumvention, an NSA specialty, but a hacker spirit that gamifies its work.

The fun and games are sometimes dispiriting to read. In the NSA's Hawaii operations center, civilian and enlisted personnel used their work machines to circulate dozens of photo memes that originated on Reddit, 4chan, and somethingawful.com. One photo showed a four-foot plastic Donald Duck with hips positioned suggestively between the legs of a pigtailed little girl. Another depicted a small boy tugging at a playmate's skirt with the caption, "I would tear that ass up!" An image of blue balls accompanied a warning to a girl in her early teens against "teasing" her boyfriend without submitting to sex. Beneath a photo of smiling middle school children, one of them in a wheelchair, another caption read, "Who doesn't belong? That's right. Wheel your ass on outta here." A similar photo, overlaid with an arrow that pointed to one of the boys, declared, "Everyone can be friends! Except for this little faggot." One more, shot at the finish line of a Special Olympics footrace, advised the joyful victor, "Even if you win, you're still retarded."

None of that could be called official business, even if distributed at work, but ethnic and other slurs find their way into NSA briefings and training resources as well. They turn up most commonly when syllabus writers are called upon to make up foreign names. Invented names are a staple of NSA course materials because analysts in training have no need to know the identities of actual foreign surveillance targets. Instructors use fictional substitutes to teach the technical and procedural fine points of target selection.

One of the first things an analyst needs to learn is what counts as an adequate reason to judge that a prospective surveillance target is a foreign national on foreign territory. (Fourth Amendment restrictions apply otherwise.) The NSA syllabus for its Smart Target Enhancement Program walks through twelve "foreignness factors" that analysts may rely upon, each illustrated with examples. Some of the ersatz target names are merely playful: Elmer Fudd, Dr. Evil, Bad Dude, Bad Girl, Bad Guy, and Super Bad Guy. Most of them descend into stereotype. Lotsa Casho is a "Colombia-based coordinator" for a drug cartel. A Beijing-based Chinese party of interest can be found online as fried rice@hotmail.com. The Turkish target (kababs4u@yahoo.com) is "Master Kabob," believed by the NSA "to have provided grilled kabobs for hungry Islamic cells."

The most derisive descriptions, and the ones used most often, are reserved for fictional Arabs and Muslims. Many are named with a bastardized reference to an Arabic term of respect for fatherhood. Abu Bad Guy, Abu Evil, and Abu Raghead make appearances, among others. Another version takes the name of the Prophet: Mohammed Bad Guy, Mohammed Evil, and so on. Weekly program updates in briefings prepared for supervisors display related tropes. One report on a surveillance operation in progress took a break from matters at hand to joke about what happens when the "mulla [*sic*] mixes his viagra with his heroin." ("Now he gets an erection but can't stand up.") Save for the last example, these are bureaucratically vetted teaching materials.

The levity extends to battlefield support for U.S. Special Forces and CIA drone operators. The work of the SIGINT Directorate, when it locates and identifies enemy combatants, can have immediate life-and-death stakes. In unguarded moments, as NSA personnel put crosshairs on an enemy, they display a gamer's detachment from bloodshed. A surveillance photo in one official briefing depicted a man in Arab headdress strumming an instrument, oblivious to what the context suggests is his impending demise. The caption on the photo is "To Catch a Guitar Hero?" after the Activision video game. The wisecracking cover names for al Qaeda's once-favorite encryption software, use of which helped mark a target for death, were EXPLETIVEDELETED and EXUBERANTCORPSE.

In the summer of 2006, a long and frustrating hunt for the leader of al Qaeda in Iraq was drawing to a close. The NSA and other U.S. intelligence agencies had labored for years to track Abu Musab Zarqawi, who spread monstrous carnage—hundreds of kidnappings, beheadings, and bombings—in his quest to expel foreign forces and terrorize Iraq's Shiite majority. When U.S. warplanes finally caught up with him on June 7, 2006, NSA analysts claimed a share of the credit in a fist-bumping status report. In it they assembled half a dozen photographs of Zarqawi's corpse. Blood pooled and congealed beneath his head, ran from his nose, and smeared his cheeks. Flies feasted on his flesh. The U.S. government later released a cleaned-up image of Zarqawi in final repose, attempting to quell any doubts about his death. The ones in the NSA document were brutal close-ups. An audio file accompanied the six frames. "*Oh noooo!*" exclaimed a nasal, cartoonish voice. It was an old meme of hilarity at someone else's disappointment or pain, a staple of flame wars since early internet chat rooms. (Flamers sometimes rendered it "oh noes!" or "oh the noes!") Television's *Saturday Night Live* may have inspired the meme with a recurring comedy sketch in the late 1970s. A clay figurine named Mr. Bill, the star of a parody children's show, closed most episodes with a high-pitched scream of "Oh noooo!" as Mr. Hands mangled, crushed, or dismembered him.

In the age of Trump, I found a new openness among my bitter critics in the intelligence community. People who had shunned contact after the Snowden revelations began to talk to me again. One of them, soon after retiring as director of national intelligence, was Air Force lieutenant general James Clapper. Both his parents had worked for a time at Fort Meade, and Clapper himself did a tour there as aide to the NSA director in the course of a half-century career. In 2014, Clapper had come as close as anyone in government to accusing me, along with Laura Poitras and Glenn Greenwald, of taking part in a criminal conspiracy with Snowden. Four years later, in the summer of 2018, he agreed to meet face-to-face. Clapper had responded crankily at first to my request for half a day of his time. "I need to know what this is about before I sit for an hours-long recorded interrogation," he wrote. I made fun of his choice of noun but replied at length. Eventually he agreed to breakfast at the McLean Family Restaurant, a CIA hangout in northern Virginia, where Clapper seemed to know half the room. He made the rounds, chatting up old friends and colleagues, then ordered an egg white omelet. During several hours of conversation, long after servers cleared our plates, he listened respectfully and responded without mincing words. I recounted some of the stories I planned to tell here.

Near the end of the interview, I asked Clapper what to make of an agency culture in which hackers and analysts feel free to mock the dead and conduct official business with ethnic and sexual slurs. "These are not necessarily the people you want to be in charge," I said.

His face tightened. "TAO," he said, referring to Tailored Access Operations, "is *supposed to be*, you know, our legitimate government officially sanctioned hackers."

"Right. They're supposed to be," I replied. "But if they're snickering about—"

He interrupted, sarcastic. "But we want them to be *nice*. We don't want to do anything that's politically incorrect. Right? Isn't that what you're saying?"

"What you want is to think there's a certain level of maturity and respect for the amount of power they have."

Clapper softened. "Well, yeah. You do. But, hey, they're human beings, too. And I'm sure we could clean that up."

Open-mindedness in a leader of Clapper's rank is not to be taken for granted. Even so, he could have probed more deeply. Language is the symptom, not the problem. NSA geeks are not like other geeks whose folkways they share. The NSA's Top Guns build and operate the machinery of a global surveillance hegemon, licensed to do things that would land them in prison if they tried them anywhere else. The eagle and serpent would not be alpha predators without them. Only judgment and self-control can govern them where there is some play in the rules, as there usually is in a sprawling enterprise. Digital weapons designers, like engineers everywhere, are inclined to do what works. The choices they make reach well beyond the terrain of Bad Girls and Bad Guys.

Some of the finest minds in the field assemble for Sigdev, or "signals development," several times a year. They are incubators of the dark arts in electronic surveillance. Prodigious creative energies conjure weapons to set loose against advances in digital defense. Collateral effects are not always well contained. In 2012, the Jamboree conference took a dangerous turn.

Researchers for the NSA and CIA had been preoccupied with Apple's iPhone since its introduction on June 29, 2007. The first mass-market smartphone was a surveillance bonanza—camera, microphone, locator beacon, and more—if the government could find a way in. That was not much of a challenge in the early years. Skillful hobbyists with far fewer resources bypassed Apple's restrictions on unauthorized code within days of each new release of the iPhone operating system. That exercise, known as jailbreaking, unlocked the firmware and induced the phone to run software that Apple had not approved. "Any untethered jailbreak is remotely exploitable," as one practitioner put it to me.

The NSA, CIA, and other U.S. agencies piggybacked on the work of those hobbyists. Jared Osborne of the Applied Physics Laboratory at Johns Hopkins University gave a classified presentation at the 2010 Jamboree that summarized "'jailbreak' methods used in the iPhone community and how those capabilities can be leveraged" by government surveillance tools. What troubled NSA hackers was that Apple, more aggressively than its competitors, kept raising the bar on iPhone security. The company released frequent software updates and a new model every year. "The Intelligence Community (IC) is highly dependent on a very small number of security flaws, many of which are public," wrote a trio of researchers from the Sandia National Laboratories in a classified presentation at Jamboree 2011. They added that "Apple is quick to address these flaws with each new release of firmware and hardware."

When Apple introduced the iPhone 4, it featured a custom-built chip, the A4, that incorporated strong cryptography into the phone's main processor. The key to the firmware, which controlled all other functions of the phone, was now enciphered with the government's own advanced encryption standard. Even the NSA could not break the cipher in a frontal attack.

In 2011, two teams of Sandia researchers attacked the problem on separate paths. Both looked promising but neither was ready by the time they reported their work at Jamboree. Importantly, use of either one would require physical access to the phone. One team explored a technique called differential power analysis, which took extremely sensitive measurements of the new Apple chip's electronic emissions. The procedure could be likened to recording the sounds of the silicon circuits as the decryption key traveled their paths. The other technique required disassembly of the phone and attachment of specialized hardware. Researchers were closing in, but they still did not know exactly where the new chip stored its keys.

Both approaches had a ways to go. If and when ready for real-world deployment, they would be suitable only for closely targeted surveillance operations. Neither method attempted or had any potential to compromise iPhones in quantity or at a distance.

The Jamboree conference of 2012 marked the end of that self-restraint. This time a more audacious plan was on the table. Clyde Rogers, the project lead, called it STRAWHORSE. His research team, he told the Jamboree audience, had already tested components of the new digital weapon. It worked. What stood out about the breakthrough was that STRAWHORSE looked to be capable of compromising iPhones in quantity—and from half a world away.

STRAWHORSE did not bother trying to break down the walls that Apple had built to prevent execution of unauthorized code. Instead, it looked for ways to induce an iPhone to drop its guard. If the device could be persuaded to unlock its defenses, the agency could build malware into apps that an iPhone would freely allow to be installed. As a bonus, the STRAWHORSE method worked just as well on Apple's laptop and desktop computers.

Ken Thompson, a celebrated computer scientist, had pointed out what he called a "chicken and egg" problem for computer security as long ago as 1984. Programmers write software in the form of source code that they can review and verify. Before a computer can run the software, however, the source code must be compiled into binary instructions that are all but impossible for humans to read. The compiler is itself a piece of software, susceptible to attack, but programmers have little choice but to trust it. If the compiler is somehow compromised, it can alter the software it builds in ways that are very hard to detect. STRAWHORSE took inspiration from that dilemma.

Apple's compiler is part of what the company calls the Xcode software development kit. Xcode is like a software factory. Car makers build their vehicles in an assembly plant. Apple developers build iPhone apps in Xcode. STRAWHORSE, the Sandia team reported, was a "whacked," or maliciously modified, version of the Apple compiler. If the tool worked as advertised, the NSA would have the means to install surveillance implants in any iPhone app created on a STRAWHORSE-infected machine.

NSA hackers would no longer need to break into one iPhone at a time. STRAWHORSE would position them as if they were factory managers who could reconfigure an assembly line to install a hidden microphone in every car.

In the executive summary of his talk, Rogers described how his Sandia team had used "our whacked Xcode" to insert a remote-controlled back door into each app it compiled. The implant had already been tested to "send embedded data to a listening post," to rewrite the iPhone's security checks, and to sign uninfected iPhone apps with a digital certificate that allowed the malware to spread.

STRAWHORSE added one more devious touch to extend its useful life: it modified Apple's software installer "to include our . . . whacks" in any future installation of Xcode on the app developer's machine.

As STRAWHORSE entered research and development, Jon Callas was nearing the end of his tour as Apple's "security privateer." It was a self-deprecating title for a pioneering software engineer. Among his other credentials, he was a principal designer of the cryptographic protocols and security architecture of the iPhone and Macintosh operating systems. When we discovered the STRAWHORSE documents, Soltani and I reached out to Callas for his assessment. His first reaction was anger. "I'm pretty irritated," he told us. "It's the reputation of the company. You know, it's my responsibility as a developer to make a secure system. You can't make security that decides whether or not you fit certain political persuasions. It's a machine. It either works or not." Callas gave special attention to a STRAWHORSE feature that removed and replaced the iPhone's built-in "security daemon," a background process that keeps continuous watch over the operating system. "If you put your own 'securityd' in there, you can do anything," he said.

The STRAWHORSE project, unlike previous attacks on the iPhone, was not designed to "target" its malware in the usual understanding of that word. On the one hand, it did not aspire to mass surveillance. The STRAWHORSE designers had no plan or plausible path to place their malware in Apple's official App Store for download by all the company's registered developers. On the other hand, STRAWHORSE could not be called a discriminate weapon. Its purpose was to infect in-house developers employed by organizations, agencies, and companies whose software might be used by an NSA surveillance target. In-house developers typically work for large companies. It was inherent in the STRAWHORSE design that it could compromise hundreds or thousands of iPhones in order to reach one or two. The malware did not take aim at software developers because they were intelligence targets themselves. It used them as stepping-stones. In order to reach a single iPhone, STRAWHORSE would infect every app on every iPhone that used any software that the developer wrote. Every car in the factory came with a microphone, but the target drove only one.

It was a perfectly rational strategy, and it fit the hacker ethos of circumvention and victory at all cost. If you can't break into one device, try slipping past the perimeter that protects them all. Power up. Beat the game. Deployment of STRAWHORSE in this way would probably comply with U.S. law, no matter how many iPhone owners were needlessly compromised, so long as it took place overseas and focused on a valid foreign intelligence target. Would it be a wise and proportionate use of awesome powers? The people who make those choices in practice, driven to breach barriers and win the game, are not trained to consider such policy questions, nor be attentive to the privacy of bystanders. That is not their culture or their job.

The Snowden files are full of operations like STRAWHORSE, some of them more ambitious still. *The Intercept* reported on another jaw-dropping example. The NSA and GCHQ tunneled jointly into a Netherlands company called Gemalto, which makes the lion's share of SIM chips used in mobile phones around the world, including those sold by Verizon, AT&T, T-Mobile, and Sprint. Each of them is embedded with a unique encryption key for use on the latest LTE mobile networks to safeguard against eavesdropping. The NSA and GCHQ broke into the online accounts of Gemalto engineers and stole tens of millions of those encryption keys. Breaking the encryption itself would have been hard, maybe too hard even for the NSA. Somebody looked at the problem, dreamed up the Gemalto gambit, and thought, "Game over." Now the two intelligence allies can listen in on conversations held on tens of millions of phones.

The game is always evolving. It never really ends. A few months after STRAWHORSE was unveiled at Jamboree, the NSA's elite hackers put out a new call for talent. One of the Rock's offensive teams, code-named POLITERAIN, sent word that it was "looking for interns who want to break things.

"We are tasked to remotely degrade or destroy opponent computers, routers, servers and network enabled devices by attacking the hardware using low-level programming," the classified announcement said. "We are also always open for ideas."

SEVEN

FIRSTFRUITS

You can't tell everybody without telling the bad guys.

—*Edward Snowden to author, December 5, 2013*

L ate that first summer of Snowden, as I made my way through the NSA archive, I came across my own name in the documents. I gawped at the screen and bit back an impulse to swear. The jolt of alarm felt naïve. I knew perfectly well that government agencies prefer not to read their secrets on the front page. Sometimes they resent a story enough to investigate. How in blazes did the reporter find that out? In serious cases maybe the Justice Department steps in. I knew all that, but I had not often felt it personally. Until Snowden upended my professional life, I seldom imagined myself a target of special attention. I put time and thought into protecting people who spoke to me in confidence, but the risks felt abstract. Most of the time I lacked conviction that anybody was watching.

I had skimmed the first page of this document and set it aside in the first tumultuous weeks after receiving the NSA archive. More than two months passed before I returned to the memo and noticed my name on page seven. Why the discovery took so long is hard to explain. I am not above a vanity check for Gellman, Barton, in the index of a book. (Did the author mention my work? Why not?) A few keystrokes would have found me in the Snowden materials, but I did not make the search. The idea seemed melodramatic.

The document that proved me wrong was more than a decade old, a TOP SECRET//COMINT//ORCON//NOFORN memorandum for the attorney general of the United States about "unauthorized disclosures . . . of high-level concern to U.S. policy makers." Three of my stories, the memo said, had been referred to the Justice Department for criminal investigation in early 1999. A sensation of exposure crawled up my spine. The FBI had been put on the case. I had no inkling at the time. How much did the bureau find out? The memo did not say. No harm, as far as I knew, had come to my sources, but I realized that in some cases I could not really say. It had been a long time.

An intriguing file name, "Denial and Deception—Ashcroft.doc," had attracted my attention to this document. John Ashcroft was attorney general under President George W. Bush when al Qaeda killed 2,996 people in the attacks of September 11, 2001. In preparation for the coming war with Osama bin Laden, the Justice Department launched a task force to deter the leak of classified secrets. The NSA was eager to take part. "We are aware that your Committee is interested in unauthorized disclosures that may have affected intelligence operations," said a nine-page memo for Ashcroft from NSA director Michael V. Hayden near the end of that year. The memo, an undated draft, nominated forty-nine recent stories with "disclosures that we deem especially egregious, and in apparent violation of federal criminal laws."

I was in good journalistic company: other bylines on the list included *New York Times* correspondents James Risen and Don Van Natta Jr., *Washington Post* reporters Doug Farah, Steve Mufson, Thomas Lippman, and Kathy Sawyer, and the *New Yorker*'s Seymour Hersh. The roster could have been a lot longer. It is not easy to write about diplomacy or war without touching on something classified. And the accounting, I noted, stopped a few weeks after 9/11. Many of us on this list did our deepest digging into national security in the decade that followed. I had to assume that my subsequent work may have come under an FBI microscope more than once.

In the three stories singled out in this memo, I had described an intelligence operation gone wrong in the aftermath of the Gulf War of 1990–91. Back then, Iraq really did have a nuclear weapons development program and an arsenal of biological and chemical munitions. Seven years after the war, United Nations arms inspectors were still finding remnants. The United States accused Baghdad of continuing to hide weapons of mass destruction. Iraqi president Saddam Hussein accused Washington of packing the UN Special Commission, or UNSCOM, with American spies. Both claims turned out to be true, my stories revealed. The U.S. government was using inspections as cover for straight-up espionage. The NSA, with CIA help, placed cleverly concealed microwave antennas inside UN facilities around Iraq, enabling the agency to listen to conversations inside the Baghdad government. UNSCOM, unbeknownst to its own personnel, had become the Trojan horse that Saddam always alleged. Technically ingenious, the U.S. operation produced a diplomatic debacle. As word of the surveillance began to circulate inside the UN Secretariat, weeks before I published my stories, UNSCOM lost the last of its political support as a neutral disarmament authority. By the end of 1999 the Security Council disbanded it.

According to the NSA "compromise assessment report," my reporting

disclosed the basic concept for a highly classified NSA collection system, as well as Iraqi diplomatic communications. This communications system was inactive prior to the disclosure, and no

efforts were made to regain access due to the increased risk following the media disclosure. A report of this disclosure was made
to the Department of Justice.

The most intriguing part of the memo was the framing of the harm
that the NSA ascribed to my stories. The harm fell into a category
called denial and deception. That is a counterintelligence term of art
for keeping valuable secrets away from prying eyes. The lessons of
history, the NSA wrote, suggest that "press leaks could result in our
adversaries implementing Denial and Deception (D&D) practices." If
adversaries know how the United States spies on them, in other words,
they can do a better job of covering their tracks. That is a legitimate
concern, but there is a flip side. Good journalism sometimes exposes
deception by the U.S. government itself—not only in tradecraft but
also in matters of basic policy and principle. The Clinton administration publicly defended UNSCOM's impartiality even as it turned the
inspectors into unwitting spies. My coverage of the ensuing meltdown
revealed the strategic price of subverting an international mission for
tactical gain. Exposure of this betrayal on the American side, from the
NSA's point of view, constituted a crime.

A whole folder in the Snowden archive was devoted to denial and
deception. It was not about foreign spies. The counterintelligence adversaries in these documents were journalists and the people who gave
us information. The memos and slide decks laid out the grave dangers
posed by news reporting in theory and practice. They also sketched
the beginnings of a plan to do something about it. National security
was a playing field on which the government was at the peak of its
advantage over journalists. U.S. elected and appointed officials held
more power here than on any other subject to prevent, discourage,
shape, and punish unwelcome disclosures. And when it came to the
Snowden story my own government might not be the most serious

threat. My reporting took place in a perilous environment, and I never had the luxury of forgetting that.

Every file in the "denial and deception" folder mentioned a cryptonym. None defined the term fully, but it seemed to be the cover name for an effort to track and trace journalistic leaks.

FIRSTFRUITS. I had heard that name before. I had thought it a myth.

B y the way," I told Snowden a few days later in a live chat, feigning nonchalance, "my name is in the file." I noted the reference to FIRSTFRUITS. He did not know what it meant.

"Maybe you should FOIA yourself and reference the program," he typed back. "Just for the delicious pages of black bars."

"Doing that. I can make street art of the redactions."

We were sharing a nerdy little joke. It was not likely that I would learn more about FIRSTFRUITS by asking nicely in a Freedom of Information Act request.

Sure enough, when the FOIA results came in, years later, the interesting ones mostly looked like the example I reproduce on page 226, an exchange among senior White House, Justice Department, and DNI officials.

Banter with Snowden, regardless of subject, came as a relief to me. It was our first contact in months. Snowden had stopped speaking to me after I wrote a newspaper profile about him in June. I deserved some of his ire. When my story referred to his alias, Verax, I inadvertently exposed an online handle that he was still using. The next day he vanished from the hidden server where we met for live chat. I had no other way to reach him.

When I logged in on August 24, 2013, and finally found him in our old meeting place, he had a new anonymous handle that he chose as a

----- Original Message -----
From: robert.litt@dni.gov <robert.litt@dni.gov>
To: (b)(3)
(b)(3)   Weissmann, Andrew;
Caitlin_M_Hayden (b)(6)   <Caitlin_M_Hayden (b)(6)   >;
Christopher_C_Fonzone (b)(6)
<Christopher_C_Fonzone (b)(6)   >; Avril_D_Haines (b)(6)
<Avril_D_Haines (b)(6)   >; Cole, James (ODAG) (JMD); Anderson,
Trisha (ODAG) (JMD); Carlin, John (NSD) (JMD); Wiegmann, Brad (NSD)
(JMD); (b)(3)
(b)(3)
Cc: (b)(3)
(b)(3)

Sent: Thu Jun 13 19:43:28 2013
Subject: FW: Two new stories

(b)(3); (b)(5)

rebuke—something akin to "Bart sucks," but subtler. I let it pass without comment. I was northbound on an Amtrak train from Washington when Snowden popped up on my screen. My encrypted link to the server cut in and out, but I had to keep him talking. There were so many more questions to ask. I could not afford a permanent breach between us.

"Thanks for coming back," I wrote. "Blowing the handle was really stupid."

"I don't care about apologies. What do you want?"

Where to start? I wanted a lot of things. One was an invitation to visit Snowden in Russia. I had said no, reluctantly, to the Hong Kong trip until after the PRISM story was published, by which time it was too late. After all this time I had yet to meet the man or hear him speak to me. It would be some kind of compensation if I could be the first reporter to interview him in Moscow. Snowden had been stranded there since June 23, when he tried to change planes at Sheremetyevo

International Airport en route to Latin America and discovered that his passport no longer worked. The State Department had revoked it with exquisitely bad timing, hoping to keep him in Hong Kong to face extradition but in fact ensuring that he remained in one of the least accessible places to American law. It was a calculated risk, a high-ranking Justice Department official told me. "Bob Mueller was near the end of his term," the official said, referring to the FBI director. "He wanted him bad." Russia held Snowden in the airport's transit zone for thirty-nine days before granting him temporary asylum on August 1. Now, just over three weeks later, it looked as though Snowden would be parked in Moscow indefinitely. Scores of reporters were looking for him. He had spoken to none of them.

I did not bring up a Moscow trip, not yet. We needed a bit of reporter-source relationship repair. Never inclined to small talk, Snowden wanted to know where my reporting would bring me next.

"My next story, already first-drafted, is on the black budget," I wrote, referring to the government's classified spending plans for intelligence programs.

"That's not going to get you invited to any Christmas parties."

"No. They're really mobilizing on this."

Three days earlier I had driven with my *Washington Post* coauthor, Greg Miller, to Liberty Crossing in northern Virginia, a high-security campus of the Office of the Director of National Intelligence. The director's office, we were told, had assembled stakeholders from across the seventeen intelligence agencies and offices to discuss our pending stories. The black budget spanned thousands of pages and enumerated $53 billion of classified spending, which made for a lot of stakeholders. A shell-shocked public affairs officer met us at the gate, fresh from a chaotic premeeting full of raised voices and swearing, as we learned later. "These guys are coming in hot," he warned us quietly. We found our way to a small raised dais at the front of a simmering auditorium.

Bob Litt, the chief intelligence lawyer, was apparently supposed to moderate this encounter, but he was running late. With no one in charge, Greg and I cleared our throats and opened the meeting with a summary of the story we planned to publish. Two dozen intelligence officers and analysts, among them only one with a name, asked hostile questions and tried to pierce us with laser beams shot from their eyes. What gives you the right to do this? someone asked. What makes you think this is okay? Greg displayed impressive composure, but we never did get to ask any questions ourselves. Litt finally turned up and said, speaking as much to the rest of the room as to Greg and me, something very much like what he regularly told us on the phone: "For the record, not only are we not giving feedback or guidance or affirmation, we are also not acquiescing or implying any acquiescence to the publishing of any classified information you may or may not have."

"What was that supposed to be?" I asked Greg when the meeting petered out and we escaped to the parking lot. He had done plenty of consultations as a *Post* intelligence reporter, he said later, "but nothing like this." I did not believe this convocation had been staged to intimidate us. It had been too much of a hot mess to call it staged at all. Few of those men and women, I guessed, had likely interacted with a reporter before. They were afraid of what we might publish and baffled that the decision was in our hands. "True disbelief that there was no way to just stop us," Miller recalled afterward.

Several days later, Air Force general James Clapper, the director of national intelligence, asked for a meeting with Marty Baron and Cameron Barr, the *Post* executive editor and national editor.

"He was dour," Baron told the newsroom team, just after returning. "Barely said hi. He said he understands there are two kinds of media, responsible and irresponsible, and—"

"He hates them both," Barr cut in, barely half joking.

"—he places us for the moment in the 'responsible' camp," Baron said.

Clapper had four top-priority requests to keep information under wraps, Baron reported. We talked them through and agreed that they were all reasonable. One request had to do with contingency plans in case a certain very bad thing happened overseas, and if we mentioned the existence of those plans they would be less likely to work. Some of the other requests were not as obvious, but persuasive when explained. Our small newsroom group also finalized a short list of summary budget tables that we would publish, a tiny fraction of the seven thousand pages we possessed in four thick volumes.

"Truth is I think there are genuine secrets there," I told Snowden. "I wouldn't advocate posting the thing. But there's a lot in there that's legit debate and we'll post some charts and tables etc."

"Yes. Just stick to the ground rules: public interest, no harm."

So much easier said than done. What counts as "harm" or "public interest," exactly? How could I discern their weight and compare them? Why should anyone trust the likes of me, or the *Post*, to make that choice? And once I decided that something was harmful, did it become my job, affirmatively, to protect the secret? I had secrets of my own: confidential sources, sensitive notes, future reporting targets. How could I keep them safe from sophisticated thieves? Whom was I even up against? Journalism used to feel a lot simpler.

I wiped off the television makeup, unclipped my lapel microphone, and emerged into a pleasant summer Sunday outside the CBS News studio in Georgetown. The Snowden story was less than two weeks old, and I had just come off a live broadcast of *Face the Nation*. In the back of a cab I pulled out my iPad. The display powered on, then dissolved into static and guttered out. Huh? A few seconds passed and the screen lighted up again. White text began to scroll across an all-black background. The text moved too fast for me to take it all in, but I caught a few fragments.

```
# root:xnu . . .
# dumping kernel . . .
# patching file system . . .
```

Wait, what? It looked like a Unix Terminal window. The word "root" and the hashtag symbol meant that somehow the device had been placed in super-user mode. Someone had taken control of my iPad, blasting through Apple's security restrictions and acquiring the power to rewrite anything that the operating system could touch. Panic fought my reporter's instinct to take notes. I fumbled for pen and paper, dropping the tablet on the seat next to me as if it were something contagious. I had a senseless impulse to toss it out the window. I must have been mumbling exclamations out loud, because the driver asked me in some alarm what was wrong. I ignored him and mashed the power button, no longer interested in finding out what would come next. I had no secrets on the iPad, but watching it turn against me was remarkably unsettling. This sleek little slab of glass and aluminum featured a microphone, cameras on front and back, and a whole array of internal sensors. An exemplary spy device.

I took a quick mental inventory. No, I had not used the iPad to log in to my online accounts. No, I kept no sensitive notes on there. No notes at all, in fact. None of that protected me as much as I wished to believe. For one thing, this was not a novice's hacking attempt. Breaking into an iPad remotely, without a wired connection, required scarce and perishable tools. Apple closes holes in its software as fast as it finds them. New vulnerabilities are in high demand by sophisticated criminals and intelligence agencies. Shadowy private brokers pay million-dollar bounties for software exploits of the kind I had just seen in action. Someone had devoted resources to the project of breaking into my machine. I did not want to be worth that kind of expenditure. I did not understand how my adversary even found the iPad. My Apple account did not use a public email address. If intruders had located this device, I had to assume that they could find my phone, too, as well as any computer I used on the internet. One thing I knew for sure: I was not meant to see the iPad do what it had just done. But for good luck, it could have happened while I slept. If the exploit worked as intended, I never would have known. The iPad would have worked normally, on the surface. It would not have been working for me.

This was the first significant intrusion into my digital life—that I knew of. It was far from the last. Working on the NSA surveillance beat exposed me to a steady stream of evidence that I faced aggressive foes.

In the last days of 2013, NSA whistleblower Tom Drake told me he had received an invitation from one of my email addresses to join me for a chat in Google Hangouts. It looked exactly like an authentic notice from Google, but Drake had the presence of mind to check whether the invitation really came from me. It did not. Somebody wanted Drake to talk to an impostor posing as me. A similar scam in mirror image caught me with my guard down. I wrote a pair of confidential messages to Tom Lowenthal, a computer scientist who sometimes advised me on security, and he wrote back to say, "I have two emails from you that I can't read because they're sent to an imposter key." Someone had placed the fake encryption key on a public directory known as a keyserver, and I had foolishly used it without checking. The impostor could read my encrypted email, but Lowenthal could not. Fake keys for "Barton Gellman," likewise, began appearing on public keyservers. Anyone who used them would be sending confidential messages to somebody else.

In early 2014, Google started refusing my login credentials on two accounts, one of them personal and one associated with my position as senior fellow at the Century Foundation. An error message popped up in my mail client: "Too many simultaneous connections." I looked under the hood and found that most of the connections came from IP addresses I did not recognize. On the Gmail web page, a pink alert bar appeared at the top: "Warning: We believe state-sponsored attackers may be attempting to compromise your account or computer. Protect yourself now."

By policy, Google will not tell a targeted user more than that. Which state sponsor? That would be nice to know. Google, fearing evasion of its security protocols, will not say. I did some further reporting and learned from confidential sources the following month that the would-be intruder in my accounts was Turkey's national intelligence service, the Millî İstihbarat Teşkilatı. I did not use email for confidential work either, but I took this as terrible news. There had to be a dozen foreign agencies with greater motive and wherewithal to go after the NSA documents, beginning with Russia, China, Israel, North Korea, and Iran. If Turkey was trying to hack me, too, the threat landscape was more crowded than I hoped. Some of the hackers were probably better than Turkey's, maybe too good to be snared by Google's defenses. Not encouraging.

The MacBook Air I used for everyday computing seemed a likely target. I sent a forensic image of its working memory to a leading expert on the security of the Macintosh operating system. He found unexpected daemons running on my machine, serving functions he could not ascertain. (A daemon is ordinarily benign, but the satanic flavor of the term seemed fitting here.) I decided to abandon the laptop. Some software exploits burrow in and make themselves very hard to remove, even if you wipe and reinstall the operating system. Ed Felten at Princeton told me he would assign his security engineering class a project: how can Bart transfer old files to a new machine without transferring any infection? He changed his mind, he said, because he came to believe the task could not be reasonably accomplished.

For my next laptop, I placed an anonymous order through the university, where I held a fellowship. I used two cutouts for the purchase, with my name nowhere mentioned on the paperwork, and I took care not to discuss the transaction by email. I thought all this might reduce the risk of tampering in transit, a technique used by the NSA, FBI, and foreign intelligence services alike. No need to hack into a machine if it comes preinfected. The new laptop, a MacBook Pro, began to experience cascading hardware failures, beginning with a keyboard that lagged behind what I typed, even with a virgin operating system. I never learned whether something untoward was at work, but the problems were beyond unusual.

I brought the balky machine for repair at Tekserve, a New York City institution that at the time was the largest independent Apple service provider in the United States. I had been doing business there since a couple of years after Tekserve set up shop in a Flatiron warehouse space in 1987. I liked the quirky vibe of the place, with a porch swing hung indoors and an ancient Coke machine that once charged a nickel a bottle. For my purposes, the most pertinent fact about Tekserve was that Service Manager Debra Travis allowed me to stand with a senior technician on the repair floor as he worked on my machine. I preferred not to let it out of my sight.

The technician, an affable guy named Anthony, tested and swapped out, seriatim, the keyboard, the logic board, the input/output board, and finally, still baffled, the power interface. After three visits, the problem remained unsolved. Typing keystrokes would produce nothing at first, then a burst of characters after a long delay. Tekserve consulted with supervisors at Apple. Nobody could explain it. I asked Anthony gingerly if he saw anything on the circuit boards that should not be there, and he said he was not equipped to detect spy gear like that. "All I know is I've replaced every single part in the machine," he told me. "We've never seen this kind of behavior before." I gave up and got another one.

I was still using a BlackBerry smartphone when the Snowden story broke. I began to receive apparently empty text messages and emails that appeared to have no content and no return address. The ghostly emails showed time stamps of midnight on January 1, 1970, which marks the beginning of time as far as Unix computers are concerned. Texts and emails without visible text are commonly used to transmit malicious payloads. I got rid of the BlackBerry and bought an iPhone, which experts told me was the most secure mobile device available to the general public. I do not do sensitive business on a smartphone, but I did not like the sense of being watched.

From time to time, I received genuine-looking emails from Michael Hayden, the former NSA director, and Attorney General Eric Holder. Each of them included a web link, which I did not click. Hayden and Holder did not actually send those emails, but the unpublished personal addresses for the two men were valid. That piqued my attention briefly, but I decided they had fallen victim themselves to a run-of-the-mill phishing attack. Most likely they had unknowingly sent the link to everyone in their address books. Memo to senior officials: close your AOL account. The security is awful.

In January 2014, I became an early adopter of SecureDrop, an anonymous, encrypted communications system for sources and journalists. It is still the safest way to reach me in confidence if you have reason for concern about repercussions. (My Twitter profile @bartongellman points to a page to get you started.) SecureDrop, which requires no technical knowledge to use, had been introduced the previous year as a newsroom tool by the Freedom of the Press Foundation, based on code written by Aaron Swartz, Kevin Poulsen, and James Dolan.

Having advertised a way to get in touch anonymously, I expected to receive malware as well as submissions from internet trolls and conspiracy theorists. I got my share of all of those, alongside valuable reporting tips. Most of the malware was run of the mill. Someone would send a standard phishing link, hoping to steal my online credentials, or a ransomware package that, if I clicked the wrong thing, would lock up my files and demand payment to unlock them. I do not, ever, run executable files or scripts that arrive by email, so these were not a big concern.

One day, however, a more interesting exploit showed up. The sender tried to make it attractive, disguising the file as a leaked presentation on surveillance. I asked Morgan Marquis-Boire, a security researcher then affiliated with the Toronto-based Citizen Lab, if he would care to have a look. "You've got a juicy one," he wrote back.

Most hacking attempts are conducted at scale. The same malicious package is sent to thousands of people at a time, or millions, as email attachments or links to infected websites. This one was customized for me. It was a class of malware known as a remote access trojan, or RAT, capable of monitoring keystrokes, capturing screenshots, recording audio and video, and exfiltrating any file on my computer. "Piss off any Russians lately?" Marquis-Boire asked me. Attribution is an imperfect art, but he had reason to ask. For one thing, the RAT was designed to link my computer to a command and control server hosted by Corbina Telecom on Kozhevnicheskiy Lane in Moscow. From there, if I had triggered the RAT, a hacker could have watched and interacted with my computer in real time. Other IP addresses called by the malware resolved to Kazakhstan. And internal evidence suggested that the coder was a native speaker of Azeri, the language of Azerbaijan and the Russian republic of Dagestan. The RAT had an interesting self-defense mechanism. The moment Marquis-Boire probed for more information, revealing an effort to trace the source, the command and control server disappeared from the internet.

———————

Now and then, outsiders merely asked that I hand over sensitive documents from the archive. "Dear Mr. Barton Gellman," came an email from a mail server in Russia, "I'd like to know could you send me original document of 'Black budget' for scientific purpose. Wait for your reply. Best wishes, Yaroslav Afanasiev." I cannot say whether this was the fellow's real name or what his affiliation might have been. I asked, out of curiosity. He did not reply.

Overtures of another kind came to my friend and colleague Ashkan Soltani soon after his byline appeared alongside mine in the *Washington Post*. Soltani was young and single and a regular user of the dating service OkCupid. Normally, as usually is the case for men, Soltani initiated contact with women on the site. "Within the span of a week, three hot, really attractive women messaged me out of the blue," Soltani later told me over beers at a downtown New York City pub. OkCupid is for relationship seekers more than quick hookups—"you're more than just a photo," the site tells its members—but two of the women made their intentions known before they even met Soltani face-to-face.

Soltani pulled out screenshots of their messages, which he had saved: "excuse my brazen demeanor but i find you incredibley cute and interesting," one of them wrote. "let's meet up?"

Then, on the day they set, she proposed to get together at his place: "it's gloomy out. makes me want to cuddle," she wrote.

"She was the one who wanted to hook up, like straight away," Soltani said. "The fact that two girls in a row were making themselves available on the first date, I was like, what the fuck? Am I being, what—there's a word for that—"

"Honey trapped," I said. "I'm glad I wasn't single for this story."

"Yeah, honey trapped. I do okay, but it usually involves going out on a couple dates or whatever. These are the only times that both girls advanced on me on the first night. I don't think I'm a bad-looking guy, but I'm not the kind of guy women message out of the blue and invite me to cuddle."

Soltani suspected an intelligence agency setup—"the Chinese government trying to get up on me" in an effort to elicit information about the NSA documents, or to steal the digital files. The two of us talked through a well-known information security scenario known as the evil maid attack, which relies on brief physical access to a computer to steal its encryption credentials. The Snowden files, as it happened, were at that time locked in a *Washington Post* vault room and kept separate from their keys, but outsiders would not know that. And if Soltani was sufficiently motivated, an attractive spy might assume, anything was possible.

Soon after these interactions, Soltani returned to OkCupid to document them in more detail. He searched for the women who had reached out to him. Their online profiles no longer existed.

Soltani wound up going out with a third woman who reached out to him around the same time, "but for the longest time I would not bring her back to my house," he said. "I wasn't comfortable. I remember that feeling. I would never leave my phone when I went to the bathroom. It's weird to have opsec when you're dating."

Did he have grounds to live this way? He did. Were they valid in any given case? No way to know.

By the time we had this conversation, in the late fall of 2015, Soltani and I had stopped writing stories for the *Post*. I was reporting for this book. Soltani had moved on. He had retired his old laptop, returned an encryption key fob to me, and shed his last connection to classified materials. "When we were wrapping up, it felt really good that I didn't have to carry this burden anymore," he told me. "I mean from the perspective of the duty to protect this stuff. There's still stuff in there that I think should absolutely never see the light of day."

He kicked a question back to me. "You still constantly have to be diligent. You've been doing it for, like, three years. How do you do on vacation?"

Well, about that. Preoccupation with surveillance had distorted my professional and personal lives. I had balked at the main gate of Disney World when I realized I would have to scan a fingerprint and wear a radio-tagged wristband everywhere in the park. Dafna, standing with our seven-year-old son, dared me with her eyes to refuse. I caved, of course. With very specific exceptions, I brought my laptop everywhere I went, even on beach and hiking trips. I refused to set my bag down at coat checks at parties. Precautions for my electronics inconvenienced my friends and embarrassed my family. "You're moving further and further into a world that I'm not a part of, and that I don't understand, and I don't want to be a part of," Dafna told me one night. I had not come to terms, until that moment, with how abnormal my behavior had become. I was absorbed with risk, and I never felt safe enough.

In the back of my mind was an episode of involuntary entanglement in the intelligence world. In December 2003 I had been traveling in Iraq, interviewing weapons scientists and engineers to reconstruct their history with WMD. One day I paid a call at the University of Baghdad campus, looking for a biologist accused by American officials of working on designer pathogens. My interpreter asked directions, listened to the answer, and then turned to me gravely. It isn't safe for you here, he said. Another man had been to campus before me, identifying himself as "Barton Gellman," and asking questions as though he were a reporter. Either that man was from the CIA, my interpreter said, passing along what he heard, or you are. U.S. intelligence policy discourages the use of journalistic cover, but there is a loophole for "extraordinary circumstances." When I confronted a CIA spokesman, he could not give me a categorical answer on whether the agency had made an exception here. The impostor, of course, could have come from anywhere.

I built ever-thicker walls of electronic and physical self-defense, and I had access to world-class expertise, but I had not been formally trained in operational security. Put less gently, I was an amateur playing against professionals. Twice I left my keys in the front door overnight. Once I met a source for a drink and agreed to a second round, then a third, a rarity for me. In the morning I could not find my laptop bag anywhere. Frantically I canvassed the possibilities. The bar had nothing in its lost and found. Could my source have slipped away with the backpack? No chance, I decided. I played and replayed the memory of my exit from the subway the night before. I had nearly missed my stop, and I distinctly remembered the way the bag slapped against my shoulders as I slid through the closing doors. So where had it gone? Fully aware of the irony, I persuaded the superintendent of my apartment building to let me review the lobby camera video. (I hear you, dear reader. Surveillance is good for you.) There I was on the little black-and-white monitor, strolling to the elevator with nothing on my shoulder. I had come home bagless. Finally I remembered the hot slice with mushrooms that I stopped to eat on the short walk home from the subway. I raced out the lobby and around the corner. Humiliated, I found my bag behind the counter at the neighborhood pizza joint.

Other lapses, though rare, continued to mortify. I had firmly requested a separate, locked room at the *Post* for use by the reporters who worked with the Snowden documents. On a subsequent visit, a facilities staff member proudly showed me the new space in a place of honor beside the company president's office. The room had one feature I had specifically asked to avoid: a wall full of windows. If you craned your neck you could catch a glimpse of the Beaux-Arts mansion half a block to the west. The Russian ambassador's residence in Washington. "You have to be kidding me," Ashkan said. Crestfallen, I asked for a change of venue to a windowless space. The *Post* dutifully found one, installed a high-security lock, put a video camera in the hall outside, and brought in a huge safe that must have weighed four hundred pounds.

I acquired a big, heavy safe in New York as well. I will not enumerate every step I took to keep my work secure, but they were many and varied and sometimes self-befuddling. The computers we used for the NSA archive were specially locked down. Ashkan and I cracked open a pair of laptops, removed the wi-fi and Bluetooth hardware, and disconnected the batteries. If a stranger appeared at the door, we merely had to tug on the quick-release power cables to switch off and reencrypt the machines instantly. We stored the laptops in the vault and kept encryption keys on hardware, itself encrypted, that we took away with us each time we left the room, even for bathroom breaks. We sealed the USB ports. I disconnected and locked up the internet router switch in my New York office every night. I dabbed epoxy and glitter on the case-bottom screws of all my machines to help detect tampering in my absence. (The glitter dries in random, unique patterns.) Detection of compromise was as important as prevention, security expert Nicholas Weaver told me, so I experimented with ultraviolet powder on the dial of the New York safe. Photographing dust patterns under a UV flashlight beam turned out to be messy. I kept my notes on multiple encrypted volumes, arranging the files in such a way that I had to type five long passphrases just to start work every day. I hardly ever typed all the passphrases right the first time. I forgot the passphrase to one seldom-used PGP key and lost access to a few of my files forever. I annoyed the hell out of newsroom colleagues who wanted to communicate about the story in anything that resembled a normal way.

At a farewell party for Anne Kornblut, who oversaw the Snowden coverage, my newsroom colleagues put on a skit that purported to depict our story meetings. Reporter Carol Leonnig, playing the role of

Anne, pulled out blindfolds for everyone in the pretend meeting. They had to cover their eyes, she explained, before Bart could speak. Funny and fair, I had to admit. I was a giant pain in the ass.

I never imagined that any single barrier was impassable. My old summer camp bunkmate, Larry Schwalb, who runs a lock and safe company, told me that few commercial vaults take an expert more than twenty minutes to crack by one means or another. Intelligence agencies have whole departments for stealthy circumvention of barriers and seals. Special antennas can read the emanations of a computer monitor through walls. All I could do was layer on defenses and make myself a less appealing target. Less appealing, if I put it honestly, than other journalists who possessed the Snowden files. Greenwald, I knew from his colleagues, took fewer precautions than I did, at least for the first several months. One colleague went to visit him and reported that he had no password on his home wi-fi router. That was not an especially honorable way to think about my problem, but it did occur to me. I did not want any theft of the files en masse to be my fault. In any case, if I could not stop a supervillain I could stop the average burglar and maybe some of the more capable ones. I had an obligation to try. I layered on so many defenses that navigating through them became a chronic drain on my time, mental energy, and emotional equilibrium.

Richard Ledgett, who oversaw the NSA's media leaks task force and went on to become the agency's deputy director, told me matter-of-factly, years later, to assume that my defenses were breached. "My take is, whatever you guys had was pretty immediately in the hands of any foreign intelligence service that wanted it," he said over lunch in suburban Maryland. "Whether it was Russians, Chinese, French, the Israelis, the Brits. Between you, Poitras, and Greenwald, pretty sure you guys can't stand up to a full-fledged nation-state attempt to exploit your IT. To include not just remote stuff, but hands on, sneak-into-your-house-at-night kind of stuff. That's my guess. I don't have any specific information on that." In reference to Russia and China, he added, "I'm sure there's a nice dossier on you in both countries, as one of his three principal interlocutors."

I asked: Weren't you watching? Or wasn't the FBI? Did you not keep an eye out for foreign spies on the hunt against American reporters? I did not much like the idea, but I realized as we spoke that I made that assumption.

"No. That would be reverse targeting," he said—unlawful surveillance of an American in the guise of watching foreigners. That was true as a legal matter, but only if there had been no judicial warrant. Proof or not, Ledgett said he saw little room for doubt.

"If some of those services want you, they're going to get you. As an individual person, you're not going to be able to do much about that."

Neil MacBride, the U.S. attorney for the Eastern District of Virginia, spotted me from the far side of a long gallery. We were bound to cross paths at this conference. Both of us were on the speakers list. Would he approach? He would. MacBride held my gaze for a beat, then ambled across the room. It felt like a metaphor. He wanted me to see him coming. MacBride was the lead prosecutor in *United States v. Edward J. Snowden.* Thus far, he had charged my source with theft of government property and two counts of espionage. Snowden, MacBride alleged, had given "classified communications intelligence information" to an unauthorized person or persons. The names of those persons were held under seal, but mine had to be one of them. The other two, Poitras and Greenwald, remained overseas on advice of counsel. If the government wanted to tag someone, I was in easy reach.

MacBride had made himself notorious in my line of work. By then he had spent the better part of three years trying to jail James Risen of the *New York Times* for refusing to testify against his source in another classified leak. Risen had recently lost his final appeal. "It's nothing personal, only business," MacBride had told me years before, when I accused him of excessive zeal against Risen. The way I heard it, Mac-Bride used that line from *The Godfather* with every new prosecutor in his office. Assistant U.S. attorneys came in two types, he would say, like the brothers in the film. Sonny Corleone's hot head got him killed. MacBride preferred Michael, the thinking man's assassin.

If I faced legal trouble, the *Post* lawyers said, it would probably look a lot like Risen's. A federal grand jury would command me to present myself and my notes in Alexandria, Virginia. Nothing good would come of it when I declined. MacBride's office, according to subsequent news accounts, had also monitored Risen's email and telephone conversations and obtained his credit and banking records.

Surely MacBride would not discuss the Snowden case here. For certain I would not. What did he have in mind? MacBride, who is taller than I am, smiled mischievously and stepped close enough that I had to raise my chin.

"I was just wondering if you'd sign my copy of *Angler*," he said. My Cheney book, he meant. He had nothing in his hands.

It seemed only polite to let him deliver the punch line.

"Sure," I said.

"Unfortunately, I forgot to bring it," MacBride deadpanned.

The exchange had nothing but subtext. I wondered what message, exactly, he meant to send. There was no sensible way to ask. (Pro tip for reporters: if your source has been charged with a federal crime, don't chat about the case with his prosecutor.) As best I could guess, MacBride had just reprised the point he made to me years before. *Nothing personal, if we meet in court. Only business.*

Soon after this encounter, NSA director Keith Alexander appeared on a peculiar broadcast produced for the Defense Department's internal television network. I did not understand its import until later. The broadcast, titled "I Spy, No Lie," had an unexpectedly amateurish look. Watching it was almost a voyeuristic experience. Aides and support staff wandered in and out of the frame through the darkened exhibition spaces of the National Cryptologic Museum, adjacent to Fort Meade, after hours. Duct tape and a bright yellow extension cord threaded across the camera shot and underneath Alexander's plain wooden chair. This was a man with a message, too impatient to wait for a professional media relations crew.

Alexander did his best to look and sound casual. He wore his four stars on an informal black zipper jacket, his white uniform shirt unbuttoned at the neck. Periodically he would ask the interviewer a rhetorical question, such as "Would that make sense to you?" The screen would fade to large block letters: "Yes sir, it does make sense." Patriotic music played softly in the background. I showed Dafna the interview and she said it looked like a *Saturday Night Live* "Wayne's World" skit set in Pyongyang.

For all the effort at folksy charm, Alexander struggled to master his emotions. Anyone in his position would be troubled by the steady stream of revelations from reporters who possessed the Snowden documents. Alexander appeared to be at his wit's end. Speaking of the journalists, not Snowden, he said, "When people die, those that are responsible for leaking it are the ones that should be held accountable." Alexander saw no legitimate debate to be had about the costs and benefits of NSA surveillance programs. "We're taking this beating in the press because of what these reporters are putting out," he said, but "nobody would ever want us to stop protecting this country against terrorists." By analogy he said the public was not qualified to disagree. "Do you have children?" he asked his interviewer. Would you let them refuse to wear seat belts? The NSA's work was a kind of seat belt, too. "You see, we've learned that lesson on how we take care of our people. These programs help us take care of our people. And we wouldn't stop, we shouldn't stop, doing them."

Alexander complained, as other officials had, that reporters were writing about things we did not understand. "It's absurd," he said. "They get it wrong. . . . The reporters who got this see this data and quickly run to the wrong conclusion." But his more urgent complaint had to do with accurate disclosures. And here came the striking departure: he called for active measures to put a halt to our work.

"What they're doing will do grave harm to our country and our allies," Alexander said. "So we gotta figure out how to fix that. . . . I think it's wrong that newspaper reporters have all these documents, fifty thousand or whatever they have, and are selling them and giving them out as if these—you know it just doesn't make sense. We ought to come up with a way of stopping it. I don't know how to do that, that's more of the courts and the policymakers, but from my perspective it's wrong. And to allow this to go on is wrong."

I did not focus closely enough on these words at the time. *A way of stopping it*. Could Alexander mean that literally? I learned later that he did. In meetings that fall, Alexander asked more than once about staging raids to seize control of unpublished Snowden documents in the hands of Glenn Greenwald, Laura Poitras, and me. He saw no reason for the government to sit back and watch as its precious secrets were spilled. It was only common sense. These were classified documents. Why in heavens should the government not take them back?

Whatever the spy novels may say, this kind of direct action is not within the NSA's bailiwick. If Alexander had prevailed, however, it might have been within the FBI's. I had feared exactly this prospect when I first understood how big and valuable the Snowden archive was. That fear drove me to devise backups that would be hard to find, seize, or destroy. It brought me nearly to tears of relief when Marty Baron agreed to safeguard a copy at the *Washington Post*. The Nixon administration had tried to halt publication of the Pentagon Papers in 1971, an act of prior restraint that the Supreme Court rejected, but even Richard Nixon did not dispatch the FBI to toss a newsroom.

Alexander did not get his way. "He was just expressing frustration," his deputy, Ledgett, told me four years later. "The director of NSA doesn't make policy." Under President Trump, he said, "I couldn't predict what this administration would do. With the previous administration that was never going to go anywhere."

Shawn Turner, who worked for Clapper, recalled later that he had this conversation repeatedly with senior program managers at the NSA. Each time a reporter prepared to reveal something new, "I'd have to go to these people and say, 'Your program is next,'" Turner recalled. "Those people got angry. They couldn't understand why we wouldn't do more. It's government property. We know where it is. Why can't we go and get it back?"

Shortly after the Alexander video came a more official harbinger of legal jeopardy. On January 29, Clapper sat down at a Senate witness table to deliver the annual assessment of worldwide threats, his most extensive public testimony of the year. This was a tour of the horizon that covered the gravest dangers facing the United States. He did not open his remarks with terrorism or nuclear proliferation or Russia or China. He opened with Ed Snowden, and within a few words he was quoting one of my stories.

> Snowden claims that he's won and that his mission is accomplished. If that is so, I call on him and his accomplices to facilitate the return of the remaining stolen documents that have not yet been exposed, to prevent even more damage to U.S. security.

I pretty much stopped listening after the word "accomplices." This was not an off-the-cuff remark. It was prepared testimony on behalf of the Obama administration, vetted for weeks across multiple departments, including the Department of Justice. And "accomplice" has a meaning in criminal law.

"I had in mind Glenn Greenwald or Laura Poitras," Clapper told me years later, unrepentant, as the remains of his egg white omelet were cleared from the table. "They conspired with him, they helped him in protecting his security and disseminating selectively what he had, so to me they are coconspirators."

"I wouldn't distinguish myself categorically from them," I replied.

"Well, then, maybe you are, too. This is the whole business about one man's whistleblower is another man's spy."

In a similar vein came remarks by the NSA inspector general, George Ellard. Twice in February 2014, both times as I sat within his sight, Ellard referred to journalists on the story as Snowden's "agents." We had done more damage, he said at a Georgetown University conference, than the notorious FBI traitor Robert Hanssen, who helped Soviet security services hunt down and kill U.S. intelligence assets. Tight-lipped and curt, he walked away when someone introduced us after the panel. When we finally spoke nearly two years later, he said, "I must confess I read your work with keen interest."

Did Clapper agree with Alexander's idea?

"I understand what Keith was saying," Clapper told me in late 2018, after retiring as director of national intelligence, publishing a book, and coming under sustained rhetorical assault from President Trump. "I understand why he would say it. Certainly at the time, when I was DNI, if there was some way we could have recovered what [Snowden] stole, I'd have been all for it. I have great reservations about that now, now that I'm part of the 'fake media.' I might have felt differently about it when I was in the government." Still, there were practical impediments. The documents were in Germany with Poitras, in Brazil with Greenwald, and doubtless hidden online. "I don't recall that [the idea] went anywhere," Clapper said.

The NSA's general counsel, Raj De, told Alexander to forget about taking the Snowden documents back, people told me later. The First Amendment protected me and the other journalists, De said, however unfortunate the effects of our work. But that was not really right, not altogether. American political culture and governing norms, not the letter of the law, were the real protection.

Copies of the Snowden documents were arguably evidence in a criminal case. They were arguably contraband as well, illegal to possess, and therefore subject to search and seizure. More significant, perhaps, they were alleged to be the fruits of espionage. The latter, I thought, might have allowed the invocation of counterintelligence tools, including secret physical and electronic searches under the Foreign Intelligence Surveillance Act. It was impossible to know for sure, because the Justice Department's policy on these things was itself classified. After a FOIA lawsuit, the FBI was obliged to release a redacted copy of its Domestic Investigations and Operations Guide. The section called "National Security Letters for Telephone Toll Records of Members of the News Media or News Organizations" was entirely blacked out, as were several pages on use of secret FISA warrants against reporters. *The Intercept* later published a leaked copy of the classified Appendix G from the fall of 2013. It said the FBI could use secret administrative subpoenas "to identify confidential news media sources" with approval from the bureau's general counsel, an executive assistant director, and the assistant attorney general in charge of the Justice Department's national security division.

Was I a valid counterintelligence target?

"Well, theoretically you could be," Clapper told me. "Given how Snowden is viewed by the intelligence community, someone who's in league with him, conspiring with him, that's a valid counterintelligence—and for that matter law enforcement—target. That's from the perspective of the intelligence community."

The FBI had the same view, as a strictly legal matter. I asked James Comey, after Donald Trump fired him as FBI director, whether the bureau could have tried to seize my notes and reporting materials.

"I think you could," he said. "Yeah, sure, you legally could. There was zero chance of that with Barack Obama as president and Eric Holder as attorney general, but I could imagine with Trump and Jeff Sessions at least exploring a search at a journalist's premises, or following a journalist" to discover his confidential sources. On the other hand, Comey said, "that would be such a departure from the norms that they'd run a tremendous risk of a leak about that.

"They could say, 'We're searching for evidence of a crime, so we should be able to get a search warrant to recover this, just like we could if it was in a storage locker.' It's in the journalist's computer. Technically you could, but . . . that would eventually become public and the world would be on fire. It's the norms, practices, traditions, culture, and external pressure that would be brought to bear by the journalists. Not just journalists but by the community."

Asked about Alexander's proposal specifically, Comey paused for some time.

"I was at the dovish end because I knew you," he said finally, "but I get it. That antagonism was real. You should have been paranoid because there were people out to get you."

It became a running joke among U.S. officials that Gellman should watch his back. In May 2014, I appeared alongside Bob Mueller, Comey's predecessor, to talk about Snowden on a panel hosted by former White House chief of staff and defense secretary Leon Panetta. Mueller cross-examined me: Were the NSA documents not lawfully classified? Were they not stolen? Did I not publish them anyway? I held out my arms toward him, wrists together, as if for handcuffs. The audience laughed. Mueller did not. I ran into Mueller again later that year in the dining room of a Saratoga Springs, New York, bed-and-breakfast. "There you are!" he boomed at me, all alpha male, as he pushed aside his plate. "We were just talking about that event we had out at the Panetta Institute."

"Hello, Director," I said.

"Are you surveilling me?" he asked, then walked out the door.

How exactly does one pack to visit a fugitive under asylum in Vladimir Putin's Russia? As I planned my first visit, I began to approach security experts with thinly veiled questions. Suppose a reporter travels to Moscow, hypothetically. No special reason. (Nudge, wink.) He knows better than to carry sensitive notes, let alone U.S. government documents. He will bring a secondhand phone, freshly wiped. An old laptop with a new solid state drive and nothing on it. He will not log in to his online accounts on the road. He'll use disposable everything. What I cannot figure out is this: how can this reporter bring notes and photos and recordings home without exposing them to either government at the borders?

There was not much I could do about Russian physical surveillance or eavesdropping when Snowden and I met. Their turf, their rules, no plausible self-defense. If the Russians wanted to listen in, they would. I would make a pro forma effort, bringing water-soluble paper in case Snowden wanted to pass me a private note, but when the time came Snowden only laughed. "Don't even bother," he told me. "Assume everything here is monitored."

Long negotiations preceded my trip. Snowden saw no need to meet with me or any journalist after leaving Hong Kong. The documents were the story. Although critics saw him as hungry for fame, and the spotlight did grow on him later, Snowden was truly reluctant to talk about himself. He had given only two interviews: to Poitras and Greenwald for his coming-out video and to a Hong Kong–based reporter as his local lawyer tried to stave off extradition. Hundreds of requests were pending from media celebrities around the world. He worried that I would hurt him "in an effort to be centrist." Speaking of himself in the third person, he said, "If you put something damaging in the article, as you have in the past, our friend may not have time to recover before the issue is dead."

"I'm not going to suck up to you," I replied. "I'm not your advocate. But I'm fundamentally interested in the same debate."

When it finally seemed that Snowden would consent to see me, I asked if I could bring him anything. Snowden, who sometimes referred to himself as "source" or "src" to preserve anonymity, said not to bother. "src lives off of ramen and chips, as always. has 400 books (as everyone brings but never has time to read). is an indoor cat, so doesn't need much. . . . something that is not public is src's natural asceticism. he has few needs." I packed a few jars of salsa to go with his chips ("in short supply," he had mentioned), and I framed the fortune from a fortune cookie that Dafna had opened as we finished a meal at our local Chinese standby. "Put the data you have uncovered to beneficial use," the fortune said in little blue letters.

Anatoly Kucherena, a Putin-connected oligarch who had been appointed as Snowden's asylum lawyer in Russia, sent me the invitation I would need for a business visa. I did not especially want to associate with him, and I did not want him knowing my travel plans. Kucherena had a bad habit of tipping off his friends in the Russian media when Snowden's family visited, and I preferred not to be met at the airport, as Lon Snowden had been, by local television crews. I applied for a tourist visa instead and touched down at Moscow's

Sheremetyevo Airport, unmolested by paparazzi, at 10:15 a.m. on December 5, 2013.

"What time exactly does your clock say?" asked the voice on the telephone that afternoon, the first words Snowden ever spoke to me aloud. I glanced at my wrist—3:22 p.m. "Good. Meet me exactly at four. I'll be wearing a backpack." Of course he would. Snowden would not leave his laptop unattended.

The rendezvous point that Snowden selected was a gaudy casino hotel called the Korston Club on Kosygina Street. Enormous flashing whorls of color adorned the exterior in homage to Las Vegas. Inside the lobby, a full-sized grand player piano tinkled with energetic pop. The promenade featured a "Girls Bar" in purple neon decor, with stainless steel chairs and mirrors competing for attention with imitation wood paneling, knockoff Persian rugs, and pulsing strobe lights on twelve-foot plastic foliage. Also, there were feathers. The place looked as though a tornado had knocked down a trailer full of old Madonna stage sets.

As I battled sensory overload, a young man appeared near the player piano, his appearance subtly altered to allow a well-known face to travel unremarked. A minder might be anywhere in this circus of a lobby, but I saw no government escort. We shook hands, thumbs up, shoulder high, and Snowden walked me wordlessly to a back elevator. In phrasebook Russian he was soon ordering room service: a burger, fries, and ice cream. For the next two days, during fourteen hours of interviews, he did not once part the curtains or step outside. He remained a target of surpassing interest to intelligence services of more than one nation. He kept his head down.

Snowden nixed a photographer, who would complicate security, so I brought a good camera. He changed into a pale blue pinstriped shirt and charcoal blazer and fussed with his appearance, preoccupied with moles on either side of his neck—"Frankenstein bolts," he called them,

unfondly. These were the first photos taken of him in Moscow and they became iconic, reproduced thousands of times after I published them in the *Post:* Snowden standing in profile, Snowden in a mirror, Snowden under a gauzy painting of a woman with a white parasol, Snowden staring thoughtfully at an unseen laptop screen, the lid adorned with a bumper sticker that declared, "I Support Online Rights." He insisted on taking my camera's memory card and reviewing every frame before I could use it. I found that irritating but tried to see it his way. These photos and this interview were his reintroduction to the world after six months of silence. His disclosures were still roiling the news. There was no bigger story in the world at the moment, and he was the mystery figure at its heart.

More than half the questions I brought collided with boundaries that Snowden set around his privacy, security, or concept of what my story should be about. What were his living conditions? "Unnecessary question," he said. Supporters in Silicon Valley had donated "enough bitcoins to live on until the fucking sun dies," but he did not want to name any sources of his support. "You know this is off the record, and it has nothing to do with the substance," he said about something else. "You're showing bad faith." Did he talk to his girlfriend? "Don't jerk me around," he said. He missed small things from home, he allowed. Milk shakes. Why not make your own? Snowden refused to confirm or deny possession of a blender. Like all appliances, blenders have an electrical signature when switched on. He believed the U.S. government was trying to discover where he lived. He did not wish to offer clues, electromagnetic or otherwise. "Raising the shields and lowering the target surface," he said, one of his security mantras. He was not wrong about the capability. U.S. intelligence agencies closely studied electrical emissions when scouting Osama bin Laden's hideout in Pakistan.

Snowden restricted the interview, in part, to try to control my story. I kept asking questions.

"You push too hard," he said. "This is not a profile. You should point out that a price has been paid. 'Look at how much this guy lost. He gave up his home, his job, this big salary, his family contact.' But I wouldn't go into the pornographic depths of voyeurism. Just enough to tell the story."

On bathroom breaks, Snowden took his laptop with him, trusting me no more than Ashkan trusted a new girlfriend. "There's a level of paranoia where you go, 'You know what? This could be too much,'" he said when I smiled at the precaution. "But it costs nothing. It's—you get used to it. You adjust your behavior. And if you're reducing risk, why not?"

I replied that I was growing discouraged about my own security.

"I've been trying to imagine that if I could just get good enough at it—" I started to say.

"—that you'd be protected."

"That I'd be protected," I agreed.

"Safe," he said, whispering in mock drama.

"So it appears there is not a purely technical answer."

"What you're forgetting is that while it is discouraging to think that you cannot be completely safe, the fact that I'm walking free today, the fact that I'm still able to communicate with you, it shows that there are cases and there are circumstances where if you do things right, if you do things carefully, you can win. Not because you're invincible but . . . you can literally win. You can beat them."

Gradually, over six hours on that first day and eight hours on the next, Snowden loosened up a bit. He explained for the first time why he had agreed to bring me in on the story the previous spring. "It was important that this not be a radical project," he said, an allusion to the politics of Greenwald and Poitras. "I thought you'd be more serious but less reliable. I put you through a hell of a lot more vetting than everybody else. God, you did screw me, so I didn't vet you enough." That first profile in the newspaper, he meant.

I had expected to find a man embattled and alone, in hiding, possibly full of regret for the life he had lost, disoriented by a language and culture he did not understand. Instead, the indoor cat appeared to be content.

"One of the very interesting things about doing the right thing is you have no trouble sleeping," he said. "You have untroubled nights. It really hasn't been the giant nightmare people assume it would be. For me, in terms of personal satisfaction and accomplishing the mission, the mission's accomplished. I already won. As soon as the journalists were able to work I got everything I wanted. I didn't want to change society. I wanted to give society the opportunity to change itself. I strongly believe in informed consent. As far as I'm concerned that's a milestone we left behind a long time ago."

As for living conditions, for Snowden's purposes, Russia and Hawaii were more alike than different.

"How many hours a day do you think you are online?" I asked.

"All the ones I am awake. It's really difficult to get me to leave the house. I just don't have a lot of needs," he said. "Occasionally there's things to go do, things to go see, people to meet, tasks to accomplish. But it's really got to be goal-oriented, you know. Otherwise, as long as I can sit down and think and write and talk to somebody [online], that's really more about the meaning of life to me than coming out and looking at landmarks. I like learning. I like reading. That makes the internet pretty attractive."

From time to time, I pushed Snowden on mysteries left unresolved in the archive, or between the lines of things he had already told me. One claim in particular from his "README_FIRST" text file, the one that accompanied his first transmission of documents, was very much on my mind. It was a startling assertion about something Snowden said he had done in order to prove that ordinary analysts could gain access to any U.S. communications they liked. It was not a claim I would publish without evidence, and he had provided none.

Here in Moscow in 2013, Snowden demurred. "That would be dead man material," he said elliptically. He was referring, as he had done with me before, to a "dead man's switch," a device or arrangement according to which the most sensitive files in his possession would somehow come to light automatically in circumstances he did not specify. Julian Assange of WikiLeaks had made an explicit arrangement like this in 2011, distributing online an encrypted "insurance file" and threatening to release the decryption key if the U.S. government did anything to harm him or shut down WikiLeaks. Snowden never made this kind of threat himself, but Glenn Greenwald did so in a published interview. "Snowden has enough information to cause more harm to the U.S. government in a single minute than any other person has ever had," Greenwald told the Argentinian daily *La Nación*. "The U.S. government should be on its knees every day begging that nothing happen to Snowden, because if something does happen to him, all the information will be revealed and it could be its worst nightmare."

In private, Snowden dismissed that whole idea as a "stupid revenge narrative." Greenwald was trying to protect Snowden, it appeared, but he was freelancing. Snowden said it would be wildly irrational to arrange things as Greenwald described, because that would "incentivize every foreign intelligence agency to shoot me in the face." Kill Snowden, release the secrets. At the same time, in those early months he did not want to give Washington too much reassurance. "If you categorically deny the existence of a dead man's switch, you take away a cloud of uncertainty that restrains the government's behavior," he said. "They've been much more careful about how they pursue people like Glenn because they're concerned that the alternative is worse."

When I pressed for answers to some kinds of questions, Snowden still resorted to the "dead man" reply. The evidence existed, he said, and it might appear one day, but he no longer had control of the material. He had not brought secret information to Russia, and possessed no decryption key. Maybe some subtler version of the doomsday device existed after all. "I'm not talking about it beyond what's already been stated, but given how much thought appears to have gone into things to this point, I think it would be fair to give our friend credit for considering obvious incentive problems and designing around them," he said. So was there a dead man's switch or not? Were there more documents that might still emerge? Maddening ambiguities like this were an irreducible fact of life with Snowden.

When we broke for the night, I walked into a hotel stairwell and down two floors, where I found an armchair in a deserted hallway. I had a chore to take care of before I returned to my room, where I assumed there would be eyes watching me. I might or might not be under surveillance right now, but this looked like my best chance to work unobserved.

I moved the audio files from the memory card of my voice recorder to an encrypted archive on my laptop, packaging up the notes I had typed as well. I locked the archive in such a way that I could not reopen it without a private key that I had left in a safe place back in New York. I uploaded the encrypted archive to an anonymous server, then another, then a third. Downloading from the servers would require another private key, also stored in New York. Once I was sure that there were redundant copies online, I wiped the encrypted files from my laptop and cut the voice recorder's unencrypted memory card into pieces. Russian authorities would find nothing on my machines. When I reached the U.S. border, where anyone can be searched for any reason, where the warrant requirement of the Fourth Amendment does not apply, I would possess no evidence of this interview. Even under legal compulsion I would be unable to retrieve the recordings and notes in transit. I hoped to God I could retrieve them when I got home.

Since the first round of NSA stories, readers had been asking me to explain what kind of information I held back from publication. After a while I came up with a parable. Imagine that the NSA supplies mind-reading earrings to the mistress of the emperor of Mars. The emperor's Earth invasion plans are discovered and stopped just in time. This is blockbuster stuff, a scoop for the ages. If I told the tale, on the other hand, a sensible reader's response might come in four parts:

Boy, was that a close call.

Didn't know the NSA could do that.

Sure am glad they did that.

Now they can't do it anymore, you son of a bitch, because you went and told the Martians all about it.

(Subsequent reports from the Red Planet describe the mistress's beheading, earrings and all.)

The analysis would have to go deeper than this, of course. Secret mind-reading tech would be a dangerous and controversial thing for the government to acquire. The public would have a strong claim to know about that development, even if I kept quiet about the operation on Mars. But the parable serves its purpose here, I think. It is supposed to be an easy case. Most people can probably agree that it would be wrong to blow the cover of the mistress and her earrings, especially with planetary conquest at stake.

Snowden and I had a conversation in Moscow about drawing lines like this. He brought up two kinds of encrypted communication. The NSA could decrypt one kind but not the other. We spoke of them elliptically, knowing that our conversation might be overheard. I said I would not be writing either of those stories.

"Why?" he asked, more curious than argumentative. He had seldom expressed an opinion about what should be published.

"Because it's—generally speaking, I don't like the idea of pointing to vulnerabilities or blind spots," I said.

"I see your point. You can't tell everybody without telling the bad guys."

"Right. And in the other case you have a particular encryption standard favored by certain parties who pretty much anyone would regard as legitimate foreign intelligence targets, and I know what the capabilities are of the NSA against those, and I'm not the least bit interested in publishing that."

I will not be specific here about the stories I chose not to write, but some of the NSA archive, I strongly believed, should not see the light of day. As I've mentioned, there were photographs of operational personnel in the field. Names of adversaries under surveillance. Particulars of the networks on which they talked. The NSA had acquired precious information that anyone who wished my country well would want the government to know. I did not consider revealing those things, which is not to say I never found hard cases.

Other people, no doubt, would draw the lines differently. "The damage is incalculable by anyone not a professional in the field. Sorry but you do not know what is damaging and what isn't," former NSA chief scientist George Cotter wrote to me. "Your view that the public has a right to know is seriously offset by an author's limited and (regrettably) non-professional judgment." Bill McRaven, Bob Litt, James Clapper—they and many of their peers believed without second thought that I should publish nothing classified, ever, full stop. The proposition seemed obvious to them. Proper authorities drew lines of secrecy, and I should defer to them. Advocates for radical transparency, on the other hand, objected in principle when I held anything back. And plenty of mainstream critics wrote that I should reveal somewhat more than I did—additional details from the black budget, for example, in service of a better-informed public debate on spending priorities.

Criticism from all sides did not mean I got the balance right. I have always thought that a fatuous argument. Logically it could also mean I made the wrong choice every time. Weighing the value of news against potential harms was bound to be a contested exercise. There was no avoiding the responsibility, in my view. Ethical journalists do not publish every secret they learn, but neither can they accept the government's judgment as final.

A lot of people are surprised to hear that we have any choice in the matter. They assume it is illegal to publish classified information, or believe that it should be so. That is not in fact the state of the law. Under prevailing legal practice, a person entrusted with classified information by the government can be charged with espionage for giving that information to someone who lacks such a clearance, even if the recipient is a reporter and not a foreign intelligence service. Reporters, however, have not been held criminally liable for publishing those secrets. The First Amendment is widely thought to prevent such a prosecution, given the central role of freedom of speech and of the press in our constitutional system. No law, for much the same reason, forbids publication of false information (with narrow exceptions such as libel). Likewise, publishing information stolen by someone else does not qualify legally as trafficking in stolen goods.

There was, as the *Post* lawyers had warned me, one catch. The government had never tried to prosecute a journalist or publisher under the Espionage Act of 1917, which is so broadly drafted that it could be read as banning any news story about "national defense information," whether classified or not. No one knew for certain how such a prosecution would fare under First Amendment analysis. In mid-2019, the Trump administration decided to test the question. In an indictment unsealed against Julian Assange, the founder of WikiLeaks, the Justice Department charged him with sixteen counts of espionage, three of them based entirely on his communication of secrets "to all the world by publishing them on the Internet." Whether you wish to call Assange a "journalist" or not, the distinction is not important legally. The elements of the crime alleged against him—disclosure of secret information to the public—are very hard to distinguish from what I did with Snowden's NSA archive, even if I was more selective about it. If Assange is extradited, tried, and convicted for publishing classified information, and if the conviction withstands a constitutional appeal, then the climate for investigative journalism on national security will change pretty starkly. At this writing, that day has yet to come.

By the time the Snowden story arrived I had done a lot of thinking about these questions. My master's thesis at Oxford explored the foundations in democratic theory for a "right to know" in the context of national security. I had twice taught a Princeton class called "Secrecy, Accountability, and the National Security State." Most of my guest speakers—including Mike Levin, a former NSA chief of information security who had once called me a "traitor" on film—agreed by the end of our three-hour seminars that there might be circumstances in which disclosing classified facts would be the right thing to do.

What if the U.S. government deliberately exposed American troops to nuclear radiation in order to learn more about the medical effects? That really happened after World War II. "It is desired that no document be released which refers to experiments with humans and might have adverse effect on public opinion or result in legal suits," wrote the responsible official at the Atomic Energy Commission in 1947, in a memo that remained classified until 1994. "Documents covering such work field should be classified 'secret.'" If reporters had known the truth then, should they have suppressed it?

What if the U.S. government deliberately infected commercial sex workers in Guatemala with gonorrhea and syphilis? That happened, too, in wildly unethical experiments between 1946 and 1948. When the sex workers failed to transmit the diseases quickly enough for scientific purposes, "the research approach changed to direct inoculation of soldiers, prisoners, and mental hospital patients," the government acknowledged in an apology in 2010.

What if a classified military investigation found "numerous incidents of sadistic, blatant, and wanton criminal abuses" against foreign detainees, in violation of the Geneva Conventions and the Uniform Code of Military Justice? That happened at the Abu Ghraib Confinement Facility in 2003. Major General Antonio Taguba's investigation was classified SECRET//NOFORN. Even oversight committees in Congress did not receive an unredacted copy until an unauthorized leak made it public. Much the same sequence of events, with classification stamps employed to conceal information that public officials could not or did not wish to justify, took place after the government tortured al Qaeda suspects in secret prisons, authorized warrantless surveillance of U.S. citizens, and lied about intelligence on weapons of mass destruction in Iraq. These were history-making events, full of political and legal repercussions, but they were hidden from public scrutiny until news stories broke through barriers of classification.

My point here is fairly modest, I think. Classification stamps do not capture the whole of the public interest when the question is whether or not to keep something secret. Even if secrecy served legitimate purposes in these examples, it also thwarted accountability for consequential choices. "Cold War secrecy became a habit," wrote Mary Graham, author of the authoritative history of executive secrecy. "Presidents expanded surveillance in order to catch spies and uncover enemies' secrets. But they also hid their mental or physical illnesses, their ethical lapses, their intrusions into the privacy of ordinary citizens, and their illicit efforts to weaken their political opponents." The Moynihan Commission, the best known of the many bipartisan panels that have studied secrecy since the 1950s, found that the classification system "is used too often to deny the public an understanding of the policymaking process, rather than for the necessary protection of intelligence activities and other highly sensitive matters."

Consider a simple question. How often does the NSA break its own privacy rules? The agency keeps internal statistics of those "compliance incidents." The statistics are classified Confidential, which is supposed to mean that disclosure would damage national security. Why should the mere number, a simple count of the errors, be treated as a state secret? Quite a lot harder to justify: the Justice Department, which prepares a similar compliance report for Congress and the FISA Court, classified exactly the same statistics as TOP SECRET//SI. That had a very practical impact. High-level clearances are rare among members of congressional staffs. Most offices had nobody eligible to read the compliance reports. You might suspect that someone preferred it that way.

Members of Congress often express frustration at their impotence to oversee secret bureaucracies in the executive branch. It is difficult, even with constitutional authority, to induce a person to tell you what you do not know how to ask. "You have to start just spitting off random questions," I once heard Representative Justin Amash say, explaining why Congress failed in its oversight of surveillance. "Does the government have a moon base? Does the government have a talking bear? Does the government have a cyborg army? If you don't know what kind of things the government might have, you just have to guess and it becomes a totally ridiculous game of twenty questions."

Sometimes an official secret is merely trivial, classified by force of habit. Steven Aftergood of the Federation of American Scientists once turned up a Navy laundry and dry cleaning manual that was stamped Secret. In the Snowden documents I found another choice example. Here is a Top Secret, compartmented paragraph in its entirety from a presentation prepared in 2003:

(TS//SI) On 4 November 1979, a mob of Iranian students stormed the U.S. Embassy in Tehran and took the diplomatic staff hostage. The students actions were soon sanctioned by Iran's revolutionary government, and a standoff developed between the United States and Iran over the issue of the 52 captive American diplomats. The standoff lasted for almost two years before the hostages were released in January 1981 (Inauguration day for Ronald Reagan).

Few events in modern history were more thoroughly covered in the news media than the hostage crisis in Iran. Still, someone at the NSA decided—more than twenty years after the fact—that mentioning the episode publicly would do "exceptionally grave damage to national security." That is the legal standard for a Top Secret classification under Executive Order 13526.

These are neither rare, wacky exceptions nor representative samples of the classified universe. There are plenty of legitimate secrets, if by "legitimate" we mean that their disclosure could bring a foreseeably bad result. But not all classified secrets meet that test, and sometimes the workings of cause and effect are hypothetical, conditional, or unclear. Sometimes the asserted harm is controversial. Does it count as harm if disclosure of classified U.S. government conduct offends an ally, provokes a lawsuit, builds pressure for legislation, shrinks the NSA's pool of recruits, or leads a private company to encrypt its email servers? All those things happened after the Snowden disclosures, and any of them may have caused a loss of collection, but if so the result was a feature, not a bug, in the systems that govern us. Diplomacy, law, politics, and free markets worked as intended.

None of this is to dismiss the idea that stories about the Snowden documents, including some of my own, resulted in genuine damage to NSA operations. I do not know the particulars, because damage of that sort would itself be classified, but I refuse to pretend that so many secrets could have spilled without any consequence. "You don't delude yourself, I hope," former NSA analyst Alan Tu told me. "Despite your efforts, you have negatively impacted some valuable work people have done, a lot of work actually. You can say it's the cost of ripping away corrosive lack of transparency in a hostile environment, but you should still know there is a cost to what you have done."

Snowden, in Moscow, resisted any such concession. "People who have the greatest, absolutely greatest incentive to tear down the reporting, to play up the harms, to invent harms as a result of this, aren't doing it," he told me. "They haven't been able to. We have no evidence at all of anything going bad."

When I pushed back, saying that some surveillance targets must have changed behavior, Snowden said I failed to understand that nothing stays the same for long in signals intelligence. The global telecommunications system is the most complicated machine ever built, its physical and virtual structures in constant flux. Facebook adjusts a protocol, Cisco updates its firmware, Mozilla squashes a bug, China upgrades the Great Firewall, someone in Russia replaces a router—any of a million things happen and something in the NSA toolkit no longer works. Every change, Snowden said, brings opportunity, too. "Sources and methods die every day," he said. "And they die for reasons that are completely unrelated to leaks or opsec or anything like that. It is just a natural product of the intelligence process. NSA and the intelligence community are a factory for generating new sources and methods."

Up to a limit, Snowden and Clapper might have agreed on this. Not long before my trip to Moscow, Clapper briefed members of Congress on the fallout from the first several months of Snowden leaks. The intelligence community, he said, had done a retrospective review of contemporary damage assessments after major security breaches. History suggested that early analysis overstated the harm. In the immediate aftermath of a breach, intelligence agencies commonly judged that their programs had been set back by a decade or more. That seldom turned out to be true, especially in signals intelligence, which generally found ways to reacquire its targets. "People must communicate," Clapper said in the closed briefing. "They want to communicate. They will make mistakes, and we will exploit them."

Still, there are significant opportunity costs in the kind of recovery that Clapper was talking about. Money and labor are diverted in large quantities to assess and repair the damage of a security breach like

Snowden's. Nobody can say much for sure about this, but the NSA will also have missed some signals, meanwhile, that it otherwise could have intercepted. There are (sometimes) costs and harms of disclosing secrets, just as there are (sometimes) costs and harms of keeping them from the public.

At heart, national security secrecy presents a conflict of core values: self-government and self-defense. If we do not know what our government is doing, we cannot hold it accountable. If we do know, our enemies know, too. That can be dangerous. That is our predicament. Wartime heightens the case for secrecy because the value of security is at its peak. But secrecy is never more damaging to self-government than in wartime, because making war is the very paradigm of a political choice.

How do we navigate this dilemma, and who gets to hold the rudder? A long list of incompetents comes to mind. Suppose we begin with me. I am not qualified to assess the harm of any given disclosure to national security, and moreover I am not responsible for the outcome. Likewise, the president and his appointees are not qualified to decide what the public needs to know to hold them accountable. I do not mean that they are unskilled in the exercise. I mean that a self-governing people cannot consent in principle for the president to conceal whatever he likes, armored with the power to impose secrecy under penalty of law.

In the American ecosystem of secrets and leaks, we have, broadly speaking, two reciprocally unqualified parties. Neither side has the power to decide alone which secrets will be kept. The government tries to keep its secrets, and usually succeeds. Journalists try to find some of them out. The news may seem to be full of unauthorized disclosures, but leaks are dwarfed by the billions of classified choices made by millions of clearance holders every year. Consequential leaks are edge cases, teaspoons from an ocean of secrecy, and the ecosystem deals with them in a process that combines competition with cooperation. Traditional mainstream media, and many of our newer cousins as well, give respectful hearings to the government when we contemplate publication of something sensitive. We negotiate a middle path, most commonly by mutual consent, however reluctant and tacit the consent may be.

At breakfast with Clapper in 2018, I began to explain the way the *Post* handles such things. I wanted to ask how he assessed the process, but Clapper lost patience before I finished a sentence.

"You know, Bart, this sounds like you're trying to justify to me, four years later, five years later, trying to sell me that you're a responsible journalist," he said, interrupting. "And my point is, that's not a reliable criterion from an intelligence perspective, protecting sources and methods."

"All I want to ask—" I began, but Clapper rolled on, exasperated.

"You put it on us to make a judgment, well, good old Bart Gellman. He'll protect us. Maybe you will. Maybe you won't. Maybe someone else won't."

True, I wanted to say. Sometimes you get a case like the so-called Shadow Brokers leak of 2016, when parties unknown placed online a whole suite of the NSA's most potent software exploits. It was a devastating loss, very likely worse than any damage done by Snowden. Doing damage, and laying the blame on the NSA, appeared to be the whole purpose of the leak. What I was hoping to talk to Clapper about was how the process ought to work when journalists and government make the best available choices.

Clapper rebelled against my claim that consultation was his best-case scenario once a journalist finds something out. But in that event the more reliable mechanisms of information control, as he understands them, have already failed. I was not going to give the Snowden archive back. I was not going to quash every story I found there. But neither did I want to do wanton damage. Most especially I was determined not to step on anything fragile without knowing what I had underfoot. I sometimes disagreed about the balance of public interests in any given disclosure, but I had to know what the government saw as a risk. And there were many times, as the Snowden story developed, when it was possible to remove details that my interlocutors cared about without undercutting the news value of a story.

In one story, for example, I wanted to grant a point to the government by noting that a controversial surveillance program had produced valuable intelligence. Three of the best examples were obvious non-starters: mentioning them would blow ongoing, productive collection against a significant U.S. adversary. Glenn Greenwald and Laura Poitras, who knew about all three of these stories, had decided independently not to publish them either. (I know that only because they did not do so. We did not coordinate on decisions like that.) When Julie Tate, my *Post* research partner, and I worked through a huge pile of intercepts, she noticed that there were four alleged terrorist suspects—all dead by then or in custody—who had been located because of the surveillance tools I wanted to write about. I approached Clapper's office. Was there any reason not to name the four men, now that they were no longer threats at large? The CIA, which took the lead in preparing an answer, asked that our story not mention two of the four. Officials there offered a reason, off the record, that persuasively explained their concern. The *Post* agreed to hold back the two names. We published the other two, and the CIA did not object.

The greatest impediment to these consultations was a catch-22 of the government's own devising. Classified information may only be discussed on secure government communications channels. I held no classified clearance and could not use those channels. The NSA and DNI's office therefore felt bound to insist that we talk about the most hair-raising secrets on ordinary email and telephone lines when we could not meet face-to-face. This made no sense to me. How could they possibly want that? The whole idea, from their point of view, was to identify information they thought would be harmful to disclose.

For months I begged interlocutors such as Vanee Vines, the NSA spokeswoman, to use commercial, off-the-shelf encryption software or hardware for our conversations. Shawn Turner, the DNI spokesman, wrote to White House spokeswoman Caitlin Hayden shortly after the Snowden disclosures began, taking note of "a change in the way Gellman wants to communicate about the information he has. He no longer wants to email us information from the document. He asked that we either meet face-to-face or use a courier to collaborate." In fact, that had been my request from the beginning. Government-certified encryption technology was available for sale to anyone. Anything would be better than nothing. Vines was in Fort Meade, Maryland. I lived in New York. Most of the time we could not speak in person, and anyway we often wound up in conference calls with people in other states. Eight months into the process, Vines told me, "We're aware of your concern. It's been stated many times. We don't have an answer for you."

Stuck with open telephone lines, we resorted to mumbly evasions.

That thing we discussed last week . . . No, the other thing, the one about that country . . . With three syllables . . . Fourth paragraph, fourth line . . . The program named after an animal . . .

I once heard myself say to Chris Inglis, then the deputy director of the NSA, that "there's a diagram with two rhyming words, and between those words is an acronym next to a box. Is that the capability you're talking about?"

On one occasion I wanted to ask about a large quantity of what seemed to be unprocessed intercepts. There were no page numbers, no author, no title, and no other way I could think of to identify the contents elliptically on the phone. There were dozens of pages. Vines suggested I email them. No way, I said. We went back and forth. Finally I agreed to send an encrypted zip file. I directed Vines to a long, complex phrase that I did not have to say on the telephone. That will be the password, I said.

The next day, Vines called back to say she could not open the zip file. "My IT guys say they don't know what's wrong," she said.

Your IT guys? The National Security Agency's IT guys cannot work a zip file?

"Can you send it again with a simple password?" she asked. "How about 'abc123'?"

She really asked that. I refused. Eventually I asked Julie Tate to print the pages and meet an emissary from the NSA outside the newspaper on 15th Street NW. Before handing over the envelope, Julie asked the man in the car to show some identification. He could not believe his ears. "You're the one—" he sputtered, then gave up and pulled out his NSA badge. The whole scene was surreal.

The first time I heard the term FIRSTFRUITS, a confidential source told me to search for it on the internet. All I turned up were ravings on blogs about spooky plots. The Bush administration, according to these accounts, had an off-the-books spying program akin to the work of the former East German Stasi. FIRSTFRUITS allegedly listened in on journalists, political dissenters, members of Congress, and other threats to the globalist order. In some versions of the story, the program marked its victims for arrest or assassination. Even the respectable left-wing opinion site *Daily Kos* included an overheated tale about FIRSTFRUITS in its unmoderated "Community" section. As best I could tell, these stories all traced back to a series of posts by a man named Wayne Madsen, who has aptly been described as "a paranoid conspiracy theorist in the tradition of Alex Jones, on whose radio show he often appears." (After reporting that foreign intelligence services had proof that Barack Obama's birth certificate was a forgery, Madsen did a follow-up story that "Obama White House Wants Wayne Madsen Killed.") I did a little bit of reading in these fever swamps and concluded that FIRSTFRUITS was a crank's dark fantasy.

Then came the day I found my name in the Snowden archive. Once again the journalism gods reminded me that grains of truth turn up in the least likely places. Sixteen documents, including the one that talked about me, named FIRSTFRUITS as a counterintelligence database that tracked unauthorized disclosures in the news media. Madsen's blog posts were full of outlandish accusations, for instance that the NSA relied on FIRSTFRUITS for "plugging any leaks of classified or other information that points to U.S. government's involvement with the terrorist attacks on September 11, 2001." Even so, the blogger knew three things that no one had reported publicly before. The NSA did have a database called FIRSTFRUITS. It focused on press leaks. And it fell under the rubric of a Denial and Deception (D&D) unit within the NSA's Signals Intelligence Directorate.

According to Top Secret briefing materials prepared by Joseph J. Brand, a senior NSA executive who was also among the leading advocates of a crackdown on leaks, FIRSTFRUITS got its name from the phrase "the fruits of our labor." Brand wrote that "adversaries know more about SIGINT sources & methods today than ever before." Some damaging disclosures came from the U.S. government's own official communications. If Washington admonished Moscow, for example, to stop funding rebels in this or that country, the admonition might reveal knowledge obtained by the NSA. This happened surprisingly often, according to Brand. He counted 399 such "demarches," as formal diplomatic communications are known, that placed sources or methods at risk between 1999 and early 2002. Other secrets were lost to foreign spies, Brand wrote, but "most often, these disclosures occur through the media." He listed four "flagrant media leakers": the *Post*, the *Times*, the *New Yorker*, and the *Washington Times*. The FIRST-FRUITS project aimed to "drastically reduce significant losses of collection capability" at our hands.

In NSA parlance, exposure of a source or method of surveillance is a "cryptologic insecurity." If exposure leads to loss of collection, that is "impairment." I was fully prepared to believe that some leaks cause impairment, but Brand's accounting—like many of the government's public assertions—left something to be desired.

By far the most frequent accusation in debates about this question is that journalists caused a devastating loss of access to Osama bin Laden's satellite phone communications. It is hard to overstate the centrality of this episode to intelligence community lore about the news media. The accusation, which as best I can discover was first made publicly by White House press secretary Ari Fleischer in 2002, relied on a sequence of events laid out in a classified presentation from Brand. As Fleischer put it, a newspaper reported that the NSA could "listen to Osama bin Laden on his satellite phone," and this caused the al Qaeda leader to abandon the device. President George W. Bush and a long line of other officials reprised this assertion in the years to come.

I carry no brief for the *Washington Times*, the newspaper in question, but the tale of the busted satphone surveillance was almost certainly untrue. It relied on the following coincidence. On August 21, 1998, the *Washington Times* wrote in the twenty-second paragraph of a profile of bin Laden, "He keeps in touch with the world via computers and satellite phones and has given occasional interviews to international news organizations." Shortly thereafter, bin Laden stopped using the phone. Some U.S. officials, including the CIA's James Bruce in the documentary film *Secrecy*, said journalists spooked bin Laden by revealing that "we had an intercept capability." No story actually said that until weeks after bin Laden went dark. The mere fact that bin Laden used a satellite phone had been published repeatedly since 1996, and bin Laden did not try to hide it. NBC News broadcast footage of the al Qaeda leader *posing* with the phone in December of that year. Bin Laden's aides actually asked a fixer for ABC News to bring a spare satphone battery for their boss when the network came for an interview in 1997.

Why, then, did bin Laden suddenly stop using the device the following summer? The answer may be inferred only circumstantially, but circumstances are awfully suggestive. On August 20, 1998, the day before the story in the *Washington Times*, the United States launched barrages of cruise missiles against al Qaeda training camps in Afghanistan and a factory in Sudan, targeting, among other sites, a facility that bin Laden had recently visited. Bin Laden went deep underground, forswearing electronic communications that might give his location away. Blaming a news story for this development, rather than a close miss on bin Laden's life, strained all logic. Somehow it became an article of faith in the intelligence community.

In 2001, according to Brand's NSA documents, the agency "stood up" a staff of leak trackers, allocating new positions for that purpose to a unit concerned with foreign denial and deception. The director of central intelligence established an interagency Foreign Denial and Deception Committee. The project, which began compiling records in May 1999, grew large enough, Brand wrote, that it "hired [a] contractor with FDDC funds to build [a] foreign knowledge database (FIRST-FRUITS)." One of its major purposes was to feed information about harmful news stories to the "Attorney General task force to investigate media leaks."

In forty-nine cases, three of them involving me, the FIRSTFRUITS project produced "crime reports to DOJ." The FBI, in turn, was left with a conundrum. What crime, exactly, was it being asked to investigate? Congress has never passed a law that squarely addressed unauthorized disclosures to reporters from public officials. There is no American counterpart to the United Kingdom's Official Secrets Act. Government employees sign a pledge to protect classified information. If they break that pledge they can lose their security clearances or their jobs. Those are civil penalties. When it comes to criminal law, there are potential charges of theft or unlawful possession of government property. The nearest analogy in the law, however, and the charge most commonly prosecuted in such cases, is espionage.

Some people will see a kind of sense in that. A secret has been spilled and damage potentially done. From the NSA's point of view, a loss is a loss. It may not matter whether a foreign adversary learns the secret from a spy or a published news report. The cryptologic insecurity is the same. Before the disclosure, the NSA had a valuable source or method. Afterward, it does not.

In other ways, espionage is a terrible analogy for a news media leak. Spying and talking to a journalist are not the same behavior at all. Spies, as we understand the term in everyday life, steal American secrets on behalf of some other country. They hope our government never learns of the breach. They have a single, stealthy customer. They intend, as the Espionage Act defines the crime, "that the information is to be used to the injury of the United States or to the advantage of [a] foreign nation." News sources, on the other hand, give information to reporters for the purpose of exposure to the public at large. They want everyone to know. They may have self-interested motives, but they commonly believe, whether rightly or wrongly, that their fellow citizens will benefit from the leak.

I am not making a legal argument. News sources have been tried and convicted of espionage. The charge is nonetheless a fiction enacted as law. The underlying conduct, which may be whistleblowing of the purest kind, is disfigured by forcing the whistleblower into the mold of a spy. If news is conceived as espionage, then it is logical for George Ellard to call me an agent of the adversary and James Clapper to call me an accomplice. It is no stretch at all, from that point, to deployment of the government's most intrusive counterintelligence powers against a journalist.

I had all this on my mind when I filed Freedom of Information Act and Privacy Act requests for copies of my records on file with the Department of Homeland Security, Justice Department, FBI, NSA, CIA, and other government agencies. Although I joked with Snowden about it, I made the requests in earnest. After more than two years of foot-dragging by most of the agencies, I filed a lawsuit to enforce the requests in 2016.

For all the limits of FOIA, which has nine kinds of exemptions and infinite opportunities for government delay, I have learned some interesting things from *Gellman v. DHS et al.* The CIA, for example, offered what is known as a Glomar response when I asked for my files. "The CIA can neither confirm nor deny the existence or nonexistence of records responsive to your request," the agency told me. "The fact of the existence or nonexistence of requested records is currently and properly classified." The DNI's office said it had withheld 435 documents about me in full, and it explained its reasoning in a classified, ex parte explanation that my lawyers at the Reporters Committee for Freedom of the Press were not allowed to read. Homeland Security personnel, I learned from another document, had produced a seventy-six-page report of every international flight I took since 1983. Customs inspectors had secretly searched my checked baggage when I returned from more than one overseas reporting trip. The reasons and results of those searches were redacted because disclosure, the Customs and Border Patrol asserted, "would disclose techniques and/or procedures for law enforcement investigations or prosecutions." When the *Post*'s Snowden coverage won honors, intelligence officials groused in an interagency email chain. "Can you believe the Pulitzer Prize announcement?" one official wrote. "So annoying." Hundreds of emails recorded behind-the-scenes reactions and internal debates about how to respond to my questions or stories. The government asked the court to withhold all of those on grounds of deliberative privilege.

I learned something else by way of FOIA. My practice, when seeking comment for a story, had been to frame my questions precisely and send them to spokesmen by email. I aimed to avoid misunderstanding and make the questions harder to dodge. It turned out, according to internal government correspondence I received in the course of my FOIA lawsuit, that the spokesmen were forwarding my emails to the FBI. The public affairs shop subsumed its work entirely to law enforcement. The spokesmen did not even have to be asked. They volunteered. "Below please find correspondence between reporter Bart Gellman and NSA & ODNI public affairs," a senior intelligence official, name redacted in the FOIA release, wrote on December 21, 2013, to a manager in the Office of the National Counterintelligence Executive, or NCIX. "In the email, Gellman references conversations he has with Edward Snowden. . . . Are these emails useful for NCIX?"

The manager replied, "Yes, these types of correspondence are useful. We will ensure they get to the FBI investigations team." The deputy assistant director for analysis and collection management passed my emails to the group chief for analysis and production, who wrote in turn to someone at FBI headquarters. "I have been asked to share the below with the appropriate FBI POCs and so am forwarding so you can pass on as appropriate," the group chief wrote. From that point forward, my emails were redirected routinely to the FBI.

None of the FOIA disclosures thus far have acknowledged the existence of FIRSTFRUITS. Two hints, nonetheless, have emerged from descriptions of documents that the government is asking the court to keep out of my hands. I knew, as I mentioned earlier, that the Foreign Denial and Deception Committee hired a contractor to manage the database that tracks news stories, reporters, and referrals for criminal investigation. In the FOIA case the government cited a contractor's "trade secrets" to justify withholding what it blandly described as "copyrighted bulletins summarizing intelligence news reports which are prepared, pursuant to contract, by a non-governmental outside vendor."

The most unsettling revelations in the case came from filings that hinted at the nature of the records that the FBI wants to withhold. According to an affidavit from David M. Hardy, a section chief in the FBI's Information Management Division, my name appears in files relating to "investigations of alleged federal criminal violations and counterterrorism, counterintelligence investigations of third party subjects." Not only the Snowden case, that is. Investigations and third parties, plural. Some of those files, Hardy said, may appear in an ELSUR database, short for electronic surveillance, that includes "all persons whose voices have been monitored."

Even the names of the FBI files, Hardy told the court, would give too much away. The file names specify "non-public investigative techniques" and "non-public details about techniques and procedures that are otherwise known to the public." The FBI is especially concerned about protecting one unspecified intelligence-gathering method. "Its use in the specific context of this investigative case is not a publicly known fact," Hardy wrote. The bureau wants to protect "the nature of the information gleaned by its use."

Those are not comforting words.

EIGHT

EXPLOITATION

I t was warm enough, barely, for an outdoor table the day I met the Google security engineer. He was not supposed to talk to a journalist, certainly not about company business, but he agreed to meet on a Sunday away from his office. I had promised to tell him something consequential to his work. Understanding it, I said, was equally consequential to mine. That sufficed as a lure. He knew what kind of work I was doing.

This begins to sound like a quid pro quo, but that was not my proposal. No trade was in the offing. On rare occasions I chose to show a document to one of my sources, not as barter but as an aid to reporting. Sometimes I could not interpret the evidence without an expert guide. Something was happening inside Google. Ashkan Soltani and I had worked out enough on our own to know it was going to be news. Now I needed insiders—from Google or the NSA, or both. They had to see what we saw in order to help us.

The engineer and I sat on a wide esplanade that edged the Hudson River on a late autumn afternoon, the sun strong and slanting low in the sky. Skateboarders honed their aerobatic tricks, grinding across the top of a low concrete wall. My source drained a beer and made small talk as I booted a laptop. We agreed on some ground rules. I turned to page fourteen of a twenty-three-page NSA file and pivoted the display in his direction. The engineer shaded his eyes.

I knew the exact moment he spotted the smiley face near the bottom of the classified diagram. His eyebrows climbed. He leaned closer to the screen. He started to say something, took a breath, and reread the page. The title was "Current Efforts—Google." Current efforts, that is, by the NSA. Against Google.

"Mo-ther-*fuckers*," he said at last, pronouncing the word with conviction. He reached for his beer, found it empty, and waved for a waiter. "I hope you publish this. I've spent years securing this network. Fuck those guys."

We talked for two more hours and agreed to meet again.

The hand-drawn cartoon I showed the engineer lent a whimsical quality to a classified presentation that was otherwise notably dense. Two fluffy clouds floated side by side against a lemon sky. The one on the left bore the label "Public Internet." The one on the right said "Google Cloud." An arrow pointed to the spot where the two clouds met, the digital borderland between Google's inside networks and the outside world. The caption said "SSL Added and removed here!" That was where the artist placed the smile emoji.

Added and removed? It hardly seemed possible. SSL, which stands for secure sockets layers, is the core technology of encryption on the internet. It is the padlock in your browser's address bar, the armor that protects information as it flows across the web. To remove SSL would be to pick the lock, pierce the armor, peel encryption away. Could the NSA somehow do that?

The drawing transfixed me. Ashkan and I spent most of a month of research and reporting to decode it. One thing was clear right away.

The emoji conveyed an unmistakable boast, a keyboard warrior's dance of victory. The NSA had triumphed over Google in some secret fashion. It had found a path, this being the point of signals intelligence, into something valuable that Google thought to be hidden from prying eyes. LOL Google, the diagram said, if you think your cloud is secure. The message resembled an old hacker meme, mocking a vanquished opponent: *All your base are belong to us.* Game over. Thank you for playing. Small wonder that my source had erupted in anger.

So simple a diagram and yet so opaque. Nothing in the adjacent pages explained how the NSA pulled off its heist. Technical details did not always matter for journalistic purposes, but they damn well did here. Every expectation of privacy on the internet, every secure transaction, depended on SSL. If the encryption was broken in some fundamental way, we were living in a different world than we had been led to believe. Maybe the diagram meant something else, but that question was front and center.

"Google definitely has a dog in this fight," the engineer told me. Not only did the company rely on SSL, but its employees were also core contributors to the shared software code that brought encryption to websites around the world.

By some means or another, the NSA was piercing the boundary between the public internet and Google's private infrastructure. On the diagram, that boundary was virtual, a digital abstraction represented by a hand-drawn box that nestled between two clouds. In the tangible world, the box had to be something concrete—physical hardware that could be seen and touched and pinpointed on a map. But where? Information crossed the globe by land, sea, and air, and Google hosted operations on four continents.

Unless the NSA had gone entirely rogue, which I did not believe, the operation had to be taking place overseas. It would be lawless, full stop, for the agency to engage in clandestine collection against a U.S.

company on American soil. Even with a federal warrant, electronic surveillance inside the United States was generally the province of the FBI. Outside the United States, the NSA's operations were considerably less constrained. The Foreign Intelligence Surveillance Act did not apply to collection abroad unless it deliberately targeted an American using equipment based inside the United States. There were other rules and regulations based on Executive Order 12333, a directive signed by President Ronald Reagan. Insiders pronounced it Twelve Triple Three. The standards set in that executive order were more permissive, implemented in classified regulations and seldom subject to oversight outside the executive branch.

"Look, NSA has platoons of lawyers, and their entire job is figuring out how to stay within the law and maximize collection by exploiting every loophole," John Schindler, a former NSA analyst who taught at the Naval War College, told me. "It's fair to say the rules are less restrictive under Executive Order 12333 than they are under FISA."

Congress and the courts stayed largely out of the picture. The FISA Court had no jurisdiction, and the intelligence committees, a top Senate committee staff member told me, "are far less aware of operations conducted under Twelve Triple Three." The staff member added, "I believe the NSA would answer questions if we asked them, and if we knew to ask them, but it would not routinely report these things, and, in general, they would not fall within the focus of the committee."

The NSA did not have to invade Google headquarters in Mountain View, California, to tap the internet giant's data stream. Google had built enormous facilities all over the world, large enough to require their own electrical power substations and industrial cooling plants. Thousands of miles of privately owned or exclusively leased fiber optic cable linked these fortresslike data centers, sixteen of them in all. "Cloud" was an insubstantial metaphor to describe this globe-spanning machinery. There must be many points of entry, potentially, for an enterprising signals intelligence agency.

The engineer and I considered several hypotheses at length. Understanding how the NSA broke in required me to ask delicate questions. How exactly did Google protect its cloud from an intrusion like this?

"I'm not going to tell you," he said.

"Not well enough, it looks like," I said.

"I'll tell you one thing—that's going to change," he said.

One mystery here was the NSA's motive to break into Google at all, no matter where it happened. There was no obvious need for stealth, or none obvious to me right away. Under PRISM, the NSA already had compulsory access to any information that Google possessed about a foreign intelligence target. This access was hardly a secret from Google, though the public knew nothing about PRISM before the Snowden disclosures. The NSA sent classified orders to Google by the tens of thousands, specifying accounts it wanted to tap. As long as the agency asserted a lawful foreign intelligence purpose and sent orders in valid form, Google had to comply. Under separate authority from the FISA Court, the NSA could also gather communications in transit through U.S. cables from one foreign country to another. All that happened under streamlined legal procedures inside the United States. Why would the NSA resort to black bag operations against Google assets somewhere else?

When I worked through related documents with Ashkan, we found nothing that spelled out the background or mechanics of the operation. More than a dozen presentations in the Snowden archive had references or brief asides that seemed relevant. We assembled one cryptic technical clue at a time: "international/fiber," "private search index," "Internal server-to-server authentication," "GCHQ access environment," "gaia protocol." A few cover names repeated themselves: WINDSTOP, MUS-CULAR, GHOSTMACHINE. Over and over we found signs of an operation that took place on a grand scale: "bulk access," "full take," "high volume." The collection systems had to cope with "truly heinous" quantities of information, one briefing said. No wonder about that. Google accounted for the lion's share of the whole world's traffic in web search, email, photographs, chat, online documents, and videos.

One week into the sleuthing, I described the Google cloud diagram to Snowden in a live chat over one of our secure links. There was more to the drawing than I have laid out here so far. I was looking at this:

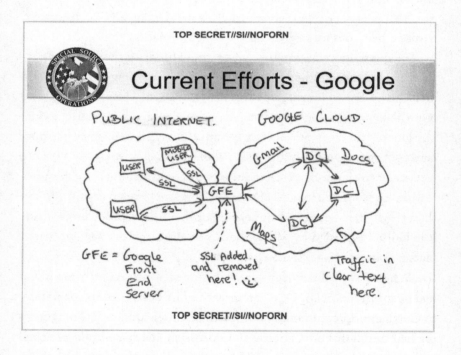

The box where encryption was "[a]dded and removed" was labeled "GFE." That stood for Google Front End. The term referred to the computer servers—there were many—that connected Google's internal systems to the browsers used by members of the public. When you check your email, your computer or smartphone is talking to a front end server. Google's private infrastructure, I explained to Snowden, was shown on the right side of the diagram. It included boxes labeled "DC," or data center. "Traffic in clear text here," a caption said. No encryption, in other words. Only outside its digital property line, on the public internet, did Google armor its data with encryption. The NSA, somehow, was inside Google's house.

Snowden and I spoke in technical shorthand, but in essence I asked him, how did the NSA break in?

"That's a complicated topic and I can't answer everything," Snowden wrote.

Then how about a more basic question: *why* would the NSA do this?

Because it could, Snowden replied. The agency saw great heaps of information flowing unencrypted through conduits it could reach. "I'm speculating, but NSA doesn't ignore low-hanging fruit," Snowden wrote.

One of the NSA documents used the same phrase. High-volume collection overseas could be "optimized," it said, by focusing first on well-known "protocols and applications—'low hanging fruit.'"

Understanding dawned on me slowly in the coming days, no more than surmise at first. The NSA must be getting something abroad that it could not get at home. Location made all the difference as a legal matter. Domestic collection under FISA was inherently a discriminative act. PRISM offered rich access to Google accounts, but the NSA had to specify individual foreign targets. NSA analysts sent "selectors" to Google, most commonly in the form of email addresses, and targeting had to follow court-approved guidelines. Another way to say this is that the NSA had to know in advance whom it wanted to spy on. It could not use mass surveillance tools to discover unknown targets— not if the tools were employed on U.S. territory, that is. If the NSA reached into the Google cloud from overseas, on the other hand, there was a lot more room to maneuver. Analysts could gather a whole data stream and sift it with selection criteria that FISA did not permit. They could decide to collect, for example, any communication that used *this* version of *that* software or mentioned *these* key words on *those* network domains. They were bound to collect much more than they wanted that way, but they could subject the take to further filtering.

One day I managed to seize an idea that had been hovering just out of reach. Usually I take notes with a keyboard, but I put this on paper.

1. What's 'here' is 'there'

The rest of it followed.

2. No bar to bulk ingest
3. Incidental
4. Collapses domestic/foreign distinction?

In a nutshell, my list assembled four thoughts that I had not put together before.

First, the information that Google stored for American account holders was just as likely to sit in Ireland as in Iowa. Google had big facilities in both places. Redundant data centers around the world, eight of them overseas, served as backup for one another and shared the workload of moving content across the internet. If one node slowed down, another picked up the slack. It had to be a lot more complex than that in a system so large, but load balancing was basic to any network design. That meant your Google data traveled overseas even if you never left the country yourself. An email from Austin to Boston might pass through Quilicura, Chile, or make its way to a backup there afterward.

Second, the NSA could and did tap into high-volume circuits

overseas—gathering data "in bulk," without discriminants. The agency did not keep everything it touched, not by a long shot, but it liked to touch whatever it could reach. And since American data passed overseas, bulk operations there were guaranteed to touch Americans at home.

Third, the NSA was allowed under Twelve Triple Three to keep "incidentally obtained information" about Americans as long as it did not target them deliberately for surveillance. "Incidentally" was a specialized legal term. It did not mean accidentally, unexpectedly, unforeseeably, or even undesirably. It meant that the NSA caught U.S. persons in nets that it cast with some other lawful purpose in mind. Collection remained incidental even when the NSA knew for certain that Americans would be swept in and was happy to have them. The NSA could hold on to the incidental data, and it did so. Once in hand, the American communications could be searched and analyzed along with the foreign stuff. With U.S. identities masked (sometimes), the information could be shared with other agencies. The law did not say "finders keepers"—it was more nuanced than that—but the NSA did not have to discard what it gathered about Americans in the course of business abroad.

Fourth, in consequence of the first three points, aggressive use of the NSA's foreign intelligence-gathering powers could have as much impact on American privacy as domestic surveillance. It might have more. Overseas operations took place on a much larger scale. If information from South Carolina could be intercepted in Singapore, the law was barring one door and leaving another wide open. Spying from a distance might blow a hole in the rules against spying up close, even without any devious intent.

There had to be, conservatively, one hundred million American accounts among the more than one billion at Google. This story was not about "foreign intelligence" as a layperson could be expected to understand the term. With scarcely a word of public debate, we had found our way to a world in which the NSA could not spy on Americans one at a time without a warrant, but it could sweep them in by the millions. This was the foreseeable result of operations in bulk—"high volume," "full take"—inside the Google cloud. And the NSA was allowed to presume, absent evidence otherwise, that information collected overseas belonged to foreigners. "Incidentally," in this context, was a powerful word.

D aniel Ellsberg, the whistleblower of Pentagon Papers fame, stepped cautiously down a weathered staircase from a deck overlooking San Francisco Bay. Intent on his mission, he barely noticed the panoramic view. Ellsberg steered past a hot tub and opened the door to what "used to be an under-basement," he explained when he gave me the tour.

A lifetime's accumulation of books and papers filled the subterranean office, a warren of interconnected rooms. There were wobbly stacks of file boxes, some topped with wire baskets holding still more files. Narrow aisles divided uneven rows of bookcases. The shelves were labeled thematically: "EVIL," "GENOCIDE," "BOMBING CIVILIANS," "BUSH." Ellsberg had lost none of his outrage at the news of the world, none of his appetite for political combat. At eighty-two, his face lined but unsoftened, he still had the bearing of a raptor on the hunt.

In 1971, then a defense analyst with a Top Secret clearance, Ellsberg had sent a classified history of the Vietnam War to the *New York Times* and the *Washington Post*—seven thousand pages, enough to shatter the lies of two presidents about the war. He became an icon of dissent, the archetype of a leaker as agent of social change. Henry Kissinger, then Richard Nixon's national security adviser, called him "the most dangerous man in America," a badge that Ellsberg carried with fierce pride. Ellsberg became the first American ever charged with espionage for providing information to the press.

Now, four decades later, the same month I met the Google engineer,

Ellsberg bent over a borrowed notebook computer. Unfamiliar software logged him into an anonymous account. Somewhere in Moscow, ten time zones away, Edward Snowden awaited Ellsberg online. Each man had played a notable role in his times. Their rendezvous, preserved as a transcript, was self-consciously historic but intended to remain tête-à-tête.

Snowden had granted no interview for broadcast or print since his arrival in Moscow. He professed not to care about his own reputation, but he kept a keen eye on his clips. He asked Ellsberg to keep their talk, even the fact of it, confidential. "The government has tried to construe some amazingly innocent things into scandalous statements, so I've been trying to minimize my footprint in the press to force a focus on the reform battle," Snowden wrote.

Ellsberg accepted Snowden's conditions, and the younger man seemed to relax. Even off the record, Snowden ordinarily calculated each word, but the older man's exuberance pierced his façade. Their temperaments and politics were almost nothing alike. Snowden, the cool libertarian, did not tend to share the passions of the left. Over the next two hours and twenty minutes, even so, Snowden slowly let down his guard.

"Wow! This is very exciting for me!" Ellsberg typed, large hands crowding the compact keyboard. "If you've seen anything I've been saying about you and what you've done, you know that you're a hero of mine."

"For us both, then," Snowden replied. "I don't think there are many out there anymore who don't respect what you've done. I deeply appreciate the things you've said and written. I think your history and clout really helped turn the PR spin around."

Ellsberg had adopted Snowden publicly as a man in his image. No leak in American history, he declared, had been more important. "I've waited and hoped for forty years for someone like you," he told Snowden as they began their chat. Three months earlier, he had written in the *Guardian* that Snowden proved "that the so-called intelligence community has become the United Stasi of America," a reference to the dreaded former East German intelligence service. Snowden avoided inflammatory images of that sort, but he found Ellsberg inspiring. He had told me he watched a documentary about the Pentagon Papers with his girlfriend, Lindsay Mills, months before he went public with the NSA archive. He told Ellsberg it "did 'harden' my resolve."

Ellsberg offered a dark theory to begin their discussion of the NSA. "[T]he reason I think they're keeping targeting of individuals secret is that it gives them blackmail capability against Congresspersons and judges; and a total ability to find sources of journalists and end real investigative reporting," he wrote. He elaborated at length. "Any thoughts on this mass- or individual blackmail potential?"

Snowden demurred. "The technical capability to do that is there," he replied. "It wouldn't even be hard. That said, I do not personally have knowledge of that (or even believe it)—if it's true, it's highly compartmented. Realistically, most day-to-day workers [at the NSA] are good people trying to do a good job. I think someone would find a way to leak that."

Ellsberg typed ahead of Snowden's replies, throwing questions, digressions, hypotheses, and parentheses at a ferocious pace. "How are your spirits in Russia? Do you see any prospect of ever leaving?"

"My spirits are fine: I'm practically autistic in my ability to function for long periods without human contact." Snowden dodged the second question.

"What got to you, pushed you over the edge?" Ellsberg asked.

Snowden gave a variety of answers to that question in public, including outrage at James Clapper's denial in Senate testimony that the NSA "wittingly" collected data on millions of Americans. (Clapper testified long after Snowden made contact with journalists but before he sent us documents.) Here Snowden offered a more personal reply, alluding to his girlfriend's online journals and the provocative self-portraits she photographed.

"Re: 'tipping point,' I can't say. I think about it a lot. I think seeing Lindsay begin developing a web presence—a huge, beautiful, creative online footprint—and realizing how vulnerable it made her and the millions of innocents like her, caused something of a crisis of faith. I can't point to any single thing. It was a recognition of the trends, and where they lead."

Ellsberg asked Snowden to respond to some of his critics. "Are you really confident that, contrary to what armchair pundits assume, Russia and China have not been able to get your data?"

"Yes. It is not possible the RU or CN could have any data from me. I can't go into the methods of protection, but it's a physical [impossibility]. To get the data would require the expenditure of more energy than exists in the entirety of the universe."

"What's your answer to the argument that Americans aren't benefited by your putting out so much about NSA spying on OTHER countries?" Ellsberg asked.

"There are two false presumptions there: 1) The whistleblower causes the harm, rather than the action (the spying). 2) That the spying is itself a benefit. I would argue that the NSA spying does not provide a public benefit commensurate to the risk. If we're going to be a moral authority, we must act as one."

By Snowden's lights, foreigners deserved no less shelter from untargeted surveillance than did Americans. If there were no solid grounds to target a person, her data should be left alone. Snowden often used "probable cause," the strict standard for a criminal search warrant, as the proper threshold for legitimate spying overseas. This was perhaps his most radical belief. Intelligence gathering abroad had never been subject to that kind of limit. Snowden disagreed at root with decades of

constitutional analysis by federal courts and the core concept, really, of
foreign espionage. Intelligence seeks information, not evidence of crimes.

"I believe our constitution protects everybody, not just citizens,"
he told Ellsberg. "The declaration of independence does not declare
that 'all US Persons are created equal,' does it? Much of my reasoning
follows from that."

Ellsberg, who had made no attempt himself to flee from American
law, praised Snowden for seeking asylum abroad against espionage
charges: "YOU COULD NOT BE FAIRLY TRIED IN THE US, UN-
DER THE CURRENT INTERPRETATIONS OF THESE LAWS."

"The espionage act should have been struck down in 1917," Snowden
agreed, and he offered a novel, if impolitic, argument. "It perverts the
system of incentives: why should a rational actor (who is not selling information to foreign governments) subject themselves to a legal system
that will punish them as though they were selling information to foreign governments? They are incentivizing treason and disincentivizing
whistleblowing. Basically, the espionage act is putting classified information (for example, the things in my head) at risk by forcing me to flee
the US rather than allowing me to stay and mount a public interest
defense (or face a reasonable penalty)."

Snowden had just acknowledged something he never entertained
with me, even hypothetically: that his presence in Russia represented
a potential security risk to the United States. Then Ellsberg asked him
where the next whistleblower should go.

"That's difficult. The obvious answer is Russia, because under
their doctrine they would never return someone who future 'actual
spies' might think of as a 'walk in / volunteer,' because it would prevent them from getting 'actual' walk-ins in the future."

This was, I knew, an authentic expression of Snowden's view, but
he would not have said it in public. The point was awkward, easy to
turn against him. Snowden meant: I am not a Russian asset, but the

Russian government protects me because I look like one to other prospective assets. Moscow, he believed, could not treat him badly without harm to its recruiting.

There was no public evidence whatever that Snowden actually gave information to Russia. No official in a position to know ever claimed to me that the government had any. Snowden could not, on the other hand, prove the negative. The nearest he ever came to addressing it was in our December 2013 interview. "I will say—hypothetically speaking—is what would happen is you'd get pulled out of the line at the [passport] control, just like they do in any country in the world, and you go into a room with a bunch of people and they say, 'Hey look, here's the situation, here's what we can offer you, blah blah blah, will you work with us? Do you have anything you can help us with?' Can we be friends, basically. And you go, 'Look, I don't think that would be appropriate.' That's not what I'm doing. That's not what this is about. And if you really wanted them to leave you alone you'd go, 'I can't have these conversations or I'm going to report them.' What do you think they would do?"

By way of circumstantial evidence for his case, Snowden pointed out that he had continuous access to the internet during the thirty-nine days he was held in limbo at Sheremetyevo Airport; he had a witness with him, Sarah Harrison, and regular contact with journalists during that time. If Russian officers had taken a hard-line approach, as many American officials speculated, Snowden would more likely have been locked up and stripped of that outside contact and support. "If you're with somebody else you're not isolated," he told me. "You don't have that psychological fear. You're in an airport that has wireless internet in every room. So they can't bullshit you because you've got a laptop in front of you where you can fact check everything they say. It's basically the strongest negotiating position you can have in a horrible situation." Snowden did not need Russian government financial support. Russia could have made his life miserable and done much more to compel him, but Vladimir Putin had a vested interest in treating him with kid gloves. Snowden's freedom posed no threat to Putin and gave considerable heartburn to the United States, keeping alive a story that disrupted U.S. diplomacy and politics. "I have no relationship with the Russian government at all," Snowden told me. "I have not entered into any agreements with them. I don't have contacts with them. It's just not how this is going." One piece of circumstantial support: Snowden discouraged me from bringing classified information to Moscow, which is hardly what a Russian asset would do. I was open to contrary evidence, but never found any.

In his conversation with Ellsberg, Snowden wrote that the "ideal" destination for someone like him would be a democracy with strong whistleblower protections and the will to stand up to pressure from Washington. It was hard to believe that such a country existed. He mentioned Iceland, Ecuador, and Uruguay, but how much would they really sacrifice to protect him, and for how long?

Over and over, Ellsberg returned to his lifelong preoccupation with leaks and leakers themselves. There were so many state crimes, so many secrets, so few the brave souls prepared to expose the truth.

"I desperately want more Snowdens," he wrote to the younger man. "Do you have any insight into the question (I've faced, and asked myself, for 40 years: without much insight, I must say): Why YOU? And not ANY of those other guys, who had comparable access AND who shared your basic values and views about the wrongness of what was happening?'"

"I can't say. I think most people are crippled by comfort, and I have few needs. It is much easier for someone who doesn't have many desires to walk away."

Later, when I came to visit, Ellsberg told me that Snowden gave only half an answer. "It's obvious why most people don't do it," he said. "They don't want to go to prison, don't want to lose their jobs. But why don't *any* of them do it? Why is it as rare as it is? The stakes are so great it would seem natural for some people to be willing to go to prison. We're talking about ending a war, averting a war, possibly a nuclear war, or ripping up the Constitution."

Ellsberg had made a point for years of interviewing every whistleblower he could identify. He documented each exchange in his exhaustive diary. ("1:46 pm: get ready for Gellman at 2," he wrote on the day we met.) "What it comes down to is an approach to it that we all shared, which seems extremely natural to us," he told me. "Since no one's going to do it, it's up to me." Still, the puzzle remained. The man or woman who picks up that burden "is not normal," Ellsberg admitted. "What is it these people have in common? I haven't found much in terms of background."

I found it fascinating that Ellsberg did not see it. True, he and Snowden bore little resemblance in life experience. The older man had served successfully as a Marine platoon and company commander; the younger had washed out through injury as an Army recruit. Ellsberg was a Harvard Ph.D. who blazed a fast track through the national security establishment, a certified member of the insider elite. He had bona fide expertise on the Vietnam study he leaked, having served on the team of three dozen scholars who wrote it. Snowden shared Ellsberg's high intellect but not his credentials or institutional roots. He was an autodidact of no fixed curriculum, an outsider who slipped through cracks of opportunity to the inside. He had the vantage point of an observer on the periphery of the NSA, far from the center but privileged to roam. Administrative roles left his talent underemployed, disastrously so, in retrospect, from the agency's perspective.

What Ellsberg and Snowden did have in common was unbreakable confidence in their understanding of right and wrong. As a journalist, I had known my share of leakers who were driven by a cause. Certitude defined them more than any other quality, even if they came to dissent after working inside the system for some time. They were allergic to compromise, estranged from workplace norms. In my experience they claimed no special knowledge of moral truth. It was characteristic of their worldview that they believed the truth was obvious to just about everyone.

The first time I met Snowden, I tried hard to pin him down on this point. Lots of people disapprove of what they see at work, I said. "Most of them just go along. It takes a lot of—I don't know, intellectual and moral self-confidence, right?" I asked.

"Or sociopathy," he joked, uncomfortable with this line of inquiry.

"You have to feel like you out of all the people who could be doing it—in this case, tens of thousands of people—that you're the one who ought to be the agent of change," I said. "The great majority would just stay and rationalize it, right? A small number would say, 'I can't be part of this,' and leave. Hardly anyone says, 'I have to be the one who stops it.'"

Snowden lit up. "I agree. And that's where my frustration was. . . . If you see that things aren't changing, and you see the gravity of the situation, you may feel compelled simply to do something. Because you realize you can. You realize you have the capability, and you realize every other motherfucker sitting around the table has the same capability but they don't do it. So somebody has to be the first."

What distinguished whistleblowers from their peers was intolerance of belief without action. There was black and there was white and they refused to avert their eyes, even—or especially—if others would not let themselves see. Going public followed inevitably. Whatever else drove Ellsberg and Snowden, their zeal was sincere.

Ashkan and I came up with four, then five, then six hypotheses about how the NSA broke into the Google cloud. Maybe, we thought, the NSA had stolen the company's master SSL certificate, enabling spies to impersonate Google services online. Your computer thought it was talking to Google, but it was talking to Fort Meade. Maybe, on the other hand, the NSA cracked the genuine certificate's encryption. Your computer really was talking to Google but the NSA listened in. Maybe the NSA could forge a certificate. Maybe it secretly ran one of the companies ("certificate authorities") that verified certificates as authentic. Maybe it found a bug in the software code that managed certificates in browsers. Maybe—the most disturbing prospect—the NSA knew of a "master flaw," as Ashkan put it, in the way cryptographic certificates worked. "We've just figured out, we think, that NSA has a master SSL cert for the entire internet," I wrote, hyperbolically, in a diary note early in our explorations.

Wrong. Completely wrong. Further reporting shot down all six of our hypotheses. That is what reporting is for, but we were making no progress.

Imagine the mystery in medieval terms. We knew the NSA could read secret messages that were supposed to be safe behind high castle walls. We did not know how the ramparts were breached or how many secrets were lost. Did the NSA have the queen's guard on its payroll? Did it know how to intercept messenger ravens in flight? Did spies slip through cracks in the castle walls, pry open the portcullis, tunnel under the moats? Did some dark magic allow them to pass through walls? Some versions of this story had bigger repercussions than others.

Another day, another engineer from Google's security team. This one met me in a dimly lit coffeehouse, table in the back. He did not swear when he saw the smile emoji, but apart from that his first words matched his colleague's exactly: "I hope you publish this."

"The diagram is a simplification of what we do," he said. "It's not fully accurate, but that does not mean they are not aware of the details." He pointed toward the right side of the sketch, where Google data centers exchanged information "in the clear" inside their own private cloud. "The fact that they've investigated that and they've got the big smiley face on it, they've clearly tapped enough to be aware of how we've architected things. On our private backbone, traffic would be unencrypted."

He gave a tight smile, angry but self-possessed. He wore the expression of an expert locksmith who just learned that the locks on his own house had been picked—over and over, for a very long time. One slide in the document dated the operation back more than six years. The NSA knew what Google's networks looked like from the inside, and there was only one way it could have discovered that, he said: "They know where the plaintext is, and they're aware of that because they went around and found it. And once they've found it, it seems highly unlikely they'd say, 'That's interesting' and then leave it alone."

Highly unlikely, but not logically impossible. In theory the NSA might have picked Google's locks, looked inside, discovered a gold mine of unsecured information, and departed without touching a thing. The agency might have found a way to collect information about Google users from somewhere else. From outside the Google castle, in other words. Over the property line. In order to nail down this story, Ashkan and I needed evidence that the NSA possessed something unique to Google's internal networks, bits and bytes that existed in no other place.

Eventually, with the help of government and company sources, we found fragments of raw collection in NSA files that matched the data structures and formats used among Google data centers. Those formats were proprietary and unique. They did not travel on the internet.

Case closed. And not only for Google. The NSA was also breaking into Yahoo, Google's Silicon Valley rival. The agency had been obliged "to develop custom demultiplexers," one presentation said, to take apart the proprietary format that Yahoo employed for "transferring entire email accounts." We found strong circumstantial evidence that Microsoft's overseas data networks were compromised, too, but not quite enough to say so definitively.

Finally we understood why all our hypotheses about Google cloud exploitation had been wrong. We had been trying to answer the wrong question. We assumed it was the NSA that stripped away ("added and removed") the SSL encryption protecting Google traffic. The question we asked was how. But that was not the way the thing worked at all. It was Google that decrypted its own traffic, as part of normal operations, just as the data left the public internet and arrived at the boundary of the company's private cloud. The NSA acquisitions directorate did not have to break through the walls of the Google castle or dig under them. Figuratively speaking, the NSA infiltrated the gatehouse and waited for Google to open the door. As a literal matter, there were places around the world where Google's "private glass," the cables that linked the company's internal networks, reached a physical junction with the fiber optic backbone of the internet. Private companies hosted the junction points. GCHQ, the NSA's British counterpart, had a special relationship with one of those companies. The GCHQ and the NSA shared access to Google's conduits at a location identified only as MUSCULAR. Wherever it was, a photograph shot inside the premises showed side-by-side racks of communications gear. One side of the photo was labeled "carrier equipment," which made the fiber optic connection to Google's network. The other side was labeled "multiplexing equipment," which diverted an extra copy of the whole data flow to the NSA's TURMOIL processing system. One copy in, two copies out, and Google none the wiser.

The scale of the operation was significant. According to a Top Secret accounting dated January 9, 2013, the NSA's acquisitions directorate sent millions of records every day from internal Yahoo and Google networks to data warehouses at the agency's headquarters at Fort Meade. In the preceding thirty days, the report said, field collectors had processed and sent back 181,280,466 new records—including "metadata," which would indicate who sent or received emails and when, along with content such as text, audio, and video. Finally, we were ready to publish.

On October 30, 2013, my story with Ashkan began like this: "The National Security Agency has secretly broken into the main communications links that connect Yahoo and Google data centers around the world, according to documents obtained from former NSA contractor Edward Snowden and interviews with knowledgeable officials. By tapping those links, the agency has positioned itself to collect at will from hundreds of millions of user accounts, many of them belonging to Americans."

We continued, "The MUSCULAR project appears to be an unusually aggressive use of NSA tradecraft against flagship American companies, especially striking because the NSA, under a separate program known as PRISM, has front-door access to Google and Yahoo user accounts through a court-approved process."

By now, prompted in part by our questions, Google had launched its own investigation. The company had held its silence on most of the surveillance stories to date, but this time it let loose with a thundering statement. "We have long been concerned about the possibility of this kind of snooping, which is why we have continued to extend encryption across more and more Google services and links," chief legal officer David Drummond said, adding, "We are outraged at the lengths to which the government seems to have gone to intercept data from our private fiber networks, and it underscores the need for urgent reform."

"There was a lot more emotion that day than on most days," Microsoft's then general counsel, Brad Smith, told me two months later. "In an industry that is very competitive, there was a lot of unity across the tech sector in terms of reaction to that news. Suddenly we realized that perhaps we didn't know everything that was going on. Our fundamental position as a technology provider was being undermined. We didn't have the control of our own facilities and data that we thought we had."

Keith Alexander, the NSA director, was attending a cyber security conference when the story broke. A reporter there asked him about it. The reporter had not read our story and slightly misstated its main point. "General," he asked, "we're getting some news that's crossing right now being reported in The Washington Post that there are new Snowden allegations that say the NSA broke into Yahoo and Google's databases worldwide, that they infiltrated these databases?" Alexander seized on the word "databases" to offer what sounded like, but was not, a flat denial. "That's never happened," he said. "This is not the NSA breaking into any databases. It would be illegal for us to do that. And so I don't know what the report is, but I can tell you factually we do not have access to Google servers, Yahoo servers." Our story, as Alexander knew by then, did not say the NSA broke into servers or databases. It said the agency, working with its British counterpart, intercepted communications on private circuits among data centers. The distinction was between "data at rest" and "data on the fly." The NSA and GCHQ did not break into user accounts that were stored on Yahoo and Google equipment. They intercepted the information as it traveled over fiber optic cables inside the company networks. Alexander then digressed to an off-topic explanation that the government obtains court orders to intercept data on U.S. territory.

Alexander and his staff had known for six days what our story was going to say. They were angry, above all, at its account of the legal context, which described "looser restrictions and less oversight" because the operations took place abroad. "Such large-scale collection of Internet content would be illegal in the United States," we wrote.

Intelligence officials took that as an accusation of bad faith. Valerie Sayre, the NSA's deputy director for legislative affairs, sent a heads-up by email two days in advance of publication to Bob Litt, the government's chief intelligence lawyer. "Bart Gellman, Washington Post, is planning to run a story possibly as early as Tuesday afternoon about certain NSA 12333 collection, which he believes is being 'backdoored' to circumvent [FISA Amendments Act section] 702 authorities," she wrote on October 28. "His analysis is wrong, of course."

What was wrong, Sayre and others believed, was our implied allegation of cheating. Litt and his NSA counterpart, Raj De, said as much when they spoke at an American Bar Association conference on the morning our story appeared. De, ordinarily an even-tempered man, expressed outrage at "the implication, the insinuation, suggestion or the outright statement that an agency like NSA would use authority under Executive Order 12333 to evade, skirt or go around FISA." Litt complained that, after all, "everything that has been exposed [in the press] so far has been done within the law."

That was actually our own point, if a news story can be said to have a point. We did not accuse the NSA of breaking the law or evading its confines. We exposed a wide gap between what the law said, as government lawyers construed it, and what Americans had been led to believe about their privacy. De and Litt were paid to find running room in a broken field of rules and regulations. They did so in good faith, for a good cause, and the NSA took full advantage of the openings they found. The question raised by the story was whether the law needed reform, as Google executives and civil libertarians urged. Sometimes, as the writer Michael Kinsley has said, the scandal is what's legal.

I n early 2015, the showrunner of Showtime's *Homeland* television series invited me to chat with the cast and creative team. The series, a spy drama entering its fifth season, had become a big hit among actual intelligence officers and national security types. The *Homeland* writers made an annual pilgrimage from Hollywood to talk to the real-world counterparts of their fictional characters. Two former CIA directors and a cabal of former station chiefs were on the list this year. Sounded fun.

Was there any chance, my friend Alex Gansa asked me, that Snowden might want to join us virtually? Unexpectedly, Snowden agreed. We decided to make his appearance a surprise. The group met at the private City Tavern Club in Georgetown, an eighteenth-century inn that had once served ale to George Washington and John Adams. There was a faint smell of leather polish and antique rugs. Halfway through lunch, as a technician fussed with a two-way video link in the clubhouse library, I told the group, "We have Snowden joining us."

"Insane," said Claire Danes, the star of the show, who played a bipolar CIA officer. She reached for a phone and texted someone. "I'm going to push back my flight," she said.

Snowden appeared onscreen like the Wizard of Oz, nothing but head, larger than life. The *Homeland* crew had heard a lot about him, none of it good, from intelligence and State Department and White House officials. He had admirers here today, but the room was split. Snowden, it turned out, was willing to tolerate more personal questions from this group than he did from journalists. Like Ellsberg, Team *Homeland* brought out his discursive side.

"Your name has come up over and over again," Gansa told him. "And honestly your name comes up, and it's like a light switch flips. And the level of betrayal that the people [in government] feel as to what's been revealed . . . I would just like to start with your feelings about hearing the level of vitriol that we got back."

"So this is actually a little bit new to me, but it's valuable to hear this," Snowden began. Official Washington had worked hard to vilify him, so "it doesn't surprise me that people say that. But I would be interested in knowing how many people you talk to have actually been close to these issues, have actually worked with this, knew me. How many people worked with these programs, and *didn't* have second thoughts."

At the working levels of the intelligence community, below the big bosses, Snowden thought he enjoyed some support. "Almost any-time you speak with these individuals privately, off the record, not a journalist—you're a friend, you're a confidant, and they really feel safe—I think you'll find more often than not there's a little bit more nuance there. They're not going to say, 'Hey, this guy's great, give him a medal and a parade,' and I wouldn't expect that. I think this is an extraordinary case. . . . But of course I'm not perfect. I'm flawed. I'm human. I could have made terrible mistakes. But I felt that I had an obligation to act."

Snowden was in a talkative mood. "I can't say that I can't be criti-cized, I can't say that I'm this champion of law, because I broke a lot of rules to do this act. But there aren't a lot of people in public today who are arguing that we'd be better off if we didn't know. I did what I could to maximize what was in the public interest and minimize what would cause harm."

"I'm really parroting to you what we heard—" Gansa started to say.

"No, no, I understand. Don't hold back."

"—and that is that the fight against the bad guys has been very severely affected."

"Did they quantify that? Did they give any specific examples? Be-cause they've been making the same arguments in the newspapers off the record. But even though we've had literally congressional hearings on this, they've never provided even a single case."

Well, Gansa said, "they're prohibited from talking about that here. We don't get to hear that classified stuff."

"They are saying, damage, damage, damage. But this is largely—if not specious, it's overblown. My last position at the NSA, I was actually targeting people with these systems. . . . I've read actual terrorist emails. I've read hackers' emails. I know how these guys operate. I know how the systems function. I know what the sources and methods are. I know what's important to us, because I had to rely on them. And I did what I could to maximize what was in the public interest and minimize what would cause harm."

Snowden's disclosures, he said, were news to ordinary people but not to terrorists and foreign leaders. They already knew they could be overheard. "[They] are not going to be surprised that Western intelligence agencies control the internet and the telecommunications sphere. That's our home turf. That's seen as our domain. They know they're in adversary territory when they're operating like that."

Danes cut in. It's one thing "to tacitly have it understood that this surveillance has been going on, but it's another for it to be formally confirmed to the world—that's another point that they made," she said.

As the conversation progressed, Snowden raised doubts periodically about the value of "bad guy" language in world affairs. "We get so caught up in these political conflicts around the world that we take sides," he said at one point. "In a fight between monsters, some people are saying, 'Godzilla, I want him to win.' Other people are saying, 'Mothra, I want him to win.' And we totally forget that when monsters fight it's the city that suffers. This is really the crux of it. There are no good guys; there are no bad guys."

Snowden reached for common ground, invoking Carrie Matheson, the CIA character that Danes plays on *Homeland*. "For CIA, for case officers, for people like Carrie I guess, the CIA makes commitments to agents when they're recruited, to their assets," he said. "It's a common trope where [a case officer is] anguished because the agency says, 'Cut this person loose.'" Sometimes, he said, a real-life Carrie is forced by headquarters to sacrifice someone she had recruited. Keeping promises to the recruit "is going to blow an operation or cause simple embarrassment for a powerful company," and Langley makes brutal choices. "They go, 'Protecting from this embarrassment is more important than the life of this asset.' This stuff really does happen. I can't get into detail here, but this is not only fiction."

This was Snowden at his most extravagant, implying inside knowledge of life-and-death events. I did not see how he could know such things from his experience as a CIA technical officer in Geneva. Team *Homeland* did not seem convinced. Snowden doubled down, telling his audience about an early conversation between the two of us. Laura Poitras and I had received the first of his leaks but had not yet begun to publish. Snowden had warned me to hurry.

"When I was talking to Bart, he thought I was being incredibly dramatic," Snowden said now. "It was still very likely that I would be interdicted. I told him, 'If the U.S. government thinks that you are the single point of failure, if they can stop this from happening by killing you, they will do that.' And he didn't believe me. He probably still has some reservations on that."

No, I did not believe the government would assassinate a reporter. Back then, before I even knew his name, I hoped that Verax did not mean it literally. Maybe, I thought, he had let fear run away with him. It bothered me that Snowden reprised the story now—as if it lent him authority as the real spy in a room full of pretenders. When we talked about it later, he called me naïve. "We wouldn't kill a journalist? Dude, we bombed Al Jazeera."

Danes, shoes off, curled up in a cashmere wrap, tucked her feet under her hips in a leather armchair. She had been scowling for some time.

"You're obviously really cynical about how the CIA works," she said. "Do you think that there's any value in a clandestine service? Do you think that it serves us as a country?"

"I do actually," Snowden replied. "And I want to be clear, that I think they're super valuable. I think they're good. I don't want to tear down the NSA or the CIA. I think the work they do is by and large very valuable. The things I take issue with are specific programs used in specific ways. Particularly the mass surveillance authorities, particularly the deception of the public, as opposed to the deception of our adversaries."

"Why did you go to China first? Did you know that you would end up in Russia?" Danes asked.

"The thing with China was that any extradition request was going to take time, and that time would allow me to communicate with the reporters everything they needed to basically report the stories, regardless of what happened to me," Snowden said. "I never thought I would end up in Russia. When I was en route to Russia, the U.S. government canceled my passport while I was up in the air, which is what froze me in place. I actually had a flight booked at the time to Ecuador."

That was correct. Snowden planned two intermediate stops that day, in Havana and Caracas. Sarah Harrison, his travel companion from Hong Kong, had furnished me copies of the confirmed reservations.

Passenger(s):		Ticket(s) #:		Seat(s):
Miss Sarah Harrison		5552102421916		N/A
Mr Edward Snowden		5552102421917		N/A

Date	From	To	Flight	Status
24 Jun 2013	MOSCOW SHEREMET, RUSSIA 14:05 TERMINAL D - DOMESTIC/INTL	HAVANA, CUBA 18:45 TERMINAL 3	SU 150	Confirmed Economy

If you had stayed at home, Gansa said, "there was no way that you were ever going to get a day in court."

Snowden agreed, citing Ellsberg. "People forget that the only reason that Daniel Ellsberg is not still in prison, the only reason that he walked, was that Nixon was involved in so much completely outrageous behavior that the judge had no choice but to throw the case out," he said, alluding to a break-in by Nixon's agents at the office of Ellsberg's psychiatrist. "If you are charged under the Espionage Act, there is no successful defense."

Danes was trying to picture Snowden's life in Russia. "Have you made friends? What's your community? Do you have dinner parties? What's life like?"

"You're asking questions that I can guarantee the FBI is like, 'Oh please, please ask more of these.'"

Danes made a sour face. "Okay, well, don't answer, then."

Some of us, Gansa said, tacking gently, have "feared for your safety" in Russia.

"I've got to say, I appreciate that," Snowden said. "But really, my work is done. I feel that in a large way, my life's work is completed. . . . If something terrible happens to me and I disappear, don't shed a tear for me."

Mandy Patinkin, who played a top CIA official in the series, shook his head sadly and said in a low voice, for the room, "'My life's work is over.' It's a boy. I have a child that's thirty-two. That's a boy." Louder, for Snowden, Patinkin asked, "Do you have bad dreams or do you sleep well at night?"

"This is actually something I've never been asked, except by my girlfriend," Snowden replied.

"Mandy gives good girlfriend," Danes cracked.

"I actually couldn't hear you, but if you said, Lindsay is a good girlfriend—"

"No, it's fine," Danes said, grinning. "It was hilarious."

Patinkin persisted: "Tell me about your dreams. And if you sleep good at night."

"I don't dream," Snowden said. "Or if I do dream, I don't remember them."

The National Security Agency, established under that name on November 4, 1952, grew up in the age of radio waves and electric current traveling on copper wires. Decades of investment built a global apparatus of antennas and switches and satellites, all assembled with the singular purpose of harvesting electronic signals of specified kinds. The age of the photon, which commenced in earnest near the end of the twentieth century, rendered a great deal of that apparatus obsolete. By the year 2000, most of the world's communications traveled as pulses of light over strands of spun glass the width of a human hair, arranged in ribbons and then twisted into braids. Fiber optic cables revolutionized data in transit. Digital storage revolutionized data at rest. The NSA had to remake itself from the ground up. When it learned to master its new domains, it attained a span of control over information that no human endeavor had ever aspired to reach.

"We were moving to *active* SIGINT, commuting to the target and extracting information from it, rather than hoping for a transmission we could intercept in traditional *passive* SIGINT," wrote Michael V. Hayden in his 2016 memoir, *Playing to the Edge*, the first by a former director of the NSA. "We also knew that if we did this even half well, it would be the golden age of signals intelligence, since mankind was storing and moving more and more data in digital form with each passing day.

"With little debate," Hayden added, "we went from a world of letting radio waves serendipitously hit our antennas to what became a digital form of breaking and entering."

You could take away the wrong impression from that summary. The NSA was plenty active in the analog years. Project BLARNEY, which co-opted telephone companies, dated back to the 1970s. But by late 2001, impelled by technological opportunity and the 9/11 terrorist attacks, the NSA began wholesale collection from major switching points of global communications networks.

Mark Klein, a technician for AT&T in San Francisco, learned in the summer of 2002 that an NSA representative had come to visit and consulted with company officers on classified business. A new secret room, Room 641A, sprang up at AT&T's facility at 611 Folsom Street, a crossroads for the whole internet on the West Coast. A crypto keypad, unusual at the facility, locked the door against entry by union construction and maintenance crews and technicians without Top Secret clearances. Documents and other hints convinced Klein that something fishy was happening there.

The building hosted peering links for the biggest internet providers in the western United States—physical connections at the intersection of information superhighways. AT&T developed a "splitter cut-in and test procedure," according to documents Klein shared with me, that showed how to make a copy of the whole data flow.

One night in 2003, Klein found himself alone on an overnight shift on the seventh floor, just above the secret room. "That gave me a chance to investigate without people wondering what I was doing," he told me later at his Alameda home, where he lived with his wife and two terriers. The floor of his cable room was the ceiling of Room 641A, with two-foot-square tiles covering the access space. He got down on one knee and began to remove the tiles, using a Fireberd test kit to trace the connections. "I'd pull up the floor, pull up one tile at a time, and you can see the cabling under there," he said. "You can just trace it, see where the cable is going." Four tiles from his starting point, he found the spot where the cables plunged down to a splitter cabinet in Room 641A. On the floor below, the sixth floor, Klein found a ladder and "poked my head up there to see—the ceiling tile was open." He confirmed that one cable went into the splitter cabinet from the seventh floor. Two came out, the second a perfect copy of the first. They were yellow cables, easy to spot. At the time they each carried gigabytes of data per second.

The NSA had many installations like that "to gain access to high-capacity international fiber-optic cables, switches and/or routers throughout the world," according to an overview briefing for members of Congress on the intelligence committees. Some were the NSA's own handiwork and some, like the MUSCULAR project against Google and Yahoo, relied on one of the Five Eyes intelligence allies. A few were "unilateral"—clandestine, and maintained in stealth. More were known to "corporate partners," including AT&T, Verizon, Motorola, and Cisco, their identities obscured in NSA paperwork by cover names such as FAIRVIEW and OAKSTAR. It did not take many such access points, strategically placed, to provide the NSA with a commanding view of communications across the globe. According to a 2011 presentation for an intelligence conference with the NSA's counterparts in the United Kingdom, Australia, Canada, and New Zealand, the "New Collection Posture" of the Five Eyes was to "Sniff it All," "Know it All," "Collect it All," "Process it All," "Exploit it All," "Partner it All." This was overstated as a description of reality, then and now, but it rang true as an aspirational goal.

The ambitions of the golden age of surveillance led to parallel anxieties in the intelligence establishment. If "collect it all" was nearly within grasp, then any missing piece felt like a culpable failure. David C. Gompert, who served as deputy director of national intelligence between 2009 and 2011, including a stint as acting director, once told me over breakfast at PJ's Pancake House in Princeton that he had testified many times in closed congressional hearings. No member of

Congress ever asked him whether he thought U.S. intelligence went too far, collected too much information, put too much privacy at risk. "The only thing they ever asked was how we failed to anticipate something, how we failed to stop it, why we did not know enough," he said. Nicholas Rasmussen, who directed the National Counterterrorism Center until 2017, told me, similarly, "If there weren't zero tolerance for any attack, any one casualty, they wouldn't be so obsessed with knowing everything. But there's no power they're willing to give up when they're being held to a standard that nothing can ever happen that you didn't know about."

In November 2014, early in his second year as FBI director, James Comey gave a fascinating illustration of that frame of mind in a keynote speech at a conference at Fordham University's Center on National Security. He warned, as his predecessor had, that the spread of encryption in consumer technology—attributable, in significant part, to the Snowden revelations—was hobbling the FBI. More and more often, investigators came across evidence that was locked out of their reach: photos on an iPhone or messages sent with WhatsApp, for example. The FBI had access to exotic cracking tools, and sometimes there were alternative paths to the evidence, but Comey said the bureau was "going dark" too often against terrorists and criminal suspects. Apple, Google, and other technology companies made a point of engineering their products in such a way that only the customer could unlock them. They refused to create back doors for government use. Comey preferred the term "lawful access." Absent such help, he said, encryption risked creating a warrant-free zone where the rule of law did not apply.

I put up my hand for a question. Comey made a wry show of reluctance, then called on me by name. We had grown to be friends several years before in the course of my work on *Angler*, when Comey was between big jobs in government. He had been to my home for dinner.

Now I was a potential witness and, in some eyes, an accomplice, to crimes under his jurisdiction. I thought we might resume our friendship when professional positions allowed, but circumstances now kept us at arm's length. A public encounter like this one was the only prudent kind.

I wanted to try out an idea I had been playing with. A search warrant entitled the government to seek, not to find. There was no guarantee of success. Encryption posed a challenge in practice, but that did not repudiate rule of law. Society did not have to configure itself for transparency. The founders themselves had used codes and ciphers in their personal correspondence long after the Revolution was won. We all had a right to conceal things we did not want others to see or hear. We could whisper out of earshot, leaving no record. We could bury a letter or burn it. The law was full of obstacles: the right to remain silent, exclusion of tainted evidence, the unanimous jury requirement. America was not built for maximum police efficiency.

"Do you see any possibility, in your respect for civil liberties, that inefficiency in terms of law enforcement and intelligence gathering at some level is a feature, not a bug?" I asked.

"I think that's actually, Bart, at the heart of the conversation we need to have: given the way we're going, will it go beyond mere inefficiency to a total darkness on the law enforcement front," he said. "I can picture a future where that information is utterly inaccessible to us, and so is that mere inefficiency? Maybe in the view of some. My view is that it would be, maybe, the mother of all inefficiencies."

If you insist that Apple create a special encryption key for the FBI, I asked, "how is this different from saying that you shouldn't be able to buy a lock without telling the lock company what combination you're setting, or you can't buy a shovel without telling the manufacturer where you're digging a hole? Why is it that you should demand perfect knowledge of what they do with their devices?"

The difference, Comey said, was that "there's no lock, there's no safe in the world that can't be opened."

A telling answer, I thought, more so than I had expected. With the right authorization, Comey could already break down any domestic physical barrier. He had the power of perfect knowledge of the inside of any vault. He wanted the same reach within the virtual realm. It sounded like much the same thing, perhaps, but it was not. Governments had not had a power like it before. Communications had never been comprehensively open to intelligence agencies. Most human interactions, even in the age of the written word, had gone unmemorialized.

It would have been inconceivable at any other time to gather a record of any conversation at will, still less all of them. Today the ambition was plausible, and some of Comey's peers in the intelligence community believed that achieving it was essential. Not to know everything, but to be capable of knowing anything. Any refuge against surveillance, any zone of effective privacy, had to be neutralized. That is why encryption, anonymity, and antivirus software were all categorized as "threats" in the NSA's internal literature. In an ideal world, NSA deputy director Chris Inglis told me, the agency would have "a universal capability" to penetrate those defenses and adversaries would not know it could do so.

I did not blame law enforcement and intelligence officials for wanting unrestricted access. The job was father to the wish. That did not mean a well-tuned republic should grant it.

Like Google and Yahoo, Microsoft had reason to believe the links between its overseas data centers had been compromised. Brad Smith, the Microsoft general counsel who would go on to become the company's president, wrote, in a blog post about our story, that "[g]overnment snooping potentially now constitutes an 'advanced persistent threat, alongside sophisticated malware and cyber attacks." Those were fighting words. Smith was comparing the NSA to a foreign adversary or a criminal syndicate. I imagined that Microsoft must have confronted the U.S. government about MUSCULAR, demanded an explanation. Two weeks later, I asked Smith how the NSA had responded. "I haven't asked, because I don't want to know," Smith told me. "Because if I'm told, then I'm going to be told the information is classified. And it may restrict my ability to speak."

There were all kinds of things Big Tech did not know or did not want to know about the NSA's use of American corporate infrastructure abroad. Twelve Triple Three, the Reagan-era executive order, gave legal cover to a multitude of intrusions. Ashkan and I shifted our attention entirely to operations of this kind, the ones that happened overseas but touched Americans at home. Critics accused Snowden, and us, of gratuitous disclosure of foreign operations. The gist of our reporting project, though, was the domestic impact.

One thing we discovered was that the NSA was standing at major intersections of the internet and pulling in anything that looked like an electronic address book—email contacts and instant messaging "buddy lists." Like an old-fashioned paper address book, these electronic listings commonly incorporated not only names and email addresses but also online handles, telephone numbers, street addresses, and business and family information. The NSA loved address books because they offered so much information about human relationships in a structured format. Computers could easily manipulate the entries and "enrich" them, in NSA parlance, with information about the same people from other repositories. Address books also helped correlate online identities when the same person used more than one.

The NSA harvested millions of address books at data crossing points around the world. Many of them, inevitably, belonged to Americans. It was the same story as the one for the Google cloud. The web did not respect geographic boundaries. Just because collection happened abroad did not mean the data was foreign.

Because of the way online services worked, they often transmitted address books when a user logged on, composed a message, or synchronized a computer or mobile device with information stored on remote servers. Rather than targeting individual users, the NSA gathered every address book it could find at its foreign outposts. The numbers grew large enough to constitute a meaningful fraction of the whole world's email and instant messaging accounts. Analysis of that data enabled the agency to search for hidden connections and to map relationships within a much smaller universe of foreign intelligence targets.

During a single representative day, the NSA's Special Source Operations branch collected 444,743 email address books from Yahoo, 105,068 from Hotmail, 82,857 from Facebook, 33,697 from Gmail, and 22,881 from unspecified other providers, according to an internal PowerPoint presentation. Those figures, described as a typical daily intake, corresponded to a rate of more than 250 million address books a year. Each day, the presentation said, the NSA collected contacts from another estimated 500,000 buddy lists on live-chat services as well as from the in-box displays of web-based email accounts. Although the collection took place overseas, two senior U.S. intelligence officials acknowledged that Americans were swept in. They declined to offer an estimate but did not dispute my contention that the number was likely to be in the tens of millions.

Early in the debate that Snowden provoked, Keith Alexander had defended bulk collection as an essential counterterrorism and foreign intelligence tool. "You need the haystack to find the needle," he said. That was a bold proposition, acknowledging the immensity of a different operation, the one that collected domestic telephone records. That one applied to metadata alone. Address books often included more than metadata: nicknames, labels, and notes fields. Sometimes the contacts were listed in email accounts with the first few lines of their most recent messages. Taken together, the data would enable the NSA to draw detailed maps of a person's life, as told by personal, professional, political, and religious connections.

The NSA had no authority from Congress or the special intelligence court that oversees foreign surveillance to collect contact lists in bulk. High-ranking officials acknowledged that the operation would be illegal from facilities in the United States. The agency avoided FISA restrictions, as it did with Google cloud exploitation, by intercepting contact lists from access points "all over the world," one senior official told me, speaking on condition of anonymity. "None of those are on U.S. territory." Because of the method employed, the agency was not legally required—and had no technical capacity—to restrict its intake to contact lists belonging to specified foreign intelligence targets, he said.

How could this be justified? I asked. American accounts were certain to be scooped up. The NSA believed the law entitled it to pretend otherwise. When information passed through "the overseas collection apparatus," the official told me, "the assumption is you're not a U.S. person." That was indeed the formal rule. In the absence of specific information to the contrary, according to the court-approved targeting rules, "a person reasonably believed to be located outside the United States or whose location is not known will be presumed to be a non–United States person."

Like other bulk programs, the address book operations were plagued by overcollection. The majority of all emails, one NSA document said, "are SPAM from 'fake' addresses and never 'delivered' to targets." Those produced a massive take of useless contact lists, and some of them had to be "emergency detasked" by the intake system. In a briefing from the NSA's Large Access Exploitation working group, the author called for narrowing the criteria for data interception. It called for a "shifting collection philosophy": "Memorialize what you need" versus "Order one of everything off the menu and eat what you want."

Mass surveillance techniques did not naturally work that way. They gathered haystacks, not straws. Another program we came across was extraordinarily ambitious: it tried to track and store the location of every device that placed a mobile telephone call, logging each phone's whereabouts over time, provided that the device could be monitored from a switch outside U.S. territorial limits. Ashkan and I discovered a set of programs that gathered nearly five billion records a day on the whereabouts of cellphones around the world, enabling the agency to track the movements of individuals—and map their relationships—on a planetary scale.

There were at least hundreds of millions of devices in this location database. The NSA had no reason to suspect that the movements of the overwhelming majority of cellphone users, individually, would be relevant to national security. It mapped the whole universe, or as much as it could touch lawfully, because the database fed a powerful set of analytic tools known collectively as CO-TRAVELER. The CO-TRAVELER toolkit allowed the NSA to find, for example, unknown associates of known intelligence targets by tracking people whose movements intersected. If I switched off my usual phone and turned on a burner at around the same time and place, the NSA could also make that connection and identify the burner phone as mine.

Here again, the NSA did not conduct this collection for the purpose of mapping Americans, but it mapped plenty of Americans nevertheless. For one thing, tens of millions of Americans lived or traveled abroad every year, and just about everyone used a mobile phone. For another, as one senior collection manager told me, "we are getting vast volumes" of location data by tapping mobile networks that served U.S. and foreign cellphones alike.

As for other bulk collection programs, we found evidence of concern in the NSA that the high volume of phone-mapping information was "outpacing our ability to ingest, process and store" data. Unlike in some other cases, the proposed cure was not to be more selective. Instead, the NSA was building more storage and processing power to handle the data flow.

In scale, scope, and potential impact on privacy, the efforts to collect and analyze location data may be unsurpassed among the NSA surveillance programs that Snowden disclosed in his leak. Analysts could find cellphones anywhere in the world, retrace their movements, and expose hidden relationships among the people using them. When aggregated over time, location data is widely regarded among privacy advocates as uniquely sensitive. Sophisticated mathematical techniques enabled NSA analysts to correlate patterns of movement with thousands or millions of other phone users who crossed paths. Cellphones broadcast their locations even when they were not being used to place a call or send a text message. "One of the key components of location data, and why it's so sensitive, is that the laws of physics don't let you keep it private," privacy advocate Christopher Soghoian told me. People who value their privacy can encrypt their emails and disguise their online identities, but "the only way to hide your location is to disconnect from our modern communication system and live in a cave." Methodical collection and storage of this geolocation database meant that the government was tracking all those devices into confidential business meetings or personal visits to medical facilities, hotel rooms, private homes, and other traditionally protected spaces.

No refuge. No haven. No place the U.S. government would accept as sanctuary.

As always, the documents available were incomplete. I did not like the wiggle room that Bob Litt, the DNI's general counsel, left in his official statement: "[T]here is no element of the intelligence community that under any authority is intentionally collecting bulk cellphone location information about cellphones in the United States." Was some other government entity doing it? Did the government buy the data or acquire it in some way that it did not count as "collection" under intelligence law? What did he mean by "bulk"? How much work did "intentionally" do in that sentence? Litt would not answer those questions.

Keith Alexander had disclosed in Senate testimony in October 2013 that the NSA ran a pilot project in 2010 and 2011 to obtain "samples" of U.S. cellphone location data. The project was discontinued because it had no "operational value," he said then. He said nothing to suggest any doubt about his legal authority. Gathering U.S. location data "may be something that is a future requirement for the country, but it is not right now," he said. Had that changed? We had no answers.

In the age of the photon, a man could take refuge in Moscow without disconnecting from the world at large. He could remain in hiding and yet emerge, virtually, to join a conversation almost anywhere. Snowden did not suffer the isolation of exiles past. "I can be involved whenever I want to be," he told me in 2015. "When I'm giving talks at Stanford, Harvard, and Princeton, things are pretty good. The government has lost their power. The only thing they can do is not let me in the border."

"The fact that I am so free to work, by virtue of the internet, and by my ability to armor my communications—that is something that's really new," he told the *Homeland* cast and creative team the same year. The latest innovation, he explained, allowed him to "sort of 'possess' a robot." He was talking about possession in the ghostly sense. From a keyboard in Moscow, Snowden inhabited a five-foot-two automaton on wheels. It was called a BeamPro, ninety pounds of sleek steel, aluminum, and glass that its manufacturer, Suitable Tech Inc., described as a "remote telepresence."

Everyone naturally called the thing a Snowbot. Snowden not only could speak and listen, see and be seen, but move around a room or down a hallway. He controlled the motion with the arrows on his keyboard. The effect reminded me of Rosie, the household robot in

the *Jetsons* cartoons. In March 2014, Snowden made his public debut with a BeamPro by giving a TED Talk in Vancouver, pivoting between the moderator and his audience.

I had to go meet the Snowbot. On the day I arrived at the sleek New York headquarters of the ACLU, which represented Snowden, he had already spent hours at the office from thousands of miles away. He attended and participated in a moot court held in preparation for appellate arguments coming soon in *ACLU v. Clapper*, which challenged the telephone metadata program. Snowden used the robot to circumnavigate the big conference table, shifting position to talk to someone face-to-face or to examine a document. Later, he wandered down the hallway, checking the name plates on the doors, saying hello, and stopped to visit one of the lawyers, Jameel Jaffer, for a one-on-one. It sounded like a gimmick, but mobility gave Snowbot a presence that video calls did not.

"The only thing there's trouble with is, this thing doesn't have any arms," Snowden told me when he beamed back in to chat that afternoon.

Ben Wizner, his principal lawyer, made an arch reference to killer cyborgs and the grand artificial intelligence in the *Terminator* films. "We're not going to have Skynet yet because you can't push the elevator buttons," he said.

Elevators. Snowden thought on that, looked ahead to the tactical problem. "If you're ever running away from a killer robot," he advised me, "go hide in the elevator, because it actually kills the wi-fi signal. So I can roll into the elevator after you, but as soon as the door closes I'm totally screwed."

"I love that," Wizner replied. "Twenty-first-century opsec."

Wizner was joking. Snowden was working the problem.

In retrospect, Snowden's tactical frame of mind could produce startling results. In 2019, amid Special Counsel Robert Mueller's investigation into Russian interference in the 2016 presidential election, I went looking for something unrelated in my notes of an interview with Snowden in 2013. I came across an exchange that had not especially struck me at the time. Snowden had been riffing on the danger that NSA surveillance could be misused for political ends. A different kind of leaker, he said, with a different kind of agenda, could have exposed communications in a devastating electoral attack.

"What if I had been a real political partisan who hated the Democrats and Obama and collected every Democratic official's emails between now and the elections coming up in the midterm, and leaked them all out as the new October surprise," he said then, referring to the 2014 midterms. "Think about the implications that has for the way our system of governance works. The way our elections work. That is the harm, that is the risk that these centers of gravity represent, that these databases represent."

This conversation took place more than two years before Russia's GRU hacked into email accounts belonging to Hillary Clinton's campaign chairman and the Democratic National Committee. "Doxing," which is short for document dumping, was not a novel concept at the time. Hackers had invented it as a tactic of revenge in the 1990s. Its use as a high-impact political tool, however, was yet to come. At the time Snowden spoke, doxing was most often discussed as a low-stakes prank. In March 2013, for example, a person or persons unknown had created a website, The Secret Files, that published personal information— phone numbers, addresses, and the like—for Michelle Obama, Ashton Kutcher, Beyoncé, Joe Biden, Donald Trump, and other celebrities. The devastating hack of the Sony Corp. by North Korea, and other episodes in what Bruce Schneier called "the rise of political doxing," did not begin until about a year later. Snowden saw the potential before it happened. His mind just naturally turned in that direction.

B y the time I met Vanee Vines in person, we had already suffered through dozens of mutually unsatisfying exchanges by email and telephone. As the lead media contact for the NSA during the Snowden drama, Vines tried to play a role that no one could have pulled off. She was a crisis manager with no authority to manage. Day after day, she bore bad news to bosses and no news at all to reporters. She had been a reporter herself, covering education at the *Virginian-Pilot* for the first few years after college at Syracuse. When she finished her master's in journalism, she switched sides. Media relations was the growth industry. For the most part Vines kept her performance cool, but exasperation often lurked offstage. On the day we met face-to-face at Georgetown Law School, she had just heard George Ellard, the NSA inspector general, compare Snowden—and me as Snowden's "agent"— to the worst traitor in the history of the FBI. Now she pulled me aside and launched a broadside. Snowden had lied to me constantly, Vines alleged, and I fell for it every time.

"You're in love with your source," she said. "Have you even considered he's spinning you?"

Spin, I thought uncharitably, was her department. I did not say it.
Vines was not really the culprit. On most days she delivered lines that
others wrote for her. There had been way too much dishonest bluster
from government officials, too many artful statements crafted to dis-
tract from the truth. Members of the intelligence establishment
loathed Snowden and wanted to tear him down. They believed his
crimes and deficiencies were the story.

Maybe I dismissed what Vines said too easily.

There were signs that Snowden was capable of an instrumental approach to truth. In conversations about my work, when I got stuck
on a hard reporting problem, he sometimes suggested that I provoke
fresh disclosures from government officials by pretending to know
more than I did.

"It sounds like I won't be able to give you the smoking gun on the
story, but I encourage you to make grave accusations when seeking
comment, even if you don't run them in the article," he told me once.
"Seems like one of the only ways to get the truth anymore."

"I don't claim to know something I don't," I responded. Snowden
let it drop.

Another time he went further, proposing that I actually publish
informed speculation as fact. If my story outran the evidence, he said,
the government would be forced to respond and thereby reveal more.
There would be a net gain for public information either way. As an
example, Snowden cited the *Washington Post* article about mobile telephone location tracking. Ashkan and I had written that the NSA gathered nearly five billion location *records* a day. We would have preferred
to say how many *phones* the agency tracked, but we did not know.

"You can't know for sure, but I would say, let the NSA clarify that,"

Snowden told me. "Leave it as 'phones' until they come out and say, oh, we're not tracking five billion phones, we're tracking 286 million."

Did he mean that seriously? At first I was not sure because he combined the point with a critique of journalistic evenhandedness. "I don't think you go far enough ideologically," he said. "You're not willing to indict them, because mainstream American media, they don't do that. They don't indict people. They don't denounce people for doing things that are clearly wrong."

"I think there's a certain role for a sharp advocate," I replied. "I think you're getting all you need of that."

Snowden, who was eating, laughed through his nose at my reference to Greenwald. He had always understood the division of labor between us. But he had a point he wanted to make, a model of the marketplace in public discourse. He said misinformation from people like Mike Hayden, supporters of the intelligence establishment, pushed the terms of debate so far off center that only rhetorical counterforce could set the record straight.

"The trouble is when you can't reach what's true in the field, because the person on one side sets one anchor and the person on the other side sets the other anchor. But there's a line tied between the two anchors. So when Hayden drags it over here, you're no longer in range of the truth, and you can't get there with the truth. That's the trouble."

"I'm not sure we agree on that," I said, trying to move on.

He insisted on an answer. I had already discussed this with him in terms of principle. I tried a practical reply. Errors undermined confidence. Readers would stop believing the stories he cared about if I proved myself unreliable.

"I really want to be sure" before I publish, I told him. "If there is one story that I have to take back that is wrong, that changes the game."

Snowden had once agreed with me about that, he said, but no

more. "I thought—I call it colloquially the zero fuckups policy—was right. I am not sure it is true. And here is my thinking on that. A wrong story can still produce public good. It can provoke the truth out of the government."

"I will leave that to somebody else," I said.

"It is not an intentional strategy. For people who are like, 'This is a disaster,' it still produces more public good than existed before the story was written," he replied.

Of all the Snowden stories I never published, the most tantalizing was something he wrote himself, not an NSA document with a classified stamp. He offered only the headline. I needed supporting detail before I could publish. Extraordinary claims require extraordinary evidence. I knew what the evidence would look like, but I never could nail it down. Two years passed before I understood why.

I have written about the text file called "README_FIRST," which Snowden composed to accompany the NSA archive when he first conveyed it to Laura Poitras and me on May 21, 2013. In it he introduced himself by name and delivered an antisurveillance manifesto. The story I never wrote was the dramatic climax of that message. Snowden recounted something he had done to prove that the NSA's surveillance apparatus could be turned against anyone. There were "limited protections" against abuse, he wrote, but "I tell you from experience that these protections can be stripped away in an instant." This is how he knew:

On the authority of nothing but a self-certification made to a software program, I have wiretapped the internet communications of Congress' current Gang of Eight and the Supreme Court.

It was a jaw-dropping claim, specific and vivid, damn near perfect as an illustration of his point. He had gone rogue to prove it could be done, he wrote. Even the great and powerful were subject to the NSA's all-seeing gaze: nine justices and eight ranking members of the House and Senate. Snowden offered this much elaboration and no more:

> May they enjoy the attention of the system they authorized. They will not suffer, as this collection will be immediately destroyed upon discovery and I [will be] punished owing to their privilege, but I pray it demonstrates the danger: what has saved them is policy rather than capability, and policies may be revised at any time. If the communications of the most powerful and protected in the world can be so trivially surveilled, what sanctity does your private correspondence enjoy?

That message from Snowden arrived with tens of thousands of documents that I had not been expecting. I had yet to find a news organization to publish me, yet to secure the archive, yet to take my first legal advice. On any other day this claim would have commanded my full attention. On that day it washed over me as part of a tidal wave. The following week, Snowden raised it again while pressuring me to publish the first story. Time was of the essence, he wrote, because "at this point there should be an active investigation into a certain act I disclosed in the 'README_FIRST' file."

As the months passed, I returned periodically to Snowden's story about the justices and the Gang of Eight. It amazed me that the tale stayed under wraps. Poitras and Greenwald, who could hardly have missed it, may have calculated, as I did, that they did not know enough. When had Snowden tapped those communications? Which accounts, which "selectors," had he targeted? (Most of the men and women on his list had no public email address.) How could Snowden prove he knew what they said?

Snowden did not want to elaborate and there was always something else to talk about. The mystery tugged at me, even so, because I believed the answers were nearly within my reach. I thought, in fact, that I might have them in hand already. There were boxes full of secrets on my hard drive that I still could not open.

This was a broader point of tension between me and Snowden. He had sent what appeared to be five encrypted containers all at once, but he provided the encryption key for only one of them. One of the containers was bigger than "Pandora," the one I could unlock. "The only thing you have is what you have plaintext access to," Snowden told me. "Anything beyond that would probably be deadman linked, time locked, or the like." He declined to explain further, saying, "discussing those mechanisms weakens them."

Whatever he meant by the dead man's switch, Snowden was proud of it. He had told Ellsberg in their chat that "I built a technical system that could ensure things would still be communicated while I was detained, but I would not be able to modify it at all while in prison, which created a number of risks." The résumé he sent to Booz Allen included this line: "invented an uncensorable method of asset communication that functions in the event of the originator's death or detainment."

When I brought up the Gang of Eight story, Snowden alluded to this spooky mechanism. I knew that Poitras and Greenwald had obtained some documents in Hong Kong that I did not possess. I asked Snowden, in a live chat in October 2013, whether those included the intercepts from the Supreme Court and the Gang of Eight.

"I've thought a lot about that," he replied, "but I'm not sure that will come out in the foreseeable future, as it would be used to 'criminalize' the disclosures. Maybe after the reform battle, but even then, it's risky. No one has that at this time. That's deadman material. It's not going to be scooped."

In June 2014, a full year after the first leaks, Snowden brought up the episode on his own initiative. I had asked him for on-the-record comment about another story. "The NSA," he wrote to me, "has access to the complete, comprehensive records of our private lives going back for five years; the scary part is any high school drop-out can wake up in the morning and decide they're going to walk out the door with copies of Nancy Pelosi's emails, and unless they send them to the *Washington Post*, nobody's ever going to know."

I got nowhere asking federal investigators whether Snowden had wiretapped famous people. "We have no evidence of that," said one official closely involved in the probe, who expressed skepticism. "He could submit tasking to sensors. He couldn't directly task sensors. There's a process where you vet the tasking. That goes through collection managers, who look at it, decide what sensors to task into, and actually implement the tasking. If you had every goober in the system inputting tasking you'd crash the system."

Snowden said he could and did enter search terms directly, without prior review. One way he might game the system, without arousing suspicion, would be to convert his query to an encoded format such as base64. Instead of risking a raised eyebrow by searching for "Pelosi," he could obscure his target as "UGVsb3Np." It would be foolish to claim with certainty that he could not find his way around restrictions, given other breaches he had pulled off. "I don't see how" he could have done it, the investigator said. "I don't want to say that's completely impossible. Systems and people are not perfect."

The thing was, I knew for sure that Snowden had access to some content collected under PRISM authority, which meant it had to come from sensors inside the United States. He had proved that by giving me a large sample of intercepted emails and online chat messages. For reporting purposes I assumed that he had the proof I needed to tell the story of the Supreme Court and Congress. My job was to shake it loose. In the summer of 2015, my second visit to Moscow, I took the opportunity to press Snowden in person.

"Here's the thing I want to talk about the most, and I've got to figure out a way to persuade you to talk about it," I told him. "In the early 'README_FIRST,' you make a very specific statement of something you did that's not been published. You said you had tapped the Gang of Eight and the justices. I can't pretend I don't have that. And again, it's one of those things, it leaves you so vulnerable to [critics who would say], 'Wow, what a crock of shit.'"

Snowden played for time. The NSA's XKEYSCORE interface allowed an analyst to enter any selector, he said. It followed that anyone could be surveilled. The thing is, I replied, the agency says there are safeguards. And you said you had actually done it.

"It's a big claim and actually would be—it's one of the most powerful images you could have," I told him. "I need more on that."

"I think we talked about this before, and I said it's unlikely it will ever come [out], and there are reasons for that," he replied. "We also talked before about Hong Kong and the fact that things were destroyed. Sometimes I have to signal that things are accessible that will never be accessible, because you're not the intended audience."

"So you had the evidence, and you destroyed it in Hong Kong?"

Snowden looked uncomfortable. He slipped into the passive voice. "The breadth of it wasn't demonstrated in the same way, but the proof of concept was," he said. "There's a named individual that's a member of that group, but that's all it was."

"But I mean in the 'README' . . . you said the Gang of Eight and the Supreme Court. We're talking about seventeen people. Did that actually happen?"

"Not all seventeen, no. I hate to disappoint you on that because I know it was a major claim."

At the time he wrote the message in question, he said, he felt that there was "no way to explain . . . that anyone would believe" how easily any person could become a target. He had to have a concrete example. "I needed you to understand, prior to the evidence, and the other journalists, that this was possible. And it is possible. I had done it. I had seen it. I had seen this for other people as well. If you type in an email, you get whatever's in the system."

But wait. What had he actually done in his proof of concept? Slowly an answer took shape. Snowden did not know the private email addresses of the justices of the high court or members of Congress. In order to spy on them, he would have needed those addresses to enter as selectors. Instead, he had found a public email listing for the office of Representative Nancy Pelosi, the California Democrat who then served as House minority leader. Something in the @mail.house.gov domain. He had entered that address into XKEYSCORE. Nothing of special interest came back.

"I overstated it a little bit," Snowden told me. He had intended to leave some ambiguity when he composed the anecdote. "I'm not sure that I stated it as forcefully as you stated earlier."

"Pretty direct."

"But really, if you semantically parse the words, was it a direct claim?"

"I didn't bring it with me because I don't bring shit across borders," I said.

"It was intended . . . to be a little bit lawyerly," Snowden replied. "But if that was the case, I really do have to apologize. . . . I would feel really badly if it was a direct claim on all of them."

Had there ever been a secret cache of additional documents? An automated switch to control their release? Yes and no. Snowden had, he now told me, written the dead man code, and "that was the original plan." He had prepared an archive of additional documents in an encrypted container. He did not share the key with anyone. That container was filled with files that he had not had time to organize. They might be even more sensitive than the others. He devised a system that would "coordinate you, Glenn, and Laura in a secret sharing scheme"— that is, a cryptographic arrangement in which he would split the decryption key and all three of us would have to combine credentials in order to open the dead man archive. "I had second thoughts," he said. "I wasn't sure that even if you agreed, it would be the right thing to do" to release that material. In the end, he did not activate the dead man mechanism at all. He destroyed the encryption key for the extra container. "That stuff's never going to come to light," he said.

Snowden's misdirection was an unwelcome discovery. It was not altogether a shock. Evasions and hyperbole were the cost of doing business as a journalist. From experience as an investigative reporter, I had yet to meet a news source who met the platonic ideal. Sometimes they shaded the truth. Sometimes they fooled themselves. They erred. They made assumptions. They offered opinions in the guise of fact or supplemented firsthand knowledge with surmise. Like a cop or intelligence officer, I cross-checked what I heard and learned a lot anyway.

Snowden was almost preternaturally articulate, which made deflection more obvious when it came. I took the passive voice or pedantic precision as a sign to be wary. I priced uncertainty into Snowden's value as a source, as I generally do, and looked for independent evidence. I did not publish his too-perfect credentials or his too-perfect anecdote. Very few of my stories actually quoted him at all, or were even about him.

All that said, I found Snowden to be more reliable than most of the critics and nameless officials who engaged me on this story. When we spoke of specific events or facts, he generally framed his claims narrowly and explained how he thought he knew. When he did not know, he told me so. He had a subjective point of view, like anyone. He could overestimate his grasp of context. I was prepared to believe that there were times when intelligence sources were right to say he did not know what he was talking about. Broadly speaking, though, when it came to nonsubjective information—particulars that I could verify, in principle—he was dependably careful.

I heard a great many word games from his opponents, who regularly trafficked in bad-faith talking points. Public officials routinely called Snowden a high school dropout, knowing about his GED and advanced certifications. They described him as a low-level technician, when in fact he had the highest-tier privileges as a system administrator and responsibilities beyond his job description. They used secret definitions of commonplace words to deny the truth as ordinary people would understand it. There were straight shooters who spoke for the government, holding silence instead of dissembling when they did not feel free to answer a question, but not as many as I would have liked.

"I was always taught you can't lie to the press," said Rick Ledgett, the former NSA deputy director, who never gave me cause to doubt him. "It's actually illegal to do that" as an intelligence official "because you're putting misinformation in U.S. channels."

"That's quaint," I said. He smiled. He knew my experience differed somewhat.

"I'm kind of naïve that way. Not a political person."

It was commonplace in national security circles, especially in the first year or two after Snowden announced himself, to brand him a traitor. I am not especially interested in the labeling debate—hero, traitor, whistleblower, criminal—but treason was a silly epithet, flung in the heat of anger. Hardly anyone tried to defend it literally, according to the constitutional test: "Treason against the United States, shall consist only in levying War against them, or in adhering to their Enemies, giving them Aid and Comfort." Government officials from James Clapper on down acknowledged that Snowden did not fit that bill. He had not pledged allegiance to or worked on behalf of another country. He had been no one's agent but his own. The interests he intended to serve—and intent was legally relevant—were those of the public at large. "I don't remember seeing evidence either of the Russians having the material or that he was an asset," James Comey said to me. "I've come to the view that he viewed himself as a white knight, that he was going to address abuses that he perceived."

Snowden came up with a pithy formula. "If I defected, I defected from the government to the public," he told me. That appropriation of democratic mandate infuriated national security leaders. "[I]n an act of supreme arrogance, he simply chose to violate a public trust without any warrant from the 330 million Americans who gave him that trust," former defense secretary Ash Carter wrote in his memoir. The "central flaw in his reasoning," Comey told me, was "that he's the one who should make the decision to share this outside the U.S. government."

Raj De, then the NSA general counsel, told me soon after the first Snowden disclosures, "Even if you agree, as I do, that we should be having public discussion about some of these issues, it's still okay to think what he did was wrong and this wasn't the way to go about it. To my mind in some ways it's pretty antidemocratic for any individual to put their judgment above everyone else's."

Yet this was always the leaker's role, taking authority upon himself to spill secrets. It was a reporter's role, too. I never heard a plausible scenario for a national reckoning with NSA surveillance in a universe that did not include a leak like Snowden's. Without those disclosures, Comey told me, "I don't think we were going to have the conversation in public, certainly. There's a good argument to make that—I won't say we're better off for it, but not as bad off as people thought we would be and said we would be, and there have been some benefits to the conversation."

I asked Raj De, "If we could have had this debate without the Snowden leaks, why didn't we?"

"I think it's because our political system is broken at some level, probably," he replied. "The national security bureaucracy is naturally tilted in a conservative way. . . . By and large, these are really good people who are trying to keep everyone safe. So, if that's your job, of course you're going to be risk-averse about being transparent. The systems are not geared to allow for greater public debate. Every incentive is to not do anything that would increase risk. Transparency is an abstract value in some ways, and a bomb going off is a concrete nightmare, and when just human beings are worried about raising the risk of one by trying to fulfill this other value it gets really hard."

Some Snowden critics acknowledged that, in principle, a leak of classified information could bring democratic benefits. There might be justifiable leaks, some said, but most of Snowden's did not qualify.

"You can make an argument—I don't fully agree with it—that the disclosure of the [domestic telephone] metadata program was in the public interest," Ledgett told me over seafood soup at the Elkridge Furnace Inn, a few miles north of Fort Meade. "The argument stretches more thinly when you talk about the PRISM program. And with all the stuff after that, it breaks down entirely."

The idea was that only those programs, if any, counted as domestic surveillance, and only domestic surveillance raised legitimate points of debate. The rest of the disclosures were "national security porn," Ledgett said, gratuitously damaging to valuable intelligence techniques.

I disagreed, or I would not have written the stories I wrote. Even if you set the bar at eavesdropping on Americans, you still had to consider the impact of collection overseas. The NSA's and the CIA's technical collection machinery tapped foreign circuits in bulk, and Americans were ubiquitous on those lines. Google and Yahoo cloud exploitation gathered American data. Location tracking in bulk tracked Americans. Address book collection swept Americans into the NSA's social networking database. Bulk acquisition methods, inherently, were as nearly comprehensive as possible.

Two years in a row, in public presentations, Gus Hunt, the CIA's chief technical officer, made exactly that point. In 2012, he displayed a slide that spelled out the reasoning behind Keith Alexander's haystack metaphor.

1. Don't know the future value of a dot today
2. We cannot connect dots we don't have
3. The old collect, winnow, dissem[inate] model fails spectacularly in the Big Data world

Therefore, Hunt said, the intelligence community had to collect all the dots, as many as data science allowed. It might sound surprising to a layperson, but scale was not an obstacle. With Big Data techniques, he wrote, "6,998,329,787 is a small number." That was the estimated population of the entire world that year. "It is nearly within our grasp to compute on all human generated information," he wrote, underscoring the word "all." One year later, at a conference held by GigaOm in New York City, he made himself still more explicit. "The value of any piece of information is only known when you can connect it with something else that arrives at a future point in time," he told the audience. "Since you can't connect dots you don't have, it drives us into a mode of, we fundamentally try to collect everything and hang on to it forever."

I had no quarrel with foreign intelligence gathering. It was essential to national defense and rational policymaking. It was simply wrong to say, however, that "everything . . . forever" could be configured to leave Americans alone. In our lunch together, Ledgett did not insist on that point, but he thought the risks it posed were fanciful. He was game to discuss the hard problems, but he was also exasperated.

"People are uncomfortable with the idea of the NSA penetrating technology and services that everybody uses," I said.

"How would you propose that we understand what the nation's adversaries are doing?" he asked. "If you could talk them into going to badguy.com, that would be cool. Then we'll only concentrate on that part."

This was the root of the problem. Intelligence targets in days gone by—the Nazi high command in the 1940s was the classic case—had used unique ciphers, codes, and communications technology. Nobody else was on those channels. The NSA's predecessor, alongside British allies, could break in without any prospect of "incidental" bystanders. Today there were still intelligence targets who used bespoke technology, but they were exceptions. Most of them used the same pipes as the rest of us.

Why not find your targets where they are and other people are not? Go after their individual devices, local networks, junction points?

"Some of that's opportunity-based," Ledgett said. "Sometimes we don't have the opportunity. Then there's efficiencies as well. Do you have enough—mainly people, but also money—to go do that everywhere you need to do that?"

We were back to efficiency and my question for Comey at Fordham. At times in its history, the NSA had achieved something like a God's-eye view of its targets on their specialized communications channels. Now, with the same goal, the agency wanted something it had never had before: efficient means to read and listen to anything on any channel at all. My instincts rebelled against a too-efficient state on this scale of operations. I worried about the Dark Mirror, so transparent on one side and so opaque on the other. The power gradient of government to citizens became too steep.

I asked Ledgett about the artificial divide between surveillance conducted at home and overseas. Even before September 11, 2001, the intelligence establishment had pressed for relief from the strictures of FISA, the 1978 law that governed electronic surveillance inside the United States. They pointed out that purely foreign communications—from Russia to Italy, for example—might pass through internet infrastructure in New York. Under the original FISA law, intercepting those communications required an individual warrant. Why, they asked, should foreigners, while located overseas, be granted the protection of the Fourth Amendment? It was a reasonable question. Congress passed the Protect America Act of 2007 and the FISA Amendments Act of 2008 to ease restrictions on operations of this kind. What legislators never really considered was the flip side. The same revolution in global telecoms sent purely domestic communications overseas, as I have described above. Almost nobody called for tightening controls on U.S. intelligence gathering abroad to account for all the Americans swept in. Congress passed no such law. Twelve Triple Three remained the only legal framework outside U.S. territory.

"The default assumption and the reason FISA applies if you're collecting inside the United States—or from a collection system based in the U.S.—is you'll run into a U.S. person, more likely than not," Ledgett said. "So you need procedures in place that are more restrictive in authorization. The default assumption in E.O. 12333 is that you're more likely to find a non-U.S. person. I don't think those assumptions are necessarily false."

But Americans are all over the foreign circuits, I pointed out.

"The fact is you run into Americans in every part of the global network," Ledgett acknowledged. "When I started in this business it was all about the Soviet Union, and if you got into a network, all it was was Soviets. They built and deployed and operated their own networks for their own use. The global system [today] means that everything's interconnected. That's why there are minimization procedures that are designed so when you inevitably encounter Americans in pursuing foreign intelligence targets—everything from targeting to collection to processing to storage to dissemination—there are gates that are designed to protect the identity of the U.S. communicant. So that they're not subjected to . . ."

He trailed off.

"There's no legal regime you can establish that can eliminate that," he finished.

Minimization," the term Ledgett used, was the intelligence community's answer to the bystander problem. It was jargon for a dense thicket of rules intended to limit intrusions into the privacy of Americans who were incidentally swept in by surveillance of others. Minimization did not stop the collection of American communications. It imposed a set of procedures after the fact. The procedures told intelligence authorities what they could and could not do with the U.S. data once they had it in their hands. "Collection rules prevent the government from having the *ability* to misuse data," as Jennifer Granick, then director of civil liberties at Stanford Law School's Center for Internet and Society, wrote in her book *American Spies*. "Minimization rules, in contrast, deny government officials *permission* to misuse data in particular ways."

Ledgett was right to say that incidental collection could not be eliminated entirely. If the NSA wiretapped only a single telephone line, it could still collect personal calls made by the target's spouse or conversations between the target and the target's American fishing buddy. Even in that simplest of cases, there could easily be more non-targets than targets in the surveillance take. Incidental collection was exponentially greater when it came to digital content. The contents of a target's laptop computer or a Gmail account, for example, could—and often did—contain personal photos and documents belonging to other people who were not pertinent to foreign intelligence. In the real world of surveillance operations at scale, this imbalance was a fact of life.

In order to demonstrate what that meant concretely, Snowden had given me the content of 160,000 actual communications intercepted in the PRISM operation. Ashkan, Julie Tate, and I did weeks of computer-assisted analysis on the cache, which filled about a quarter million pages. Picture it as one big pile of conversations intercepted by the NSA. In it were the texts of chats and emails along with photos and other kinds of files sent as attachments. We counted the number of unique accounts in the pile. More than 9 out of 10 of the accounts we found were not the intended targets of NSA surveillance.

That figure—9 out of 10—represented the "incidentally collected" bystanders. They accounted for more than 10,000 of the 11,400 unique accounts whose contents were intercepted. Some of the by-standers knew the NSA targets and conversed with them. Many others fell into the pile by joining a chat room, regardless of subject, or using an online service hosted on a server that a target used for something else.

Half of the files that held those intercepted conversations included Americans. The NSA ingested so much content as it spied on 1,250 foreign targets that it had to black out 65,000 references to U.S. citizens and green card holders. We also found roughly 900 U.S. accounts that NSA analysts had neglected to black out.

Even when the analysts explicitly described intercepted files as useless for intelligence purposes, the NSA retained them. The contents had an intimate, even voyeuristic quality. They told stories of love and heartbreak, illicit sexual liaisons, mental health crises, political and religious conversions, financial anxieties, and disappointed hopes. They included medical records sent from one family member to another, résumés from job hunters, and academic transcripts of schoolchildren. In one photo, a young girl in religious dress beamed at a camera outside a mosque. Scores of pictures showed infants and toddlers in bathtubs, on swings, sprawled on their backs, and kissed by their mothers. In some photos, men showed off their physiques. In others, women modeled lingerie, leaning suggestively into a webcam or striking risqué poses in shorts and bikini tops.

All of those examples were from nontargets. "None of the hits that were received were relevant," two Navy cryptologic technicians wrote in one of many summaries of nonproductive surveillance. "No additional information," wrote a civilian analyst. If a target entered an online chat room, the NSA collected the words and identities of every person who posted there, regardless of subject, as well as every person who simply "lurked," reading passively what other people wrote. "1 target, 38 others on there," one analyst wrote. She collected data on them all. In other cases, the NSA designated as its target the internet protocol, or IP, address of a computer server used by hundreds of people.

The NSA treated all content intercepted incidentally from third parties as permissible to retain, store, search, and distribute to its government customers. Raj De testified that the NSA did not generally attempt to remove irrelevant personal content, because it was difficult for one analyst to know what might become relevant to another.

Minimization was fiendishly difficult to explain because there were so many nuances and conditional clauses. Bob Litt described it this way for a lay audience at the Brookings Institution: "Minimization procedures are procedures . . . that must be 'reasonably designed in light of the purpose and technique of the particular surveillance, to

minimize the acquisition and retention, and prohibit the dissemination, of nonpublicly available information concerning unconsenting
United States persons consistent with the need of the United States to
obtain, produce, and disseminate foreign intelligence information.'"
Later, in another public appearance, he said it had taken him years to
understand the safeguards. With rules so complex, as Granick noted,
it was reasonable to worry about their application and effectiveness in
practice.

At the simplest level, minimization required that the names of
Americans be redacted before the NSA distributed an intelligence report. Usually. Contingently. The practice was qualified. For one thing,
the names were masked, not deleted. They could be unmasked at will,
and unmasking was fairly routine.

If the NSA had reported on the telephone call I received from the
Israeli prime minister near the end of March 1997, when I was the
Washington Post Jerusalem correspondent, the report would have conveyed that Benjamin Netanyahu "told MINIMIZED U.S. JOURNAL-
IST that his story 'was bullshit and you know it's bullshit and you did it
on purpose.'" If, however, a recipient of that report asked for more details, including my name, in order to understand the meaning or significance of the intercepted telephone call, then the NSA would identify
me. Probably. Contingently. There was some discretion involved. The
names of Americans could also be unmasked and reported to the FBI or
another law enforcement agency if the NSA believed it had come across
evidence of a crime. That alone was a significant exception because the
evidence, in such a case, would have been obtained without a criminal
warrant.

It was apt that Ledgett used the term "gates," not "prohibitions," to
describe the limits imposed by minimization procedures. Every barrier set by the rules could be opened. Nonpertinent information about
Americans was supposed to be deleted from NSA data stores, for

example, but that restriction applied only if the information "could not be" foreign intelligence and an analyst had affirmative reason to believe the person in question was an American. If the communication was "enciphered" or "reasonably believed" to have secret meaning, the government could keep the contents regardless of the time limits that otherwise would apply. (Cryptanalysis might break the cipher later.) Some of the minimization procedures, moreover, were classified. If you did not have a government clearance, you could not even read what the standards were supposed to be. And as Litt pointed out, the rules "can and do differ depending on the purpose of the surveillance and the technique used to implement it." He described the tailoring of rules, despite their secrecy, as "an important way in which we provide appropriate protections for privacy." It would be easier to have confidence in privacy safeguards that were a lot less opaque. Based on my interviews and the evidence in the files, I believed that NSA personnel took the procedures seriously, as best they could understand them; that they wanted to do the right thing; and that minimization could reduce the harms of overcollection. Granick, I thought, took skepticism too far when she wrote that "malleable secret rules are a lot like no rules at all."

Still, minimization could easily be oversold. It was sometimes depicted as a cure for whatever ailed electronic surveillance in its contemporary form, especially when it came to bulk collection. The intelligence establishment would say, in as many words: We know we collect too much ("incidentally"), and American communications are swept in, but you need not worry because we minimize the results after the fact—we close our eyes to prevent ourselves from looking at things we are not supposed to see. There was nothing wrong with that argument if you read it narrowly. Overcollection was bound to happen, and after-the-fact safeguards reduced the impact on privacy. But sometimes the argument was offered more broadly, as though minimization disposed of any question about whether to limit collection in the first place. That did not follow. It would not have followed even if minimization were a great deal stricter, a great deal clearer in its meaning, and a great deal more transparent to the public.

Try a thought experiment. Return to the science-fictional technology of mind reading that I described in chapter 7. The writer Conor Friedersdorf proposed a version of that scenario in the *Atlantic*. Suppose the government really could read human thoughts. Should "surveillance professionals shy away from breaking into everyone's minds, thereby 'going deaf' to threats against the United States?" he asked. For my purposes here, let's add a few details. Suppose the National Mind Reading Agency collected thoughts in bulk from passengers at transportation hubs around the world. By law it was allowed to presume that those thoughts belonged to foreigners, because the passengers were, after all, located overseas. Millions of Americans incidentally passed through the thought-reading sensors as well. Leave aside the dystopian flavor of the operation as a whole. Focus for the moment only on the protection of American privacy. Would we be satisfied by procedural rules that said the thought-readers did not target American minds, would not read American thoughts except for lawful foreign intelligence purposes, and would (usually) remove the names of Americans from thought-reading reports? Would we be content with the intentional collection of all thoughts, for that matter, so long as the results were "minimized"?

Ledgett was nothing but cordial at our long lunch, which stretched past the three-hour mark, but he found it hard to take some of my questions seriously. He believed that people who worried about bulk surveillance and minimization loopholes, who did fantastical thought experiments, fundamentally misapprehended the world in which he had worked.

"What I struggle with is to convince people that the government really doesn't care about them, in that sense. You're just not that interesting. People wearing tinfoil hats in the hinterlands with a basement of food and do their own ammunition making, I get that they are concerned that the government is listening to their communications, but the government just doesn't care. Things they're doing are not interesting enough from a national security point of view."

Speaking directly to me, he added, "The National Security Agency doesn't care about you."

What the government cares and does not care about is fluid over time. The national security point of view had once cared a great deal about the loyalty of German and Japanese Americans, black civil rights leaders, Vietnam War protesters, and the designated enemies of Richard Nixon and J. Edgar Hoover. It still cared about worshippers at mosques to a degree that some judges found untoward. Not all of this history was the NSA's, and there had been reforms, but the contingent nature of government interest was one of Snowden's strongest points. Many advances we take for granted now in civil rights and social justice—women's suffrage, desegregation, the right to form unions, gay marriage—relied on organized resistance against the law of their times. The Underground Railroad could not have run in a time of pervasive surveillance. The same could be said of the American Revolution. "They wouldn't have been able to coordinate," Snowden said of the founders. "They would have been individually popped off the street and thrown in King George's jail." Comprehensive transparency in service of comprehensive law enforcement, he said, would mean "freezing in place the status quo of that society forever."

In the early twenty-first century, the NSA had amassed a degree of latent power that Snowden believed to be an inherent threat. The machinery of electronic surveillance, and in particular of bulk collection, spanned so broad a reach that its mere potential for misuse was cause for alarm. "The only things that restrict the activities of the surveillance state are policy," he said. Policy could change, he told Poitras and Greenwald in his first taped interview. "And there will be nothing the people can do at that point to oppose it. It will be turnkey tyranny."

Senator Frank Church, back in the Nixon era, famously preceded Snowden in that observation. He chaired an eponymous congressional committee that investigated intelligence abuses after Watergate. On August 17, 1975, he appeared on NBC's *Meet the Press*. At a time when NSA capabilities were far less advanced, and the name of the agency was seldom mentioned, he offered a warning.

We have a very extensive capability of intercepting messages wherever they may be in the airwaves. Now, that is necessary and important to the United States as we look abroad at enemies or potential enemies. We must know, at the same time, that capability at any time could be turned around on the American people, and no American would have any privacy left, such is the capability to monitor everything—telephone conversations, telegrams, it doesn't matter. There would be no place to hide.

If this government ever became a tyranny, if a dictator ever took charge in this country, the technological capacity that the intelligence community has given the government could enable it to impose total tyranny, and there would be no way to fight back because the most careful effort to combine together in resistance to the government, no matter how privately it was done, is within the reach of the government to know. Such is the capability of this technology.

The Church Committee inspired many reforms and a culture of respect for rules inside the NSA, among other agencies. But by the time I sat down with Ledgett, the United States had elected a president who showed flagrant indifference to legal niceties and governing norms.

"Does Donald Trump make you reconsider in any way the powers and practices that seemed okay to you because you trusted the people who held them?" I asked.

"I didn't trust the system because of the president or his minions, whether in the White House or cabinet. I trust the system because of the people that operate it, because of the decades of culture and experience and training and ethos that NSA has and the respect they all have for the Fourth Amendment."

And if the president tried to direct surveillance against his political enemies, as he tried to direct investigations in the Justice Department?

"As convinced as I am of the gravity of that, if there were attempts to do something improper like that, people would refuse, and it would become known pretty quickly to Congress, to the DNI and the attorney general," Ledgett said.

I thought he overestimated the resilience of those institutions against presidential influence, but that was a bigger question, one of the central questions of the Trump years. I asked instead about a force in Trump's favor: the reverential respect, in the NSA as in all Defense Department components, for the chain of command.

"You were never in the military," Ledgett replied. "You don't swear an oath to the president. You swear an oath to the Constitution that is bigger and lasts longer than any president—and that's [also] true of civilians. The idea that just because the president says it, people are going to jump and do it, is a little bit of a falsehood, especially when it's something that is so clearly out of bounds."

Trump's genius, I said, was suborning people who thought they knew their limits. He led them into transgression one unexpected step at a time. Was Ledgett really confident that people in the NSA or anywhere else would recognize exactly when they began to cross a line? In the end, he conceded, the president might have his way.

"Could he decide to drop in a B-52 and drop a nuclear bomb on anyone he wants to? Sure. Am I losing sleep over that?"

Ledgett shook his head. That was an old fallacy, a hand-waving exercise. Yes, it seemed paradoxical to worry about lesser contingencies when the president could lay waste to the world in a nuclear war. Ledgett was too smart to think that answered my question.

I had had a similar conversation long before with Raj De back in 2013. Maybe, I proposed, the government had granted itself too much power over information. Maybe an apparatus of pervasive surveillance, capable of seeing anything, anywhere, was too dangerous to build. Maybe we should want to defer that decision. The NSA could not "collect it all" yet, but it was headed there. Did he not fear the results if the wherewithal should fall into malignant hands?

De had worked in Barack Obama's White House. He trusted the president, trusted the presidency, trusted the norms of the institutions he knew. To him the dark turn I hypothesized was beyond unlikely, and shackling the NSA to prevent its misuse made no sense.

"The idea of having some categorical ability to prevent tyranny is just a fool's errand," he said. "Shit, Hitler was elected in a democratic society at the time. You can't categorically prevent that. And I don't think that should be the driving force to set what we should be doing to protect ourselves" with foreign intelligence. "If you really want to prevent a surveillance state that could be abused by a tyrant, the only thing is to not have surveillance."

James Clapper, then the DNI, might have said about the same thing at the time. Five years later and recently retired, he had begun to rethink. Trump had accused the Deep State of spying on him. When we met at the McLean Family Restaurant two mornings after Trump lashed out at Clapper and threatened to revoke his security clearance, I asked Clapper if he thought Trump was projecting his own intent.

"There's all kinds of things he could do, I guess," he said. "I can think up scenarios. I don't think he'd bother to rewrite Twelve Triple Three. It doesn't strike me that he's all that hung up on what executive orders say. He'd just do it."

"You're probably not going to like this, but this is one of the first points that Snowden made," I told Clapper. "He called it turnkey tyranny. The idea that there are so many latent powers in the system— that despite all the safeguards now, they can be switched off."

A sour look crossed Clapper's face. He took a swipe at Snowden, doubting his motives, but he surprised me by agreeing with the main point.

"If you view that in the context of pre-Trump, well, that's kind of unthinkable," he said. "In the absence of congressional oversight, well, yeah, he can do a lot. When you have an unprecedented situation like that, all the previous rules, norms and standards are O.B.E."—overcome by events. "So, sure. The system is not ironclad. It's fragile. It's based on people behaving in a certain way, in conformity with the principles of this country and the Constitution and long-standing practice, procedure. And all that is really, you know, out the window because of Trump. Anything people thought pre-Trump is very different. It's almost the innocent age."

There must be people in the intelligence world, I said, who believed reform had gone too far in the 1970s and 1980s. I wondered: Would Trump have willing allies inside the system, ready to scale back privacy rules? People who would help him reinterpret standards or find room between the lines? Clapper nodded.

"Well, I suppose people make individual judgments about their frustrations with either rules that are in place or rules that they wish we had, so yeah, sure. That's human nature. I can't argue with it."

"So here's where it leads me," I said. "And I don't know for sure the answer but I have an instinct that worries me—that once you come to that conclusion, that it really is true that someone could do the wrong things with all that latent power, does it change your views on the creation of machinery that offers that much power? Does it make you think that maybe the machinery, its very existence, goes too far? Maybe that it's not a great thing that the apparatus can do all that it can do?"

"Well, now we find ourselves asking those questions. The reason all that machinery was built was ostensibly to keep the nation safe and secure. In that spirit, I guess, yeah, there's potentially room for abuse."

"To put a fine point on it, is it possible that what Trump teaches us is that maybe you want to scale back capabilities?"

"The problem when you say 'scale back capabilities,' you put a governor on the technical capacity that you have. The technical capacity is always going to be there. You can't unring the technology bell. The only way you can put a governor on that is to make a decision to do that. But the technology is still there. The problem is, Bart, if you set your mind to it, you can reinstitute, you can recapture capacity or capability that's lost or forsworn. Because as long as the tech is there, mankind devised that technology, so mankind can turn around and exploit it or de-exploit. And no amount of rule making or law passing can undo that."

Clapper had no cure to propose. De thought a cure was not possible. Ledgett believed rules and culture would win out.

Snowden, who had sounded the alarm, put his own faith in technology to ward off overreach by the NSA. "Let us speak no more of faith in man, but bind him down from mischief by the chains of cryptography," he said in his first signed communication, rewriting Thomas Jefferson's ode to the Constitution. "Our future depends on the efforts of the open source community." In an interview later, he told me, "The people who are going to change this and change it lastingly are grad students today. They're kids in college. . . . People are writing dissertations and proposing new models that are robust against surveillance systems."

From Moscow, Snowden spent much of his time in virtual meetings with tech executives and engineers, advocating for greater security in commercial products. He worked with developers on exotic tools, including one project to turn a smartphone into a tamper-detection device and another to automate "secret sharing" for cryptographic keys—the concept behind his abandoned dead man's switch. Periodically he would say things to me like, "I'm doing some really fulfilling stuff with nested virtualization now."

In history, as Snowden told it, "communications were always private, simply because of access. You couldn't plant a government spy in everybody's house in the 1800s. We start to get electronic communications, everything suddenly gets more open, until we reach the point of about ten years ago, where everything can be monitored. Encryption was very rare. Basically you could find some information about anybody anywhere. So the entire communications space [was] observable. That dynamic is beginning to change now. We're shifting it. We're basically reclaiming spots and making parts of it more private again. And these actually aren't unsolvable problems. If you can make security work in the most common settings, you can shift the focus of surveillance resource spending from watching everybody to watching the people who are actually suspicious."

The Snowden effect shifted popular culture. It brought about legal, diplomatic, political, and legislative challenges to the prevailing model at the NSA. Alongside all that, and perhaps most significant, came demand for greater resistance in the private sector against NSA bulk surveillance techniques. Security and privacy became marketing points for the internet giants. Google accelerated plans to encrypt all its services for consumer and business customers, and it tightened up security inside its cloud, too. "I am willing to help [the U.S. government] on the purely defensive side of things," Eric Grosse, Google's chief security engineer, said in a published interview, referring to cyber security. "But signals intercept is totally off the table." Google would not cooperate with government there, he said, adding, "No hard feelings, but my job is to make their job hard."

The year after our Google cloud exploitation story, Grosse's team released the source code for a new software library called End-to-End. It was a free tool that other software developers could use for encryption of email. Google security engineers left a blunt fuck-you for the NSA in a comment embedded in the source code, harking back to the smiley face in the cloud cartoon:

```
--ssl-added-and-removed-here-;-)
```

Snowden and the U.S. government made occasional, inconclusive efforts to reach a negotiated agreement for his return to the United States. The efforts were most intensive in late 2013 and early 2014, when the stakes were highest for U.S. intelligence. The secrets Snowden had stolen were still fresh. The government did not know how many might yet be exposed. Ledgett believed that Snowden could resolve expensive uncertainties.

"He's already said, 'If I got amnesty I would come back,'" CBS News correspondent John Miller said to Ledgett in a December 15, 2013, interview. "Given the potential damage to national security, what would your thought on making a deal be?"

"So, my personal view is, yes, it's worth having a conversation about," Ledgett replied. "I would need assurances that the remainder of the data could be secured and my bar for those assurances would be very high. It would be more than just an assertion on his part."

The more time passed, the more the government mitigated its losses. Forensic detective work gave greater clarity about what Snowden took. There was always strong opposition to a negotiated arrangement with Snowden, and gradually the case for compromise diminished. Snowden, meanwhile, made a new life in Moscow. His girlfriend, Lindsay, joined him there. They married in 2017. He built an online community among English-speaking activists. As this book was completed, both sides had settled into a long-term waiting game.

"Neither of us," Snowden told me, "have a driving need to see any kind of resolution."

ACKNOWLEDGMENTS

My first thanks belong to Edward Snowden, who took me into his confidence and gave life to a vital public debate about the boundaries of secret intelligence in a free society. For introducing us, and for our early collaboration, I thank Laura Poitras. For helping us navigate a complex relationship, I owe Ben Wizner, Snowden's lawyer at the ACLU, the world's tallest beer.

Hundreds of people in the U.S. and foreign governments, military and intelligence services, private industry, NGOs, think tanks, and universities have enriched my understanding of the worlds I describe in this book. There are far too many to thank by name, and some cannot be named. I am grateful to all of them. Any errors of fact or interpretation, as always, are my own.

Ashkan Soltani was outfitting his van for a long road trip when I recruited him to help research this book. By then we had closed down our partnership at the *Washington Post*, where we pieced together hard puzzles from the Snowden archive. Ashkan had been glad to shed the burden, relinquishing his encryption keys and relaxing the precautions he took to protect our work. He almost said no when I asked him to suit back up. "Imagine being completely free of this, never leaving your machine unwatched and all that, and [then] being pulled back down into it," he wrote to me. Happily, he gave in. His insights and expertise were invaluable, especially to chapters 6 and 8.

Research and writing can be solitary work, but I had a lot of help. I relied most often and most heavily on Sam Adler-Bell, who produced countless research memos, brainstormed about mysteries, chased down leads, challenged my assumptions, fact-checked every chapter, and produced a first draft on Snowden's early life for chapter 2. Sam influenced my thinking particularly on the intersections of justice and privacy, taking the lead on our long report* about the disparate impact of surveillance on people of color. He is a resourceful reporter, gifted writer, and passionate critic, well launched now into his own career, and I can't wait to see what he produces next.

A platoon of talented young women and men provided additional research assistance at various stages: Victoria Beale, Erica Portnoy, Rachel Adler, Jordan Larson, Harrison Cramer, James McAuley, Colson Lin, and Dina Lamdany.

Since the spring of 2013, before the NSA disclosures began, my professional and intellectual home has been the Century Foundation, a bipartisan public policy research institute in New York that punches above its weight in the world of ideas. I owe debts to the late Janice Nittoli, who hired me; her successor as president, Mark Zuckerman, who gave me the luxury of time as the book progressed; and the board of trustees for its interest in and substantial support for my work. Under Century's umbrella, Mark sponsored a series of policy papers on surveillance and privacy, and he arranged for the foundation to cohost Snowden's first public debate. I am grateful, not least, for the laughter and comradeship of my colleagues. My work at Century received generous support from the Addy Foundation, the Open Society Foundations, and the Ford Foundation.

Princeton University was a second professional home before and

*Barton Gellman and Sam Adler-Bell, "The Disparate Impact of Surveillance," Century Foundation, December 21, 2017, at http://perma.cc/WV8A-ZMV3.

ACKNOWLEDGMENTS

during the research for *Dark Mirror*. I twice taught a seminar on national security secrecy at the Woodrow Wilson School of Public and International Affairs, where I learned a great deal from my students and the questions they posed. Later I had the good fortune to become a visiting research collaborator at the Center for Information Technology Policy, a prodigiously creative and stimulating environment. I owe particular debts there to Ed Felten, Jonathan Mayer, Tithi Chattopadhyay, and Laura Cummings-Abdo. Grants to the center from the John D. and Catherine T. MacArthur Foundation and the Microsoft Foundation helped support my work.

When I needed a place to hide and write, Columbia Law School graciously provided an office and anointed me a distinguished visiting journalist. I enjoyed the opportunity, while there, to guest-teach a class for an interdepartmental course on cyber security offered by the high-powered team of Matthew Waxman, Steve Bellovin, and Jason Healey.

My work on the NSA disclosures began at the *Washington Post*, where I had grown up as a reporter and spent the larger part of my journalistic career before departing in 2010. I returned in 2013 as a freelance writer with the Snowden documents in hand and found an extraordinary newsroom leader in Marty Baron. Marty committed himself to the story in every way I could have asked, with guts and resources and never a foot wrong. Anne Kornblut managed the team and held my wits together; she was the one I called late at night when I was well and truly stuck. Among the many colleagues who played important roles in our NSA coverage, I want to recognize editors Kevin Merida, Jeff Leen, Cameron Barr, Jason Ukman, and Peter Finn; reporters Greg Miller, Ellen Nakashima, Carol Leonnig, Craig Timberg, Steven Rich, Marc Fisher, and Craig Whitlock; and researchers Alice Crites, Jennifer Jenkins, and above all Julie Tate. Julie, who has collaborated on more of my work than anyone alive, also fact-checked this manuscript, saved me from foolish errors, and improved the citations. The *Post* supported our work with clear-eyed legal advice from Jay Kennedy and James McLaughlin, reinforced by Kevin Baine and Barry Simon of Williams & Connolly. As I struggled with some of my early decisions, I thought more clearly after consulting two distinguished *Post* alumni: Bob Kaiser and Steve Coll. Len Downie, the *Post*'s former executive editor, helped me work through a hard question that came up later.

My agent, Andrew Wylie, guided me with a sure hand through unusual terrain in the course of *Dark Mirror*'s journey. I am obliged for above-and-beyond support from the Wylie Agency's James Pullen, Jessica Calagione, Jacqueline Ko, and Katie Cacouris.

It is my honor and privilege to work with Penguin Press, which is everything an author could want. Ann Godoff, the founder and president, earned Penguin Press's place long ago as the house of choice for serious nonfiction. I am especially fortunate to have the brilliant Scott Moyers, Penguin Press's publisher, as my editor. He saw the shape of this story before it took form on the page, steered me through delicate choices, encouraged me when I faltered, and sharpened the manuscript with every stroke of his pen. Scott put himself on the line for this book, and I will not forget that. As I write this, the Penguin team is ramping up production, copyediting, legal review, and preparation for publicity and marketing. I want to give special thanks to Bruce Giffords, Roland Ottewell, Yuki Hirose, Colleen McGarvey, Danielle Plafsky, and Mia Council for the energy and focus they bring to the enterprise.

Litigation continues at this writing in *Gellman v. DHS*, the freedom of information case that has produced both questions and answers for this book. I tip my hat to the dedicated and ferocious lawyers of the Reporters Committee for Freedom of the Press, who have represented me throughout: Katie Townsend, Adam Marshall, Linda Moon, Gunita Singh, Selina MacLaren, and Hannah Bloch-Wehba.

ACKNOWLEDGMENTS

Secrecy is a complex subject at the heart of this book, and I want to acknowledge some of the people who influenced my thinking on the subject, in conversation and in their published work. Special thanks go to Mary Graham, David Pozen, Jack L. Goldsmith, Fritz Schwarz, and Steven Aftergood. Aftergood's *Secrecy News* blog at the Federation of American Scientists is an essential resource on the workings of FOIA and the classification apparatus.

It is hard to single out friendships, but these especially helped me keep my balance when the book threatened to swallow everything else: Robin Miller, Craig Snyder, Debora Cahn, Michael Heller, Freyda Spira, and Ben Slavin.

Finally, closest to the core, I am grateful for family: my late mother, Marcia Jacobs; my father, Stuart Gellman; my late stepfather, Abe Jacobs; my sisters, Sheri Throlson and Cheryl Jacobs; and my brother, Alan Gellman. Alan, a marketing executive turned executive coach, lent me his coaching superpowers this year when I needed them. My children—Abigail Gellman, Micah Gellman, Lily Gellman, and Benjamin Gellman—enrich my life and fill me with pride. Dafna Linzer, my partner in all things, gave me the gifts of her honesty, counsel, and love, and sustained our family life when book writing kept me away. I look ahead with hope for decades to come.

NOTES

PREFACE

xi **"How did you do it?":** Snowden and I did not use standard commercial chat services from Skype, Yahoo, or Google, which are easy for authorities to monitor. We used channels that were both encrypted (our words unreadable by others) and anonymized (our locations and identities concealed). For the technically minded: we used Pidgin on the Tails operating system, connected to Jabber accounts over Tor hidden services, with Off the Record encryption.

xii **panels of blue-black glass:** The architect Jack Self described the elegant cuboid structure of OPS2A/B, the NSA's operations center, in an article titled "The Authorised Information Available on This Building Could Be Published in a Single Tweet," *Dezeen*, March 26, 2015, at https://perma.cc/S8P7-MWJ8. Wikimedia hosts a public-domain photograph of the headquarters building at https://perma.cc/9J6A-WGDN.

xii **"golden age of SIGINT":** The term appears in a high-level policy planning paper titled "SIGINT Strategy," February 23, 2012, and shared with allied services from the United Kingdom, Canada, New Zealand, and Australia. The paper has been reproduced online at https://perma.cc/CL7E-6VY9. It was first described publicly in James Risen and Laura Poitras, "N.S.A. Report Outlined Goals for More Power," *New York Times*, November 22, 2013, https://nyti.ms/31ToL5T.

xiv **"I'm not sure I'll ever":** Edward Snowden and Barton Gellman, live encrypted chat, October 2013.

xv **his memoir last year:** Edward Snowden, *Permanent Record* (New York: Henry Holt, 2019).

xvi **a book about power:** See, for example, Jeffrey Vagle, "Surveillance Is Still About Power," *Just Security*, February 9, 2016, www.justsecurity.org/29240/surveillance-power/.

CHAPTER ONE: PANDORA

1 **brought her an enigmatic tip:** Poitras, conversation with author, February 2, 2013. According to Micah Lee, who helped arrange the first contact with Poitras, the would-be confidential source wrote to him on January 11, 2013, saying, "I need to get information securely to Laura Poitras and her alone, but I can't find an email/gpg key for her. Can you help?" Lee sent the source her key and verified that it was authentic (by tweeting its forty-character "fingerprint") on January 28, 2013. Poitras emailed me three days later, on January 31, and we met on February 2. Micah Lee, "Ed Snowden Taught Me to Smuggle Secrets Past Incredible Danger. Now I Teach You," *Intercept*, October 28, 2014, http://interc.pt/1DXiB2S.

1 **NSA's "Q Group":** The NSA is opaque in public about its organizational structure. Internal charts made available by Snowden, on file with author, use "Q" to designate internal security (not to be confused with the fictional Q Branch of the British Secret Intelligence

NOTES

Service, which makes spy gadgets for James Bond). Formally, it went by Associate Directorate for Security and Counterintelligence. As a relatively small office, in comparison to S (Signals Intelligence), T (Technology), and others, it was known as a "group." Confidential source, interview with author, February 22, 2016.

There have been very few public references to Q Group. The best one I found is Eli Lake, "Inside the 'Q Group,' the Directorate Hunting Down Edward Snowden," *Daily Beast*, June 10, 2013, http://thebea.st/1oYatwL.

2 **Top Secret, compartmented:** The markings on the document were "TOP SECRET//SI//ORCON//NOFORN." Among other meanings, which I will take up later, those designations signify that the material includes "sensitive compartmented information" about signals intelligence sources and methods. Compartments are used to segregate classified information so that even people with sufficient clearances are not permitted to see the contents without an approved "need to know." Although the PRISM slides were not marked "ECI," a still more restricted category that stands for "exceptionally controlled information," the accompanying speaker's notes said that portions of the briefing should be treated as such. For more on classification markings, see "Intelligence Community Classification and Control Markings Implementation Manual," Office of the Director of National Intelligence, May 31, 2011, www.fas.org/sgp/othergov/intel/capco_imp.pdf.

2 **Under the cover name PRISM:** PowerPoint presentation, "PRISM/US-984XN Overview," April 2013 (hereafter cited as "PRISM Overview"), on file with author, published in part at www.washingtonpost.com/wp-srv/special/politics/prism-collection-documents/. Other news sites have published portions of additional slides. They are aggregated at https://nsa.gov1.info/dni/prism.html. See also Barton Gellman and Laura Poitras, "U.S., British Intelligence Mining Data from Nine U.S. Internet Companies in Broad Secret Program," *Washington Post*, June 7, 2013, http://wapo.st/1LcAw6p.

Several U.S. government officials mocked our use of the term "program" in that headline and story, saying we demonstrated ignorance of the subject. Robert S. Litt, the general counsel of the Office of the Director of National Intelligence, habitually referred to "the so-called PRISM program" in public remarks. See his remarks, "Privacy, Technology, and National Security," July 18, 2013, at https://perma.cc/U3ZL-UCSX, and "Facts on the Collection of Intelligence Pursuant to Section 702 of the Foreign Intelligence Surveillance Act," June 8, 2013, at https://perma.cc/Z567-NZ6M. The latter said PRISM was simply a name for "an internal government computer system." That claim was misleading. In NSA argot, PRISM is a "sigad," or "signals intelligence activity designator." A sigad represents a point of access to data that the NSA wants to collect and a method of tapping into it. I do not know a better term than "program" to describe it for a lay audience.

2 **Yahoo, Google, Microsoft, and Facebook accounts:** The full list encompassed nine companies, also including AOL, Skype (owned by Microsoft), Apple, YouTube (owned by Google), and Paltalk. According to the briefing, similar access to Dropbox was imminent.

3 **had six miles to travel:** The distance is measured as the crow flies for illustration. Email does not actually follow a linear path across the internet. Standard network protocols break the message into "packets," each of which is routed independently before the message is reassembled at its destination. Data takes the cheapest or fastest path, which may not be the shortest. The next endnote explains what was different about the precautions that Poitras and I took.

3 **anonymous relays around the world:** Ordinarily, when a computer connects to a website or an email server, it broadcasts a numeric string called its internet protocol address. That address identifies the device and its location. In order to protect our anonymity, Poitras and I connected to the internet using Tor, a free proxy service that routes each connection through three randomly chosen relays, many of them overseas. See the Tor Project, https://torproject.org. For an interactive graphic of the system, see "Data Flow in the Tor Network," https://torflow.uncharted.software/.

3 **spoof their hardware and network addresses:** Every device that connects to the internet has a network interface card with a unique address of twelve letters and numbers. This MAC address, short for "media access control," identifies the hardware. Another string, a set of

NOTES

numbers arranged in four groups and known as the internet protocol, or IP, address, assigns the machine a local network identity. The latter usually corresponds closely to geographic location. See "What Is a MAC Address?," http://whatismyipaddress.com/mac-address. Using software tools, one can randomize both of those addresses and thereby avoid many forms of tracking. Such tools, for example, are built into an operating system called Tails, which is based on Debian Linux and optimized for privacy. See "The Amnesic Incognito Live System," https://tails.boum.org.

3 **the ciphertext looked like this:** Poitras to author, email, May 21, 2013. The ciphertext I quote here is for illustration. It is an encrypted version of the words Poitras wrote, verbatim, but it is not the same encrypted version she sent. For purposes of this book, I decrypted her message and reencrypted it with a different key. In effect, I changed the lock, which changed the ciphertext. If I reproduced her message exactly as sent, an intelligence agency could match it against internet traffic that it might have captured on the day she sent it. Such a match would identify our anonymous accounts and could compromise other confidential aspects of our work.

This risk is not remote. U.S. intelligence rules on "minimization," the official term for limits placed on surveillance of U.S. citizens and residents, ordinarily require the NSA to discard the communications of U.S. citizens and residents if they are not relevant to a foreign intelligence purpose, and in any case after five years. The limits do not apply to encrypted messages. Still-classified regulations allow "retention of all communications that are enciphered or reasonably believed to contain secret meaning" for "any period of time" until the NSA is capable of decrypting them or no longer cares.

In the summer of 2013, after the Snowden revelations began, the Office of the Director of National Intelligence published a censored version of its 2011 minimization guidelines. The redacted document, which blacked out the provisions about encrypted text, was "Minimization Procedures Used by the National Security Agency in Connection with Acquisitions of Foreign Intelligence Information Pursuant to Section 702 of the Foreign Intelligence Surveillance Act of 1978, as Amended" (redacted), submitted by the U.S. Department of Justice to the U.S. Foreign Intelligence Surveillance Court on October 31, 2011, at https://perma.cc/R5JG-B356. Two months before the ODNI release, I published the full, unredacted text of the same document as submitted to the FISC on July 29, 2009. It is reproduced on Scribd at http://bit.ly/1oQ97DL and also at https://edwardsnowden.com/wp-content/uploads/2013/10/FAA-Minimization-Procedures.pdf. The accompanying story was Ellen Nakashima, Barton Gellman, and Greg Miller, "New Documents Reveal Parameters of NSA's Secret Surveillance Programs," *Washington Post*, June 20, 2013, http://wapo.st/1QMis6c. Shortly after that story, the ODNI issued a news release but made no reference to the provisions on encrypted text. See "ODNI Fact Sheet," June 25, 2013, http://wapo.st/1NpW28K.

5 **"I feel a little bad":** Poitras to author, email, December 22, 2010.

5 **Politics on the radical side:** Mary Greendale, "Filming the Ravages of War: After Winning Peabody Award, Holliston Native Set to Focus on Iraq," *MetroWest Daily News* (Framingham, MA), June 13, 2004, at https://perma.cc/9AXE-3ESR.

5 **Grew up near Boston:** Liz Karagianis, "Fulfilling a Dream," *MIT Spectrum* (Spring 2008), http://spectrum.mit.edu/articles/fulfilling-a-dream-2/.

5 *My Country, My Country*: Praxis Films, press kit, 2006, www.praxisfilms.org/images/uploads/mycountrymycountry.presskit.pdf. The film's broadcast premiere was October 25, 2006, on the Public Broadcasting Service. See www.pbs.org/pov/mycountry/. For the 2007 Academy Award nomination, see https://to.pbs.org/1QJZkGk.

5 **failed attempt to install democracy:** "Interview: Laura Poitras, Director of 'My Country, My Country,'" *Indiewire*, July 31, 2006, www.indiewire.com/article/indiewire_interview_laura_poitras_director_of_my_country_my_country.

5 **her latest,** *The Oath*: See Zeitgeist Films, press kit, 2010, https://zeitgeistfilms.com/media/films/182/oath.presskit.pdf.

5 **pulled aside for interrogation and search:** This account, which Poitras gave to me at the time, has not been disputed by the U.S. government. Later, it became public. See Dennis

Lim, "An Eye on America Is Also Under Watch," *New York Times*, May 6, 2010, http://nyti
.ms/1ppyRaH; and Glenn Greenwald, "U.S. Filmmaker Repeatedly Detained at Border,"
Salon, April 8, 2012, www.salon.com/2012/04/08/u_s_filmmaker_repeatedly_detained
_at_border/.

5 **stating no reason:** Two possible explanations emerged later, but authorities notified Poitras
of neither. The first involved an ambush of Oregon National Guard soldiers in Baghdad in
2004. Poitras was said to be filming from a nearby rooftop when it happened. According to
documents she obtained under the Freedom of Information Act from the FBI, a lieutenant
colonel from the unit reported her to the Army's Criminal Investigation Division, saying
he "strongly believed POITRAS had prior knowledge of the ambush" and could have
alerted U.S. forces. Government documents offer no basis but coincidence for the officer's
belief. See Poitras FOIA release at Poitras-65, displayed at a 2016 exhibition at the Whitney Museum in New York and available at https://cryptome.org/2016/02/poitras-docs
-whitney.jpg.

A second possible explanation came in a *New Yorker* article, which noted that she
transferred money to the principal subject of her film, a Sunni doctor and clinic director
named Riyadh al-Adhadh, as his family fled the civil war in 2006. See George Packer, "The
Holder of Secrets," *New Yorker*, October 20, 2014, http://nyr.kr/ZliVIV. The FBI document Poitras-64 described the doctor's neighborhood as "very pro–SADDAM HUSSEIN."

The watch-listing bureaucracy seems to have made no attempt to justify the adverse
inferences it drew from these superficial facts or to supply any other evidence to Poitras or
the public. Like many other journalists in Iraq, I had also witnessed dangerous encounters
for U.S. forces, and I had contributed toward the resettlement of an Iraqi stringer, himself
nostalgic for Hussein, who endangered his family by working for the *Washington Post*. For
a critique of the watch-listing process, see "U.S. Government Watchlisting: Unfair Process
and Devastating Consequences," American Civil Liberties Union, March 2014, www.aclu
.org/us-government-watchlisting-unfair-process-and-devastating-consequences.

5 **"confiscated my laptop":** Affidavit of Laura Poitras, paragraph 35, August 24, 2016, in
Poitras v. Department of Homeland Security, Civil Action No. 15-cv-01091-KBJ.

5 **U.S. government's pretense:** In 2008, the Ninth Circuit held "that reasonable suspicion is
not needed for customs officials to search a laptop or other personal electronic storage devices at the border," accepting the government's contention that laptops and hard drives are
analogous to other closed containers. See United States v. Arnold, 523 F.3d 941 (9th Cir.
2008), https://caselaw.findlaw.com/us-9th-circuit/1162807.html. The Fourth Circuit had
already found no First Amendment exception to border search doctrine for "expressive
materials." See United States v. Ickes, 393 F.3d 501 (4th Cir. 2005), https://caselaw.find
law.com/us-4th-circuit/1308274.html.

6 **right of a citizen to be left alone:** This formulation was famously articulated by Samuel D.
Warren and the future Supreme Court justice Louis D. Brandeis in "The Right to Privacy,"
Harvard Law Review, December 15, 1890, http://groups.csail.mit.edu/mac/classes/6.805
/articles/privacy/Privacy_brand_warr2.html.

6 **judges had only just begun to question it:** The leading cases were still to come, or progress-
ing through trial courts. In 2013, the Ninth Circuit revisited some of the issues in *Arnold*.
It found that reasonable suspicion is required to conduct a forensic search of an electronic
device, which is considerably more intrusive than a conventional search. See United States
v. Cotterman, 709 F.3d 952 (9th Cir., en banc, 2013), https://caselaw.findlaw.com/us-9th
-circuit/1624272.html. In 2014, the Supreme Court held that law enforcement officers
need a warrant to search a cellphone taken incident to arrest. The case is likely to have
implications for border searches, especially if a device gives authorities access to information in cloud storage. See Riley v. California, 573 U.S. ___ (2014), https://caselaw.findlaw
.com/us-supreme-court/13-132-nr3.html.

For further discussion, see Gretchen C. F. Shappert, "The Border Search Doctrine:
Warrantless Searches of Electronic Devices After *Riley v. California*," *United States Attorney's Bulletin*, November 2014, 1–14; and Thomas Mann Miller, "Digital Border Searches

NOTES

After *Riley v. California*," *Washington Law Review*, December 9, 2015, http://papers.ssrn .com/sol3/papers.cfm?abstract_id=2701597.

6 **hiring private investigators:** In 2006, private investigators hired by Hewlett-Packard illegally obtained the phone records of several journalists as part of an investigation into leaks by members of the company's board of directors. See Damon Darlin, "Hewlett-Packard Spied on Writers in Leaks," *New York Times*, September 8, 2006, http://nyti.ms/1xk61Jh.

6 **not to reveal our confidential sources:** Even before the Snowden revelations, privacy advocates were making this point. See Christopher Soghoian, "When Secrets Aren't Safe with Journalists," *New York Times*, October 26, 2011, http://nyti.ms/1RskMQl.

6 **another word for "somebody else's computer":** Graham Cluley, "Don't Call It 'the Cloud.' Call It 'Someone Else's Computer,'" blog post, December 3, 2013, www.grahamcluley .com/2013/12/cloud-privacy-computer/.

7 **GPG, TrueCrypt, OTR, SOCKS proxies, Tor:** The most important link I sent to Poitras was the Electronic Frontier Foundation's excellent guide "Surveillance Self-Defense," https://ssd.eff.org, which explains most of those acronyms. More valuably, the EFF lays out a method for thinking about the particular "threat model" in each case. I also sent one of the occasional blog posts I wrote for *Time* online, "The Case of the Stolen Laptop: How to Encrypt, and Why," *Techland*, August 6, 2010, http://ti.me/1Qjdu5f.

7 **the cypherpunks of the 1990s:** See Steven Levy, *Crypto: How the Code Rebels Beat the Government, Saving Privacy in the Digital Age* (New York: Viking, 2001). See also Eric Hughes, "A Cypherpunk's Manifesto" (1993), www.activism.net/cypherpunk/manifesto.html; and John Perry Barlow, "A Declaration of the Independence of Cyberspace," Electronic Frontier Foundation, February 8, 1996, www.eff.org/cyberspace-independence.

7 **invented "onion routing":** Among the seminal papers by Naval Research Laboratory employees was David Goldschlag, Michael Reed, and Paul Syverson, "Onion Routing for Anonymous and Private Internet Connections," *Communications of the Association for Computing Machinery*, January 28, 1999, www.onion-router.net/Publications/CACM-1999 .pdf. Onion routing relays an internet connection through a series of hops, each of them encrypted, ensuring that no single network operator can see both the origin and the destination. Today's Tor Project (originally an acronym for "The Onion Router") offers a free, easy-to-use anonymous browser at www.torproject.org.

8 **GPG, the gold standard of email and file encryption:** GPG, also known as Gnu Privacy Guard and GnuPG, is a free, open-source implementation of the encryption standard pioneered by Phil Zimmermann in the commercial software package called Pretty Good Privacy, or PGP. (Already we have four names for the same basic product, five if we add OpenPGP.) The original author of GPG remains sole custodian of the code. He marked its first decade in a post to an email listserv, archived here: Werner Koch, "GnuPG's 10th birthday," December 20, 2007, https://lists.gnupg.org/pipermail/gnupg-announce /2007q4/000268.html. See also Julia Angwin, "The World's Email Encryption Software Relies on One Guy, Who Is Going Broke," ProPublica, February 5, 2015, http://propub.li /223gPN8.

8 *Time* **magazine overrode a reporter's objections:** The case was *United States v. I. Lewis Libby*. Libby was eventually convicted of perjury and obstruction of justice in 2005. See Daniela Deane, "Prosecutor Demands Time Reporter Testimony," *Washington Post*, July 5, 2005, http://wapo.st/1Tthli J. Also see Matthew Cooper, "What Scooter Libby and I Talked About," *Time*, October 30, 2005, http://ti.me/1QovJVB. The chief editor of Time Inc. defended his decision in a memoir. See Norman Pearlstine, *Off the Record: The Press, the Government, and the War over Anonymous Sources* (New York: Farrar, Straus & Giroux, 2007). For my part, I did not want an editor or publisher to be capable of making the decision for me.

8 **even experts foundered:** Disheartening proof is easy to find in the GnuPG-users listserv, an email forum populated exclusively by geeks, where hundreds of thousands of words have been spilled on the software's mysteries. See the GnuPG-users Archives, http://lists .gnupg.org/pipermail/gnupg-users/.

8 **manual could swallow:** The horror classic runs to about twenty-five thousand words. GPG boasts a sixteen-thousand-word manual and eleven thousand words of "frequently asked questions." See Robert Louis Stevenson, *The Strange Tale of Dr. Jekyll and Mr. Hyde*, www .gutenberg.org/files/42/42.txt; "The GNU Privacy Handbook," www.gnupg.org/gph/en /manual.html; and "GNUPG FREQUENTLY ASKED QUESTIONS," www.gnupg.org /faq/gnupg-faq.txt. After drafting this comparison, I found a fine blog post with a similar comparison to the forty-thousand-word novel *Fahrenheit 451*. See Moxie Marlinspike, "GPG and Me," February 4, 2015, www.thoughtcrime.org/blog/gpg-and-me/.

Even the commercial PGP software, which had a friendly graphical interface, was baffling to ordinary users. In a controlled test with a dozen beginners, three accidentally made public their secret encryption keys (which defeated the main protection of PGP), all twelve disregarded instructions to choose a complex passphrase, one forgot her passphrase, and one never managed to send an encrypted message at all. See Alma Whitten and J. D. Tygar, "Why Johnny Can't Encrypt: A Usability Evaluation of PGP 5.0," *Proceedings of the 8th USENIX Security Symposium*, August 23, 1999, 169–84, www.gaudior.net/alma /johnny.pdf.

8 **"You should probably have":** Author to Poitras, email, January 14, 2011.

8 **"Do you have time to grab a coffee":** Poitras to author, email, January 31, 2013.

9 **conversation had begun five days before:** The intermediary who helped the source make contact with Poitras said the secure channel was established on January 28, 2013, when he confirmed the forty-character "fingerprint" of Poitras's encryption key for the source. See Lee, "Ed Snowden Taught Me to Smuggle Secrets Past Incredible Danger." Lee's tweet may be found at https://twitter.com/micahflee/status/296119710485979136.

9 **domestic surveillance in my last book:** Barton Gellman, *Angler: The Cheney Vice Presidency* (New York: Penguin Press, 2008). For the NSA surveillance narrative, see especially chapters 6, 11, and 12.

9 **no better than a coin toss:** According to Malcolm Gladwell, systematic lie detection tests, based on videotaped interviews, "have been given to policemen, customs officers, judges, trial lawyers, and psychotherapists, as well as to officers from the F.B.I., the C.I.A., the D.E.A., and the Bureau of Alcohol, Tobacco, and Firearms—people one would have thought would be good at spotting lies. On average, they score fifty per cent, which is to say that they would have done just as well if they hadn't watched the tapes at all and just guessed." See Malcolm Gladwell, "The Naked Face," *New Yorker*, August 5, 2002, http:// nyr.kr/1Rsoae4. Also see Paul Ekman, "8 Myths About Lying," www.paulekman.com/psy chology/8-myths-about-lying/.

10 **interviewed an Israeli settler named Yigal Amir:** I found the notes of that interview and wrote about them on the night of Rabin's assassination. Barton Gellman, "In June, Suspect Talked of Israel's Weak Backbone," *Washington Post*, November 5, 1995, http://wapo.st /20qTJ1X. The June story, which did not mention Amir, was Barton Gellman, "Jewish Settlers Grab Land as Arab Self-Rule Nears; Israel Does Little to Halt West Bank Moves," *Washington Post*, June 26, 1995.

11 **Top Secret reference site:** The CIA disclosed the existence of a Top Secret "Intellipedia," shared by other agencies, in 2006. See Cass R. Sunstein, "A Brave New Wiki World," *Washington Post*, February 24, 2007, http://wapo.st/1oKv9IF. The online "IT Law Wiki" first posted a description of NSANet in 2011, at http://itlaw.wikia.com/wiki/NSANet, according to this date-based Google search: https://goo.gl/j0Jc8y.

12 **short film on another NSA critic:** Laura Poitras, "The Program," *New York Times*, August 23, 2012, http://nyti.ms/1TBmnJp, was a profile of the whistleblower William Binney for the newspaper's "Op-Docs" series.

12 **failed to elicit a reply from Greenwald:** Edward Snowden used the handle Cincinnatus, not Verax, for contact with Greenwald. Micah Lee, then a staff technologist at the Electronic Frontier Foundation, said the anonymous source (writing to Lee as "anon108") first began trying to reach Greenwald in December 2012. When Greenwald did not respond, the source

"moved on" to Poitras and asked Lee for her secure contacts on January 11, 2013. It was not until May 13, when Snowden renewed his effort to bring in Greenwald, that Lee sent a thumb drive with encryption tools to Greenwald in Brazil. It was delayed in transit and arrived on May 27, which is also the date of the source's "first encrypted conversation directly with Greenwald." See Lee, "Ed Snowden Taught Me to Smuggle Secrets Past Incredible Danger."

12 **a how-to video on encryption:** See anon108, "GPG for Journalists—Windows Edition | Encryption for Journalists | Anonymous 2013," Vimeo, January 6, 2013, https://vimeo .com/56881481.

12 **a less tractable panelist:** In fairness, the discussion flew out of control when NPR's Dina Temple-Raston told him angrily from the floor that she knew more than he did about the evidence in one of her recent stories. Greenwald counterattacked, and the exchange went south. Puzzled about the hostility, I asked Greenwald afterward, "Did you happen to run over her dog recently?" He smiled and said, "Actually, I kind of did." He had branded Temple-Raston a patsy in a recent column about reporters who swallow U.S. intelligence claims without proof. See Glenn Greenwald, "Government Accusations: No Evidence Needed," *Salon*, November 1, 2010, www.salon.com/2010/11/01/awlaki_2/. The NYU panel took place on November 5, 2010. The video, uploaded three days later, is at https:// youtu.be/nyJU2Ceq83s.

13 **huge scoop about secret overseas prisons:** See Dana Priest and Julie Tate, "CIA Holds Terror Suspects in Secret Prisons," *Washington Post*, November 2, 2005, http://wapo.st /1fk1wVN.

14 **seized the press run, and burned it:** See "Smiles or Tears for Town Crier?," *Student Press Law Center Report* (Fall 1979), 28, http://issuu.com/splc/docs/v2n3fall79. I recounted this story at length in a 2014 speech marking the fortieth anniversary of the Student Press Law Center, which assisted us in our legal battle. The speech and accompanying slides are available in full on YouTube, https://youtu.be/bSMnfzGyn08.

14 **a First Amendment lawsuit:** Gellman v. Wacker, U.S. District Court for the Eastern District of Pennsylvania, 1977. I brought the case with fellow students Craig Snyder and Robert Gordon. Many of the filings and hearing transcripts are available in the Barton Gellman Papers, box 10, Mudd Manuscript Library, Princeton University. See http://findingaids .princeton.edu/collections/MC262/c011.

14 **poison note for my college application file:** During my freshman year of college, I obtained a copy from the admissions office. (I had not waived my right under the Buckley Amendment, 20 U.S.C. § 1232g, to see my recommendations.) The principal filled out nothing on the four-page form, save for one sentence: "I do not feel as though I could give a recommendation that would be helpful toward Barton's acceptance by your institution." A copy is on file in the Gellman Papers.

14 **a *Philadelphia Inquirer* photograph:** The photograph accompanied Marc Schogol, "Confiscated School Paper May Lead to Court Fight," *Philadelphia Inquirer*, October 29, 1977. A copy is available in the Gellman Papers.

14 **express his contempt for my work:** See, for example, *Face the Nation*, CBS, September 18, 2011, http://cbsn.ws/1PXLdT6.

> **Bob Schieffer:** Barton Gellman, who wrote a biography on you, "Angler," said your book shows mutual disillusionment that developed between you and President Bush. Is that accurate?
> **Dick Cheney:** No, I don't think it is. I didn't think Gellman's original book was all that accurate either. I believe it's called "Angler," which is my Secret Service code name. He got that part right.

14 **ten-page letter to Congress:** Assistant Attorney General William E. Moschella to Senator Arlen Specter, chairman of the Senate Committee on the Judiciary, November 23, 2005, http://wapo.st/1TagwuW. See also Christopher Lee, "Report on FBI Tools Is Disputed,"

NOTES

Washington Post, November 30, 2005, http://wapo.st/1PR4g1r. The article in dispute was Barton Gellman, "The FBI's Secret Scrutiny: In Hunt for Terrorists, Bureau Examines Records of Ordinary Americans," *Washington Post*, November 6, 2005, http://wapo.st/1KmBrrl.

A year and a half later, on the same day the Justice Department's inspector general issued a scathing report, the department retracted most of its previous letter and promised to "correct, as necessary, any erroneous statements made in . . . correspondence to Congress." See Office of the Inspector General of the Department of Justice, *A Review of the Federal Bureau of Investigation's Use of National Security Letters*, March 9, 2007, https://oig .justice.gov/special/s0703b/final.pdf; and Acting Assistant Attorney General Richard A. Hertling to Senator Arlen Specter, March 9, 2007, http://wapo.st/1UEMpZB.

14 **CIA had mounted a fierce campaign:** "Statement by Dr. David Kay, Special Advisor to the DCI [director of central intelligence]," November 3, 2003, published as a CIA news release and sent to scores of news organizations. It is available at https://perma.cc/8CL8-U3AB. Kay oversaw the CIA-led Iraq Survey Group, which was searching for weapons of mass destruction after the fall of the Iraqi president, Saddam Hussein. His statement, and his private letter to the executive editor demanding that my story be retracted, were reactions to Barton Gellman, "Search in Iraq Fails to Find Nuclear Threat: No Evidence Uncovered of Reconstituted Program," *Washington Post*, October 26, 2003, http://wapo.st/1ZnfdZD.

In 2006, Kay told me he knew at the time that the 2003 story was accurate. The nuclear accusations, he said, were "a gross manipulation of data," but pressure from the CIA's deputy director, John McLaughlin, and Cheney made it impossible for him to acknowledge the truth publicly until he made his formal report to Bush the following year. David Kay, interview with author, August 3, 2006.

15 **offered publicly to put me in a field:** The story he disliked was Barton Gellman, "U.S. Bombs Missed 70% of Time," *Washington Post*, March 16, 1991, available on the Stanford University website at http://stanford.io/1KSNLdM.

16 **"So it is decided!":** Verax to Poitras and author, email, May 2013, on file with author. Verax used cover names, even in encrypted correspondence, to add one more layer of security.

20 **did not invoke any official grievance procedure:** In a statement sent by email to reporters, the NSA public affairs office wrote, "There are numerous avenues that Mr. Snowden could have used to raise . . . concerns or whistleblower allegations. We have searched for . . . indications of outreach from him in those areas and to date have not discovered any engagements related to his claims." NSA statement, May 29, 2014.

20 **a recent presidential directive:** President Obama's directive extended whistleblower protections for the first time to intelligence community employees. It made no mention of contractors. In any case, its procedures did not come into effect until July 2013, a month after the first Snowden disclosure. See "Presidential Policy Directive 19," October 10, 2012, http://fas.org/irp/offdocs/ppd/ppd-19.pdf. Also see Glenn Kessler, "Edward Snowden's Claim That He Had 'No Proper Channels' for Protection as a Whistleblower," *Washington Post*, March 12, 2014, http://wapo.st/1RMjylz.

The Intelligence Community Whistleblower Protection Act of 1998, Public Law 105-272, at https://perma.cc/JJ64-WC43, provides a secure means for employees—including contractors—to report to Congress or an agency's inspector general on matters of "urgent concern" regarding classified information. According to the Defense Department, however, it offers no protection "from reprisal for whistleblowing." The statute's definition of "urgent concern" specifically excludes "differences of opinions concerning public policy matters." See "About the ICWPA," Department of Defense Office of the Inspector General, www.dodig.mil/programs/whistleblower/icwpa.html; and Daniel D'Isidoro, "Protecting Whistleblowers and Secrets in the Intelligence Community," *Harvard Law School National Security Journal*, September 29, 2014, http://harvardnsj.org/2014/09/protecting -whistleblowers-and-secrets-in-the-intelligence-community/.

22 **Three digital vaults:** The Pandora and Verax vaults were in TrueCrypt format, with Verax inside Pandora. The innermost vault, Journodrop, which was inside Verax, was an encrypted, compressed archive in a format called 7z, an alternative to the more familiar zip format.

22 **one gigabyte could hold:** The forensic security firm Setec has published a reference sheet, "How Many Pages per Gigabyte and Megabyte?," www.setecinvestigations.com/resources /techhints/Pages_per_Gigabyte.pdf.

25 **My master's thesis:** "Secrecy, Security and the 'Right to Know': Some Grounds and Limits of Open Government" (M.Litt. thesis in Politics, University of Oxford, 1988).

25 **twice taught a Princeton course:** The course, WWS 384, was called "Secrecy, Accountability, and the National Security State." See https://registrar.princeton.edu/course-offerings /course_details.xml?courseid=011833&term=1132.

25 **cover names, handling caveats, and access controls:** The authoritative source is "Intelligence Community Authorized Classification and Control Markings," Controlled Access Program Coordination Office, Office of the Director of National Intelligence, March 30, 2012, https://perma.cc/M9W2-SY3Z. For a slightly more user-friendly guide, see "Marking Classified National Security Information," Information Security Oversight Office, Revision 4, January 2018, https://perma.cc/6N2K-2SZB.

26 **surveillance program created by Dick Cheney:** See Gellman, *Angler*, chapters 11 and 12.

26 **"Wish I knew the underlying details":** Author to Poitras, August 7, 2012.

27 **Years later he told me:** Edward Snowden, interview with author, July 1, 2015, Moscow.

28 **one final breach of NSA defenses:** I tell this story in the final chapter of this book.

29 **"Edward Joseph Snowden, SSN":** The redaction of his Social Security number is mine, not Snowden's. He provided it to us in full.

29 **"Former Senior Advisor":** I take up later in this book whether Snowden exaggerated the nature or seniority of his positions. The titles he used here were imprecise.

CHAPTER TWO: HEARTBEAT

31 **steered his new Integra:** For Snowden's daily commute from his home at 94-1044 Eleu Street in Waipahu to the Kunia Regional Security Operations Center, see Google Maps, https://goo.gl/4vwT8w.

31 **It was March 2012:** Snowden, interview with author, July 1, 2015, Moscow.

31 **half an hour's drive from the Baskin-Robbins:** Peter Serafin, "Punahou Grad Stirs Up Illinois Politics," *Honolulu Star-Bulletin*, March 21, 2004, http://archives.starbulletin.com/2004 /03/21/news/story4.html. For the drive time, see Google Maps, https://goo.gl/SY1673.

31 **shabby with age:** The physical description of Kunia's underground facility is based on interviews with former members of the workforce there. Its origins, design, and successive tenants are described in "History of NIOC Hawaii," Navy Information Operations Command, www.public.navy.mil/fcc-c10f/niochi/Pages/AboutUs.aspx; and Donna Miles, "Beneath the Pineapple Fields," *Soldiers*, January 1995, 26–27, https://fas.org/irp/news/1995/soldiers _jan95_p26.htm.

32 **did not break ground:** See Michael A. Lantron, "NSA/CSS Hawaii Breaks Ground for New Operations Security Center," U.S. Navy news release, September 7, 2007, www.navy.mil /submit/display.asp?story_id=31660.

32 **was still "Charlie Foxtrot":** The NSA announced completion of the new Captain Joseph J. Rochefort Building just before Snowden arrived. Sources with firsthand knowledge told me that much confusion accompanied the move, with the usual complaints and growing pains. Years later, the Kunia Tunnel remained in use, with many offices still divided between the two facilities. See NSA press release, "NSA/CSS Unveils New Hawaii Center Designed to Boost Intelligence Integration, Collaboration," January 6, 2012, at https://perma.cc /JV6V-75WZ.

32 **scanned his green contractor's badge:** NSA badges are color-coded for quick identification: blue for employees, green for contractors, red (with a big "V") for visitors, black for photographers, and so on. Snowden, interview with author, December 6, 2013, Moscow; agency sources who wish to remain unnamed, interviews with author.

32 **miles of fluorescent bulbs:** "History of NIOC Hawaii" reports that there are roughly five thousand bulbs, each forty inches long. End to end, they would stretch for more than three miles.

32 **"It's like a Bond villain's lair":** Snowden, encrypted live chat with author, February 14, 2014.

33 **other *noms de code*:** At various stages of interaction with Laura Poitras, Glenn Greenwald, and me, Snowden used alter egos including Cincinnatus, anon108, and Citizen Four.

33 **"I was starting to operationalize":** Snowden, interview with author, July 1, 2015, Moscow.

33 **he blamed "tabloid values":** Snowden, interview with author, December 6, 2013, Moscow.

34 **serious epileptic seizure:** Snowden described a "really big epilepsy scare" and "a pretty serious event" that prevented him from driving again under Maryland law. He declined to provide further details. Snowden, chat with author, February 14, 2014.

34 **Dell Advanced Solutions Group:** Snowden's business card, examined by author, said only Dell. The division he worked for was also known as Dell Services Federal Government.

34 **intended to pedal to work:** In his memoir, Snowden implies but does not quite say that he actually commuted by bicycle. He told me, in a lengthy exchange of emails, that he had planned to bike but changed his mind and drove despite the small risk of an epileptic seizure. See Edward Snowden, *Permanent Record* (New York: Henry Holt, 2019), 215.

34 **six seizure-free months before driving:** Hawaii's law was actually stricter than Maryland's, which forbade driving by anyone who had had a seizure in the three previous months. See Epilepsy Foundation, "Driver Information by State," www.epilepsy.com/driving-laws/2008696, and HAW. REV. STAT. § 286-4.1 (2011).

34 **NSA's National Threat Operations Center:** Formally, it is the NSA/CSS Threat Operations Center, the CSS being Central Security Service. See *National Cyber Incident Response Plan*, September 2010, www.federalnewsradio.com/wp-content/uploads/pdfs/NCIRP_Interim_Version_September_2010.pdf. For an advertised position similar to Snowden's, see National Security Agency, "Computer Network Defense (CND) Analyst," NTOC, Hawaii, archived at https://archive.is/ioxyb.

35 **CACI International:** CACI International was one of four prime contractors at the time under an NSA umbrella program called AXISS (Agency Extended Information System Services), for information technology and security services. See Brian Friel, "Spy Agency Multiple-Award Contracts Bring 80 Companies $20 Billion," Bloomberg Government, November 20, 2012, reposted at http://iissonline.net/spy-agency-multiple-award-contracts-bring-80-companies-20-billion/. A sampling of current AXISS contract jobs at the company may be found at http://careers.caci.com/key/Axiss-NSA.html.

35 **"a half hour a day":** Snowden, live chat with author, February 13, 2014.

35 **One baffled colleague:** Correspondence released by the NSA in FOIA case 78137E, on file with author. See Jason Leopold, Marcy Wheeler, and Ky Henderson, "Exclusive: Snowden Tried to Tell NSA About Surveillance Concerns, Documents Reveal," *Vice News*, June 4, 2016, https://news.vice.com/article/edward-snowden-leaks-tried-to-tell-nsa-about-surveillance-concerns-exclusive. The full correspondence is at www.documentcloud.org/documents/2852366-Leopold-FOIA-NSA-Emails-About-Snowden-Concerns.html.

36 **Off-the-books arrangements:** Confidential sources, interviews with author, February 2014. A Dell spokesman declined to comment. For background, see U.S. Government Accountability Office, "Civilian Intelligence Community: Additional Actions Needed to Improve Reporting on and Planning for the Use of Contract Personnel," January 2014.

36 **Microsoft-certified systems engineer:** The MCSE, a frequently required credential in technology jobs, has since been renamed "Microsoft-certified solutions expert." It signifies expertise in designing, building, and maintaining technology systems for large enterprises. See Microsoft, "Explore Microsoft Certifications," www.microsoft.com/en-us/learning/mcse-certification.aspx.

36 **"three tiers of system administrators":** Ben Wittes and Robert McChesney, podcast with Lonny Anderson, *Lawfare*, December 18, 2013, www.lawfareblog.com/lawfare-podcast-episode-54-inside-nsa-part-iii-wherein-we-talk-lonny-anderson-chief-nsas-technology.

36 **"I was also helping out":** Snowden, interview with author, July 1, 2015, Moscow.

37 **"art of technology":** See "Welcome to Ars Technica," *Ars Technica*, May 8, 1999, https://archive.is/PPRME.

NOTES

37 **hosted online salons:** See Kara Swisher, "Ars Technica's Ken Fisher Speaks!," *All Things Digital*, April 17, 2008, http://allthingsd.com/20080417/ars-technicas-ken-fisher-speaks/.

37 **the man behind that handle:** See Kristina Cooke and John Shiffman, "Exclusive: Snowden as a Teen Online: Anime and Cheeky Humor," Reuters, June 12, 2013, https://archive.is/SZbRn; and Joe Mullin, "NSA Leaker Ed Snowden's Life on Ars Technica," June 12, 2013, http://arstechnica.com/tech-policy/2013/06/nsa-leaker-ed-snowdens-life-on-ars-technica.

37 **free to speak anonymously:** Snowden, interview with author, July 1, 2015, Moscow.

37 **In the Army slang:** See U.S. Army, "Soldier-Speak: A Brief Guide to Modern Military Jargon," March 8, 2015, at https://perma.cc/KC34-TS88.

37 **"belligerent, self-important":** See TheTrueHOOHA, "Building a Web Server?," *Ars Technica* OpenForum, December 30, 2001, https://arstechnica.com/civis/viewtopic.php?p=16430380#p16430380.

37 **"It's my first time":** See TheTrueHOOHA, "Building a Web Server?," *Ars Technica* OpenForum, December 29, 2001, https://arstechnica.com/civis/viewtopic.php?p=16430380#p16430380.

38 **Shrike and Belgarion:** Snowden, *Permanent Record*, 48.

38 **His father, Lonnie G. Snowden Jr.:** Edward Snowden and a family confidant, interviews with author, 2015 and 2016. See also Bryan Burrough, Sarah Ellison, and Suzanna Andrews, "The Snowden Saga: A Shadowland of Secrets and Light," *Vanity Fair*, May 2014, www.vanityfair.com/news/politics/2014/05/edward-snowden-politics-interview.

38 **Snowdens moved north:** In 1993, the Snowdens bought a house on Knights Bridge Turn in Crofton, Maryland. See Julie Bykowicz and Greg Giroux, "NSA Leaker Was Shy, Computer-Bound Teenager in Maryland," Bloomberg, June 11, 2013, http://bloom.bg/25eHvZn.

38 **with precocious chatter:** Snowden, interview with author, July 1, 2015, Moscow; family confidant, interview with author, December 10, 2015.

38 **Teachers at the Crofton Woods:** Greg Toppo, "Former Neighbor Remembers Snowden as 'Nice Kid,'" *USA Today*, June 10, 2013, http://usat.ly/1VgZmfk.

38 **his IQ score:** Snowden family confidants, interviews with author on condition of anonymity, 2014 and 2015. For a table of IQ score distributions, see iqcomparisonsite.com/iqtable.aspx. Also see James Bamford, "The Most Wanted Man in the World," *Wired*, August 22, 2014, www.wired.com/2014/08/edward-snowden/.

39 **Snowden's older sister:** Federal Judicial Center, "Annual Report" (2015), https://archive.fo/yhlza.

39 **She skipped a grade:** Family confidant, interview with author, July 22, 2014.

39 **He refused to bother:** Family confidant, interview with author, October 12, 2015.

39 **His grades were erratic:** Family confidant, interview with author, July 22, 2014.

39 **refused to return to school:** Edward Snowden, interviews with author, 2015. See also Snowden, *Permanent Record*, 65.

39 **"The public education system":** The accent in "spikéd" and the confusion of "its" and "it's" are from the original. See "Profile: Ed Snowden," Ryuhana Press, Wayback Machine, April 27, 2002, http://web.archive.org/web/20031018021255/http://ryuhanapress.com/ed.html.

39 **"I'm from the Los Alamos National Laboratory":** Family confidant, interview with author, August 2016.

39 **asked if Snowden was looking for work:** Snowden, *Permanent Record*, 60.

41 **seemed to be choosing almost at random:** Snowden and a family confidant, interviews with author, 2014 and 2015. See also Jean Marbella, Shashank Bengali, and David S. Cloud, "Details About Edward Snowden's Life in Maryland Emerge," *Baltimore Sun*, June 10, 2010, www.baltimoresun.com/news/maryland/bs-md-snowden-profile-20130610-story.html.

41 **"I'm not paying for you":** Snowden family confidant, interview with author, December 10, 2015.

41 **The results and his diploma arrived:** Test scores and diploma No. 269403 from the Maryland Department of Education are on file with author, courtesy of the Snowden family.

41 **course in Windows system engineering:** Snowden, interview with author, July 1, 2015, Moscow; family confidant, interview with author, December 10, 2015. See also Matthew Mosk

et al., "Timeline: Edward Snowden's Life as We Know It," ABC News, June 13, 2013, http://abcn.ws/21lizMS. Johns Hopkins University cut its ties with the for-profit entity seven years later, and the company was reported to be shut down. See *South China Morning Post*, June 22, 2013, www.scmp.com/news/world/article/1266209/booz-allen-hired-snowden-despite-discrepancies-his-resume; and an archived version of the CCI website in 2004, https://web.archive.org/web/20040611145138/http://www.jhutrain.com/about.aspx.

42 **syllabus spanning 4,416 pages:** At that time the relevant corpus was the five-volume *Microsoft Windows 2000 Core Requirements Training Kit* (2nd ed., Microsoft Press, 2002). See also the subsequent Daniel Petri, "Windows 2000 MCSE Certification Requirements," Petri IT Knowledgebase, January 8, 2009, www.petri.com/windows_2000_mcse_certification_requirements; and *MCSE: Windows 2000 Exams in a Nutshell*, Safari Books Online, www.safaribooksonline.com/library/view/mcse-windows-2000/0596000308/ch01s03.html.

42 **identification number 2661071:** The author reviewed Snowden's certificate, dated 2002, on June 14, 2016, courtesy of the Snowden family.

42 **"I'm not convinced I'm actually that intelligent":** Snowden, interview with author, July 1, 2015, Moscow.

42 **"Can you redeem your degree":** TheTrueHOOHA, *Ars Technica* OpenForum, May 12, 2003, https://arstechnica.com/civis/viewtopic.php?p=12895678#p12895678.

43 **ran a pair of businesses:** They were not always successful. As a friend wrote on her blog in 2003, Snowden could be hard to keep on task: "Ed was easily distracted from work by shiny objects . . . like monitors with games on them." See Katie Bair, "Counting Unhatched Chickens," *Katie Bair's Art Emporium & Petting Zoo*, April 16, 2003, https://web.archive.org/web/20030608093220/http://www.katiebair.com.

43 **a web design company:** "Clockwork Chihuahua Studios," Wayback Machine, July 8, 2002, https://web.archive.org/web/20030604101959/http://clockworkchihuahua.com/index.html. In his memoir, Snowden disguises the name as "Squirreling Industries." See Snowden, *Permanent Record*, 70.

43 **online showcase for anime:** "Ryuhana Press," Wayback Machine, November 3, 2001, http://web.archive.org/web/20020408171636/http://ryuhanapress.com/home.html.

43 **brought a lot of money:** Snowden, interview with author, July 1, 2015, Moscow.

43 **"Editor/Coffee-Boy":** Ed Snowden profile, Ryuhana Press, Wayback Machine, April 27, 2002, http://web.archive.org/web/20031018021255/http://ryuhanapress.com/ed.html.

43 **"Ed is positive":** "Ahhh . . . Birthdays Are a Blessed Time," Ryuhana Press, Wayback Machine, June 21, 2002, http://web.archive.org/web/20031008215713/http://ryuhanapress.com/edbirthday.html.

43 *otaku* **for obsessive fans:** Annalee Newitz, "Anime Otaku: Japanese Animation Fans Outside Japan," *Bad Subjects*, April 1994, http://www.udel.edu/History-old/figal/Hist372/Materials/animeotaku.pdf.

43 **this time taking his friends:** Katie Bair, "Yes Folks, She's Still Standing!," *Katie Bair's Art Emporium & Petting Zoo*, August 13, 2002, https://web.archive.org/web/20030130163154/http://www.katiebair.com/news081302.html.

43 **"very few are roguish enough":** TheTrueHOOHA, "Ah, the Memories," *Katie Bair's Art Emporium & Petting Zoo*, April 1, 2004, http://katiebairsartemporiumandpettingzoo.yuku.com/topic/1069/I-Hate-Technology.

44 **They wasted demons:** Jodon Bellofatto, "Yeah . . . I'm Lazy and Busy . . . Not a Good Combo . . . ," TheRuse.net, September 19, 2002, http://web.archive.org/web/20020925190719/http://theruse.net/.

44 **in a nearby dojo:** Jodon Bellofatto, "I'm Not Dead Yet!," TheRuse.net, May 22, 2003, http://web.archive.org/web/20030620031441/http://www.theruse.net/.

44 **"Edo begging every last fool":** Jodon Bellofatto profile, Ryuhana Press, Wayback Machine, July 9, 2003, http://web.archive.org/web/20030709083138/http://www.ryuhanapress.com/jodon.html.

44 **move-by-move reaction times:** See Edward Snowden, writing as TheTrueHOOHA, "Tekken Fans Rite This Way," *Ars Technica* OpenForum, April 28, 2003, https://arstechnica.com/civis/viewtopic.php?p=12972113#p12972113.

44 **Armed with this granular knowledge:** TheTrueHOOHA, "Tekken Fans Rite This Way," *Ars Technica* OpenForum, April 30, 2003, https://arstechnica.com/civis/viewtopic.php?f=22&t=689447&p=12972042&hilit=tekken+500+matches#p12972042.

44 **"I have a buddy":** Samurai77, *Ars Technica* OpenForum, April 21, 2003, http://arstechnica.com/civis/viewtopic.php?f=22&t=693468.

45 **"I wouldn't want God himself":** TheTrueHOOHA, "In-Depth Theory Questions: How Proxies WORK. (Difficulty: Guru)," *Ars Technica* OpenForum, October 14, 2003, https://arstechnica.com/civis/viewtopic.php?f=10&t=618700&p=11737503&hilit=layman%27s+version+of+how+remote+proxies#p11737503.

46 **"I was really swept up":** Snowden, interview with author, July 1, 2015, Moscow.

46 **program known as 18X:** For a description and training schedule, see U.S. Army, "Special Forces Candidate (18X)," www.goarmy.com/careers-and-jobs/browse-career-and-job-categories/intelligence-and-combat-support/special-forces-candidate.html.

46 **"I liked the idea":** Snowden, interview with author, July 1, 2015, Moscow.

46 **After twenty-five years in uniform:** According to his LinkedIn profile, Lon Snowden joined the U.S. Coast Guard in October 1978.

47 **got only one question wrong:** Snowden, interview with author, July 1, 2015, Moscow. Snowden's score cannot be confirmed independently, but it verifiably reached the high standard required for acceptance as a Special Forces candidate.

47 **Defense Language Aptitude Battery:** Rod Powers, "All About the DLAB," USmilitary.about.com, October 23, 2015, http://usmilitary.about.com/cs/joiningup/a/dlab.htm.

47 **Private First Class Edward Snowden:** Snowden's Army discharge papers, on file with author, include his dates of service from June 3, 2004, to September 28, 2004, his rank as private first class, and his pay grade as E3. He was discharged without obligation, as if he never enlisted.

47 **"If you jump out of an airplane like that":** In his memoir, Snowden renders the quote slightly differently from the way he told it to me, writing that the doctor told him, "Son, if you jump on those legs, they're going to turn into powder.'" Snowden, *Permanent Record*, 91.

47 **"recycle" into a subsequent basic training class:** The Army sometimes seizes on injury to get rid of troublesome trainees, rather than reschedule their basic training, but by Snowden's account the Army doctor offered to recycle him. In that case, however, he would no longer be part of the 18X Special Forces program. Snowden also covers this ground in *Permanent Record*, 91–92.

48 **He accepted an administrative discharge:** The U.S. Army chief civilian spokesman George Wright told the *Guardian* in a June 2013 email, "[Snowden's] records indicate he enlisted in the army reserve as a special forces recruit (18X) on 7 May 2004 but was discharged 28 September 2004." See Spencer Ackerman, "Edward Snowden Did Enlist for Special Forces, US Army Confirms," *Guardian*, June 10, 2013, www.theguardian.com/world/2013/jun/10/edward-snowden-army-special-forces.

48 **After an interlude of recovery:** Snowden, interview with author, July 1, 2015, Moscow.

48 **post as security guard:** Ibid. A journalist for *Campus Reform* obtained documents via a public records request from the University of Maryland, confirming that Snowden worked at CASL from January 28, 2005, through November 11, 2005. See Oliver Darcy, "Exclusive: Snowden Earned Annual Salary of $29K in First NSA Job," *Campus Reform*, July 12, 2013, www.campusreform.org/?ID=4843.

48 **classified spaces for secret NSA research:** Asawin Suebsaeng, "What Happens in the University of Maryland NSA Facility Where Edward Snowden Worked?," *Mother Jones*, June 12, 2013, www.motherjones.com/mojo/2013/06/university-maryland-edward-snowden-nsa.

49 **assigned himself an IP address:** Snowden, interview with author, July 1, 2015, Moscow.

49 TECHEXPO Top Secret: An archived copy of the web page is at https://web.archive.org /web/20041030032011/http://www.techexpousa.com/.

49 offered him a job on the spot: Snowden, interview with author, July 1, 2015, Moscow. In his memoir, Snowden writes that COMSO was a hiring agent for BAE Systems, a subdivision of British Aerospace, which in turn held a contract with the CIA. Snowden, *Permanent Record*, 118.

49 Only two years earlier: TheTrueHOOHA, "How Much Time Do You Spend Gaming per Day?," *Ars Technica* OpenForum, October 26, 2003, http://arstechnica.com/civis /viewtopic.php?f=22&t=615139&p=11679190&hilit=and+two+playing+Tekken+at +Kung+Fu.#p11679190.

49 Now he was doing the work: Snowden, interview with author, July 1, 2015, Moscow. The CIA spokesman Dean Boyd declined by email on June 22, 2016, to comment on Snowden's assignments or performance.

50 What separated Snowden: Snowden, interview with author, July 1, 2015, Moscow.

50 From 6:00 p.m. to 6:00 a.m.: TheTrueHOOHA, "Who's Working Non 9–5 Shifts?," *Ars Technica* OpenForum, April 23, 2006, https://arstechnica.com/civis/viewtopic.php?f=23& t=311911&start=40.

50 "masters of the universe": Snowden, interview with author, July 1, 2015, Moscow.

50 had "incredible access": Ibid.

51 coloring far outside the lines: Snowden, *Permanent Record*, 132–34.

51 "I want to expatriate!": TheTrueHOOHA, *Ars Technica* OpenForum, https://arstechnica .com/civis/viewtopic.php?f=10&t=868906&p=16121406#p16121406.

51 The wish came true: Family confidant, interview with author, December 10, 2015.

51 telecommunications information security officer: For the contemporary CIA job description, see https://web.archive.org/web/20100324173658/https://www.cia.gov/careers/oppor tunities/support-professional/copy_of_telecommunications-information-systems -officers.html.

51 no substantive changes: Archived pages on the Wayback Machine are at https://web.archive .org/web/*/https://www.cia.gov/careers/opportunities/support-professional/copy_of _telecommunications-information-systems-officers.html.

52 six-month training course: Snowden's résumé describes "6 months of classified technical training." "Ed Snowden, PMP, CISSP, MCSE," July 2011, on file with author.

52 actual museum pieces: The Crypto Museum in Washington, D.C., has a full description, for example, of the KG-84 military digital line encryptor at www.cryptomuseum.com /crypto/usa/kg84/.

53 for CRITIC reporting: The reporting standard, the maxim on what to do when in doubt, and the example from the Iraqi invasion of Kuwait come from a classified PowerPoint presentation on file with author. National Security Operations Center, "Overview of CRITIC Reporting," February 24, 1998.

53 "cost of escalation": Snowden, *Permanent Record*, 146.

54 "nightmarishly expensive and": Joe Mullin, "In 2009, Ed Snowden Said Leakers 'Should Be Shot.' Then He Became One," *Ars Technica*, June 26, 2013, http://arstechnica.com/tech -policy/2013/06/exclusive-in-2009-ed-snowden-said-leakers-should-be-shot-then-he -became-one/.

54 he traveled TDY: Snowden, interviews with author, 2013 and 2015.

54 attend a NATO summit: Steven Erlanger and Steven Lee Myers, "NATO Allies Oppose Bush on Georgia and Ukraine," *New York Times*, April 3, 2008, http://nyti.ms/1TGdayY.

55 One involved a pair of case officers: Snowden, *Permanent Record*, 158–59. He first told a version of this story in Glenn Greenwald, Ewen MacAskill, and Laura Poitras, "Edward Snowden: The Whistleblower Behind the NSA Surveillance Revelations," *Guardian*, June 11, 2013, www.theguardian.com/world/2013/jun/09/edward-snowden-nsa-whistleblower -surveillance.

55 "We deal with some really ugly people": Confidential source, interview with author, 2016.

55 **"They'd be like":** Snowden, interview with author, July 1, 2015, Moscow.

55 **crisis of conscience:** Anderson was one of the only former acquaintances of Snowden's to come forward in the days after the first leaks. Mavanee Anderson, "Who Is Ed Snowden? Friend Shares Memories, Offers Support for NSA Leaker," *Chattanooga Times Free Press*, June 12, 2013, www.timesfreepress.com/news/opinion/freepress/story/2013/jun/12/who -is-ed-snowden/110584/.

55 **considered blowing a whistle in Geneva:** Snowden, interviews with author, 2013 and 2015.

56 **"shot in the balls":** Mullin, "In 2009, Ed Snowden Said Leakers 'Should Be Shot.'"

56 **The supervisor placed a "derog":** Eric Schmitt, "C.I.A. Warning on Snowden in '09 Said to Slip Through the Cracks," *New York Times*, October 10, 2013, http://nyti.ms/1OK5VAm.

56 **There was a derog in Snowden's file:** Eric Schmitt, "C.I.A. Disputes Early Suspicions on Snowden," *New York Times*, October 11, 2013, http://nyti.ms/1TvQ9LA.

56 **he identified a vulnerability:** The vulnerability was of a kind called XSS, or cross-site scripting. See Amit Klein, "Cross Site Scripting Explained," June 2002, https://crypto .stanford.edu/cs155/papers/CSS.pdf.

56 **"too smart to be doing":** Burrough, Ellison, and Andrews, "Snowden Saga."

57 **concentrations of silica dust:** The health impact can be significant. See "Silica," National In- stitute for Occupational Safety and Health, www.cdc.gov/niosh/topics/silica/default.html.

57 **The Geneva station packed up:** Snowden family confidant, interview with author, July 22, 2014.

57 **"dear friend and supervisor":** A confidential source, who held a copy of the letter, read it to author verbatim in 2015.

57 **"dreamed of being able":** TheTrueHOOHA, "Has Anybody Considered Working as IT Se- curity in Japan," *Ars Technica* OpenForum, February 18, 2002, https://arstechnica.com /civis/viewtopic.php?f=10&t=868906&p=16108430#p16108430.

57 **the Joint Counterintelligence Training Academy:** See Department of Defense Instruction, "Joint Counterintelligence Training Academy (JCITA)," November 13, 2013, www.dtic .mil/whs/directives/corres/pdf/524027p.pdf.

57 **"My team and I":** C. Danielle Massarini, interview with author, August 12, 2016.

59 **invited Snowden to teach again:** Letter from JCITA course chair C. Danielle Massarini to Ed Snowden, August 2010, on file with author.

59 **The seeds of EPICSHELTER:** Snowden, interview with author, July 1, 2015, Moscow.

59 **Serbian protesters set fire:** Bostjan Videmsek and Dan Bilefsky, "Protesters Attack U.S. Embassy in Belgrade," *New York Times*, February 22, 2008, http://nyti.ms/1tc0nbb.

60 **global array of network storage:** Snowden to author, email, August 15, 2016.

60 **"society really seems to have":** TheTrueHOOHA, "Cisco's Wiretapping System Open to Exploit, Says Researcher," *Ars Technica* OpenForum, February 4, 2010, http://arstechnica .com/civis/viewtopic.php?p=503777.

60 **That year he added credentials:** Copies of the certificates named in this passage are on file with author, courtesy of the Snowden family.

60 **scored 96 out of 100:** "EC-Council Certified Security Analyst Examination Score Report," 2010, on file with author, courtesy of the Snowden family.

60 **DoD Directive 8570:** See DoD 8570.01-M, "Information Assurance Workforce Improvement Program," December 19, 2005, http://dtic.mil/whs/directives/corres/pdf/857001m.pdf.

61 **his business card:** Transcribed by author from a verified original, the card read:

Ed Snowden
solutions consultant / cyber referent
Advanced Solutions Group
Dell Inc
8270 Willow Oaks Corp. Drive
Fairfax, VA 22031
ed_snowden@dell.com

NOTES

61 **designated him as the man to see:** Snowden, interview with author, July 1, 2015, Moscow.

61 **"Project Frankie":** Project Frankie was Dell's internal name for the project. The company later rebranded it as "Yes, Now! Cloud" for large enterprise sales. See Dell, "Say Yes to Cloud Apps," https://security.dell.com/say-yes/cloud-apps.aspx; and Eric Savitz, "Out of the Cloud, and into the Business of 'Yes, Now,'" *Forbes*, May 23, 2011, https://archive.fo/PQVO3.

61 **rival bid from Amazon:** Frank Konkel, "Sources: Amazon and CIA Ink Cloud Deal," *FCW*, March 18, 2013, https://fcw.com/articles/2013/03/18/amazon-cia-cloud.aspx.

62 **approached Massarini with a proposal:** Snowden to Massarini, email, May 31, 2011, on file with author. They continued their correspondence periodically through July.

63 **through the lens of an FBI investigation:** Shortly after Snowden went public as the source of the first NSA stories, FBI agents questioned Massarini and copied her correspondence with Snowden. C. Danielle Massarini, interview with author, August 12, 2016.

63 **an unclassified curriculum vitae:** "Ed Snowden, PMP, CISSP, MCSE," July 2011, on file with author.

63 **teenage job at a two-person firm:** In his memoir, Snowden uses a pseudonym, Squirreling Industries, for his part-time employer. Snowden, *Permanent Record*, 70. The firm was actually called Clockwork Chihuahua Studios.

64 **"The truth is going to get out":** Edward Snowden, interview with author, Moscow, December 6, 2013.

64 **he donated $250:** Snowden's campaign contributions, as distinguished from those of a theatrical producer and a tech executive of the same name, were dated March 18 and May 6, 2012, according to records maintained by the Federal Election Commission and accessible at http://fec.gov/finance/disclosure/norindsea.shtml. See also CNN Political Unit, "Ron Paul Gives Thanks to Leaker," CNN, June 10, 2013, http://cnn.it/28Lj7Xx.

65 **he wore a hoodie:** Andy Greenberg, "An NSA Coworker Remembers the Real Edward Snowden: 'A Genius Among Geniuses,'" *Forbes*, December 16, 2013, http://onforb.es/1YWdXMc.

65 **eagle wearing comically oversized headphones:** Aaron Jue, "NSA Spying Hoodies," Electronic Frontier Foundation, October 16, 2012, www.eff.org/deeplinks/2012/10/nsa-spying-hoodies.

65 **He also kept a copy:** Greenberg, "NSA Coworker Remembers the Real Edward Snowden."

65 **Runa Sandvik:** Snowden (as "Cincinnatus") to Sandvik, Novmber 18, 2012, copy on file with author. At this writing, Sandvik is chief of information security at the *New York Times*. Her personal website is https://encrypted.cc.

65 **the Tor Project:** I discussed Tor in chapters 1 and 2. See www.torproject.org.

65 **fastest "exit relays":** Snowden hosted the relays, rated at two gigabits per second, on virtual private machines he rented at Voxility.com in Romania. He registered them with the email address yopackets@lavabit.com. There were fewer than a thousand exit relays in the world at the time, and Snowden's were in the top 10 percent for speed. See Tor Metrics at https://metrics.torproject.org/relayflags.html?start=2012-11-01&end=2012-11-30&flag=Running&flag=Exit.

65 **"letters from law enforcement":** Runa Sandvik, interview with author, May 21, 2014.

65 **stickers and T-shirts:** Snowden told Sandvik he had seen her offer that kind of Tor swag in one of Reddit's "Ask Me Anything" forums, https://archive.is/nzT1B.

65 **cohost a "cryptoparty":** Runa Sandvik, interviews with author, May 21, 2014, and June 2014. Portions of this anecdote were first recounted in Kevin Poulsen, "Snowden's First Move Against the NSA Was a Party in Hawaii," *Wired*, May 21, 2014, www.wired.com/2014/05/snowden-cryptoparty/.

66 **sent Sandvik his full name:** Snowden to Sandvik, November 20, 2012, on file with author.

66 **"there is no traffic fairy":** Confidential source, interview with author, 2016. The traffic fairy makes her appearance now and then in NSA classified slides, in one case taking the form of Disney's Tinker Bell.

68 **"he used his sys admin privileges":** Wittes and McChesney, podcast with Anderson, *Lawfare*, December 18, 2013.

69 **FISA Amendments Act, Section 702:** Public Law 110-261, July 10, 2008, www.gpo.gov /fdsys/pkg/PLAW-110publ261/pdf/PLAW-110publ261.pdf.

69 **"not access to what":** Wittes and McChesney, podcast with Anderson, *Lawfare*, December 18, 2013.

69 **Snowden found and copied them:** Those files were the basis for Barton Gellman, Julie Tate, and Ashkan Soltani, "In NSA-Intercepted Data, Those Not Targeted Far Outnumber the Foreigners Who Are," *Washington Post*, July 5, 2014, http://wapo.st/28Uxwgj; and Barton Gellman, "How 160,000 Intercepted Communications Led to Our Latest NSA Story," *Washington Post*, July 11, 2014, http://wapo.st/1Mq04zI.

70 **cover names for ECI compartments:** One such list, "Exceptionally Controlled Information (ECI) Compartments," classified CONFIDENTIAL//REL TO USA, AUS, CAN, GBR, NZL, January 2013, is on file with author.

71 **met onstage at Duke:** The post-debate exchange was unrecorded. The debate was headlined "Leakers or Whistleblowers? National Security Reporting in the Digital Age." It took place at Duke University's Sanford School of Public Policy on November 11, 2013, and is available on YouTube, http://youtu.be/kfbHbht081E.

72 **Based on my own analysis of the metadata:** For example, by using the Terminal command "mdls" on the inspector general's report, I obtained values for kMDItemFSOwnerUserID and kMDItemFSOwnerGroupID that matched other files known to be under Brand's control.

72 **"The biggest hurdle":** Snowden, online chat with author, February 24, 2014.

72 **the Kunia coat of arms:** The patch, with "KUNIA RSOC" lettered at the top and "SILENT SENTINELS" at the bottom, may be found on an unofficial web page maintained by the Navy's Counterterrorism Community, navycthistory.com. Author has archived the image file at http://archive.is/qc7MT.

73 **based on a worst-case surmise:** There is an obvious distinction to be drawn between the number of documents Snowden could "touch"—had access to—and the number he actually copied and took with him. Current and former U.S. government officials elided the difference, asserting variously that he stole 900,000 classified documents, 1.5 million, 1.7 million, or 1.77 million, among other estimates. The former NSA director Mike McConnell, vice chairman of Snowden's final employer, Booz Allen Hamilton, was the first to make the claim that Snowden stole "1.7 to 1.8 million" documents. See Rachael King, "Ex-NSA Chief Details Snowden's Hiring at Agency, Booz Allen," *Wall Street Journal*, February 4, 2014, http://on.wsj.com/29aRY0Z; and Margaret Hartmann, "Booz Allen Exec Describes How Snowden Deceived His Former Employer," *New York*, February 5, 2014, http://nym.ag/297XMad. For a sampling of other estimates, see Declaration of David G. Leatherwood, DIA, in Leopold v. Department of Defense, CA-14-0197, U.S. District Court for the District of Columbia, May 21, 2015, http://archive.is/8pZ63; and "A Deal for Snowden," *60 Minutes*, CBS, December 12, 2013, www.cbsnews.com/videos/a-deal-for -snowden/. The then DIA director, Lieutenant General Michael T. Flynn, whose agency wrote a briefing for Congress that cited 1.77 million stolen documents, acknowledged that the estimate was a surmise based on the number Snowden was capable of reaching. "Everything that he touched, we assume that he took," Flynn said. See David Sanger and Eric Schmitt, "Snowden Used Low-Cost Tool to Best N.S.A.," *New York Times*, February 8, 2014, http://nyti.ms/298WZa8. Shortly after retiring as NSA director, Keith Alexander also acknowledged, "I don't think anybody really knows what he actually took with him, because the way he did it, we don't have an accurate way of counting. What we do have an accurate way of counting is what he touched, what he may have downloaded, and that was more than a million documents." See Christopher Joye, "Interview Transcript: Former Head of the NSA and Commander of the US Cyber Command, General Keith Alexander," *Australian Financial Review*, May 8, 2014, http://archive.is/ilSpO.

73 **all journalists combined:** Based on reporting I am unable to disclose, I am confident that I know what Snowden gave each of the four journalists he worked with—Poitras, Greenwald, the *Guardian*'s Ewen MacAskill (for documents originating from the UK's General Communications Headquarters), and myself.

NOTES

73 **"have blown up any logs":** Snowden, interview with author, July 1, 2015, Moscow.

73 **"help me get this right":** Snowden, encrypted chat with author, February 13, 2014.

74 **the U.S. intelligence community:** There are seventeen agencies and organizations in all, including the NSA. See "Intelligence Community," Office of the Director of National Intelligence, www.dni.gov/index.php.

74 **"a rat's nest":** Snowden, interview with author, July 1, 2015, Moscow.

75 **The NSA was paying Dell:** In an email exchange on February 26, 2014, Dell's director of corporate media, David Frink, wrote, "We don't discuss specifics regarding any individual's role. We won't have additional comment, on, or off the record."

75 **"It's not an exaggeration":** Snowden, chat with author, February 13, 2014.

75 **"If you had a guy":** Greenberg, "NSA Coworker Remembers the Real Edward Snowden."

76 **published an automated notice:** The lists were published as self-updating RSS feeds, an acronym for "really simple syndication."

76 **crawl around digital networks:** The best-known spider on the open internet is Google's constantly updating search index. For a general explanation, see Google, "Crawling & Indexing," *Inside Search*, https://goo.gl/k2vFw1. The first public mention of spiders in connection with Snowden came in Sanger and Schmitt, "Snowden Used Low-Cost Tool to Best N.S.A." Officials quoted in that story expressed bafflement that he could automate so many downloads, apparently unaware of the Heartbeat project.

76 **wget and rsync:** The rsync utility, in use for decades, synchronizes files and directories across different networks. It is built into Unix operating systems and available on others. See https://rsync.samba.org/. The wget utility downloads the content of web pages or websites, including the pages hyperlinked from their original target.

77 **"admitted to FBI Special Agents":** The brief account for Congress, unclassified to permit public release, came in Ethan Bauman, NSA director of legislative affairs, "Memorandum for Staff Director and Minority Staff Director, House Committee on the Judiciary," February 10, 2014, on file with author and available at https://fas.org/irp/news/2014/02/nsa-021014.pdf.

78 **The command may look opaque:** According to two sources with firsthand technical knowledge, this is the correct form of the command that Snowden entered. For simplicity, I assume the name of the manager's certificate was "bosskey" and that it was stored in the Terminal's current working directory. After this, one more command would move the certificate to the Heartbeat Digital Identity Store.

79 **"At the very beginning":** Snowden, interview with author, July 1, 2015, Moscow.

80 **"I read your journal.nsa entry":** Snowden to NSA intern, internal NSA email, January 24, 2013. Their exchange, on file with author, continued into January 25.

81 **"What I was actually doing":** Snowden, interview with author, July 1, 2015, Moscow.

82 **The then FBI director:** Robert Mueller, interview with author, March 11, 2011.

82 **stole the answers:** McConnell was quoted in King, "Ex-NSA Chief Details Snowden's Hiring at Agency, Booz Allen."

82 **"Let's look at it this way":** Snowden, chat with author, February 13, 2014.

83 **a double rainbow overhead:** The photograph accompanied an NSA press release, "NSA/CSS Unveils New Hawaii Center," January 6, 2012, www.nsa.gov/news-features/press-room/press-releases/2012/a4-hawaii-final.shtml and archived at https://archive.is/vScSE.

83 **Roach Fort:** Two confidential sources who worked at Rochefort independently mentioned the nickname to author.

83 **"I'm much more interested":** Snowden, interview with author, July 1, 2015, Moscow.

84 **he had sought out the contract:** Lana Lam, "Snowden Sought Booz Allen Job to Gather Evidence on NSA Surveillance," *South China Morning Post*, June 24, 2013, https://archive.is/VLzcT.

84 **"The idea was that NTOC analysts":** Confidential source, interview with author, 2014.

85 **Ned NTOC:** Course syllabus for "OVSC 1400—Dual Authorities: SIGINT/IA," March 2012, classified SECRET//COMINT//REL TO USA, AUS, CAN, GBR, NZL, on file with author.

85 **"You believe it is":** Ibid., 72–73.

86 **"with the assistance":** See Public Law 110-261, Foreign Intelligence Surveillance Act of 1978 Amendments Act of 2008, https://archive.is/4YMNx. See also www.law.cornell .edu/topn/fisa_amendments_act_of_2008.

86 **He could "task":** NSA instruction materials, "Entering New FAA-Authorized DNI Tasking in the Unified Targeting Tool (UTT)/Gamut," March 30, 2010, classified S//SI//REL, on file with author.

86 **CAPTAINCRUNCH:** Confidential source, interview with author, 2015.

86 **In his first filmed interview:** Laura Poitras and Glenn Greenwald, "NSA Whistleblower Edward Snowden: 'I Don't Want to Live in a Society That Does These Sort of Things,'" *Guardian*, June 9, 2013, www.theguardian.com/world/video/2013/jun/09/nsa-whistleblower -edward-snowden-interview-video.

88 **boarded a flight to Tokyo:** Most accounts have reported erroneously that Snowden took a direct flight from Honolulu to Hong Kong. He told me in Moscow in 2015 that his itinerary passed through Tokyo.

CHAPTER THREE: HOMECOMING

89 **Seven Pulitzers?:** The count was indeed seven for Leen as reporter or supervising editor, first at the *Miami Herald* and then at the *Post*. The following year, 2014, he shared in an eighth when the paper split the Pulitzer Prize for Public Service with the *Guardian*.

89 **three executive editors:** Leen joined the paper in 1997 under the executive editor, Leonard Downie, who was succeeded by Marcus Brauchli in 2008 and Marty Baron at the end of 2012. The publisher, Don Graham, meanwhile, relinquished that job to focus on the larger Washington Post Company, giving way to Boisfeuillet Jones Jr. in 2000 and then to Graham's niece Katharine Weymouth in 2008.

89 **series about Vice President Dick Cheney:** The four-part series, available at http://wapo.st /1PbY0us, began with Barton Gellman and Jo Becker, "A Different Understanding with the President," *Washington Post*, June 24, 2007, https://wapo.st/1nOzs4j.

89 **an awkward conversation:** I have reconstructed this conversation with notes I took after the fact, drawing equally on Leen's recollections. The call was memorable for us both, but it is not rendered verbatim. The two of us believe it is close. Jeff Leen, interview with author, March 16, 2016.

91 **"a faint note of fear":** Ibid. Leen gave a similar account in Roy J. Harris Jr., *Pulitzer's Gold: A Century of Public Service Journalism* (New York: Columbia University Press, 2015), excerpted at www.pulitzer.org/article/14085: "'So I was completely not in work mode,' Leen recalls. 'I was surprised to hear from him, and frankly a little annoyed. He was very secretive and cryptic.' Then came the conditions Gellman said the *Post* would have to accept. . . . 'My mind was reeling a bit at all the demands.' But he knew Gellman. 'It's like E. F. Hutton: You listen,' Leen says."

92 **Katharine Graham's memoir:** Katharine Graham, *Personal History* (New York: Alfred A. Knopf, 1997). Attorney General John Mitchell, who later notoriously said Graham would "get her tit caught in a big fat wringer" if the *Post* printed a different story, threatened criminal charges against the Washington Post Company in the Pentagon Papers case. I take up the implications in the next note.

92 **she risked losing the company:** Profitable local television stations accounted for a substantial fraction of the Washington Post Company's revenue. Felons are barred from owning a broadcast license. Graham was counting on an infusion of funds from an initial public stock offering, which could also have been jeopardized by a criminal suit. See ibid., 448–50.

92 **Graham hired a new lawyer and published:** Among many accounts of that moment, along with her own fine chapter in ibid., is Donald Graham, "Ben Bradlee, a Hero to the Post Newsroom," *Washington Post*, October 21, 2014, http://wapo.st/1UlWk94. The change of lawyers brought in Edward Bennett Williams, whose firm, Williams & Connolly, would help shepherd the NSA stories of 2013.

NOTES

History vindicated the *Post* and the *New York Times*, which had the story first, as well as their source, Daniel Ellsberg, who provided them with the Pentagon Papers. The previously classified history of the Vietnam War, unredacted, is now available from the National Archives as Vietnam Task Force, Office of the Secretary of Defense, *United States–Vietnam Relations, 1945–1967*, www.archives.gov/research/pentagon-papers/. Nixon's solicitor general, who told the Supreme Court in 1971 that publication would cause grave damage, acknowledged later, "I have never seen any trace of a threat to the national security from the publication." Erwin Griswold, "Secrets Not Worth Keeping: The Courts and Classified Information," *Washington Post*, February 15, 1989, http://wapo.st/25ssi86.

92 **fought the case to the Supreme Court:** The New York Times Co. v. United States, 43 U.S. 713, June 30, 1971, www.law.cornell.edu/supremecourt/text/403/713, said the government had not met its high burden for prior restraint of publication. More than one justice noted, however, that they had made no holding on whether the papers could be prosecuted after the fact. The government did not bring criminal charges.

92 **rescind my credentials:** The State Department episode is recounted briefly in chapter 1. In 1997, Israel's Government Press Office threatened to revoke my status as an accredited foreign correspondent after I published the name of the director of the Shin Bet internal security service, Carmi Gillon. His identity was an official secret but widely known. (Even directory assistance operators knew his name. I once called to ask for Gillon's home phone number, just to see what would happen. After a long pause, the operator replied, "You know I can't tell you that.") I was ordered to begin submitting my stories to the government censor. I declined, as did *Post* correspondents before and since. The press office eventually dropped the matter.

92 **a memorably profane call:** The prime minister was enraged by my interview with his ultra-Orthodox interior minister, who said Israel would stop recognizing Jews converted by Reform and Conservative rabbis overseas. Netanyahu was about to travel to New York, where the "Who is a Jew?" debate was a minefield. He accused me of deliberately sabotaging his trip and demonstrated a fluent command of idiomatic American swear words. I later learned that senior aides, standing alongside him in the prime minister's office, had urged him to cool off before making the call.

92 **took me to the woodshed:** Fortunately for me, Len Downie never began a conversation with "This is going to be an important meeting for you." That was said to be the executive editor's opening line in his second-to-last meeting with an employee whose job was on the line.

93 **"salon dinners":** The story broke in Michael Calderone and Mike Allen, "WaPo Cancels Lobbyist Event," *Politico*, July 2, 2009, http://politi.co/1RrrENG. When the paper equivocated about it for days, I took the unusual step of calling the publisher, Katharine Weymouth. I urged her to let the full story out instead of hoping the scandal would go away. The paper's central mission demanded it. "I don't know why any company would do that to itself," she told me. I liked Weymouth, and she did not flinch from the risks of the Snowden story when I returned in 2013, but I found that reply disappointing. I made the same phone call, on the same day, to the executive editor, Marcus Brauchli. He took no position on full disclosure, save that his position was complicated. Later, he was obliged to acknowledge that he made false claims in an interview about the scandal with the *New York Times*. See Jad Mouawad, "Newspaper Apologizes for Seeming to Sell Access," *New York Times*, July 5, 2009, http://nyti.ms/1RoL1do; and "NYT Accuses Washington Post Editor Marcus Brauchli of Lying to NYT Reporter About 'Off the Record' Dinners," *NYTPicker*, October 17, 2009, www.nytpick.com/2009/10/nyt-accuses-washington-post-editor.html.

93 **Patriot militias:** Barton Gellman, "The Secret World of Extreme Militias," *Time*, September 30, 2010, http://ti.me/1XR17hv. For the story on Romney's political childhood, see Barton Gellman, "Dreams from His Mother," *Time*, June 4, 2012, http://ti.me/1ZxUaDo.

94 **"I've got a line on a document":** Duffy and Calabresi, encrypted chat with author, May 7, 2013.

94 **"Circumstances not encouraging":** Calabresi, encrypted chat with author, May 14, 2013.

95 **close to a hundred magazines:** See Time Inc., Our Iconic Brands, www.timeinc.com /brands/.

95 **Cappuccio, a conservative powerhouse:** See Peter Lattman, "Time Warner's Don 'Pooch': Part of the Vast Right Wing Conspiracy?," *Wall Street Journal*, February 10, 2006, http:// on.wsj.com/1RLE7fe, citing Edward P. Lazarus, *Closed Chambers: The Rise, Fall, and Future of the Modern Supreme Court* (New York: Times Books, 1998).

95 **call Baruch Weiss:** Weiss served as acting deputy general counsel of the Department of Homeland Security from 2003 to 2006. See partner profile, Arnold & Porter, www.arnold porter.com/en/people/w/weiss-baruch; and LinkedIn profile, "Baruch Weiss," www.linke din.com/in/baruch-weiss-2156491b.

96 **joined me around a speakerphone:** I reconstruct this scene from contemporary notes and additional notes and memories from Duffy and Calabresi. Mike Duffy and Massimo Calabresi, interviews with author, April 5, 2016.

96 **aggressive legal tools:** Josh Gerstein, "Holder Walks Fine Line on Prosecuting Journalists," *Politico*, May 13, 2013, http://politi.co/1N0zlit; Tom McCarthy, "Eric Holder: Justice Department Will Not Prosecute Reporters Doing Their Job," *Guardian*, June 6, 2013. In July 2013, a month after the first Snowden leaks, Holder announced rules narrowing the circumstances under which law enforcement could obtain journalists' records. See Charlie Savage, "Holder Tightens Rules on Getting Reporters' Data," *New York Times*, July 12, 2013, http://nyti.ms/1SBOOSY.

97 **held back publication for more than a year:** The *Times* had the main facts of the story by the late fall of 2004. It did not publish the story until the end of 2005. See James Risen and Eric Lichtblau, "Bush Lets U.S. Spy on Callers Without Courts," *New York Times*, December 16, 2005, http://nyti.ms/1y8izFc. Also see Margaret Sullivan, "Lessons in a Surveillance Drama Redux," *New York Times*, November 9, 2013, http://nyti.ms/1VT9Q60; and Eric Lichtblau, "The Education of a 9/11 Reporter," *Slate*, March 26, 2008, http://slate.me /15tLUNU.

97 **I doubted that cowardice explained:** The delay was harshly criticized by commentators on the left, many of whom insisted the scoop could have changed the outcome of the 2004 election. See, for example, Lawrence Velvel, "The NYT's Unconscionable Decision to Sit on the NSA Story for a Year," *CounterPunch*, January 7, 2006, www.counter punch.org/2006/01/07/the-nyt-s-unconscionable-decision-to-sit-on-the-nsa-story -for-a-year/.

99 **men and women with badges:** Although I never thought it probable, the risk of a raid was not trivial. I suspected, and later confirmed, that there were high-ranking U.S. government advocates of an operation to seize the files from me, Poitras, and Greenwald. I take this up in chapter 7.

99 **the Espionage Act:** 18 U.S.C. § 793, "Gathering, transmitting or losing defense information." Most pertinent for my purposes are sections (b), (c), and (e), at www.law.cornell.edu/uscode /text/18/793. For a commentary, see Stephen Vladeck, "The Espionage Act and National Security Whistleblowing After Garcetti," *American University Law Review*, June 2008, http://digitalcommons.wcl.american.edu/cgi/viewcontent.cgi?article=1048&context=aulr.

99 **A narrower and more recent statute:** 18 U.S.C. § 798, "Disclosure of classified information," specifically forbids anyone to "publish" classified information about "the communication intelligence activities of the United States or any foreign government." For the text of the statute, see www.law.cornell.edu/uscode/text/18/798.

99 **no lawful course for me:** Retaining or distributing information "connected with the national defense" (whatever that means), whether or not classified, is a ten-year felony under the Espionage Act. Snowden had not yet been charged with a crime, but even so erasing or discarding the files could arguably constitute destruction of evidence or obstruction of justice.

99 **even from judges:** When the domestic surveillance began under President George W. Bush, it was explicitly designed to operate without judicial or legislative review. Over time the White House agreed to provide limited briefings to the so-called Gang of Eight (the party

leaders and the chairs and ranking members of the intelligence committees in each house of Congress) and to the chief judge, but not the other judges, of the Foreign Intelligence Surveillance Court. See Gellman, *Angler*, 143; 150–51. The government acknowledged an obligation to disclose to defense lawyers in a criminal case whether evidence against their clients derived from secret FISA surveillance. In 2012, Solicitor General Donald Verrilli Jr. assured the Supreme Court that federal prosecutors honored that obligation. See Verrilli's brief in Clapper v. Amnesty International, 568 U.S. ___ (2013), at http://bit.ly/2bDj3vF. In fact, they did not, in part for fear that the secret surveillance could be subjected to constitutional challenge. See Charlie Savage, "Door May Open for Challenges to Secret Wiretaps," *New York Times*, October 16, 2013, http://nyti.ms/2b3OacO. In November 2013, the government admitted having used FISA-derived evidence to convict Mohamed Osman Mohamud of plotting to set off a car bomb in Portland, Oregon. See the Government's Supplemental FISA Notification: United States v. Mohamud, Case No. 3:10-cr-00475-KI (D. Ore. Nov. 19, 2013), at http://bit.ly/2b5UZQ2. Mohamud's motion to vacate the conviction was denied. United States v. Mohamud, Case No. 3:10-cr-00475-KI-1, 2014 WL 2866749 (D. Or. June 24, 2014), at https://archive.is/YcCKE.

100 **skill set I had to teach myself:** There are unlikely to be many *kinds* of hiding places that people who search for a living have not encountered. The challenge is to use methods, physical and virtual, that remain secure even if the other party knows the methods exist. Given a large enough forest, it may not help a searcher much to know that people sometimes hide things under trees.

100 **hide information in digital alcoves:** Some of the physical space on a hard drive is typically invisible to, or disregarded by, an operating system like Windows, Apple OS X, or Linux. Examples include unassigned blocks or sectors, free space alongside the master boot record, and the "slack" that remains when a file or partition does not fill all its reserved space. A technically proficient person could put data in one of those places, which an ordinary copy would not reproduce. For an explanation of "digital warrens where data may go unnoticed," see Hal Berghel, David Hoelzer, and Michael Sthultz, "Data Hiding Tactics for Windows and Unix File Systems," *Advances in Computers* 74 (2008), www.berghel.net/publications /data_hiding/data_hiding.php.

100 **bit-by-bit clones:** A computer bit, the smallest unit of data in digital form, is a binary number consisting of 0 or 1. All other units of data are based on that. (There are 8 bits in a byte, 1,024 bytes in a kilobyte, 1,024 kilobytes in a megabyte, and so on.) Ordinary backup copies include only the bits that are allocated, or mapped, by the operating system. They leave a lot of stray data behind. A clone, also known as a forensic image, captures the "digital warrens" described in the previous note. There are commercial software packages for making clones, but I did the job quick and dirty with a command-line tool ("dd") built into Unix-based operating systems such as OS X. See the manual pages at http://apple.co /21rZMAm and www.gnu.org/software/coreutils/manual/html_node/dd-invocation.html.

102 **they made the same request:** The *Washington Post* general counsel, Jay Kennedy, and deputy general counsel, James McLaughlin, interviews with author, March 31, 2016.

104 **"I will confess":** Jay Kennedy, interview with author, March 31, 2016.

105 **metaphors of cryptography are stupid:** In 2014, Princeton undergraduates in Arvind Narayanan's Privacy Technologies seminar conducted a study to test whether better metaphors could improve the experience of nontechnical users with email encryption. See Wenley Tong et al., "Why King George III Can Encrypt," June 6, 2014, http://random walker.info/teaching/spring-2014-privacy-technologies/king-george-iii-encrypt.pdf.

109 **opened the PRISM slide deck:** National Security Agency, "PRISM/US-984XN Overview, or the SIGAD Used Most in NSA Reporting," April 2013, on file with author in full and published in redacted form at www.washingtonpost.com/wp-srv/special/politics/prism -collection-documents/.

110 **starbursts, charts, tables, arrows:** When the PRISM slide deck became public, it was widely mocked by graphic designers, at least three of whom offered their services, tongue in cheek, to the NSA. The substitute designs were pretty good, actually. See Holly Allen and Chad

Lorenz, "Those PRISM Slides Are Hideous: Here, NSA. We Redesigned Them for You," *Slate*, June 7, 2013, http://slate.me/1Qqnfd7; Victoria Nece, "PRISM PowerPoint Redesign," June 8, 2013, http://victorianece.com/2013/06/prism-powerpoint-redesign/; Emiland, "Dear NSA, Let Me Take Care of Your Slides," June 11, 2013, www.slideshare.net/Emi landDC/dear-nsa-let-me-take-care-ou.

111 **Skype, YouTube:** These two companies were brought into PRISM before Microsoft and Google, respectively, acquired them.

111 **Exabytes of user information:** As far as I know, the big internet companies do not disclose the volumes of data they store. By one outside estimate, a single Google data center holds ten to fifteen exabytes. Given that Google has multiple data centers, and some of its rivals store comparable volumes, it is possible that their collective holdings encompass zettabytes of information, or thousands of exabytes. See Colin Carson, "How Much Data Does Google Store?," Cirrus Insight, November 18, 2014, www.cirrusinsight.com/blog/how-much -data-does-google-store.

111 **thousands of millions of billions of bytes:** See Roy Williams, California Institute of Technology, "Data Powers of Ten," archived at https://web.archive.org/web/19990508062723 /http://www.ccsf.caltech.edu/~roy/dataquan/.

111 **"the dawn of civilization":** Eric Schmidt, remarks at Techonomy conference, August 4, 2010, http://readwrite.com/2010/08/04/google_ceo_schmidt_people_arent_ready_for_the _tech/. His full quotation was "There was 5 exabytes of information created between the dawn of civilization through 2003, but that much information is now created every 2 days."

111 **Some people questioned his numbers:** Robert J. Moore, "Eric Schmidt's '5 Exabytes' Quote Is a Load of Crap," R.J. Metrics, February 7, 2011, https://blog.rjmetrics.com/2011/02/07 /eric-schmidts-5-exabytes-quote-is-a-load-of-crap/. Moore estimated that it would be more accurate to say the world produced as much information every seven days as it did in all of 2002.

111 **legal authority that Congress granted:** In 2007, Congress passed the Protect America Act, S. 1927 (110th Cong., 1st sess., enacted August 5, 2007), www.govtrack.us/congress/bills /110/s1927/text. The following year it passed the FISA Amendments Act, H.R. 6304 (110th Cong., 2nd sess., enacted July 9, 2008), www.govtrack.us/congress/bills/110/hr6304/text. The statute, which rewrote major portions of the Foreign Intelligence Surveillance Act of 1978, was renewed in 2012. See especially Section 702.

111 **The court nearly always granted:** See "Foreign Intelligence Surveillance Act Court Orders, 1979–2015," Electronic Privacy Information Center, https://epic.org/privacy/wiretap/stats /fisa_stats.html#footnote21.

112 **Once a year:** Ellen Nakashima and Barton Gellman, "Court Gave NSA Broad Leeway in Surveillance, Documents Show," *Washington Post*, June 30, 2014, http://wapo.st/1MZVvkP.

112 **The first one laid out rules:** See "Procedures Used by NSA to Target Non-US Persons: Exhibit A—Full Document," *Guardian*, June 20, 2013, www.theguardian.com/world/inter active/2013/jun/20/exhibit-a-procedures-nsa-document. Original copy on file with author.

112 **The second one specified procedures:** "Procedures Used by NSA to Minimize Data Collection from US Persons: Exhibit B—Full Document," *Guardian*, June 20, 2013, www .theguardian.com/world/interactive/2013/jun/20/exhibit-b-nsa-procedures-document. Original copy on file with author.

112 **The court would not know:** One of my favorite colleagues confirmed this in a rare interview with the chief judge of the Foreign Intelligence Surveillance Court, who was then the U.S. district court judge Reggie Walton. See Carol Leonnig, "Court: Ability to Police U.S. Spying Program Limited," *Washington Post*, August 15, 2013, http://wapo.st/1WSZLVp.

114 **"Can I have a private word?":** I have not spoken before of this private meeting, which was exceptionally meaningful to me. I reconstruct the exchange from notes I took after the fact, using quotation marks only for the words I wrote down. The rest is paraphrased from my memory, checked against Baine's and Baron's.

114 **legal culture of twenty-first-century America:** My friend Jack Goldsmith makes the point that our legal culture has all but ruled out the application of black letter law to national

NOTES

security journalism. I do not know whether he agrees with me that this constraint applies more strongly when mainstream news organizations test the legal limits. See Jack Goldsmith, *Power and Constraint: The Accountable Presidency After 9/11* (New York: Norton, 2012), esp. chapter 3.

CHAPTER FOUR: PRISM

117 **five thousand miles away:** I have taken a small liberty in rounding. According to a standard online reference, the distance between the nearest civilian airports serving Fort Meade and the Kunia facility is 4,853 miles. See Air Miles Calculator, www.airmilescalculator.com /distance/hnl-to-bwi/.

117 **three intelligence reports:** Slide 16, "# of End Product Reports Citing US-984XN/PRISM (Sept 2007 to Feb 2013)," in "PRISM/US-984XN Overview, or, The SIGAD used Most in NSA Reporting," April 2013, on file with author. Selections have been published in the *Post*, the *Guardian*, and independent news sites. Much of the presentation remains unavailable to the public.

117 **wire diagram of the NSA:** The agency has never released an organizational chart of any detail in unclassified form. Over many months I assembled my own chart from fragments I came across in memos and briefings. In late 2015, the NSA director tore up the map and announced a reorganization plan called "NSA21." See Jane Edwards, "Adm. Michael Rogers: NSA to Undergo Reorganization in January," ExecutiveGov, December 17, 2015, www .executivegov.com/2015/12/adm-michael-rogers-nsa-to-undergo-reorganization-in -january/, archived at https://archive.fo/hU4cr.

117 **a lesser federal agency:** Among the eighty members of the association for small federal agencies, the average employee roster is said to number 625. See "About the Small Agency Council," www.sac.gov/about/.

117 **defend and attack:** There are NSA directorates, such as Research (R), Technology (T), and Legal (OLC), that support both missions. A third major element at Fort Meade, the Central Security Service, oversees the cryptologic organizations of each branch of the armed services.

A classified introduction to the NSA, prepared for new members of the House and Senate intelligence committees and their staffs, provided capsule definitions of the information assurance mission ("Protect U.S. Telecommunications and Computer Systems Against Exploitation") and the signals intelligence mission ("Intercept and Exploit Foreign Signals"). Mark Young, then chief of legislative affairs, described the two missions as complementary. "Of course, lessons learned in protecting U.S. information systems feeds NSA's ability to perform its SIGINT mission," he told legislators, according to his speaker's notes. "The cryptologic effort comes full circle as NSA uses its understanding of the vulnerabilities within foreign information systems to help secure classified national security and sensitive U.S. government information systems." Mark D. Young, "National Security Agency / Central Security Service Overview Briefing," 2006, classified SECRET//NOFORN//X1, on file with author.

118 **"Swallowing the sea":** Joel F. Brenner, "Information Oversight: Practical Lessons from Foreign Intelligence," Heritage Lecture #851, delivered at the Heritage Foundation in Washington, D.C., September 30, 2004, on file with author.

118 **"Fetch It, Etch It and Retch It":** A longtime colleague, who worked with Cotter on the NSA's senior technical review panel, credited him with that phrase. Bill Binney, interview with author, summer 2013. When asked about it, Cotter described the quotation as "a variation of many heard over the years." Cotter to author, email, December 1, 2016. Cotter retired in 2009. For his official biography, see the National Aeronautics and Space Administration conference notes for "Security in the National Grid," October 10, 2012, https:// istcolloq.gsfc.nasa.gov/fall2012/speaker/cotter.html.

118 **"serialized reports":** A good explanation of this term: "Serialized intelligence reports are distinguished from both raw intelligence reports and special intelligence reports. Raw

NOTES

intelligence is immediately reported by the collector and serves as the basis for serialized reporting (daily, weekly, monthly, etc.) by subject or geographic location. Special intelligence reports are those reports—like National Intelligence Estimates or individual subject reports—that are produced on request or as needed. Both serialized and special reports are considered finished intelligence (and often referred to as FINTEL)." See Dana Priest and William M. Arkin, *Top Secret America: The Rise of the New American Security State* (New York: Little, Brown, 2011).

119 **"PRISM is one of":** Slide 41, "PRISM/US-984XN Overview."

119 **the project's deepest secret:** As Rick put it, "The PRISM project is not protected under an ECI [for exceptionally compartmented information]. Project details are handled at the TS//SI//NF level. However, the sensitivity of the project details requires enhanced OPSEC in which only those with a need to know will have access to these details. The sensitive details are the identification of PRISM providers and details of our relationship with them through the FBI." Speaker's notes, slide 11, "PRISM/US-984XN Overview."

120 **"The internet is on principle":** Snowden to author, May 31, 2013.

121 **mostly listened in on telephone calls:** Sometimes, of course, the fictional NSA did other things like dispatching assassins to track down political enemies. See Tony Scott's classic *Enemy of the State* (Touchstone Pictures, 1998). My friend Barry Eisler, a CIA officer turned thriller writer, takes some liberties along these lines in *The God's Eye View* (Seattle: Thomas & Mercer, 2016). For the record, the NSA does not have death squads and does not control live video feeds from space.

121 **the project's Skype interface:** The "User's Guide for Skype PRISM Collection," dated August 2012, is on file with author. In 2014, *Der Spiegel* published the guide with light redactions at www.spiegel.de/media/media-35530.pdf.

121 **Analysts could ask for instant notifications:** The presentation alluded to these as RTN, which stands for "real-time notification." Slide 34, "PRISM/US-984XN Overview."

121 **could monitor keystrokes:** This was not a capability built into PRISM. The NSA accomplished this form of live surveillance by other methods, including exploitation of the Remote Desktop Service built into Microsoft Windows. Then deputy director Chris Inglis told me on June 14, 2013, that PRISM, by contrast, offered "replay" of conversations rather than live monitoring. "It's a packetized world," he said. "If you recorded the session you could play it back later and you could get it in a streamed way, but . . . you don't have the opportunity to see this in real time."

121 **a total of 8,233 articles:** The statistics for the President's Daily Brief come from the speaker's notes for slide 18, "PRISM/US-984XN Overview."

122 **"much of the world's communications":** All direct quotations here are from the speaker's notes for slide 4, "PRISM/US-984XN Overview."

122 **overseen by Vice President Cheney:** See Gellman, *Angler,* chapters 6, 11, and 12.

122 **cover name WHIPGENIE:** According to the NSA's internal classification guide for the warrantless surveillance, "Information that would provide an understanding of the partnership/location for the program is covered by the ECI WPG SSO compartment." ECI means "exceptionally compartmented information," the WPG trigraph is a short form of WHIPGENIE, and SSO stands for Special Source Operations, which refer in this context to "corporate partnerships" with large telephone and internet companies. "STELLARWIND Classification Guide (2-400)," January 21, 2009, on file with author. The *New York Times* posted this document, which it obtained under a sharing agreement with the *Guardian,* at http://nyti.ms/2gqIfHt.

123 **"in briefings and declarations":** "STELLARWIND Classification Guide."

123 **A rebellion in the Justice Department:** Gellman, *Angler,* chapters 11 and 12.

123 **Protect America Act of 2007:** Public Law 110-55, 121 Stat. 552, at http://legislink.org/us/pl-110-55.

123 **FISA Amendments Act of 2008:** Formally it was the Foreign Intelligence Surveillance Act of 1978 Amendments Act of 2008, Public Law 110-261, at https://archive.is/4YMNx. See also www.law.cornell.edu/topn/fisa_amendments_act_of_2008.

123 **"The [United States] overwhelmed"**: Speaker's notes, slide 5, "PRISM/US-984XN Overview."

124 **"PRISM access is 100% dependent"**: Speaker's notes, slide 10, "PRISM/US-984XN Overview."

124 **"NSA can't simply walk up"**: Intelligence source, interview with author, summer 2013.

124 **Unified Targeting Tool:** Slides 30 and 31, "PRISM/US-984XN Overview."

126 **Bystanders filled its data repositories:** I return to this later in the book. See Barton Gellman, Julie Tate, and Ashkan Soltani, "In NSA-Intercepted Data, Those Not Targeted Far Outnumber the Foreigners Who Are," *Washington Post*, July 5, 2014, http://wapo.st /1Mvootx; and Barton Gellman, "How 160,000 Intercepted Communications Led to Our Latest NSA Story," *Washington Post*, July 11, 2014, http://wapo.st/1Mq04zI.

126 **LOVEINT:** Short for "love intelligence," the term refers to rogue NSA employees who "channeled their agency's enormous eavesdropping power to spy on love interests," according to the news story that popularized it. "The practice isn't frequent—one official estimated a handful of cases in the last decade—but it's common enough to garner its own spycraft label: LOVEINT." See Siobhan Gorman, "NSA Officers Spy on Love Interests," *Wall Street Journal*, August 23, 2013, http://on.wsj.com/19NGBbE.

127 **"NSA was operating"**: Joel F. Brenner, "Forty Years After Church-Pike: What's Different Now," address at the National Security Agency, May 15, 2015, on file with author.

127 **"You may have time constraints"**: Author to Edward Snowden, email, May 18, 2013. Our conversation that day was prospective, as I did not yet have the document in hand. I was trying to understand his urgency, but his seventy-two-hour countdown had not yet begun.

127 **"Alright, let's talk"**: Snowden email, May 25, 2013. The misspelling of "whistleblower" is in the original.

128 **something bigger to think about:** See chapter 3.

128 **"has not been edited or changed"**: Snowden to author, email, May 16, 2013.

128 **akin to a royal seal:** Cryptographers use mathematics to do what kings and dukes once did with their wax stamps. Aside from attesting to the authenticity of a message, a signature enforces what cryptographers call "non-repudiation." A signer cannot disavow a document after signing it. I was hoping for a U.S. government signature because those are backed by a verifiable chain of digital trust called the public key infrastructure, or PKI.

128 **"It creates a 'chain of custody'"**: Snowden to author, email, May 17, 2013.

128 **The result was disappointing:** I have simplified the file names and file paths in my rendering of the command. I have also blacked out the alphanumeric identity of the Verax key, because that could be used to discover the email address Snowden used. Although some of his anonymous addresses have become public, this one has not. Experts will also note that a standard government PKI signature would have used a different file format than the one Snowden sent me.

129 **"I used to work in our U.N. spying shop"**: Snowden's reference here was to his assignment as technical officer at the CIA station in Geneva, the home of several large UN agencies, not to the United Nations headquarters in New York.

130 **Poitras and I did not need:** Verax had signed, as well as encrypted, all his emails to us, so a separate signature on the PRISM file added nothing to our knowledge of its provenance.

130 **Snowden could demonstrate:** In order to prove he was our source, Snowden could generate a signature that matched the one we published online. Only someone who possessed the unique Verax key and knew its passphrase could do that.

130 **"well-founded fear of being persecuted"**: That is the language of the controlling authority in international law, the Convention Relating to the Status of Refugees, Chapter I, Article 1(A)(2), July 28, 1951, at www.ohchr.org/EN/ProfessionalInterest/Pages/StatusOfRefu gees.aspx.

130 **And I was the one:** Snowden could not easily prove that he was our source by showing someone the signature himself. Anyone could download and sign the PRISM document once we published it. The time stamp would demonstrate at least that he possessed the file

before publication, and there were other technical options available to Snowden, but no proof would be nearly as persuasive as the *Post*'s own affirmation that he was our source.

130 **He wanted me to help him:** I told Snowden in another context that I would be happy to publish his name and an interview, if that was what he wanted. The purpose of the cryptographic signature was to allow him to expose his identity in private to foreign diplomats, not to an audience of news consumers at large.

131 **"I just read his email":** Transcript of anonymous, encrypted chat between author and Laura Poitras, May 25, 2013. I am aware that this exchange with Poitras may be quoted selectively by critics who have long accused Snowden of betraying his country. As I note explicitly, it is now quite clear that I was wrong. I rested a worst-case conclusion on ambiguous words that turned out to mean something else.

133 **"I am not sure I will have":** Snowden to author, email, May 24, 2013.

133 **"I look forward to meeting":** Author to Snowden, email, May 24, 2013.

135 **"This all makes me":** Poitras to author, email, May 27, 2013.

135 **"I thought I was pretty good":** Author to Poitras, email, May 27, 2013.

135 **"Implying an affair":** Poitras to author, email, May 24, 2013.

137 **"The response in the last few days":** Snowden to Poitras, email, May 26, 2013. Poitras and I were sharing all our correspondence with him then.

137 **"working hard to do":** Snowden to author, email, May 26, 2013.

137 **"What a nightmare":** Poitras to author, email, May 27, 2013.

137 **"Please understand that the only":** Author to Snowden, email, May 27, 2013.

138 **When I mentioned this sequence:** Barton Gellman, "Code Name 'Verax': Snowden, in Exchanges with Post Reporter, Made Clear He Knew Risks," *Washington Post*, June 9, 2013, http://wapo.st/2a4lo2Q, archived at https://archive.is/dNEqk. When I wrote this story, the day Snowden went public in a *Guardian* video, I was unable to reach Poitras or Snowden before deadline. Though accurate, my story was therefore highly incomplete, omitting the central role that Poitras played and what little I knew of Snowden's history with Greenwald. Most of my interactions with Snowden and Poitras were still strictly off the record.

138 **"Bart Gellman's claims":** That was the first of several angry declarations in the next several days. Tweet by Glenn Greenwald (@ggreenwald), June 9, 2013, https://twitter.com/ggreenwald/status/343960115227025408, archived at https://archive.is/B67nS. Greenwald was responding to the following lines in a story I wrote that day: "Snowden replied succinctly, 'I regret that we weren't able to keep this project unilateral.' Shortly afterward he made contact with Glenn Greenwald of the British newspaper the Guardian." As I explain in the previous note, my account was accurate but unavoidably incomplete. Gellman, "Code Name 'Verax,'" *Washington Post*, June 9, 2013.

138 **"Laura Poitras and I":** Tweet by Glenn Greenwald (@ggreenwald), June 10, 2013, https://twitter.com/ggreenwald/status/344040301972815872, archived at https://archive.is/VMnMk. See also Mackenzie Weinger, "Gellman, Greenwald Feud over NSA," *Politico*, June 10, 2013, http://politi.co/1WJKx4W, archived at https://archive.is/ou3py.

138 **an unwelcome "new turn":** The gist of Greenwald's account was that I obtained last-minute access to a limited number of documents, pertaining solely to PRISM, amid his own ongoing work on the larger story. None of that was correct. Glenn Greenwald, *No Place to Hide: Edward Snowden, the NSA, and the U.S. Surveillance State* (New York: Metropolitan Books, 2014), 16–18.

138 **the *Post* and I assembled lawyers:** Ibid. This was a curious reproof, I thought, from a former litigator. Every news organization consulted lawyers on the NSA story. The *Guardian*, Greenwald's newspaper at the time, killed some of its stories for legal reasons and delayed others for months; editors there destroyed a copy of the Snowden documents under threat of the more draconian British law. The *Intercept* and its parent company, First Look Media, which Greenwald helped found in late 2013, hired the *New Yorker*'s media lawyer, Lynn Oberlander. Greenwald was not against legal advice for himself when considering whether to visit the United States. For nearly a year he said publicly that his lawyers advised him it would be too risky because of his role in disclosing the NSA documents.

138 **cut the balls off our story:** Greenwald, *No Place to Hide*, 55, 56. Greenwald said the *Post* "would dutifully abide" by unwritten rules "which allow the government to control disclosures and minimize, even neuter, their impact."

138 **as he told the *Huffington Post*:** "Greenwald set up the encryption software and began speaking directly with Snowden in late March or early April, he said," according to that story. Michael Calderone, "How Glenn Greenwald Began Communicating with NSA Whistleblower Edward Snowden," *Huffington Post*, June 10, 2013, http://huff.to/1pBnqfl, archived at https://archive.is/fFeol.

138 **unaware that Verax was the Cincinnatus:** Greenwald, *No Place to Hide*, 82.

138 **"clueless on the security-technical side":** Laura Poitras, "Berlin Journal," in *Astro Noise: A Survival Guide for Living Under Total Surveillance* (New York: Whitney Museum of American Art, 2016), 95.

138 **Verax connected with Greenwald:** In his book, Greenwald wrote that his first encrypted communications with the still-anonymous source took place "during the week of May 20." As shown in my next note, the date must have been May 27. Greenwald wrote that he asked Verax for a sample of the classified material on the following day, which makes it May 28, and that it took "a couple of days" more before he figured out how to receive and decrypt the twenty-five documents that Verax sent in reply. If a couple of days means two, he opened the sample on May 30, by which point Poitras and I had been working through the full Pandora archive for ten days. Greenwald, *No Place to Hide*, 19.

During the summer and fall of 2013, Greenwald adjusted the timeline to demonstrate the primacy of his role. According to the *New Yorker*'s media writer, "Greenwald told me that Snowden initially sent him a small number of encrypted documents through Poitras," and then later, "in May, Snowden offered to share extensive government documentation of what the N.S.A. was doing." Ken Auletta, "Freedom of Information," *New Yorker*, October 7, 2013, www.newyorker.com/magazine/2013/10/07/freedom-of-information. In reality, Greenwald had no substantive contact with Snowden until the end of May, and Poitras had no documents she could have shared with him until May 21, when she and I received them. What Poitras showed Greenwald when she met with him in April were two of the still ambiguous emails from her pseudonymous source. She did not hand Greenwald the Pandora archive until the two of them boarded their flight to Hong Kong on June 1, which is also when Greenwald learned Snowden's identity.

138 **I will not belabor the timeline:** The following dates are drawn from the author's contemporary, time-stamped notes and emails, many of them cited in chapters 1, 3, and 4; and from Micah Lee, "Ed Snowden Taught Me to Smuggle Secrets Past Incredible Danger. Now I Teach You," *Intercept*, October 28, 2014, http://interc.pt/1DXiB2S; Greenwald, *No Place to Hide*, especially 7–26; the "Berlin Journal" extracts reproduced in Laura Poitras, ed., *Astro Noise: A Survival Guide for Living Under Total Surveillance* (New York: Whitney Museum of American Art, 2016); screen shots from the documentary film *Citizen Four* (Praxis Films, 2014); and Edward Snowden's pseudonymous video, anon108, "GPG for Journalists—Windows edition | Encryption for Journalists | Anonymous 2013," Vimeo, January 6, 2013, https://vimeo.com/56881481. I know of no essential omission or conflicting documentary record.

December 1, 2012—Snowden, as "Cincinnatus," writes to Glenn Greenwald, asking him to send an encryption key. Greenwald says he does not know how.

January 6, 2013—As anon108, Snowden sends Greenwald an instructional video on encryption. Greenwald does not reply.

January 11, 2013—anon108 shifts focus to Laura Poitras, asking technology activist Micah Lee of the Electronic Frontier Foundation to supply a trustworthy encryption key for her.

January 28, 2013—As "Citizen Four," Snowden sends his first substantive email to Poitras.

January 31, 2013—Poitras, writing from Berlin, asks to meet me, saying she needs advice.

NOTES

February 2, 2013—At a New York café, Poitras tells me about her source and his (still vague) story. I offer to help her validate it. According to her journal, she is also asking advice from privacy advocate and technologist Jacob Appelbaum in Berlin.

March 30, 2013—Citizen Four sends Poitras a link to an encrypted file called "astro_ noise," but not the key to open it.

April 19, 2013—Poitras learns that Greenwald is visiting New York. She asks to meet and shows him two emails from Citizen Four, suggestive but still vague about the story.

April 22–28, 2013—Poitras meets twice more with Greenwald, joined the second time by Appelbaum and ACLU lawyer Jameel Jaffer. She finds Greenwald "clueless on the security-technical side of things," which rules out long-distance collaboration or direct contact with the source.

May 7, 2013—Poitras and I agree to partner on the story. She vouches for me with Snowden, who now goes by "Verax." We expect a document any day.

May 9, 2013—Poitras, who still hopes Greenwald can join the reporting, asks Micah Lee to teach him how to communicate securely.

May 13, 2013—Lee sends Greenwald a thumb drive with encryption software, instructions, and preconfigured email and chat accounts. The package is held up in Brazilian customs for two weeks.

May 16, 2013—Poitras and I begin to meet intensively, sharing some of our separate correspondence with Verax.

May 20, 2013—Verax sends us the forty-one-page NSA slide deck on PRISM.

May 21, 2013—Verax tells us his name and employment history and sends the keys to Pandora, an archive of tens of thousands of classified documents.

May 24, 2013—Poitras and I sign contracts to write the PRISM story for the *Washington Post*. We plan to fly to Hong Kong together.

May 25, 2013—Snowden tells us he intends to seek foreign asylum. He presses us to post online a small digital file, called a cryptographic signature, which he can use to prove to foreign diplomats that he is our source.

May 26, 2013—Poitras and I decline the request and cancel our Hong Kong plans.

May 27, 2013—Snowden tells me he is withdrawing the *Post* exclusive. He chats online for the first time with Greenwald.

May 30, 2013—Greenwald receives and opens a sample of about twenty-five documents from Snowden.

June 1, 2013—Poitras flies to Hong Kong with Greenwald, joined by the *Guardian*'s Ewen MacAskill. Just before the flight she hands Greenwald a thumb drive containing the classified archive we received on May 21.

June 3, 2013—Poitras, Greenwald, and MacAskill begin several days of meetings with Snowden, obtaining additional NSA documents in person. I continue to talk to Snowden by encrypted email and chat.

June 5, 2013—Greenwald, alerted by Poitras to my story plans, publishes his first NSA article in the *Guardian*. It reveals bulk collection of telephone calling records.

June 6, 2013—The *Post*, followed by the *Guardian*, publishes the PRISM story.

June 9, 2013—Snowden identifies himself publicly as the source of the NSA disclosures.

139 **"audacious journalism":** He described his "fearlessness," "courage," and "audacious journalism" in Greenwald, *No Place to Hide*, 51, 58, and periodically in comparable terms elsewhere.

139 **"timid, risk-averse government obeisance":** We were also "fear-driven," "muddled," "subservient," "pro-government," and "obsequious." Ibid, pp. 18, 58, 68, 77.

139 **"to pursue the truth":** Marty Baron, Acceptance Remarks at the Hitchens Prize Dinner in New York, November 28, 2016, www.vanityfair.com/news/2016/11/washington-post -editor-marty-baron-message-to-journalists.

139 **holding power to account:** I discussed this, with examples, in chapter 1.

NOTES

139 **were trembling servants:** Greenwald, *No Place to Hide*, p. 89, with similar language at pp. 18, 58, 68, 77.

139 **"Hey Bart":** Glenn Greenwald to author, June 11, 2013.

140 **behind-the-scenes account:** Savage was referring to Gellman, "Code Name 'Verax,'" *Washington Post*, June 9, 2013. In that story, I mistakenly used the term "cryptographic key" when I meant "cryptographic signature."

140 **all my communications with Snowden:** I did not share all our live chats and correspondence even with Poitras, though she certainly took part in exchanges about the digital signature. For security reasons, Snowden did not keep copies of our emails and chats, and he periodically discarded the keys we used to encrypt them. When I asked, he told me categorically that he had not showed a word of our correspondence to Greenwald.

140 **"Charlie Savage tells me":** Author to Glenn Greenwald, June 11, 2013.

140 **"I never said":** Glenn Greenwald to author, June 11, 2013.

140 **reporters were still:** Most commonly, the reporters told me that Greenwald described internal *Post* legal and editorial deliberations in unflattering terms, asserting falsely, for example, that the paper ran away from tough NSA stories and forbade me to travel to Hong Kong. I declined to comment for publication. Sometimes I asked the reporters off the record how they imagined Greenwald could know these things. Two among many of those queries came in the reporting for Janet Reitman, "Snowden and Greenwald: The Men Who Leaked the Secrets," *Rolling Stone*, December 4, 2013, http://rol.st/1bIGujx, and Auletta, "Freedom of Information." See also Peter Maass, "How Laura Poitras Helped Snowden Spill His Secrets," *New York Times Magazine*, August 13, 2013, http://nyti.ms/2eAYykb.

   Now and then, when critics accused him of treason, of selling classified secrets for profit, or of endangering American lives, Greenwald pulled me into his foxhole. I had done the same things he did, he told his accusers. Why not shoot at me, too? Still, if he paid a passing compliment ("I respected Gellman . . ."), the punch line was not usually far behind (". . . but not the *Washington Post*"). Greenwald, *No Place to Hide*, 54.

141 **I had an exceptionally sensitive story:** Author to Ben Rhodes, June 5, 2013. I summarize from old notes, but neglected to save the original email before a scheduled purge of older content from the *Post* exchange servers.

142 **described him as deceptive:** See Gellman, *Angler*, 147–49.

142 **That evening, June 5:** I was sorry to learn from Greenwald's book that he got regular updates on my story plans from the notes I sent Poitras, who was still my coauthor and on contract with the *Post*. Evidently she found herself in an awkward position, and I suppose she hoped to deconflict our work. Greenwald had other ideas. He used the inside knowledge, he wrote, to ensure that he—not "the *Washington Post*, with its muddled, pro-government voice, its fear, and its middle-of-the-road-ese"—would define the story. Greenwald, *No Place to Hide*, 58, 77.

142 **first story from the Snowden archive:** See Glenn Greenwald, "NSA Collecting Phone Records of Millions of Verizon Customers Daily," *Guardian*, June 6, 2013, www.theguardian.com /world/2013/jun/06/nsa-phone-records-verizon-court-order, archived at https://archive.is /OgNKZ. Notwithstanding the dateline, which reflected the print edition, the story appeared online on June 5.

143 **unique hardware identifiers:** There are two such identifiers. The International Mobile Subscriber Identity, or IMSI, belongs to the SIM card for each customer account. The International Mobile Station Equipment Identity, or IMEI, is unique to the mobile telephone itself. It does not change when a customer inserts a new SIM card.

143 **"comprehensive communications routing information":** Judge Roger Vinson, "Foreign Intelligence Surveillance Court Secondary Order," April 25, 2013, on file with author. The *Guardian* posted the order online at https://assets.documentcloud.org/documents/709012 /verizon.pdf.

143 **"relevant to" an authorized investigation:** Section 215 of the USA Patriot Act of 2001 was enacted into public law as 50 U.S.C. § 1861, "Access to certain business records for foreign

NOTES

intelligence and international terrorism investigations," at www.law.cornell.edu/uscode /text/50/1861.

144 **The computational methods:** A general account of the methods employed were published in an unclassified NSA report two weeks before the Verizon story broke. See Paul Burkhardt and Chris Waring, "An NSA Big Graph Experiment," U.S. National Security Agency Research Directorate—R6, Technical Report NSA-RD-2013-056002v1, May 20, 2013, archived at https://archive.is/3ra8T.

144 **a principal drafter of the Patriot Act:** See Ryan J. Reilly, "Jim Sensenbrenner, Patriot Act Author, Slams 'Un-American' NSA Verizon Phone Records Grab," *Huffington Post*, June 6, 2013, www.huffingtonpost.com/2013/06/06/jim-sensenbrenner-nsa_n_3397440 .html. See also the letter from Sensenbrenner to Attorney General Eric Holder, September 6, 2013, http://sensenbrenner.house.gov/uploadedfiles/sensenbrenner_letter_to_attorney _general_eric_holder.pdf. Two high-ranking intelligence officials, speaking on condition of anonymity, have told me that Sensenbrenner refused to take part in classified briefings that would have revealed the breadth of telephone record collection. Any member of Congress could, in theory, ask to read the legal documents inside a vault where they could take no notes. Very few employed a staff member with sufficient clearance to read and provide analysis of the material.

144 **The court's order:** The Snowden archive provided only a "secondary order" in which Judge Vinson renewed legal authority that the court had granted previously. Snowden did not have or did not supply the original opinion. Later, under pressure of the public disclosures, the Office of the Director of National Intelligence released a redacted version of the original legal reasoning. See "DNI Clapper Declassifies and Releases Telephone Metadata Documents," Office of the Director of National Intelligence, July 31, 2013, archived at https://archive.is/9n0SK.

145 **"I'm not generally given":** I typed live notes during this conversation on June 6, 2013.

147 **"If the harm that you're asserting":** Ibid. I take better notes on what other people say than what I do. I reconstructed my own comments shortly after we hung up.

147 **We moved the PRISM story:** Barton Gellman and Laura Poitras, "U.S., British Intelligence Mining Data from Nine U.S. Internet Companies in Broad Secret Program," *Washington Post*, June 6, 2013, http://wapo.st/1LcAw6p, archived at https://archive.is/cYyFe. Greenwald's version, which followed, disclosed nothing that the *Post* held back. Glenn Greenwald and Ewen MacAskill, "NSA Prism Program Taps In to User Data of Apple, Google and Others," *Guardian*, June 6, 2013, www.theguardian.com/world/2013/jun/06/us-tech -giants-nsa-data.

147 **"For Internet content selectors":** Working draft of NSA Inspector General's Report ST-09-0002, history of STELLARWIND surveillance, March 24, 2009, p. 20, on file with author.

148 **"The actual architecture is very":** Chris Inglis, interview with author, June 14, 2013.

148 **a twelve-minute video:** "NSA Whistleblower Edward Snowden: 'I Don't Want to Live in a Society That Does These Sort of Things'—Video," *Guardian*, June 9, 2013, www.theguard ian.com/world/video/2013/jun/09/nsa-whistleblower-edward-snowden-interview-video.

148 **"I'm scrolling through my Twitter feed":** C. Danielle Massarini, interview with author, August 12, 2016.

CHAPTER FIVE: BACKLASH

151 **"We're not going to open":** Dennis Blair to author by telephone, July 10, 2013.

152 **an angular six foot two:** Or so his deputy spokesman, Kenneth McGraw, told me in November 2011. Some press accounts describe him as up to six foot four.

152 **two miles of free fall:** McRaven was taking part that day in an exercise to maintain proficiency in the technique known as the HALO jump, which stands for "high-altitude, low opening." The high start and last-minute pull of the ripcord are intended to maximize stealth.

NOTES

152 **"split me like a nutcracker"**: McRaven had not, as far as I knew, spoken publicly of the accident before. I profiled him as a runner-up for Person of the Year in 2011. See Barton Gellman, "William McRaven: The Admiral," *Time*, December 14, 2011, archived at https://archive.is/6q7bq.

152 **"the tension between"**: Michael Isikoff, then of NBC News, moderated a panel that featured NSA general counsel Raj De and ACLU executive director Anthony Romero. The other panelists were Neil MacBride, U.S. attorney for the Eastern District of Virginia, Jeh Johnson, the former Pentagon general counsel, and former representative Jane Harman (D-CA), who now ran the Woodrow Wilson International Center for Scholars. Video of the panel is at www.youtube.com/watch?v=kJiTjCAMjLY.

152 **"We didn't have another 9/11"**: Admiral William McRaven to author, July 18, 2013. I took notes immediately after he walked off.

153 **"was the voice of Walter Cronkite"**: McRaven had live video links during the bin Laden raid to his forward troops, the CIA, and the White House Situation Room. For the Cronkite comparison: Michael Leiter, former director of the National Counterterrorism Center, interview with author, December 7, 2011. Another participant, who did not want to be named, agreed with Leiter and added that others on the video briefing "were shitting their pants. I know I was."

153 **majored in journalism**: McRaven earned his journalism degree in the class of 1977 at the University of Texas, where he also trained as a Navy reserve officer. Gellman, *Time*, December 14, 2011.

153 **a treatise on special warfare**: McRaven's master's thesis ran to 612 pages and is said to have helped change the U.S. military doctrine of special warfare. William H. McRaven, "The Theory of Special Operations," Naval Postgraduate School, Monterey, CA, June 17, 1993, on file with author and archived at https://archive.is/jNhf.

153 **"This will go down in history"**: William McRaven, interview with author, December 5, 2011.

154 **self-government and self-defense**: I will have more to say about the dilemmas of news reporting on national security in chapter 7.

154 **my thesis on wartime**: Barton Gellman, "Secrecy, Security and the 'Right to Know': Some Grounds and Limits of Open Government" (M.Litt. thesis in Politics, University of Oxford, 1988).

154 **"but I would much rather"**: Author to William McRaven, email, January 10, 2017.

154 **"I'm happy to chat with you"**: William McRaven to author, email, January 10, 2017.

154 **John Wayne coffee mug**: The description of McRaven's office decor is from a photograph published with Brian D. Sweany, "The Four-Star Chancellor," *Texas Monthly*, October 2015, at www.texasmonthly.com/the-culture/the-four-star-chancellor/.

154 **"what precipitated my outburst"**: William McRaven, telephone interview with author, January 11, 2017.

156 **kept in the dark**: Only the chief judge of the FISA Court and the "Big Eight" in Congress—the Speaker of the House, House minority leader, majority and minority leaders in the Senate, and the chairs and ranking members of the intelligence committees—were privy to the warrantless surveillance in the early days. See Gellman, *Angler*, chapters 11 and 12.

156 **"I don't like it much"**: Conference call with Dennis Blair and John Negroponte, July 10, 2013. I typed notes audibly throughout, and Blair identified a few specific points, not these, that he wanted to keep "on background" or off the record.

157 **"It's safe to say"**: For video of the panel discussion with Blair and Negroponte, see "Mission Accomplished? Has the Intelligence Community Connected All the Dots?," Aspen Security Forum, July 18, 2013, https://youtu.be/QdxWWSG5f8Y.

157 **"One of the reasons"**: Dzhokhar Tsarnaev was convicted for the April 2013 bombing. His older brother, Tamerlan, died after Dzhokhar ran him over while trying to escape police.

158 **"talking to the terrorists"**: Senator Lindsey Graham, *Fox & Friends*, June 6, 2013. The video is at https://youtu.be/UjTcs5T1jpQ.

158 **"It seems like to me"**: The former president used this benign-sounding formula after the *New York Times* disclosed the warrantless surveillance program. "President Bush Delivers

Remarks on Terrorism," Louisville, KY, January 11, 2006, https://georgewbush-whitehouse
.archives.gov/news/releases/2006/01/20060111-7.html.

158 **Trillions of calls:** The government has not released a number or estimate, and the Snowden
archive does not provide one. Several officials, including Dennis Blair during the Aspen
panel, said the number is in the trillions.

159 **a base of two:** Beginning on the second day, the penny count is calculated as two to the first
power, then two squared, two cubed, and so on. On the twenty-eighth day, the pot reaches
2^{27} cents (two to the twenty-seventh power) plus the first day's penny, or $1,342,177.29.

159 **a tenfold increase:** This is a simplified account for illustration. For any large number of telephone accounts, some of my contacts, or contacts of contacts, will overlap with someone
else's. The number of unique contacts in the chain will increase at a somewhat slower rate
than my simplified description. The general point on exponential growth remains valid.

159 **John C. Inglis:** Inglis, who goes by Chris, announced his retirement in early 2014. He gave
a valedictory interview to National Public Radio on January 10, 2014, archived at https://
archive.is/5j5Yg.

159 **"go out two or three hops":** Testimony of John C. Inglis, "The Administration's Use of FISA
Authorities," House Committee on the Judiciary, July 17, 2013, https://fas.org/irp/con
gress/2013_hr/fisa.pdf.

159 **data scientists estimated:** Among the early works in this field was Michael Gurevitch,
whose 1991 doctoral dissertation, "The Social Structure of Acquaintanceship Networks,"
may be found at https://dspace.mit.edu/handle/1721.1/11312.

159 *Six Degrees of Separation:* The play, which opened in previews on October 30, 1990, won
the New York Drama Critics' Circle Best Play of 1990. John Guare, *Six Degrees of Separation: A Play* (New York: Random House, 1990), ISBN 0-679-40161-X. The original play-
bill is archived at www.playbill.com/show/detail/11250/six-degrees-of-separation.

159 **"Six Degrees of Kevin Bacon":** The game led to television appearances alongside Bacon, and
then a book. See Craig Fass, Brian Turtle, and Mike Ginelli, *Six Degrees of Kevin Bacon*
(New York: Plume, 1996).

159 **inspired a website:** The Oracle of Bacon, http://oracleofbacon.org.

160 **Two hops, through Rourke:** The Oracle of Bacon site uses the term "Bacon Number" in
place of "hop." It assigns Johansson, for example, a Bacon Number of 2.

160 **three links in the chain:** See, for example, Stanley Milgram, "The Small World Problem,"
Psychology Today 1, no. 1 (1967).

160 **"Under three hundred":** A panel appointed by President Obama later disclosed that the
number was 288. See President's Review Group on Intelligence and Communications
Technologies, *Liberty and Security in a Changing World,* December 12, 2013, p. 102, https://
obamawhitehouse.archives.gov/sites/default/files/docs/2013-12-12_rg_final_report.pdf.

161 **I worked through the arithmetic:** For purposes of simplicity, I used back-of-the-napkin assumptions that probably overstated the result. Although each caller has one hundred contacts in this example, there may be some overlap in their contact lists. The aggregate
number of unique contacts in the records of any ten callers, that is, may be fewer than a
thousand. On the second and third hops, which produce much larger numbers, such overlap is statistically likelier. With appropriate adjustments, the calculation was nonetheless
roughly correct.

161 **Multiply by one hundred:** Five months later, U.S. district judge Richard Leon used the
same working estimate, which he described as conservative, when he found the metadata
collection to be unconstitutional. Klayman v. Obama, Civil Action 13-0851, U.S. District
Court for the District of Columbia, December 16, 2013, at https://s3.amazonaws.com
/s3.documentcloud.org/documents/901810/klaymanvobama215.pdf.

161 **had he known back then:** Blair did not join in pre-election letters in 2015 and 2016 that
called Donald Trump unfit to be commander in chief. His only public criticism came in
response to reports that Trump was thinking of abolishing his old job. "Elimination of the
DNI position would be a major setback for the kind of integrated intelligence that the U.S.
will need in the future," he said. Matthew Cole and Jenna McLaughlin, "Donald Trump

Hopes to Abolish Intelligence Chief Position, Reverse CIA Reforms," *Intercept*, November 18, 2016, archived at https://archive.is/VFnV3.

162 **deputy chief technology officer of the United States:** Leadership staff, Office of Science and Technology Policy, archived at https://archive.is/ZLEol. See also https://obamawhitehouse .archives.gov/blog/2015/05/11/white-house-names-dr-ed-felten-deputy-us-chief -technology-officer.

162 **"Individual pieces of data":** Declaration of Professor Edward W. Felten, August 26, 2013, in ACLU v. Clapper, U.S. District Court for the Southern District of New York, archived at https://archive.is/w3n04.

162 **A presidential review group:** Appointed by President Obama, the group concluded, "Our review suggests that the information contributed to terrorist investigations by the use of section 215 telephony meta-data was not essential to preventing attacks and could readily have been obtained in a timely manner using conventional section 215 orders." See President's Review Group, *Liberty and Security in a Changing World*, p. 104.

163 **criticized some of my stories:** See, for example, Stewart Baker, "The Washington Post's Doubtful Privacy Statistics," *Washington Post*, July 6, 2014, http://wapo.st/2jvSSg7. My response is at Barton Gellman, "How 160,000 Intercepted Communications Led to Our Latest NSA Story," *Washington Post*, July 11, 2014, http://wapo.st/1Mq04zI.

163 **"Metadata absolutely tells you":** Stewart Baker, quoted in Alan Rusbridger, "The Snowden Leaks and the Public," *New York Review of Books*, November 21, 2013.

163 **"We kill people":** Michael V. Hayden remarks, "The Price of Privacy: Re-evaluating the NSA," Johns Hopkins University, April 1, 2014, at https://youtu.be/UdQiz0Vavmc?t=27s.

164 **"we don't hold data":** Keith Alexander, "Cyber Security Threats to the United States," American Enterprise Institute, July 9, 2012. The video is at the 50-minute mark of www .c-span.org/video/?306956-1/cybersecurity-threats-us. He made similar remarks at the Def Con security conference in Las Vegas two weeks later. See Kim Zetter, "NSA Chief Tells Hackers His Agency Doesn't Create Dossiers on All Americans," *Wired*, July 27, 2012, www.wired.com/2012/07/nsa-chief-denies-dossiers/.

164 **"Does the NSA collect":** The full exchange, and Clapper's explanation nearly three years later, are on "IC on the Record," the DNI's Tumblr account, in a posting dated February 7, 2016, at https://icontherecord.tumblr.com/post/139489829858/why-did-you-lie-about -nsa-surveillance-in-front-of. It is also available at www.youtube.com/watch?v=nsmo 0hUWJ08. Clapper initially told NBC's Andrea Mitchell that his reply to Wyden was the "least untruthful" response he could offer in an unclassified setting. In the 2016 posting, he said, "I simply didn't think of the business records telephony metadata" as he replied. "Instead, I thought of content."

164 **accused him of perjury:** On March 12, 2018, the five-year statute of limitations for such a charge expired. See Steven Nelson, "James Clapper Avoids Charges for 'Clearly Erroneous' Surveillance Testimony," *Washington Examiner*, March 10, 2018, https://perma.cc/DE8B -7UDL.

165 **made a clumsy job of it:** Wyden's staff sent advance word to Clapper that the senator would ask that question, but Litt, the DNI lawyer, said the message got stuck on his desk in the crush of business. Clapper, he said, did not see it coming. Robert Litt, interview with author, 2014.

166 **only twenty-one such orders:** Statistical tables based on government disclosures are assembled by the Electronic Privacy Information Center at www.epic.org/privacy/surveillance /fisa/stats/.

167 **cleaned up the list:** Several months later, an independent government report confirmed this surmise. "Upon the arrival of new records at the NSA, agency technical personnel perform a number of steps to ensure that the records, which come from different telephone companies, are in a standard format compatible with the NSA's databases." Privacy and Civil Liberty Oversight Board, *Report on the Telephone Records Program Conducted Under Section 215 of the USA PATRIOT Act and on the Operations of the Foreign Intelligence Surveillance Court*, January 23, 2014, perma.cc/Y7F3-EZBX (PDF).

NOTES

167 **"database of ruin":** Paul Ohm, "Broken Promises of Privacy: Responding to the Surprising Failure of Anonymization," *UCLA Law Review* 57 (2010): 1701, available at SSRN: https://ssrn.com/abstract=1450006.

167 **"if revealed, would cause":** Paul Ohm, "Don't Build a Database of Ruin," *Harvard Business Review*, August 23, 2012, https://hbr.org/2012/08/dont-build-a-database-of-ruin.

168 **Chekhov's famous admonition:** The best-known version is: "If in Act I you have a pistol hanging on the wall, then it must fire in the last act." Donald Rayfield, *Anton Chekhov: A Life* (New York: Henry Holt, 1997). Chekhov meant that a playwright should not break an implicit promise to the audience, but the expectations behind that promise have their roots in observed experience of the world. Most weapons are used eventually. In surveillance as in war, capabilities once invented are put to use.

168 **"Is It the End":** The presentation was prepared by technical managers tasked with improving data quality. "Is It the End of the SIGINT World as We Have Come to Know It? Do You Feel Fine?," May 10, 2012, on file with author.

169 **"the vice president's special program":** See Gellman, *Angler*, chapters 11 and 12.

169 **fifty state-of-the-art computer servers:** "FY-2002 Signals Intelligence Directorate (SID) Project Baseline Standards and Architecture Assessment Activity," on file with author.

169 **ship them to another customer:** This is described in a near-final draft copy of the classified NSA Inspector General's *Review of the President's Surveillance Program*, p. 16, footnote 4. On file with author. The IG report does not mention the vendor's name. Kirk Wiebe, who was then chief of staff to the Signals Intelligence Automation Research Center, identified the supplier as Dell.

169 **incorporating some two hundred machines:** "FY-2002 Signals Intelligence Directorate (SID) Project Baseline Standards and Architecture Assessment Activity."

170 **The price surpassed $102 million:** Draft Inspector General report, p. 27.

170 **amplify the power of surveillance:** Ibid.

171 **"the Big Awesome Graph":** Ibid.

171 **"the BAG":** From "KSP (aka the 'BAG'): Connecting the Dots," *SID Today*, September 3, 2003, an internal NSA newsletter on file with author.

171 **a large network diagram:** Ibid. FALLOUT is one of several systems that process internet metadata, not relevant here. FASCIA does the same for some phone metadata before it reaches MAINWAY. EKS stands for the NSA's broad infrastructure upgrade to an Extended Knowledge System.

171 **"metadata flow sourced from billing records":** Extract from "FAIRVIEW Data Flow Diagrams," April 2012, on file with author. FAIRVIEW is the NSA's cover name for AT&T, which it describes as a corporate partner. In late 2016, the *Intercept* published the whole presentation, save for the speaker's notes, at https://theintercept.com/document/2016/11/16/fairview-dataflow-charts-apr-2012/.

172 **"call detail record warehouse":** "SID Project Baseline Technical Assessment, Project: MAINWAY," July 2002, on file with author. SID stands for the Signals Intelligence Directorate of the NSA.

172 **"MAINWAY Precomputed Contact Chaining Service":** *SSO Dictionary*, on file with author.

173 **"You have to establish all those relationships":** Rick Ledgett, interview with author, August 22, 2017.

173 **"operating on a 7x24 basis":** "FY-2002 Signals Intelligence Directorate (SID) Project Baseline Standards and Architecture Assessment Activity," on file with author.

173 **billion new records a day:** The Felten declaration, cited above, estimated a volume of three billion telephone calls each day in the United States. I assume here that at least one-third of them were captured in the NSA's call records database.

174 **the Graph-in-Memory:** This briefing, dated May 10, 2012, and prepared by a member of the Large-Access Exploitation Group, was titled "Is it the End of the SIGINT World as We Have Come to Know It?" On file with author.

174 **a rough and ready diagram:** In December 2013, Judge Richard Leon made a comparable and little-noticed point in *Klayman v. Obama:* "The Government . . . describes the

advantages of bulk collection in such a way as to convince me that plaintiffs' metadata—indeed everyone's metadata—is analyzed," he wrote. *Klayman v. Obama*, p. 39. Felten, the Princeton computer scientist, added strength to Leon's analysis on a technology website. "The plaintiffs' data—and your data as well—is not just used occasionally; it is probably used in most every contact chaining calculation done by the NSA," he wrote. Ed Felten, "Judge Leon Explains Why the NSA Uses Everyone's Metadata," *Freedom to Tinker*, December 17, 2013, https://freedom-to-tinker.com/2013/12/17/judge-leon-explains-why-the-nsa-uses-everyones-metadata/.

174 **Binney, a mathematical cryptographer:** See also "Bio: Bill Binney and J. Kirk Wiebe," Government Accountability Project, undated, at https://perma.cc/9KEF-BBRK.

175 **"you mean 'Cosmic Fart'?":** Bill Binney, interview with author, summer 2013.

175 **a colleague, Ben Gunn:** James Bamford, the pioneering NSA journalist, described this scene in an article published the year before the Snowden leaks. See "Shady Companies with Ties to Israel Wiretap the U.S. for the NSA," *Wired*, April 3, 2012, at https://perma.cc/TF9R-YCBS.

176 **new and more permissive rules:** SID Management Directive 424, November 29, 2010, on file with author.

177 **"it enables large-scale graph analysis":** Internal NSA memo, "(S//SI//REL) New Contact-Chaining Procedures Allow Better, Faster Analysis," January 3, 2011, on file with author.

177 **"Spot the Fed" contest:** According to the contest rules, "if enough people think it's a true fed, or fed wanna-be, or other nefarious style character, you win a 'I spotted the fed!' shirt." See www.defcon.org/html/defcon-15/dc-15-stf.html.

177 **"No, we don't":** Kim Zetter, "NSA Chief Tells Hackers His Agency Doesn't Create Dossiers on All Americans," *Wired*, July 27, 2012, www.wired.com/2012/07/nsa-chief-denies-dossiers/.

178 **stretches coast to coast:** The thought experiment is fanciful, but we may as well do the math. Using 12-point type, I get about 60 lines of text per foot on a computer printout. Assuming our imaginary clerks can write that small, they fill a mile of parchment for every 316,800 lines of telephone logs. In round numbers, that is three miles of parchment per one million lines, or 3,000 miles per billion. The distance from Miami to Seattle is 2,735 miles. I likewise assume arbitrarily that each notebook weighs a quarter pound and 100 million notebooks therefore weigh 12,500 tons. I rounded down.

180 **Only twenty-two top officials:** Privacy and Civil Liberties Oversight Board, *Report on the Telephone Records Program Conducted Under Section 215 of the USA PATRIOT Act and on the Operations of the Foreign Intelligence Surveillance Court*, January 23, 2014, p. 8, www.pclob.gov/library/215-Report_on_the_Telephone_Records_Program.pdf.

181 **invited King to kill himself:** Yale historian Beverly Gage was the first to unearth a full copy of the anonymous letter that FBI domestic intelligence chief William Sullivan sent to King. Sullivan set a deadline and wrote, "There is only one thing left for you to do. You know what it is." Beverly Gage, "What an Uncensored Letter to M.L.K. Reveals," *New York Times*, November 11, 2014, http://nyti.ms/2k2JTUT.

181 **most heavy-handedly:** Barton Gellman and Sam Adler-Bell, "The Disparate Impact of Surveillance," Century Foundation, December 21, 2017, at http://perma.cc/WV8A-ZMV3.

182 **learned from *Der Spiegel*:** Laura Poitras, Marcel Rosenbach, Fidelius Schmid, and Holger Stark, "NSA Spied on European Union Offices," *Der Spiegel*, June 29, 2013, at https://archive.is/5So5r.

182 **Standard Form 312:** Office of the Director of National Intelligence, SF-312, "Classified Information Nondisclosure Agreement," Rev. 7-2013, at www.archives.gov/files/isoo/security-forms/sf312.pdf.

182 **"support and defend the Constitution":** By statute, anyone appointed to federal office, the military, or civil service must swear these words, also known as the Oath of Office. See 5 U.S.C. § 3331, at www.law.cornell.edu/uscode/text/5/3331.

182 **"As a test of your concern":** George R. Cotter to author, email, December 1, 2016.

NOTES

183 **"a massive shift in attitudes":** The poll surveyed 2,014 registered voters, who supported the "go too far" response by 45 to 40 percent. Quinnipiac University, "U.S. Voters Say Snowden Is Whistle-Blower, Not Traitor, Quinnipiac University National Poll Finds; Big Shift on Civil Liberties vs. Counter-Terrorism," July 10, 2013, https://poll.qu.edu/national/release-detail?ReleaseID=1919.

183 **"Guy boards an airplane":** The reference was to Umar Farouk Abdulmutallab, who tried to set off a bomb on a Christmas Day 2009 flight to Detroit. TATP is triacetone triperoxide, a high-explosive chemical. Abdulmutallab pleaded guilty in October 2011 to eight charges, including attempted use of a weapon of mass destruction, and received a life sentence the following year. See U.S. Department of Justice, "Umar Farouk Abdulmutallab Sentenced to Life in Prison for Attempted Bombing of Flight 253 on Christmas Day 2009," February 16, 2012, archived at https://archive.is/LSPM3. A Senate report concluded that "systematic failures across the Intelligence Community" allowed Abdulmutallab to smuggle high explosives onto the plane. See Senate Select Committee on Intelligence, "Report on the Attempted Terrorist Attack on Northwest Airlines Flight 253," May 24, 2010, www.intelligence.senate.gov/publications/report-attempted-terrorist-attack-northwest-airlines-flight-253-may-24-2010.

184 **marked TOP SECRET//COMINT/NOFORN/X1:** The first page, which provided a very high-level view of surveillance capabilities, had no "portion markings" to identify classified information by paragraph, which is NSA's standard practice. At that level of generality it revealed nothing sensitive. Details on subsequent pages were more sensitive and are not reproduced here.

Careful readers will know by now that the markings on this document stood for "communications intelligence" and "no foreign distribution." The designation X1 was a claim of exemption from automatic declassification review after ten years. The governing rule at the time was Information Security Oversight Office, "ISOO Directive No. 1," October 13, 1995, archived at https://fas.org/sgp/isoo/isoodir1.html. Updated rules, which ended the X-series exemptions, came in Information Security Oversight Office, "Marking Classified National Security Information," December 2010, at www.archives.gov/files/isoo/training/marking-booklet.pdf. I am indebted to Steven Aftergood, author of the *Secrecy News* blog at the Federation of American Scientists, for explaining this to me.

184 **"critical national assets":** "NSA/CSS Mission: PROVIDE AND PROTECT VITAL INFORMATION FOR THE NATION," October 24, 2001, on file with author.

185 **a special achievement award:** The draft nomination, on file with author, covered the period from February 2001 through January 2002. I withhold the name of the woman in question, whose civil service rank was GG-13 on a scale of 15.

185 **"just get all the American people":** A transcript of my exchange with Alexander is archived at https://archive.is/tg9pB.

186 **Maybe a review of the video:** The panel with Negroponte and Blair was recorded in its entirety and may be viewed at "Clear and Present Danger: Cyber Crime; Cyber Espionage; Cyber Terror; and Cyber War," Aspen Security Forum, 2013, https://youtu.be/Ncc0zPRrV04?t=58m21s.

186 **video evidence of waterboarding:** Mark Mazzetti and Scott Shane, "Jose Rodriguez, Center of Tapes Inquiry, Was Protective of His CIA Subordinates," *New York Times*, February 20, 2008, archived at https://archive.is/j5B2.

CHAPTER SIX: JAMBOREE

187 **toothpaste bombs:** Bond, the fictional British spy, used a toothpaste bomb supplied by Q in the film *Licence to Kill*, 1989. See Jordan Hoffman, "23 of James Bond's Most Memorable Gadgets," *Popular Mechanics*, October 15, 2012, www.popularmechanics.com/culture/movies/g985/23-most-memorable-james-bond-gadgets/.

187 **"circumvent or exploit":** Invitation, TCB Jamboree 2012, on file with author. TCB stands for Trusted Computing Base, which refers to the core hardware, firmware, and software components essential for security safeguards on a digital device.

188 "discreet control of the radio": Ibid.

188 Stealing foreign secrets: David Martin, "Former Intel Head Michael Hayden on Stealing Others' Secrets," CBS News, February 21, 2016, www.cbsnews.com/news/former-intel -head-michael-hayden-on-stealing-others-secrets/.

188 eagle astride the globe: I described this seal, belonging to the NSA's Special Source Operations unit, in chapter 3.

188 norms, admittedly ironic: Ironic but not contradictory. As I argue in chapter 7, oversight by the public is not properly comparable to surveillance of the public by government.

188 has been known as Jamboree: Unsigned article, "Jamboree," Intellipedia, TS//SCI, on file with author.

188 songs of peace: According to the official Scouting site, a Jamboree "is above all an educational event to promote peace and understanding." See "World Scout Jamboree," Scouts, at www.scout.org/jamboree.

189 a TS/SCI conference space: In 2012, the defense contractor Lockheed Martin hosted Jamboree in a squat, six-story office building equipped with "secure, compartmented information facilities" for classified work at 13560 Dulles Technology Drive in Herndon, Virginia. "Jamboree 2012," Intellipedia, on file with author. A SCIF is enclosed in fine metal mesh and other materials to block electromagnetic signals from coming in or going out.

189 Jamboree celebrates technical: One definition of "jamboree" is, in fact, a revel or carousal. See Oxford English Dictionary, online at www.oed.com/view/Entry/100700?redirected From=jamboree.

189 "As many of you know": Quoted in "InSIDers View of History: A Lesson Learned in Personal Accountability," SID Today, December 24, 2004, first published in The Intercept.

190 relied upon exceptional colleagues: A partial list of others, not named here, included Alice Crites, Jeff Leen, Jason Ukman, Peter Finn, Craig Timberg, Steven Rich, Peter Wallsten, Todd Lindeman, Marc Fisher, Craig Whitlock, and Jennifer Jenkins.

191 from slide 3 to slide 4: NSA briefing slides, "SSO Collection Optimization," January 7, 2013, on file with author.

191 read "Emo Cat": This combines two common photographic memes. For a guide, see the reference site Know Your Meme at https://knowyourmeme.com/memes/subcultures/cats and https://knowyourmeme.com/memes/cultures/emo. For the ubiquity of cat memes, a neural network trained by programmers to categorize images taken from YouTube found more with cats than any other subject. See Andrew Ng and Jeff Dean et al., "Building High-Level Features Using Large Scale Unsupervised Learning," Proceedings of the 29th International Conference on Machine Learning, Edinburgh, Scotland, 2012, https://arxiv.org/pdf /1112.6209v3.pdf.

192 "I know these guys": Ashkan Soltani, September 19, 2013.

192 "I, like a lot of people": Ashkan Soltani to author, email, June 2017. Emphasis in original.

192 "'men in black' types": Barry Sonnenfeld's 1997 film depicted a secret agency that protected Earth from dangerous aliens. See "Men in Black," Internet Movie Database, www .imdb.com/title/tt0119654/.

193 567-question psychological test: This is the Minnesota Multiphasic Personality Inventory, or MMPI-2. See https://psychcentral.com/lib/minnesota-multiphasic-personality-inventory -mmpi/.

193 SF-86 Questionnaire: The Questionnaire for National Security Positions is available at www.gsa.gov/forms-library/questionnaire-national-security-positions.

193 Alan Tu: The author verified Tu's identity by his driver's license and his NSA assignment by a document in the Snowden archive.

195 Soltani's father had grown: Ashkan Soltani requested that the author not include the full names of family members.

195 fled to America: Family history courtesy Ashkan Soltani's older sister, July 2018. The family prefers that I not name the siblings and parents.

198 my first NSA story: Barton Gellman and Laura Poitras, "U.S., British Intelligence Mining Data from Nine U.S. Internet Companies in Broad Secret Program," Washington Post, June 6, 2013, http://wapo.st/1LcAw6p, archived at https://archive.is/cYyFe.

199 **piece of the backbone:** What is known as the backbone of the global communications network is a complex infrastructure with major components including trunk lines of fiber optic cable, high-capacity switches known as core routers, cable landing stations where undersea cables join terrestrial networks, and Internet Exchange Points. The majority of worldwide telephone and internet traffic passes to, from, or through U.S. infrastructure.

199 **$394 million:** FY 2013 Congressional Budget Justification, Volume 1, National Intelligence Program Summary, on file with author. See Craig Timberg and Barton Gellman, "NSA Paying U.S. Companies for Access to Communications Networks," *Washington Post*, August 29, 2013, at https://perma.cc/4C9Y-HLJW. For more on the so-called black budget, see www.washingtonpost.com/wp-srv/special/national/black-budget/.

199 **tunnel just about anywhere:** Even overseas, the NSA may not target a U.S. person for surveillance without a warrant from the FISA Court, but that does not stop it from tapping the infrastructure of U.S. companies. (See chapter 8.) By agreement, with few exceptions, the NSA also restrains itself from clandestine surveillance in Canada, the United Kingdom, Australia, and New Zealand—the other four members of the Five Eyes intelligence partnership. Undisclosed operations inside other allied countries are regarded as risky but not out of bounds.

199 **man in the middle:** In a man-in-the-middle attack, the NSA places or takes control of equipment directly in the path of digital traffic from one server to another. This enables the agency to read—and alter, for example by injecting malware—the data flow between source and destination.

199 **man on the side:** A man-on-the-side attack gives the NSA access to but not control of equipment, such as a router or switch, that stands between the source and destination of digital traffic. This allows the agency to read but not alter the flow of data.

200 **in NSA parlance, interactive:** PowerPoint presentation, "NIOC Maryland Advanced Computer Network Operations Course," slide 7, on file with author.

200 **2,588 such interactive missions:** Ibid, slide 21.

200 **Tailored Access Operations:** A colleague reported in 2017 that the unit has been renamed Computer Network Operations. Ellen Nakashima, "NSA Employee Who Worked on Hacking Tools at Home Pleads Guilty to Spy Charge," *Washington Post*, December 1, 2017, www.washingtonpost.com/world/national-security/nsa-employee-who-worked-on-hacking-tools-at-home-pleads-guilty-to-spy-charge/2017/12/01/ec4d6738-d6d9-11e7-b62d-d9345ced896d_story.html.

200 *Decipio—Circumvenio—Latrocinor:* The author thanks Yelena Baraz, associate professor of classics at Princeton, for the translation.

200 **an actual cartoon:** Unsigned NSA diagram, "Network Shaping," classified TS//SI//REL, on file with author, and reproduced online at www.documentcloud.org/documents/2922412-Shaping-Diagram.html. For a much more detailed NSA explanation, see the eighty-one-page "Network Shaping 101" slide deck at https://perma.cc/K7AB-MKLQ. For the civil liberties risks associated with network shaping, see Axel Arnbak and Sharon Goldberg, "Loopholes for Circumventing the Constitution: Unrestrained Bulk Surveillance on Americans by Collecting Network Traffic Abroad," *Michigan Telecommunications and Technology Law Review* 21, issue 2 (2015), at https://papers.ssrn.com/sol3/papers.cfm?abstract_id=2460462.

200 **take control of a switch:** I use the term generically. The switch might be, for example, a "core router" with very high capacity that directs traffic on internet cables.

201 **They name a Windows implant ODDJOB:** There is no reference to ODDJOB in the Snowden files. The Windows command and control implant was revealed in a leak of NSA hacking tools by a person or group that went by the name Shadow Brokers, generally believed to be a front for a foreign intelligence service. See Joseph Cox, "Shadow Brokers Dump Alleged Windows Exploits and NSA Presentations on Targeting Banks," *Motherboard*, April 14, 2017, at https://perma.cc/5STA-VRZ5.

201 **"denial and deception":** Undated NSA memo, "Denial and Deception Action Plan Review." Based on Microsoft Office metadata, the memo was first saved on December 19, 2001. On file with author.

NOTES

202 **with "Cover Payroll":** Ibid.

202 **MISS MONEYPENNY:** A compendium of every scene in which Moneypenny appears in a Bond film is at "All the Miss Moneypenny Scenes 1962–2015," YouTube, www.youtube .com/watch?v=jEL3bZSdokM.

202 **"I had a blue force tracker":** Confidential source, interview with author, 2018. The source worked in a comparable expeditionary role, not in Unit S3283.

203 **not going to write about those things:** I am not sure I would have described the unit at all, given the risks, if its work and equipment had not been made public in more detail in a widely reproduced article and original NSA document called the ANT Catalog. Jacob Appelbaum and Christian Stöcker, "Shopping for Spy Gear: Catalog Advertises NSA Toolbox," *Der Spiegel*, December 29, 2013, www.spiegel.de/international/world/catalog-reveals -nsa-has-back-doors-for-numerous-devices-a-940994.html.

203 **ROOFIE:** Slang for Rohypnol, roofie is the street name for a notorious drug that sexual predators use to incapacitate women. Fact Sheet, "Date Rape Drugs," Office on Women's Health, U.S. Department of Health and Human Services, at www.womenshealth.gov/a-z -topics/date-rape-drugs.

203 **"Introduction to BLINDDATE":** Syllabus for seven-part training course, on file with author.

203 **("Grab a partner!"):** The toolkit encompassing BLINDDATE, HAPPYHOUR, NIGHTSTAND, BADDECISION, and SECONDDATE is described in "Introduction to BADDECISION," December 15–16, 2010, on file with author and published in redacted form by the *Intercept* at https://perma.cc/N855-Q5LX; "Introduction to WLAN / 802.11 Active CNE Operations," December 15–16, 2010, at https://perma.cc/3PGN-BA3D; and training slides called "Foxacid," at https://perma.cc/AA3W-TSC7. In some documents, NIGHTSTAND is spelled NITESTAND. Dutch authorities in the fall of 2018 uncovered a closely parallel toolkit used by Russia's military intelligence service, the GRU. See "The GRU Close Access Operation Against the OPCW in Perspective," *Electrospaces*, October 9, 2018, at https://perma.cc/ANH3-AUMB.

204 **into "a backdoor":** Technically, in this case, the PANT_SPARTY tool embedded an NSA decryption key into a 2012 version of OpenSSH Portable, a commonly used software package for secure communication with a Unix server. A surveillance target would believe he or she had a secure link to the server, but the NSA could read the traffic at will. "SNIPs of SIGINT: Monthly Notes for June 2012," on file with author.

204 **PANT_SPARTY:** See "Pants Party," Urban Dictionary, at https://perma.cc/8FC9-24CD.

204 **"workforce that was incredibly young":** Alan Tu, interview with author, July 5, 2018.

205 **defend the practice:** Alexandra Robbins, "Nurses Make Fun of Their Dying Patients. That's Okay," *Washington Post*, April 16, 2015, at https://perma.cc/AJN8-7SBF.

205 **Scandals have ensued:** See, for example, Emily Yahr, "What Went Wrong with Joan Rivers's Last Medical Procedure: Lawsuit," *Washington Post*, January 28, 2015, at https://perma.cc /HMM8-CFG3; Yanan Wang, "Patient Secretly Recorded Doctors as They Operated on Her. Should She Be So Distressed by What She Heard?," *Washington Post*, April 7, 2016, at https:// perma.cc/QNM8-3NX9; and Tom Jackman, "Anesthesiologist Trashes Sedated Patient—and It Ends Up Costing Her," *Washington Post*, June 23, 2015, at https://perma.cc/N5K3-DLY7.

205 **He had put a lot of effort:** See James Comey, *A Higher Loyalty: Truth, Lies, and Leadership* (New York: Flatiron Books, 2018), beginning with this observation on p. xi: "Ethical leaders can mold a culture by their words and, more important, by their actions, because they are always being watched."

205 **history of marijuana use:** Charles Levinson, "Comey: FBI 'Grappling' with Hiring Policy Concerning Marijuana," *Wall Street Journal*, May 20, 2014, at https://perma.cc/T2AS-E4KZ.

205 **"That's a great question":** James Comey, interview with author, October 16, 2018.

206 **assign its cover names at random:** NSA historian James Bamford, for example, explained NSA cover names this way in Tom Bowman, "Why Does the NSA Keep an EGOTISTICALGIRAFFE? It's Top Secret," National Public Radio, November 10, 2013, at https:// perma.cc/2FLJ-MM9N. The late Matthew Aid, author of *The Secret Sentry: The Untold*

NOTES

History of the National Security Agency, likewise said in a newspaper interview, the reporter wrote, "that most of the NSA's code names are no more than computer-generated sequences of words." Emily Heil, "What's the Deal with NSA's Operation Names," *Washington Post*, October 22, 2013, at https://perma.cc/J67L-MNXB.

206 **VOYEUR:** NSA briefing document, "TRANSGRESSION Branch: A Discovery Collaboration Effort," November 1, 2010, on file with author. For a GCHQ description of VOYEUR, see "Fourth Party Opportunities," first published by *Der Spiegel* at www.spiegel.de/media /media-35684.pdf. For an unclassified reference to VOYEUR, see Collin Anderson and Karim Sadjadpour, "Iran's Cyber Ecosystem: Who Are the Threat Actors?," Carnegie Endowment for International Peace, January 4, 2018.

206 **SCISSORS:** "FY-2002 Signals Intelligence Directorate (SID) Project Baseline Standards and Architecture Assessment Activity," July 2002, p. 203, on file with author.

206 **evoke the "brotopia":** Emily Chang, *Brotopia: Breaking Up the Boys' Club of Silicon Valley* (New York: Portfolio, 2018).

206 **BOUNDLESSINFORMANT:** Glenn Greenwald and Ewen MacAskill, "Boundless Informant: The NSA's Secret Tool to Track Global Surveillance Data," *Guardian*, June 11, 2013, at https://perma.cc/2VLS-S587.

206 **TRANSGRESSION:** NSA briefing document, "TRANSGRESSION Branch," cited above.

206 **PITIEDFOOL:** "SNIPs of SIGINT: Monthly Notes for June 2012," on file with author.

207 **"They *really* want to win":** Tom Donilon to author, October 29, 2013.

207 **"The approach we've been using":** "I hunt people who hack routers (part 5)," December 2012, on file with author. Emphasis in original.

207 **nerds use "dork":** A quick and dirty search of the Snowden archive turned up 120 occurrences of "dork" or "dorked" in this meaning.

208 **"are honing their skillz":** "I hunt people who hack routers (part 5)," December 2012.

208 **"There are 10 types of people":** Training slides, "Public Key Cryptography & Public Key Infrastructure," 2002, on file with author.

208 **by switching on:** CAPTIVATEDAUDIENCE is described in an NSA wiki article titled "QUANTUMTHEORY CT Successes," on file with author.

211 **"Everyone can be friends!":** A folder full of these "awesome pics" is on file with author.

211 **Smart Target Enhancement Program:** Course syllabus, "12 FAA FOREIGNNESS FACTORS WITH EXAMPLES," undated, on file with author. I rely here also on a tutorial titled "Entering New FAA-Authorized DNI Tasking in the Unified Targeting Tool (UTT) / Gamut," March 30, 2010, on file with author.

211 **The most derisive descriptions:** The examples in this paragraph are found in "Entering New FAA-Authorized DNI Tasking in the Unified Targeting Tool (UTT) / Gamut," March 30, 2010; "12 FAA FOREIGNNESS FACTORS WITH EXAMPLES"; and "Target Analyst Rationale Instructions Final," October 20, 2009.

212 **EXUBERANTCORPSE:** *Special Source Operations Weekly*, March 14, 2013, slide 9, on file with author.

212 **When U.S. warplanes:** Ellen Knickmeyer and Jonathan Finer, "Insurgent Leader Al-Zarqawi Killed in Iraq," *Washington Post*, June 8, 2006, at https://perma.cc/BH3X-CZ2P. See also Lawrence Joffe, "Abu Musab al-Zarqawi Obituary," *Guardian*, June 8, 2006, at https://perma.cc/8T2C-NZFP.

212 **fist-bumping status report:** On file with author.

213 **taking part in a criminal conspiracy:** See chapter 7.

213 **Eventually he agreed to breakfast:** James R. Clapper, interview with author, August 17, 2018.

217 **as long ago as 1984:** Kenneth Thompson, "Reflections on Trusting Trust," Turing Award lecture, reproduced in *Communications of the ACM*, August 1984, at https://perma.cc /NL2L-7JX3.

219 **the Gemalto gambit:** This story came to light in Jeremy Scahill and Josh Begley, "The Great SIM Heist," *Intercept*, February 19, 2015, https://theintercept.com/2015/02/19/great-sim -heist/.

220 **"looking for interns":** The call for applicants, posted on the NSA's classified WikiInfo board, is titled "S3285/InternProjects," on file with author.

CHAPTER SEVEN: FIRSTFRUITS

222 **al Qaeda killed 2,996 people:** Brad Plumer, "Nine Facts About Terrorism in the United States Since 9/11," *Washington Post*, September 11, 2013, at https://perma.cc/47DN-JQWV.

222 **a nine-page memo for Ashcroft:** Untitled and undated draft memo from NSA director Michael V. Hayden to Attorney General John Ashcroft, on file with author. Metadata from the electronic file date it to March 19, 2002, but internal evidence suggests that the bulk of it was finished in December 2001. The period covered in this accounting of leaks ended on November 23, 2001.

223 **the three stories singled out:** The NSA memo for Ashcroft cited Barton Gellman, "Annan Suspicious of UNSCOM Role," *Washington Post*, January 6, 1999; Thomas Lippman and Barton Gellman, "U.S. Says It Collected Iraq Intelligence Via UNSCOM," *Washington Post*, January 8, 1999; and especially Barton Gellman, "U.S. Spied on Iraqi Military Via UN; Arms Control Team Had No Knowledge of Eavesdropping," *Washington Post*, March 2, 1999, at https://perma.cc/ZTY6-9W2U.

223 **still finding remnants:** But some of my stories reflected a gradual decline of diplomatic backing for unrestricted weapons inspections in Iraq. Barton Gellman, "US Fought Surprise Inspections," *Washington Post*, August 14, 1998; Barton Gellman, "US Tried to Halt Several Searches," *Washington Post*, August 27, 1998; and Barton Gellman, "Inspector Quits UN Team, Says Council Bowing to Defiant Iraq," *Washington Post*, August 27, 1998.

223 **continuing to hide:** Stymied by Iraqi obstruction, inspectors from the UN Special Commission, known as UNSCOM, developed aggressive intelligence methods in response. Barton Gellman, "A Futile Game of Hide and Seek: Ritter, UNSCOM Foiled by Saddam's Concealment Strategy," *Washington Post*, October 11, 1998; Barton Gellman, "Arms Inspectors 'Shake the Tree': UNSCOM Adds Covert Tactic," *Washington Post*, October 12, 1998. This series, titled "Shell Games," was a finalist for the Pulitzer Prize for National Reporting.

223 **concealed microwave antennas:** Gellman, "U.S. Spied on Iraqi Military Via UN." The story reported that "unbeknownst to UNSCOM, the U.S. signals and sensor technicians who installed and maintained the system were intelligence operatives, and the repeater stations they built had a covert capability. Hidden in their structure were antennas capable of intercepting microwave transmissions, and the U.S. agents placed some of them near important nodes of Iraqi military communications."

223 **Security Council disbanded it:** United Nations Security Council Resolution 1284, adopted on December 17, 1999, shuttered UNSCOM and replaced it with a much less aggressive inspection regime under the United Nations Monitoring, Verification and Inspection Commission, or UNMOVIC. The text is at https://undocs.org/S/RES/1284(1999).

223 **"disclosed the basic concept":** This was an active surveillance program when I discovered it. The U.S. government shut it down when I told Clinton administration officials, as I reported on the story, that the UN Secretariat was asking about it.

224 **counterintelligence term of art:** The methods of D&D encompass both concealment and misdirection. Denial, for example, is hiding a weapons lab under a barn so that spy satellites cannot see it. Deception is laying a false trail of shipping records to hint that the lab is located somewhere else. See the entries for "denial" and "deception" in Mark L. Reagan, ed., *Counterintelligence Glossary—Terms & Definitions of Interest for CI Professionals* (Office of the National Counterintelligence Executive, June 9, 2014), at https://fas.org/irp/eprint/ci-glossary.pdf.

227 **"My next story":** We eventually ran a series of stories about the secret intelligence spending plan. The first was Barton Gellman and Greg Miller, "'Black Budget' Summary Details U.S. Spy Network's Successes, Failures and Objectives," *Washington Post*, August 29, 2013, at https://perma.cc/2ELY-WBK7. My colleagues produced a splendid online data visualization at www.washingtonpost.com/wp-srv/special/national/black-budget.

NOTES

227 **"These guys are coming in hot":** Shawn Turner, who said that to me and Greg Miller, recalled the moment in an interview on May 30, 2019.

228 **"True disbelief that":** Greg Miller, message to author, May 16, 2019.

231 **million-dollar bounties:** Zerodium, which calls itself "the world's leading exploit acquisition platform," buys software flaws that it can weaponize for government clients. It made the public million-dollar offer in 2015. See "ZERODIUM's Million Dollar iOS 9 Bug Bounty (Expired)," September 21, 2015, at https://perma.cc/AF7A-C5K8.

232 **"Warning: We believe":** The Google warning appeared on my accounts on February 19, 2014.

233 **largest independent Apple:** "Computers and Electronics," Mayor's Office of Film, Theater, and Broadcasting, City of New York, archived at https://perma.cc/N749-ZMLP.

235 **Morgan Marquis-Boire:** I knew Morgan as a talented hacker and security researcher. He provided me with advice and did several pro bono forensic investigations on my behalf, for which I am grateful. In 2017, credible accusations of sexual assault were levied against him. He disappeared from public view and has not, to my knowledge, responded to the accusations. See Sarah Jeong, "In Chatlogs, Celebrated Hacker and Activist Confesses Countless Sexual Assaults," *Verge*, November 19, 2017, at https://perma.cc/J583-ZJKV.

236 **"Within the span":** Ashkan Soltani, interview with author, October 16, 2015.

241 **"My take is":** Rick Ledgett, interview with author, August 22, 2017.

242 **two counts of espionage:** These were initial criminal charges in support of an extradition request to Hong Kong authorities. The grand jury empaneled in Norfolk very likely has handed up a sealed indictment alleging additional criminal counts. See Criminal Complaint of Edward Snowden, United States v. Edward J. Snowden, Case No. 1:13 CR 265, U.S. District Court for the Eastern District of Virginia, at https://perma.cc/M2T8-KZB8. Each of the three publicly disclosed charges carries a maximum sentence of ten years in prison. See 18 U.S.C. § 793 (a)—(f), § 798(a)(3)(1)—(4) (2012); 18 U.S.C. § 641 (2012).

242 **trying to jail James Risen:** MacBride oversaw the prosecution of Jeffrey Sterling, beginning in 2010, for unauthorized disclosure of classified information to Risen, and repeatedly called Risen before a grand jury to testify against his alleged source. The initial indictment refers to Risen as "Author A." See United States v. Jeffrey Alexander Sterling, at https://assets.documentcloud.org/documents/2106787/sterling-indictment.pdf. When Risen refused, the government moved to have him jailed for contempt of court. The Fourth Circuit Court of Appeals ruled against Risen in 2013 and the Supreme Court followed suit in 2014. See Adam Liptak, "Supreme Court Rejects Appeal from Times Reporter over Refusal to Identify Source," *New York Times*, June 2, 2014.

243 **lost his final appeal:** Later, on the brink of Risen's confinement, the Justice Department abruptly withdrew the subpoena. As the trial judge prepared to hold Risen in contempt, prosecutors announced without explanation in January 2015 that they no longer required him as a witness. See Matt Apuzzo, "Times Reporter Will Not Be Called to Testify in Leak Case; Legal Fight Ends for James Risen of the New York Times," *New York Times*, January 12, 2015.

243 **"It's nothing personal":** Neil MacBride to author, June 1, 2011.

243 **command me to present myself:** Rule 17, Subpoena, Federal Rules of Criminal Procedure, at www.law.cornell.edu/rules/frcrmp/rule_17.

243 **credit and banking records:** Michael Isikoff, "DOJ Gets Reporter's Phone, Credit Card Records in Leak Probe," MSNBC, February 25, 2011.

244 **"I Spy, No Lie":** The video interview with Keith Alexander originated on the Defense Department's official science blog. Jessica L. Tozer, "I Spy, No Lie," *Armed with Science*, October 24, 2013, at https://perma.cc/P6SR-X7HJ. Also available on YouTube at www.youtube.com/watch?v=6Kc5Xvr24Aw.

246 **"I'd have to go to these people":** Shawn Turner, interview with author, May 30, 2019.

246 **"Snowden claims that he's won":** James Clapper, testimony before the Senate Select Committee on Intelligence, January 29, 2014, transcribed at http://wapo.st/2b26smO and

archived at https://archive.is/QxYVN. The relevant video excerpt is https://youtu.be /CowlDnng2Zc.

247 **Snowden's "agents":** The NSA inspector general compared Snowden and his journalistic "agents" unfavorably to notorious FBI traitor Robert Hanssen, saying "Hanssen's theft was in a sense finite whereas Snowden is open-ended, as his agents decide daily which documents to disclose." George Ellard, panel remarks, "A New Paradigm of Leaking," Symposium on Leakers, Whistleblowers and Traitors, February 25, 2014, transcript available at *Journal of National Security Law & Policy* 8, no. 1 (2015). Ellard used identical language at a February 24, 2014, conference at Georgetown University Law Center, as I sat less than ten feet away. See Conor Friedersdorf, "A Key NSA Overseer's Alarming Dismissal of Surveillance Critics," *Atlantic*, February 27, 2014, at http://theatln.tc/My1aQ8.

247 **"I must confess":** George Ellard, interview with author, December 9, 2014.

247 **"I understand what Keith was saying":** James R. Clapper, interview with author, August 17, 2018.

248 **was entirely blacked out:** See FBI, Domestic Investigations and Operations Guide, updated September 28, 2016, released in two volumes at https://perma.cc/6YD4-VG3D and https://perma.cc/K7FR-6VTQ.

248 **classified Appendix G:** The appendix is reproduced in its entirety at https://assets.docu mentcloud.org/documents/2934087/DIOG-Appendix-Media-NSLs.pdf. The accompanying story is Cora Currier, "The FBI's Secret Rules," *Intercept*, June 30, 2016, republished on January 31, 2017, at https://perma.cc/HRW5-ETNP.

251 **his coming-out video:** The *Guardian* posted the videotaped interview: Laura Poitras and Glenn Greenwald, "NSA Whistleblower Edward Snowden: 'I Don't Want to Live in a Society That Does These Sort of Things,'" *Guardian*, on June 9, 2013, www.theguardian .com/world/video/2013/jun/09/nsa-whistleblower-edward-snowden-interview-video.

251 **Hong Kong–based reporter:** Lana Lam, "EXCLUSIVE: Whistle-Blower Edward Snowden Talks to South China Morning Post," *South China Morning Post*, June 12, 2013, at https:// perma.cc/7BM6-7DBQ.

251 **"Put the data you have uncovered":** Dafna tweeted a photo from the restaurant. "I just got @bartongellman's fortune cookie," she wrote on October 27, 2013, https://perma.cc /9KP2-RNPD.

252 **"Girls Bar":** There were indeed young women, provocatively dressed, who made more eye contact than might be expected, but I did not take that personally. For photos, see www .korston.ru/en/moscow/restaurants/promenade_bar/.

257 **"Snowden has enough information":** The Reuters news agency translated the interview. See "Glenn Greenwald: Snowden Documents Could Be 'Worst Nightmare' for U.S.," Reuters, July 13, 2013. The original was in Alberto Armendáriz, "Glenn Greenwald: 'Snowden tiene información para causar más daño,'" *La Nación*, July 13, 2013, at https://perma.cc /8R6R-PFG4.

258 **without a private key:** The PGP encryption software allows a user to encode a file to a "private key" without possessing the key itself. I would need the private key, which remained in New York, to decrypt my own recordings and notes. Doing it this way allowed me to travel without means of access to my confidential work. Likewise, I sent the encrypted files to online servers that were set to permit uploads but not downloads. In order to download the files at home, I would need an "SSH private key" that I did not bring on the trip.

258 **Fourth Amendment does not apply:** See "Notes: The Border Search Muddle," *Harvard Law Review* 132, no. 8 (June 1, 2019): 2278–92, https://harvardlawreview.org/2019/06/the -border-search-muddle/.

260 **"The damage is incalculable":** George Cotter, email to author, December 1, 2016.

260 **Advocates for radical transparency:** Julian Assange of WikiLeaks and John Young of the leak website Cryptome often criticized me, along with Glenn Greenwald and Laura Poitras, for holding back any documents at all. See, for example, "Snowden Long Drip Pie Charts," March 14, 2014, at https://perma.cc/FZ9M-ZXPF.

261 **trafficking in stolen goods:** Publishing information obtained by theft is not trafficking in stolen goods in part because the Supreme Court interprets the National Stolen Property Act, 18 U.S.C. §§ 2314 and 2315, as limited to tangible "goods, wares, or merchandise." See Dowling v. United States, 473 U.S. 207 (1985).

261 **"national defense information":** See 18 U.S.C. § 794, "Gathering, transmitting or losing defense information." The question is whether a news story may constitutionally be prosecuted as willful communication of national defense information to a person not entitled to receive it.

261 **"to all the world":** Superseding indictment, United States v. Julian Paul Assange, May 23, 2019, Case 1:18-cr-00111-CMH, counts 15 through 17.

261 **Assange a "journalist":** He has done many things that a traditional journalist would not do, but there is little room to doubt that he has functioned as the publisher of WikiLeaks.

262 **twice taught a Princeton class:** The course, WWS 384, was called "Secrecy, Accountability, and the National Security State." See https://registrar.princeton.edu/course-offerings /course_details.xml?courseid=011833&term=1132.

262 **called me a "traitor":** Levin's comment came in the 2008 documentary film *Secrecy*, by directors Peter Galison and Robb Moss. The relevant excerpt is at www.youtube.com/watch ?v=0p5AWEalj0k.

262 **"It is desired that no document":** Memorandum from Colonel O. G. Haywood Jr., Army Corps of Engineers, for the Atomic Energy Commission, April 17, 1947, at https://perma .cc/6S6A-K9GN.

262 **infected commercial sex workers:** U.S. Department of Health and Human Services, "Fact Sheet on the 1946–1948 U.S. Public Health Service Sexually Transmitted Diseases (STD) Inoculation Study," October 1, 2010, at https://perma.cc/D7V9-YCVF.

262 **found "numerous incidents":** Major General Antonio M. Taguba, "Article 15-6 Investigation of the 800th Military Police Brigade," at https://perma.cc/VZ5L-PJP4.

263 **lied about intelligence:** I use the word "lied" advisedly for a limited subset of the many incorrect claims by members of the Bush administration about Iraqi WMD. Some of the claims were merely exaggerated, and some were based on mistaken intelligence assessments made in good faith. On Iraq's alleged—and nonexistent—nuclear weapons program, however, Vice President Dick Cheney and other top officials said things that they had good reason to believe were false. See, e.g., Gellman, *Angler*, 217, and Barton Gellman and Walter Pincus, "Depiction of Threat Outgrew Supporting Evidence," *Washington Post*, August 10, 2003, at https://perma.cc/WER2-82ZR.

263 **"Cold War secrecy":** Mary Graham, *Presidents' Secrets: The Use and Abuse of Hidden Power* (New Haven, CT: Yale University Press, 2017), 4.

263 **"is used too often":** Report of the Commission on Protecting and Reducing Government Secrecy, Senate Document 105-2, 1997, p. xxi.

264 **"You have to start":** The occasion was a conference on surveillance at the Cato Institute in Washington. Andrea Peterson, "Obama Says NSA Has Plenty of Congressional Oversight. But One Congressman Says It's a Farce," *Washington Post*, October 9, 2013, https://wapo .st/2Wwg6ql.

264 **laundry and dry cleaning manual:** Naval Sea Systems Command, *Naval Ships' Technical Manual*, chapter 655, "Laundry and Dry Cleaning," S9086-V4-STM-010/CH-655. Steven Aftergood first brought this to my attention in a presentation called "Confronting Government Secrecy," March 1, 2012.

264 **"On 4 November 1979":** This Top Secret statement of a well-known public event came in "CRITIC Seminar 4," a training course dated July 24, 2003, on file with author.

265 **"exceptionally grave damage":** This is the standard set for Top Secret classification under Part 1, Sec. 1.2, Executive Order 13526 of December 29, 2009, "Classified National Security Information," Federal Register—U.S. National Archives and Records Administration, vol. 75, no. 2, p. 707, at https://perma.cc/8PNY-NC5L.

266 **"People must communicate":** I am indebted to Greg Miller for this reporting on Clapper's congressional briefing, which took place on September 10, 2013.

267 **a conflict of core values:** I discussed these dilemmas at considerably greater length in a pair of lectures at Princeton, ten years before the Snowden story broke. See "Secrecy, Security and Self-Government: An Argument for Unauthorized Disclosures," September 17, 2003, archived at https://perma.cc/RH4J-S55U; and "Secrecy, Security and Self-Government: How I Learn Secrets and Why I Print Them," October 9, 2003, archived at https://perma .cc/6T9F-R2LG.

268 **Shadow Brokers leak:** See Bruce Schneier, "Who Are the Shadow Brokers?," *Atlantic*, May 23, 2017, at https://perma.cc/4E4C-Q2SC.

270 **"a change in the way":** Email from Shawn Turner to Caitlin Hayden, August 12, 2013, obtained in a FOIA lawsuit by author. In truth I had been asking for a secure channel since the first days of the story. I grew more insistent in the summer.

270 **"We're aware of your concern":** Vanee Vines, interview with author, February 27, 2014.

271 **"How about 'abc123'?":** Vanee Vines, telephone call with author, May 21, 2014, memorialized in an email by author the same day.

271 ***Daily Kos:*** The story was Frank Vyan Walton, "Operation FirstFruits: NSA Spied on Dissenters and Journalists?," *Daily Kos*, January 19, 2006, at https://perma.cc/WJ7E-S2RD. The post bore this warning in parentheses: "This content is not subject to review by Daily Kos staff prior to publication."

272 **Wayne Madsen:** For example, see Wayne Madsen, "Hayden's Heroes: A Tale of Incompetence and Politicization at America's Super-Secret Intelligence Agency," *Wayne Madsen Report*, May 8, 2005, reposted on Cryptome at https://perma.cc/WYF5-CRQG; and "NSA Spied On Own Employees, Journalists, Other Intel," *Wayne Madsen Report*, December 29, 2005. Madsen's blog is behind a paywall, but the second article may be found on sympathetic sites such as the anti-Semitic *Rense News*. For information on Rense, see Heidi Beirich, "Jeff Rense: In His Own Words," Southern Poverty Law Center, April 27, 2015, at https://perma.cc/P6P8-HZV6.

272 **"a paranoid conspiracy theorist":** Michael Moynihan, "NSA Nutjob: Anatomy of a Fake 'Observer' Story," *Daily Beast*, July 1, 2013, at https://perma.cc/H9VE-NBDB.

272 **"plugging any leaks":** Wayne Madsen, "NSA Security Running Amok to Plug Leaks About 9/11," *Wayne Madsen Report*, July 7, 2009, republished at https://perma.cc/7J8C-HRPJ.

273 **"listen to Osama bin Laden":** White House press secretary Ari Fleischer made the accusation soon after Brand's report: "In 1998, for example, as a result of an inappropriate leak of NSA information, it was revealed about NSA being able to listen to Osama bin Laden on his satellite phone. As a result of the disclosure, he stopped using it." The 9/11 Commission adopted this story in 2004: "Worst of all, al Qaeda's senior leadership had stopped using a particular means of communication almost immediately after a leak to the *Washington Times*." See the commission's report at p. 127 at www.9-11commission.gov/report/. Bush adopted the narrative in 2005: "The fact that we were following Osama bin Laden because he was using a certain type of telephone made it into the press as the result of a leak. And guess what happened? Saddam—Osama bin Laden changed his behavior." As recently as 2018, White House spokeswoman Sarah Sanders reprised the claim. See Glenn Kessler, "The Zombie Claim That Won't Die: The Media Exposed bin Laden's Phone," *Washington Post*, August 2, 2018, https://wapo.st/2MtsC6t.

273 **almost certainly untrue:** I bring new evidence here, but my argument relies in part on Jack Shafer, "Don't Blame the Washington Times for the Osama Bin Laden Satellite Phone 'Leak,'" *Slate*, December 21, 2005, at https://perma.cc/W73Y-UMSR; and Glenn Kessler, "File the Bin Laden Phone Leak Under 'Urban Myths,'" *Washington Post*, December 22, 2005, https://wapo.st/2Ij5WAs.

273 **"He keeps in touch":** Martin sieff, "Terrorist Is Driven by Hatred for U.S., Israel," *Washington Times*, August 21, 1998.

274 **No story actually said that:** The *Washington Times* story did not report that the U.S. government could eavesdrop on bin Laden's phone. The first story to do so was Paul Richter, "Bin Laden May Use Stone Age Tactics to Elude High-Tech Hunt," *Los Angeles Times*, September 7, 1998.

274 **facility that bin Laden had recently visited:** The CIA is said to have told President Clinton that it believed bin Laden departed the Zawhar Kili camp several hours before the missiles struck, but the agency could not be sure. Steve Coll, *Ghost Wars: The Secret History of the CIA, Afghanistan, and bin Laden, from the Soviet Invasion to September 10, 2001* (New York: Penguin Press, 2004), 411.

275 **"that the information is to be used":** Espionage Act, 18 U.S.C. § 793(a).

275 **tried and convicted:** Jeffrey A. Sterling, for example, was convicted of espionage for telling James Risen, then of the *New York Times*, about a botched CIA operation in Iran. See Matt Apuzzo, "C.I.A. Officer Is Found Guilty in Leak Tied to Times Reporter," *New York Times*, January 26, 2015, at https://perma.cc/5DRT-973G.

276 *Gellman v. DHS et al.*: U.S. District Court for the District of Columbia, Case No. 1:16-cv-0635 (CRC).

276 **Glomar response:** The term has its origins in a FOIA lawsuit about the *Glomar Explorer*, a classified intelligence-gathering ship. Phillippi v. CIA, No. 76-1004, United States Court of Appeals for the District of Columbia Circuit, 178 U.S. App. D.C. 243, 546 F.2d 1009.

276 **"The CIA can neither confirm":** Letter from CIA to author, January 28, 2015, on file with author.

276 **every international flight I took:** TECSII—Primary Query History, Passenger Activity, January 30, 2015, redacted copy obtained by FOIA, on file with author.

278 **"copyrighted bulletins":** Government's Motion for Summary Judgment, Gellman v. DHS, April 3, 2019.

278 **"investigations of alleged":** Redacted declaration of David M. Hardy, Gellman v. DHS, April 3, 2019.

CHAPTER EIGHT: EXPLOITATION

280 **The hand-drawn cartoon:** The diagram appeared on a page titled "Current Efforts—Google" in a 2013 presentation called "SSO Collection Optimization" and classified TOP SECRET//SI/NOFORN, on file with author. I reproduced the diagram in Barton Gellman and Ashkan Soltani, "NSA Infiltrates Links to Yahoo, Google Data Centers Worldwide, Snowden Documents Say," *Washington Post*, October 30, 2013, http://wapo.st/1UVKamr.

280 **the core technology of encryption:** "FAQ: What is SSL," SSL.com, https://info.ssl.com/article.aspx?id=10241.

281 *All your base*: The phrase appeared in a poorly translated video game in 1991 and passed into the ranks of internet memes. It remains a staple of hackers and gamers when declaring victory. See "All Your Base Are Belong to Us," Know Your Meme, https://knowyourmeme.com/memes/all-your-base-are-belong-to-us.

281 **on four continents:** See "Data center locations," About Google, www.google.com/about/datacenters/inside/locations/index.html.

282 **Executive Order 12333:** "United States intelligence activities," 46 FR 59941, 3 CFR, 1981 Comp., p. 200, www.archives.gov/federal-register/codification/executive-order/12333.html.

282 **Google had built:** For a video tour, see "Inside a Google Data Center," YouTube, https://youtu.be/XZmGGAbHqa0.

285 **"protocols and applications":** SSO Collection Optimization, on file with author.

287 **"incidentally obtained information":** Executive Order 12333, section 2.3(i).

287 **one billion at Google:** By early 2016, Google surpassed the billion-user mark with seven separate services. Combined, they reached a billion accounts long before that. See Xavier Harding, "Google Has 7 Products with 1 Billion Users," *Popular Science*, February 1, 2016, www.popsci.com/google-has-7-products-with-1-billion-users/.

289 **"Wow!":** Transcript of live chat on Jabber instant messaging service between Edward Snowden and Daniel Ellsberg, September 8, 2013, on file with author.

290 **"that the so-called intelligence community":** Daniel Ellsberg, "Edward Snowden: Saving Us from the United Stasi of America," *Guardian*, June 10, 2013, at https://perma.cc/F7RD-LK5V.

295 **bore little resemblance:** Some have seen these differences as essential to the legitimacy of their respective leaks, comparing Snowden unfavorably to Ellsberg. See Malcolm Gladwell, "Daniel Ellsberg, Edward Snowden, and the Modern Whistle-Blower," *New Yorker*, December 19 and 26, 2016, at https://perma.cc/YU2E-EY8W.

297 **then six hypotheses:** Ashkan typed out a quick and dirty list:

1 brute forcing 1024 (or possibly longer) SSL certificates
2 flaw in SSL implementation (i.e linux flavor of openSSL)
3 obtaining companies' SSL session tickets (for those use PFS)
4 obtaining companies' SSL private cert (i.e hacking into the server)
5 getting a root/trusted CA that to sign a cert for them (or secretly being the trusted cert)
6 they have a master flaw in ALL SSL

298 **more than six years:** SSO Collection Optimization ("Midpoint_TLC_Optimization_w_Google_Exploitation.pptx"), slide 17, had a sample that was classified on January 8, 2007.

299 **a photograph shot inside the premises:** From a TOP SECRET//COMINT//NOFORN presentation titled "Special Source Operations: The Cryptologic Provider of Intelligence from Global High-Capacity Telecommunications Systems" (UODDS2Overview_v1_1.pptx), p. 14, on file with author.

300 **"We have long been concerned":** Google statement on NSA infiltration of links between data centers, October 30, 2013, at https://perma.cc/8M7G-UVA7.

300 **"continued to extend encryption":** Craig Timberg, "Google Encrypts Data Amid Backlash Against NSA Spying," *Washington Post*, September 6, 2013, at https://perma.cc/E55V-ELVZ.

301 **"That's never happened":** Barton Gellman, Ashkan Soltani, and Andrea Peterson, "How We Know the NSA Had Access to Internal Google and Yahoo Cloud Data," *Washington Post*, November 4, 2013, at https://perma.cc/2F3P-6FUU.

302 **"Bart Gellman, Washington Post":** Valerie Sayre email to Shawn Turner, Jeffrey Anchukaitis, and Robert Litt, October 28, 2013, obtained by author in a Freedom of Information lawsuit.

302 **"everything that has been exposed":** Robert S. Litt, remarks at the American Bar Association, 23rd Annual Review of the Field of National Security Law, Washington, D.C., October 31, 2013, at https://perma.cc/CDR5-A4WH.

302 **the scandal is what's legal:** Michael Kinsley, "The Conspiracy of Trivia," *Time*, March 10, 1997, at www.cnn.com/ALLPOLITICS/1997/03/10/time/kinsley.html.

309 **November 4, 1952:** George F. Howe, *The Early History of NSA*, declassified on September 18, 2007, at https://perma.cc/N4PQ-X5NH.

309 **"We were moving":** Michael V. Hayden, *Playing to the Edge: American Intelligence in the Age of Terror* (New York: Penguin Press, 2016), 134. Emphases in original.

310 **"splitter cut-in and test procedure":** AT&T technical manual, provided to author by Mark Klein.

310 **Klein found himself alone:** Mark Klein, interview with author, February 18, 2015.

311 **"New Collection Posture":** Presentation first made public in Glenn Greenwald, *No Place to Hide*. It is among those included at http://glenngreenwald.net/#BookDocuments.

312 **was "going dark":** James B. Comey, November 3, 2014, video at "James Comey at Today's Terrorism: Today's Counterterrorism," YouTube, www.youtube.com/watch?v=0LRVGdmr000.

313 **The founders themselves had used codes:** Rachel B. Doyle, "The Founding Fathers Encrypted Secret Messages, Too," *Atlantic*, March 30, 2017, at https://perma.cc/AR3V-UZYH.

313 **"Do you see any possibility":** Transcript of exchange with James B. Comey, November 3, 2014, courtesy of Karen Greenberg at the Center on National Security at Fordham Law School.

314 that "[g]overnment snooping": Brad Smith, "Protecting Customer Data from Government Snooping," Microsoft *Technet* blog, December 4, 2013, at https://perma.cc/UWH8 -VPL5.

315 an electronic address book: Barton Gellman and Ashkan Soltani, "NSA Collects Millions of E-mail Address Books Globally," *Washington Post*, October 14, 2013, at https://perma .cc/ZR32-EC4Q.

317 "a person reasonably believed": To accompany an article I coauthored with Ellen Nakashima and Greg Miller, the *Washington Post* published a 2009 version of the targeting and minimization rules. See "Classified Documents Show Rules for NSA Surveillance Without a Warrant," https://apps.washingtonpost.com/g/page/politics/top-secret-documents -show-rules-for-nsa-surveillance-without-a-warrant/248/.

318 nearly five billion records a day: Barton Gellman and Ashkan Soltani, "NSA Tracking Cellphone Locations Worldwide, Snowden Documents Show," *Washington Post*, December 4, 2013, at https://perma.cc/PS3M-Y5HJ.

320 automaton on wheels: "Meet BeamPro," Suitable Tech Inc., https://suitabletech.com/products/beam-pro.

323 The Secret Files: Christine Pelisek, "Doxxing: It's Like Hacking, but Legal," *Daily Beast*, March 13, 2013, www.thedailybeast.com/doxxing-its-like-hacking-but-legal.

323 "the rise of political doxing": Bruce Schneier, "The Rise of Political Doxing," *Vice*, October 28, 2015, www.vice.com/en_us/article/z43bm8/the-rise-of-political-doxing.

323 She was a crisis manager: Vanee Vines portrayed herself this way in her LinkedIn profile, www.linkedin.com/in/vaneevines/.

323 to the worst traitor: I wrote about George Ellard's comment, comparing Snowden and his "agent" journalists to FBI traitor Robert Hanssen, in chapter 7.

324 "It sounds like I won't": Snowden chat with author, November 22, 2013.

326 require extraordinary evidence: The aphorism was popularized by astronomer Carl Sagan in his 1980 television show *Cosmos*. It is a staple in the worlds of science, intelligence, and journalism.

326 "Gang of Eight": The Gang of Eight referred to the chairs and ranking members of the two intelligence committees and the top two Democrats and Republicans of each chamber in Congress.

328 "The only thing you have": Snowden chat with author, October 22, 2013.

328 "I've thought a lot about that": Snowden to author, October 2, 2013.

329 "has access to the complete": Snowden chat with author, June 9, 2014.

332 "secret sharing scheme": Secret sharing is a mathematical algorithm for splitting a cryptographic key into parts that must be recombined in order to work. Snowden said he based his system on a famous paper by an MIT cryptographer. See Adi Shamir, "How to Share a Secret," *Communications of the ACM* 22, no. 11 (November 1979), at www.cs.tau.ac.il /~bchor/Shamir.html.

333 the labeling debate: For a fine and subtle essay on how Snowden does and does not fit into theoretical models of legitimate civil disobedience, see David Pozen, "Edward Snowden, National Security Whistleblowing and Civil Disobedience," *Lawfare*, March 26, 2019, www .lawfareblog.com/edward-snowden-national-security-whistleblowing-and-civil -disobedience. The essay was adapted from the forthcoming volume *Whistleblowing Nation: Disclosing U.S. National Security and the Challenge of Dissent*, ed. Kaeten Mistry and Hannah Gurman (New York: Columbia University Press, 2019).

334 "Treason against the United States": U.S. Constitution, Article III, Section 3.

334 "[I]n an act of supreme arrogance": Ash Carter, *Inside the Five-Sided Box: Lessons from a Lifetime of Leadership in the Pentagon* (New York: Penguin, 2019), 338.

335 "national security porn": Ledgett was paraphrasing James Comey, who used the term "intelligence porn" to describe large-scale document dumps by WikiLeaks, not Snowden or the NSA journalists. See Tessa Berenson, "James Comey: WikiLeaks Is 'Intelligence Porn,' Not Journalism," *Time*, May 3, 2017, https://time.com/4765358/fbi-james-comey-hearing -wikileaks/.

NOTES

336 **"6,998,329,787 is a small number":** In another version of the presentation, delivered earlier, the figure was slightly lower (6,987,139,094) and explicitly labeled "World Population" on Hunt's presentation slide. See Ira A. (Gus) Hunt, *Big Data: Challenges and Opportunities*, https://info.publicintelligence.net/CIA-BigData-2.pdf.

336 **"nearly within our grasp":** Ira A. (Gus) Hunt, CIA Chief Technology Officer, "Beyond Big Data: Riding the Technology Wave," Government Big Data Forum, March 2012, at www.slideshare.net/brianahier/perspectives-on-big-data-mission-and-needs-gus-hunt-cia-cto.

336 **"The value of any piece":** Matt Sledge, "CIA's Gus Hunt on Big Data: We 'Try to Collect Everything and Hang On to It Forever,'" *Huffington Post*, March 20, 2013, at https://perma.cc/W35E-W4G8.

339 **"Collection rules prevent":** See Jennifer Stisa Granick, *American Spies: Modern Surveillance, Why You Should Care, and What to Do About It* (Cambridge: Cambridge University Press, 2017), 153. Emphasis in original.

340 **160,000 actual communications:** I write about these at greater length in Barton Gellman, Julie Tate, and Ashkan Soltani, "In NSA-Intercepted Data, Those Not Targeted Far Outnumber the Foreigners Who Are," *Washington Post*, July 5, 2014, https://wapo.st/1MVootx; and Barton Gellman, "How 160,000 Intercepted Communications Led to Our Latest NSA Story," *Washington Post*, July 11, 2014, https://wapo.st/1Mq04zI.

341 **Minimization was fiendishly difficult:** A four-paragraph definition of "minimization," full of contingency clauses, may be found in 50 U.S.C. §§ 1801(h)(1), at www.law.cornell.edu/uscode/text/50/1801.

341 **for a lay audience:** Litt cited the statutory definition under FISA law, which does not apply to surveillance under Executive Order 12333. The concepts are similar but the rules are not identical under the executive order. See Robert S. Litt, "Privacy, Technology and National Security: An Overview of Intelligence Collection," remarks prepared for delivery at the Brookings Institution, July 19, 2013, at https://perma.cc/L9BM-EYYP.

342 **years to understand:** Granick, *American Spies*, 152.

342 **With rules so complex:** One set of procedures, dating to 2013, is at "Minimization Procedures Used by the National Security Agency in Connection with Acquisitions of Foreign Intelligence Information Pursuant to Secton 702 of the Foreign Intelligence Surveillance Act of 1978, as Amended," hosted by the National Security Archive at George Washington University, https://nsarchive2.gwu.edu/NSAEBB/NSAEBB436/docs/EBB-026.pdf.

342 **"told MINIMIZED U.S. JOURNALIST":** This was an actual telephone call from Israeli prime minister Benjamin Netanyahu to author. I mentioned the call in a subsequent story without quoting the profanity, noting only that Netanyahu "took heated exception" to a piece about non-Orthodox Jewish conversions, a subject that caused him political trouble. See Barton Gellman, "Many Israelis Dispute Power of Rabbinate," *Washington Post*, April 3, 1997, https://wapo.st/2yVQc1V.

343 **you could not even read:** The DNI's office, to its credit, declassified some of the safeguards. But Granick describes the sequence this way: "[I]n 2013, Snowden disclosed the NSA's FISA minimization procedures for section 702 collection. The intelligence community ultimately declassified the FBI and the CIA minimization procedures from 2014 in September of 2015. In November 2015, the procedures for all three agencies were secretly revised." For collection overseas under Executive Order 12333, the full minimization procedures were never declassified. Granick, *American Spies*, 155.

343 **"malleable secret rules":** Granick, *American Spies*, 154.

344 **"surveillance professionals shy away":** Conor Friedersdorf, "If the NSA Could Hack into Human Brains, Should It?," *Atlantic*, December 5, 2013, www.theatlantic.com/politics/archive/2013/12/if-the-nsa-could-hack-into-human-brains-should-it/282065/.

346 **Senator Frank Church:** *Meet the Press*, NBC, August 17, 1975, viewable at www.youtube.com/watch?v=YAG1N4a84Dk.

348 **"The idea of having":** Rajesh De, interview with author, July 18, 2013.

351 **tamper-detection device:** This project, called Haven, was coauthored with security developer Nathan Freitas. See Micah Lee, "Edward Snowden's New App Uses Your Smartphone

to Physically Guard Your Laptop," *Intercept*, December 22, 2017, https://theintercept.com/2017/12/22/snowdens-new-app-uses-your-smartphone-to-physically-guard-your-laptop/.

351 automate "secret sharing": This project, called Sunder, was eventually abandoned. See Conor Schaefer, "Meet Sunder, a New Way to Share Secrets," Freedom of the Press Foundation, May 10, 2018, https://freedom.press/news/meet-sunder-new-way-share-secrets/.

352 "I am willing to help": David E. Sanger and Nicole Perlroth, "Internet Giants Erect Barriers to Spy Agencies," *New York Times*, June 6, 2014, www.nytimes.com/2014/06/07/technology/internet-giants-erect-barriers-to-spy-agencies.html.

352 End-to-End: Source code for the encryption library, which has yet to be released in final form, is at https://github.com/google/end-to-end. Google's announcement may be found at "Making End-to-End Encryption Easier to Use," *Google Security Blog*, June 3, 2014, https://security.googleblog.com/2014/06/making-end-to-end-encryption-easier-to.html.

352 comment embedded in the source code: Brittany A. Roston, "Google Takes a Dig at NSA with Easter Egg," SlashGear, June 4, 2014, www.slashgear.com/google-takes-a-dig-at-nsa-with-easter-egg-04332176/.

352 "He's already said": See "NSA Speaks Out on Snowden, Spying," CBS News, December 15, 2013, transcript at https://cbsn.ws/2P4ZkfI.

INDEX

Page numbers above 360 refer to notes.

INDEX

INDEX

Aspen Institute plenary session moderated
by, 155–66, 181–82
in attempts to authenticate leaked
documents, 3, 17–18
attempt to learn ES's identity rejected
by, 17
black budget story of, 227–28
and catch-22 in consultation about
classified materials, 270–71
Century Foundation fellowship of, 93
compromised Google accounts of, 232
cyber security tradecraft acquired by,
xvi–xvii, 2–4, 6
digital trail of, xvi
ES and, *see* Snowden, Edward
fake encryption keys for, 231
first NSA story published by, 198
Freedom of Information Act requests of,
276–78
Google engineers' meetings with, 279–81,
283, 297–98
government attempts to discredit reporting
by, 14–15
on Greenwald's contributions to NSA
story, 141
Greenwald's false accusations against, 138,
140–41, 387–90
hacking of computer and devices belonging
to, 229–35
Hayden's relationship with, 141–42
high school lawsuit of, 14
Hong Kong trip abandoned by, 135–36
intelligence community's ostracism
of, 186
as investigative reporter, xii–xiii
journalistic fallibility of, 9–10
Mueller on panel with, 249–50
NSA story offered to *Post* by, 89–91, 98
Pandora files received by, 99
Poitras and, *see* Poitras, Laura
as possible counterintelligence target,
248–49
Post career of, 91–93
PRISM files received by, 99
PRISM slides shown to Baron by, 109–13
in search for safe repository of Pandora
backups, 99–100, 102
secrecy issues as long-standing concern
of, 262
security lapses of, 239
security measures for NSA story outlined
by, 105–7
Soltani hired by *Post* to work with, 189–91,
198–99

as subject of files in Pandora archive,
221–22, 272, 274
surveillance as increasing preoccupation of,
93, 234–35, 238–42, 255
viewed as ES's "accomplice," 323
gellman.us/pgp, encryption tools at, 8
Gellman v. DHS et al., 276–78
Gellman v. Wacker, 14
Geneva, ES's CIA posting to, 54
gigabytes, 22
Gladwell, Malcolm, 366
Gompert, David C., 311–12
Goodlatte, Bob, 163
Google, 76, 111, 336
foreign facilities of, 282, 286
hacking of BG's accounts on, 232
illegal spying by, 198
PRISM and, 283, 285, 300
Google cloud, 317, 352
boundary between public internet and,
281–82
GCHQ in penetration of, 299, 301
NSA's penetration of, 279–88,
297–302, 408
Google Front End, 284–85
governing norms, 248–49, 347–48
government:
secrecy and, *see* secrecy, government
in standoff with ES, 352–53
trust and, 180–84
GPG (GnuPG), 8, 365, 366
Graham, Don, 103
Graham, Katharine, 92, 379
Graham, Lindsey, 158
Graham, Mary, 263
Granick, Jennifer, 339, 342, 343
Graph-in-Memory, 174, 177, 179, 180, 181
Greenberg, Karen, 4
Greenwald, Glenn, 213, 241, 255, 325
Alexander's proposed raid on, 245–46,
247–48, 249
BG on contributions to NSA story by, 141
BG's view of, 12
in claims about ES's unreleased files,
257–58
in decision not to publish some material
from Pandora, 269
ES's decision to leak documents to, 16
ES's first approaches ignored by, 12,
366–67
ES's first contact with, 66
ES's interviews with, 138, 346
ES's relationship with, xiii
and ES's wiretapping claims, 327

INDEX

Angler

The Cheney Vice Presidency

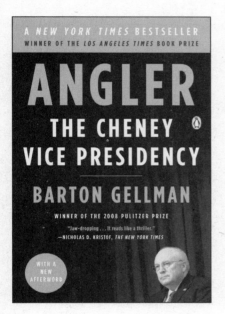

Barton Gellman shared the Pulitzer Prize in 2008 for a keen-edged reckoning with Dick Cheney's domestic agenda in *The Washington Post*. In *Angler*, Gellman goes far beyond that series to take on the full scope of Cheney's work and its consequences, including his hidden role in the Bush administration's most fateful choices in war. Packed with fresh insights and untold stories, Gellman parts the curtains of secrecy to show how the vice president operated and what he wrought.

"Jaw-dropping . . . It reads like a thriller."
–Nicholas D. Kristof, *The New York Times*